A HISTORY OF JEWISH CRAFTS AND GUILDS

ALSO BY MARK WISCHNITZER:

Die Universität Goettingen und die Entwicklung der liberalen Ideen in Russland im ersten Viertel des 19ten Jahrhunderts, Berlin, 1907.

"The Message of the Frankist Sect of 1800" (Russian), Mémoires de l'Académie des Sciences de St. Pétersbourg, XII.3, 1914.

The Memoirs of Ber Bolechow (1723-1803), Oxford, 1922.

Die Juden in der Welt. Gegenwart und Geschichte des Judentums in allen Laendern, Berlin, 1935.

To Dwell in Safety. The Story of Jewish Migration since 1800, Philadelphia, 1949.

Visas to Freedom. The History of Hias, New York, 1956.

EDITED BY MARK WISCHNITZER:

The Jews in Russia, vol. II, by Louis Greenberg, New Haven, 1951.

A HISTORY OF JEWISH CRAFTS AND GUILDS

by

MARK WISCHNITZER, PH.D.

Foreword by *Salo W. Baron*

Introduction by *Werner J. Cahnman*

Sponsored by Yeshiva University
and The Conference on Jewish Social Studies

JONATHAN DAVID, *Publishers*
New York

A History of Jewish Crafts and Guilds

Library of Congress Catalog Card Number: 64-66205

JONATHAN DAVID PUBLISHERS, INC.
131 East 23rd Street
New York, N.Y. 10010

Printed in The United States of America

Table of Contents

FOREWORD

It is with melancholy feelings that I am writing these lines in memory of an old friend and co-worker. Professor Mark Wischnitzer (1882-1955), a native of eastern Europe, belonged to the early pioneers in the study of Jewish history and sociology in Russia and Poland. He subsequently moved to Berlin where, as Secretary-General of the *Hilfsverein der Deutschen Juden* he had the opportunity of applying some of his own teachings in practice, particularly during the tragic years of the 1930's when it was his task to try to find homes for thousands of European Jews living under the Nazi menace. On that occasion he broadened the scope of his scholarly activities as well, and greatly contributed to our knowledge of Jewish communities in many other lands.

Among Dr. Wischnitzer's major fields of interest was the history of the Jewish artisan class and the artisan guilds. Beginning with a German essay, printed in 1921, he published a number of learned studies (including one in *Jewish Social Studies)* on this ramified subject. Once again, this was not merely a theoretical problem. All over the world the rising tide of European anti-Semitism was nurtured from the constantly reiterated accusations that Jews were neither economically nor intellectually productive, but had always served only as middlemen. Jews themselves were so greatly impressed by these arguments that they created various ideological movements aiming at the restratification of their masses so as to take them out of the "unproductive" areas of commerce and moneylending, and to turn them into "productive" workers in industry and agriculture.

In eastern Europe these never-ending accusations had a hollow sound. Historical records and contemporary reality revealed that sometimes as many as a third of Russo-Polish Jewry consisted of craftsmen and their employees. In many cities within the Tsarist Pale of Settlement the Jews constituted the vast majority of all artisans. Outside Russia, too, there often were sufficient numbers of craftsmen to form their own guilds. Such associations existed in Salonica where Jewish longshoremen so completely dominated that city's famous harbor that all work was usually suspended on the Jewish Sabbath. David Ben Gurion still occasionally reminisces about the impression these Salonican longshoremen made on him when he visited the city on his way to Palestine. Their example reaffirmed his conviction that Palestinian Jewry, too, could become a well-stratified society, providing all the manpower needed for manual labor as well as for intellectual endeavors.

Despite this obvious need, no one has ever written in any language a comprehensive study of the history of Jewish guilds. Going back to remote antiquity when, for instance, the Alexandrian Jewish guilds served as major employment agencies, and an association of Jewish shipmasters was rendering specific services to the Roman Empire, through ancient and medieval Babylonia, Spain, and early modern Bohemia or Poland, these guilds played a significant role in the socio-economic evolution of their people. Apart from their occupational functions, they served as religious brotherhoods, often establishing synagogues and schools of their own. They thus represented a peculiar segment of the Jewish community with different approaches to life as well as to Jewish law and learning. Scholars as well as interested laymen will, therefore, be very grateful to Dr. Wischnitzer for placing before them this comprehensive and well-documented story.

SALO W. BARON

Preface

Mark Wischnitzer began to collect material on the history of Jewish crafts and craft guilds when, after having received his doctorate at Berlin University, he became editor of the *Yevreyskaia Entsiklopedia* (Jewish Encyclopedia) published in St. Petersburg. He dealt with the subject in a series of articles, a list of which is appended in this volume.

The book was almost completed when Dr. Wischnitzer died on October 16, 1955. He was then visiting in Israel, on leave from Yeshiva University, where he had been Professor of Jewish History and Institutions since 1948.

The manuscript was edited by Dr. Werner Cahnman and myself. Dr. Cahnman wrote the introduction. Mr. Shaiah Trunk brought up to date the chapters on Poland and Lithuania, except chapter XXI dealing with arts and crafts, particularly in Poland and Lithuania, which I wrote. My husband wanted me to do this chapter and I utilized his suggestions. I also revised the data on archaeology and art history throughout the book.

Professor Salo W. Baron generously extended his advice and wrote the foreword. I am much indebted to Dr. Boaz Cohen and to Dr. Shlomo Eidelberg for valuable help in revising the footnotes. Dr. Abraham G. Duker read the proofs, and I am very grateful for his suggestions. Dr. Morris Epstein and Rabbi Alfred J. Kolatch assisted me in preparing the manuscript for the press.

Thanks are due to Mr. Abraham Berger, Director of the Jewish

Division of the New York Public Library, to Mrs. Emery Tabor of the Library of The Hebrew Union College-Jewish Institute of Religion in New York for their many courtesies, and to Miss Dina Abramowicz, librarian of the YIVO Institute for Jewish Research.

Transliteration of Russian, Hebrew and Yiddish words presented many problems. Apologies may be due for some inconsistencies. Talmudic references have not been indexed because of their large number.

Grants from the Gustav Wurzweiler Foundation and from the Conference on Jewish Material Claims against Germany, through the sponsorship by the Conference on Jewish Social Studies, have made this publication possible. I am truly grateful for the assistance received from these bodies. I am also indebted to the Alexander Kohut Foundation for its subsidy. Assistance from the Lucius N. Littauer Foundation enabled Dr. Wischnitzer to do research at Harvard and other United States libraries in preparation of the book.

My heartfelt thanks are due to Dr. Samuel Belkin, Mr. Eric M. Warburg, Dr. J. H. Lookstein, Mr. Leon Shapiro, Dr. Harry A. Wolfson, Mr. Harry Starr, Dr. Shalom Spiegel and Mr. Jacob G. Frumkin to whose friendship for my husband I owe the strength that was needed to complete this project.

RACHEL WISCHNITZER

A HISTORY OF JEWISH CRAFTS AND GUILDS

Introduction: Role and Significance of the Jewish Artisan Class

by Werner J. Cahnman

The economic activities of the Jews in the post-exilic period are considered as having been primarily, and even exclusively, commercial in nature. Whether the Jews are seen as "international bankers" of the type of the Rothschilds, or as miserable peddlers in the image of the "old clo'es Jews," whether they are described as a *Pariavolk* by Max Weber or as the epitome of a "marginal trading people" by Howard Becker, the near-unanimity in this respect of proverbial saying and fairy-tale, of political pamphlet and scholarly treatise remains impressive. Jewish authors, perhaps because they were preoccupied with ideological and political matters, have not challenged, or even scrutinized, this view seriously—so much so that, a great many valuable monographs notwithstanding, a comprehensive economic history of the Jews, written by a Jewish scholar, is still lacking. Prof. Mark Wischnitzer's "History of Jewish Crafts and Craft Guilds" therefore fills a gap in our knowledge and affords a welcome opportunity to test the thesis of the essentially commercial character of Jewish economic activities.

Prof. Wischnitzer tells the story of Jewish artisanship from its beginnings in the biblical period until the late eighteenth century and up to the threshold of the industrial era. Within the time covered, he has recorded the activities of Jewish artisans and the structure of their guilds in many lands. He has clarified the position Jewish artisans occupied in the Jewish community as well as in the larger society. He has followed up the struggles of the Jewish artisans against the dominant Christian guilds, and the struggles of the journeymen within the Jewish guild system. He has presented his data in such a way as to enable us to check previously held notions with newly ascertained facts and to confirm or modify them, according to the findings.

What conclusions do the data permit? Historically speaking, we discern two periods in Prof. Wischnitzer's story. The earlier period covers the formation of Jewish artisanship and the establishment of craft guilds in ancient Palestine and their extension from Palestine into the oriental and Mediterranean Diaspora. The later period covers the centuries since the Middle Ages and has its locale chiefly in northern and eastern Europe.

In the earlier period, the ancestors of the Jewish people grew from a wandering tribe into a settled community in their own land, where they developed agricultural skills and the traditions of craftsmanship. After the fall of the Kingdoms of Israel and Judah, these skills and traditions were carried to the neighboring mid-eastern and Mediterranean territories into which the Jews of Palestine migrated. These territories may be called the countries of the first migratory settlement, or the first Diaspora. In them, the social structure of the Palestinian Jewish community was largely preserved. The transfer of craftsmanship was most immediate with regard to Babylonia, into which country Nebuchadnezzar had especially transported those artisans who, he feared, might have recreated an independent armaments industry in Palestine. However, agriculture remained for a long time as important as artisanship among the descendants of the exiles.

This situation continued under Persian overlordship and came to an end only after the Moslem conquest of the Sassanian empire. In Christian lands, a similar situation lasted well up to the period in which the Roman Church established its hold over the society of the Mediterranean area.

Prof. Wischnitzer reports that in Mesopotamia, then the center of the Diaspora, the Jews abandoned farming only from the end of the eighth century onward. The reason was not, as Max Weber assumed, that agriculture was incompatible with growing religious orthodoxy, but rather that agricultural pursuits by Jews were incompatible with feudal obligations. The land taxes imposed by the

Caliphs were onerous and Jewish owners were more heavily taxed than others. In addition, political unrest and brigandage, the brunt of which was borne by the minority populations, made the countryside insecure and drove farmers into the cities. The Jewish artisan class in the urban centers therefore increased considerably, swelling the established groups of artisans with masses of newcomers. In Christian countries, ecclesiastical discrimination and, frequently, outright bigotry exerted the same kind of pressure. Such was the case in early medieval Sicily and in Visigothic Spain. As a result, Jewish farmers either accepted baptism and stayed on the land, or remained Jews and migrated to the cities.

In the area of first settlement, the Jews were part and parcel of an indigenous population. Such was the heritage of the Roman and Sassanian empires and the intermingling of populations in the rapidly growing urban centers. The Jewish artisan class continued to be an important segment of the total artisan class and, at the same time, a conspicuous element within the Jewish community. This was true in Mesopotamia and Egypt, the Byzantine lands, Italy, the Provence, Spain and North Africa. Even in Salonica and other Turkish Jewish communities which grew into prominence after the Jewish expulsion from Spain, this *character indelibilis* of Mediterranean Jewry was maintained. Jews either had their own guilds or, among Moslem populations, were admitted into Moslem guilds. In some places, as in Thebes in Greece, in Lucena in Spain and in Salonica under the Turks, they held a virtual monopoly of guild membership.

The situation as it shaped up in the area of second settlement, or the second Diaspora, was quite different. The Jews became estranged from handicrafts during the middle ages in northern Europe, where they appeared as late-comers, outsiders, and strangers. There, Church ideology and the interests of the native middle classes worked hand in hand to exclude the Jews from Christian guilds, to prevent the formation of their own guilds and to relegate them to the position of petty traders and moneylenders. The image of the Jews as an economically restricted and socially depressed caste of hucksters and usurers is of northern and central European coinage. This image was not modified until much later, when a new Jewish artisan class arose in what may be called an area of third settlement in eastern Europe. This further development, as related in the last chapters of this book, culminates in the modern Jewish labor movement and in the Zionist colonization of Palestine.

The historical considerations are borne out by statistical analysis. To be sure, the scarce statistical data which the sources yield are merely illustrative in nature. An important factor is whether a Jewish settlement constituted a small minority or a large minority within a total territorial society. By a small minority, we mean a community amounting to only a few per cent (occasionally less than one per cent) of the entire population of a country and rarely more than between ten and fifty families in any particular locality. Such was the proportion of Jews in the territories of northern and western Europe. The Jews of England, France, Germany and northern Italy played a more or less important role in the economic life of their respective countries, but their numbers remained small. It will be observed that these are the countries where Jews were excluded from the guilds and where the permission for them to establish a community was predicated upon their relegation to purely commercial activities, especially in connection with pawnbroking and the extension of consumer credit. In such countries, Jewish artisans were chiefly confined to crafts of a ritual nature, such as bookbinding and illuminating, printing, prayer scarf weaving, barbering, butchering and the like. They catered to a predominantly, even exclusively, Jewish clientele and, consequently, there were very few of them.

Only where larger Jewish communities existed, do we find a Jewish artisan class of considerable size and diversity working for a wider market. This was the case in many oriental and Mediterranean communities, from Babylonia to Spain and from Yemen to Salonica, and likewise in eastern Europe from the fifteenth century onward. In particular, wherever economic conditions deteriorated in the Jewish group while, at the same time, its numbers were swelling, a large Jewish artisan class would come into existence. In other words, the size of a Jewish artisan class stands in direct proportion to the size of a Jewish community, but in inverse proportion to its prosperity.

A sociology of the Jewish artisan class would have to consider the role which he plays within the general community. Contrary to Max Weber's assumption about the preference of rabbinical

Judaism for the money trade, talmudic literature, as quoted by Prof. Wischnitzer, abounds in admonitions to learn a craft and in the praise of craftsmanship. Since scholarship was considered a sacred service rather than a profession, many of the sages of Palestine and Babylonia were humble craftsmen who lived by the work of their hands. But this does not mean that craftsmen as such enjoyed a high social status. More often than not the opposite was the case. Apart from crafts that were capable of producing for wider markets, such as the brewing of date wine and gold-smithing in Babylonia, and apart from learned crafts that attained professional status, such as cartography, pharmacy and medicine in medieval Spain, manual labor and artisanship retained the marks of low status.

The reasons are not far to seek. In Babylonia, as in other countries of the Near and Middle East, the number of craftsmen increased through the migration of dispossessed villagers into the cities, causing a surplus of hands seeking employment. At other times and places, the influx was caused by restriction in commercial activities and by outright expulsion from neighboring localities or distant countries. Whenever the influx was of considerable magnitude, as in Salonica in the sixteenth century, the wealthier members of the Jewish communities had to set up employment opportunities for their poorer brethren or to provide relief.

These social problems are reflected in rabbinic writing. Juridical opinions and decisions, the most significant of which are quoted or referred to by Prof. Wischnitzer, amount to an impressive body of social legislation in favor of the working man. To be sure, the craftsman, or laborer, had to render an honest day's work, repair damages he had caused, provide for a substitute in case of absence from work and so forth, but it is a distinguishing feature of Jewish legislation, as compared with similar legislation elsewhere, that the laborer's interests were no less protected than those of his employer. For instance, the workingman's right to insist upon immediate payment, which is established in the Mishnah (*Baba Meziah* IX, 12), is unique. On the other hand, it must not be overlooked that some of the privileges of a religious nature allowed workingmen, such as permission to shorten the prayer of grace after meals in order to save time, or permission to work until noon on the day before Passover, are negative privileges, denoting a lowered status.

Wealthy men, having more leisure to learn, could accumulate more *mizvoth*. In this regard, Max Weber is vindicated.

However, in times of stress, when confronted with the threat of confiscation of their earthly goods, the rich were prone to desert their faith in order to preserve their status. Salomon Alami, a Spanish scholar who witnessed the pogroms of 1391, blamed the rich for "the ruin of their people," while he expressed high regard for the steadfastness of the artisans.

The antagonism between the upper and the lower classes, a continuing theme in Jewish history, has never been adequately described. A history of Jewish artisanship, while not primarily centered on that theme, affords an opportunity to discern the internal class struggle at many points. As a rule, the Jewish communities in the Diaspora were dominated by commercial interests. But the heritage of nomadic equality in ancient times and the fervent message of social justice propounded by the prophets, were elaborated by the sages of pharisaic and talmudic Judaism to such a degree that the welfare of the laboring man was sufficiently protected. Accordingly, Babylonian Jewry in the period of the great academies achieved a considerable measure of social equilibrium; the task of formulating the rules of Jewish living after the loss of political independence overshadowed everything else.

But the more the Jews migrated westward and northward from the Palestinian and Babylonian centers and the more they became exposed to peripheral pressures, the more firmly established became the predominance of the men of means. We know of Jewish communities which were preponderantly communities of artisans, but their status was either depressed, as in Yemen, or they failed to stand up to the vicissitudes of fortune, as in Greece and Sicily. The Jewries of southern Italy and Sicily are a case in point. In the reign of Emperor Frederick II of Suabia, the silk-weavers and dyers of these territories were fashioned into a state monopoly, but when that organizational device crumbled, the artisans were left without effective leadership. At the time of the Spanish expulsions, the Jews of Sicily, by then almost exclusively a community of craftsmen, were too impoverished to maintain intellectual activities and a vigorous community life.

The prime examples of heightened class antagonism are found in medieval Spain and in eastern Europe, especially in the old

Kingdom of Poland. Prior to the emancipation movement of the nineteenth century, Spain was the country in which individual Jews climbed highest on the ladder of socio-economic success. The court and the Jews were in firm alliance and the Jewish courtiers participated in the splendor of their noble connections. Spanish Jewry also comprised a broad middle class of traders, artisans and their apprentices who, as all of Spain, depended on the King and enjoyed patronage, protection and autonomous status; nonetheless, in the Jewish community councils, or *aljamas,* the influence of wealthy financiers and entrepreneurs predominated. This changed to some degree after the pogroms and antisemitic campaigns of 1391 and 1412-14. So many frightened men of means deserted the Jewish faith that the *aljamas* lost the majority of their administrative and juridical officers and artisans had to replace them. However, as documentary evidence from the city of Saragossa shows, the baptized Jews retained sufficient contact with Jewish affairs to sneer at the ignorant craftsmen and to remain at the disposal of the King when he called upon them to restore a competent conduct of affairs.

The story of class antagonisms within the Jewish community can be illustrated with examples from many lands. In Italy, in the seventeenth century, two different sorts of "Jewry-law" existed, one for the privileged loan bankers and one for the *università degli ebrei,* a miserable proletariat of peddlers, second-hand dealers, woolcarders and ragpickers. In the Bohemian registrations of the eighteenth century, artisans ("wretched tailors") figured at the very bottom of the list, following merchants, lessees and traders. But it is only in Poland, likewise in the eighteenth century, that we find instances of actual class struggle.

Contrary to the situation in Spain, the Jewish craft guilds in eastern Europe were not autonomous, but depended on the elders of the Jewish communities for confirmation. Prof. Wischnitzer reports about controversies and violent clashes between the *Kahals,* the official Jewish communities, and the Jewish craft guilds. The *Kahals* of Minsk, Vitebsk and other cities, which were dominated by businessmen, were accused by the representatives of the artisans of arbitrary taxation and other abusive practices, even of floggings and capricious arrests. The *Kahal's* offices were physically attacked by the artisans, but the wealthy householders retained the reins of power. Even more depressed than the status of the masters was that of the journeymen, who grew increasingly restless, as they failed to gain representation even within the Jewish guilds. Prof. Wischnitzer's story grows dramatic at this turning point in Jewish history. What we are witnessing here are the first stirrings of the Jewish labor movement. Jewish villagers fleeing before Ukrainian pogromists and Jewish traders succumbing to competition swelled the ranks of the artisan class to such an extent that it grew into a proletariat.

In terms of Jewish-Gentile relations, a number of statements can be made. Wherever a sizeable Jewish artisan class existed, the typical antisemitic image of the Jew as an idle exploiter and a money-monster could not arise. To be sure, this did not prevent discriminations, persecutions and expulsions, but it forestalled their congealment into a devil-ideology of Jewish existence. This devil-ideology grew into predominance in Germanic lands where it corresponded to the actual anomaly of Jewish status. In this regard, then, the Jewish artisan appears as the antagonist of the Jewish moneylender. In a structural view, however, the existence of a Jewish artisan class is not contradictory to the theory which characterizes the Jews as a "marginal trading people." The Jewish artisan, as a rule, is not a merchant or trader, but he shares in the intermediacy of the trader's role.

In order to substantiate this thesis, we will have to review the list of Jewish crafts that can be drawn from Prof. Wischnitzer's study. One group of crafts and craftsmen has to be excluded, though, namely those that exclusively serve the internal needs of a Jewish community. Among these are butchers, bakers, winemakers, soapmakers, barbers, embroiderers, *tallit* and *tzitzit* weavers, parchment-makers, scribes, bookbinders, printers and similar trades. Occasionally, engravers and gold-and silversmiths may be added to that list. All these trades have one thing in common, namely, that they are more or less ritualistic in nature; they are necessary for the conduct of a "holy congregation." Consequently, these are the trades which were represented even in countries where powerful Christian guilds excluded Jews from membership. Some of the trades mentioned were carried on in Jewish homes as a sideline; some, like the scribe's or the ritual slaughterer's trade, were regarded as holy vocations. None of them were part of the power structure of a Jewish community; none were in any but the most superficial communication with the outside world. However, the borderline is hard to draw, as in the case of the butchers who have to dispose of the ritually unclean hind-parts of animals and who have always enjoyed a reputation for quality meats among the Gentiles.

Turning to crafts that provide for a wider market, one encounters those that are connected with the position of the Jews in the fields of monetary and cultural exchange. To the monetary group belong minters, jewelers, gold–and silversmiths and medal engravers; to the cultural group—bookbinders, illuminators, papermakers, printers, cartographers, designers of nautical instruments, pharmacists and medical practitioners. These are the privileged crafts that come closest to banking and the international trade in metals and precious stones on the one hand and to artistic and professional activities on the other hand. The Jews at all times dealt with gold and precious stones, because of the easy transferability of this kind of capital investment. Throughout the Mediterranean region and in the countries of the Near East, they traded in these and related commodities. This brought them in contact with the courts, the nobility and even the monasteries, either as providers of luxury articles and utensils or as creditors who took such articles in pawn. The artisans who worked in precious stones and metals brought techniques from afar, worked to specifications and refashioned according to local taste. Spanish Jews excelled in this field and some oriental Jewish communities, such as those of Libya and Yemen, specialized in it. Even in Central Europe, otherwise an area of stunted Jewish craftsmanship, the court Jews of the seventeenth and eighteenth centuries brought Jewish jewelers and engravers in contact with high-born clients. The connection of Jewish minters with monetary activities is obvious.

The Jews were intermediaries in the cultural field as well as in the world of finance. The foremost example is provided by the Jews of Spain who, along with the Moors, brought to Christian Spain the scientific knowledge of the Greeks in Arabic garb and many of the techniques of the older civilizations of the East. The Jews had a tradition of learning and utilized it for making a living in fields where scholarship and manual skill had to be combined. Linguistic and mathematical knowledge was utilized in calligraphy, cartography, the making of astronomical and nautical instruments;

linguistic and naturalistic knowledge in such highly professional skills as pharmacy and medicine. The Jewish printing enterprises which were established in Italy, in Bohemia and in the Netherlands in the sixteenth and seventeenth centuries served both internal Jewish purposes and the needs of Christian Hebraists, and thus contributed to the spread of intercultural contacts. Similarly, Jewish musicians in eastern Europe entertained both at Jewish weddings and at the parties of the Bohemian and Polish nobility.

Mentioning the symbiosis of Jews and nobles does not exhaust the topic of privileged Jewish crafts. The insecurity of the social position of the Jews, which made them dependent on the protection of Moslem and Christian rulers, lent itself to fiscal exploitation and the promotion of monopolistic industries. The fact that the Jews of southern Italy and Sicily held an important position in the various branches of the silk industry, made the Norman and Suabian rulers of these regions intent on using their skills as a source of income. During his raids on Byzantium, Roger II of Sicily went so far as to carry away as captives Jewish silkworkers of Thebes and other Greek cities in order to employ them in his royal factory in Palermo. As the industry took root, the Hohenstaufen Emperor Frederick II transformed it into a state monopoly, with Jews as administrators, buyers, supervisors and workers. The profit flowed into the Emperor's treasury.

In the sixteenth and seventeenth centuries, the armies of the Turkish Sultans were clad in uniforms produced by Jewish woolen manufacturers in Salonica. At the same time, Jewish armorers provided the Turkish army with weapons. Similarly, in early capitalistic Europe, Jewish skill found an outlet in those industries which were not organized in guilds. This is true with regard to diamond cutting and tobacco dressing in Holland and such fine arts as seal engraving, gold and silver embroidery and the like in eighteenth century Prussia. In the nineteenth century, such new industries as the manufacture of cotton fabrics, ready made clothes, and tobacco products employed considerable numbers of Jewish workers in Russia.

Numerically more important than the privileged crafts, and sociologically as significant, are the depressed crafts. Since Jewish economic activities were frequently interstitial in nature, Jewish craftsmen found themselves often relegated to despised, dirty and unhealthy tasks, repair work, and finishing work. For instance, the tanning and dyeing trades formed a Jewish monopoly in many Mediterranean countries because the Gentile population did not care for the dirty work. In Morocco, where the degradation of the Jews reached its nadir, Jews were occupied as scavengers and as cleaners of latrines, and they were charged with disposing of the corpses of executed criminals.

Tailoring, which has remained a Jewish occupation through the centuries, is likely to be unhealthy work, carried on in cramped quarters and associated with cramped postures. A typical Jewish occupation in the Italian ghettos was the sewing and mending of old clothes and the remaking of used mattresses, activities which led to diseases of the eye and skin, to headaches, coughs and consumption. Also detrimental to health are the glassblowers' craft, which was plied in the countries of the Near East, and the work of house painters and furriers, in which many Jews in eastern Europe were employed.

Repair work means employment in auxiliary and subservient occupations. Italy was not the only country in which Jewish craftsmen were thus employed. Jewish men in Yemen, in southern Arabia, used to spend the week in specified Arab villages where they tinkered and hammered and fused and mended until they returned to their homes and families on Friday. This is reminiscent of the Jewish peddler's role among the peasants in central Europe. But the analogy goes even further. Prof. Wischnitzer reports that, in the sixteenth and seventeenth centuries, Jewish pawnbrokers and second-hand dealers in Bohemia began to patch up old shoes, bags, trousers, furs and other damaged articles which they had acquired and to sell them at reduced prices to their clientele. The process seems to be best documented for Prague, but it assumed historical importance in the Kingdom of Poland. The second-hand trade and the repair business were the soil out of which the emerging Jewish artisan class in Poland drew a large part of its sustenance.

Generally, it must not be thought that the occupation of a Jewish craftsman and the historical function of the Jew as a creditor are contradictory. True, Jewish artisans frequently were engaged in manual occupations which did not entail sale of the product and delayed payment for services rendered. The Jewish silk weavers, dyers, potters, leather and metal workers in the Mediterranean countries and, in later centuries, the woolen and clothing workers, the armorers, porters and longshoremen of Salonica are examples. But the Jewish workingmen were employed exclusively by Jewish employers and it was these who remained in contact with the non-Jewish community to whom the products of their industries were sold. The same applies to the Jewish working classes in eastern Europe in the nineteenth and twentieth centuries, and to the New York garment industry. We do not know a historical example of a Jewish working class being employed by non-Jewish employers. Hence, the image of the Jewish workingman remained remote to the Gentiles.

However, the cited examples notwithstanding, Jewish artisans in many instances were individual entrepreneurs, selling their products in their own booths, stalls, and stores and extending credit to their customers. Indeed, in the pawnbroking business, which had become the mainstay of Jewish economic activities in many parts of central and eastern Europe by the close of the Middle Ages, credit operations were of the essence, and the repair crafts that grew out of them were secondary in nature until, by the end of the eighteenth century, the roles appeared reversed. By then, the Jewish artisan class, soon to merge into a modern working class, had become a factor in its own right. A particularly potent example for what we have in mind is provided by one of the most typically Jewish crafts in eastern Europe, namely, distillery and innkeeping. Polish noblemen leased to Jews the right to distill brandy on their estates and the liquor was then sold to the estate's peasants on credit. Here, the craftsman and the creditor are fused in one and the same image, and the intermediate and interstitial nature of this kind of Jewish craftsmanship is unmistakably evident.

A last point remains to be clarified. We have seen that Jewish crafts were widespread and their exercise uncontested in the area of first settlement, in the Near East and in the countries around the Mediterranean Sea, and that they were stunted in the area of second settlement, in northern and western Europe. How, then, did the new growth of Jewish artisanship in the area of third settlement, in eastern Europe, come about? If powerful Christian guilds succeeded in excluding Jewish artisans from membership and consequently from the exercise of their crafts in England, France, Germany, and northern Italy, and if they further succeeded in stifling the growth of Jewish guilds, as in Spain, how were effective Jewish guilds and a Jewish artisan class capable of new and independent development in eastern Europe? The answer is that Poland, Lithuania and large parts of the Ottoman Empire in Europe and Asia had no native middle classes and that the Jews were called upon to fill a void in the social structure of these countries.

The rulers of Poland, Lithuania and Turkey welcomed Jewish immigrants to promote trade and the useful crafts and to provide much-needed revenue. The Jews were all the more welcome because there were competitors on the scene. The Turks, having swallowed Byzantium, had become dependent in commerce and in the crafts as well as in administration on the ever-present but unreliable Greeks; they used their new Jewish subjects as a politically innocuous counterpoise. The situation in Poland and Lithuania was not dissimilar. The Jews settled in the cities and towns of these countries alongside German burghers who were considered indispensable for purposes of economic development, but at the same time feared as political antagonists. Hence, the Sultans, the Grand Dukes and the Kings fostered Jewish economic activities and protected the Jewish guilds. In the Ukrainian and Byelo-Russian parts of Poland, again, Jewish artisans along with Jewish traders were useful as revenue producers and economic auxiliaries to the crown and the nobles. When the power of the crown declined and the by-then polonized Christian urban middle classes asserted themselves, the nobles continued to encourage Jewish artisans to settle in the localities which remained under their control. The Jews and their guilds profited from a doubly and triply interstitial position. This was the reverse side of the coin whose face was political weakness and exposure to violence.

Additional circumstances furthered the growth of a Jewish artisan class and their guilds. The growing Jewish population in Poland and Lithuania constituted an inner market of considerable magnitude. In this respect, Prof. Wischnitzer observes, conditions had never been so favorable for Jewish artisanship since the days of the Sassanian empire. The Jewish community in Poland and Lithuania grew away from the caste-like aspect of Jewish existence and assumed the character of a society. By and large, Jewish customers sustained Jewish artisans. On this basis, some of them, like the lace-makers of Cracow and the furriers of Lwow along with

Jewish carpenters, glaziers, and house painters, gained clientele among the Polish nobility. But their decisive advantage was that Jewish artisans could undersell the guild-monopolists and thus serve a mass clientele of Christians as well as Jews.

The Jews were forced onto this revolutionary avenue by a variety of circumstances. Fiscal discriminations in the field of commercial activities and the general impoverishment of the Jewish community in the wake of the Ukrainian pogroms of the seventeenth century drove the Jewish masses into manual occupations, sometimes in connection with petty trade. These marginal craftsmen had to earn a living by hook or by crook. Having learned their craft by trial and error, frequently with the assistance of runaway Christian journeymen, their work was likely to be of a shoddy quality and had to be sold at a reduced price. Wherever a craft grew out of the pawnbroking business and the trade in used goods, the refurbishing of worn and damaged merchandise added another incentive in favor of doing business by price-cutting. That the Jew at any rate was expected to grant credit added the final touch to the mechanism which had been set in motion. The modern economic role of the Jews in catering to the needs of a growing mass market is thus foreshadowed in the history of the Jewish artisan class in eastern Europe.

To summarize, the history of Jewish crafts and craft guilds disposes of the prejudicial image of Jewish economic activities as chiefly those of hucksters and usurers—with an upper layer of bankers—which had grown out of the earlier fixation of social historians on the history of the Jews in central Europe. If the history of the Jews in the Mediterranean countries, on the one hand, and in eastern Europe, on the other, is taken into proper consideration, the importance of Jewish artisanship becomes obvious. Although lack of documentary evidence prevented Prof. Wischnitzer from including the history of Jewish crafts in the *Maghreb* (Morocco, Algeria, Tunisia, Libya) and in Yemen in his study, the picture that emerges is one of a remarkably wide spread of manual skills and craft activities. The textile and clothing crafts, especially tailoring, but also leather work, and the food and beverage trades predominate, but hardly any activity of the human hand is unrepresented. There is no such thing as a "racial" disinclination of the Jews to engage in manual labor. However, the general characteriation of Jewish economic activities and of their role in the larger society as intermediate and interstitial is not invalidated by that statement. Invariably, the Jews form a middle layer in the societies in which they live, between the aristocracy and the laboring classes, and Jewish artisans are a part of that middle layer. With one proviso, though: when the middle layer is numerically small, the Jewish artisan class is small also. When the middle layer grows in numbers, the Jewish artisan class tends to grow into a broad working class. In this sense, the existence of a large Jewish artisan class appears as the prerequisite for the emergence of Jewish peoplehood and national consciousness.

Abbreviations

AASOR.....	Annual of the American Schools of Oriental Research.
BA.........	Biblical Archaeologist.
BASOR.....	Bulletin of the American Schools of Oriental Research.
HUCA......	Hebrew Union College Annual.
JAOS.......	Journal of the American Oriental Society.
JBL........	Journal of Biblical Literature.
JGGJCR....	Jahrbuch der Gesellschaft fuer Geschichte der Juden in der Cechoslovakischen Republik.
JPOS.......	Journal of the Palestine Oriental Society.
JQR........	Jewish Quarterly Review.
JSS.........	Jewish Social Studies.
MGWJ......	Monatsschrift fuer Geschichte und Wissenschaft des Judentums.
MJV........	Mitteilungen fuer Juedische Volkskunde.
ORT.......	Organisation for Rehabilitation through Training.
REJ........	Revue des Études Juives.
YIVO.......	Institute for Jewish Research.

Chapter I

Trades and Guilds in Ancient Israel

The Trades

At the beginning of recorded history, guilds of artisans, merchants, priests and other professional groups were already in existence, having been formed for the mutual economic, social, political and cultural benefit of their members. The nucleus of the guild was the family of the artisan or merchant. The head of the artisan family taught his son the skills he had acquired from his ancestors. Later, families working in the same craft joined together in clans, thus preparing the ground for the organization of the guild.[1]

From earliest times the family of the artisan included apprentices who came from outside the family group. In early Babylonia, the institution of apprenticeship is recorded in the Code of King Hammurabi (ca. 1728-1686 B.C.E.).[2] In the Neo-Babylonian period young slaves would be sent by their owners to learn a trade, but for the great governmental projects free labor had to be hired in addition to the slave labor force. A source of the Neo-Babylonian period illustrates the strength of a stonecutters' organization. The men were employed on a temple building project. When the months Sivan and Tammuz had elapsed and no wages had been paid, the stonecutters "spoke violently, declaring: 'the men are not pleased and will not do the king's work.' "[3] This is the earliest known reference to a strike.

Apart from craft guilds there existed merchants' guilds and even cult associations of prophets and seers.[4] The cult associations centered around the temples; the craft guilds congregated in their own quarters of the city. The Babylonian authorities recognized the guilds and handled matters of taxation with them.[5]

Opinions are divided as to the origin of artisan associations in ancient Israel. Some scholars date them to the Hellenistic epoch. I. Mendelsohn, however, who has studied the problem from literary and archaeological evidence in Mesopotamian and Palestinian sources, holds that guilds existed in ancient Palestine "centuries before the Hebrews came in contact with the Hellenistic world."[6]

When the Israelites began to settle in Canaan (in the thirteenth century B.C.E.), they attempted a peaceful penetration of the country by occupying the less densely populated, wooded, hill country. They tilled the soil, tended their flocks and possessed the primitive skills for making tools, building tents and huts, tanning skins and fashioning earthenware, harps and pipes. The women did the spinning and weaving. Cisterns were constructed and cemented to prevent water from seeping away through the porous limestone.[7] The term *harash,* artificer, was originally associated with woodwork.[8] The Israelites' progress in the occupation of the country was long thwarted by their lack of knowledge of how to smelt iron and to forge tools and arms,[9] an advantage possessed by the Canaanites (*Joshua* 17:18). The hundreds of iron war chariots of the Canaanite king Jabin decided the outcome of the battle of Hazor (*Judges* 4:2). The setback in the battle with the Philistines at Eben Ezer (ca. 1050 B.C.E.) was also due to the superiority of the enemy in iron equipment. The Philistines cut off the Israelites from the iron market which they controlled to such an extent that "there was no smith found throughout all the land of Israel; for the Philistines said: 'lest the Hebrews make themselves swords or spears;' but all the Israelites went down to the Philistines, to sharpen every man his plowshare, and his coulter, and his axe, and his mattock" (*I Samuel* 13:19 f.).

The situation changed considerably under the monarchy. King Saul withstood the pressure of the Philistines and fought victorious battles against them. He was able to equip his army with adequate weapons. David had sufficient iron for military and industrial purposes. Copper was mined in David's and Solomon's time (ca. 1000-922 B.C.E.). There is an interesting passage in *I Kings* 7:15-46 about the casting of brass pillars and vessels for Solomon's Temple. The casting was done in the plain of the Jordan "in the clay ground between Succoth and Zarethan" which Albright locates in the valley east of the Jordan and north of the Jabbok.[10]

Edom with its deposits of copper in the Wadi Arabah, on which much light has been thrown by the excavations of Nelson Glueck, had been conquered by David (*II Samuel* 8:13-15; *I Kings* 11:15-16). Glueck believes that David exploited the mines and that Solomon intensified their exploitation. The copper refinery was at Ezion-geber, the ancient port and industrial center on the north shore of the Gulf of Aqaba, today called Tell-el-Kheleifeh, where Solomon's fleet of trading ships was built and where "gold, silver, ivory, apes, and peacocks" were brought from Ophir. The refinery built in the tenth century B.C.E. was regained by the Edomites who revolted under King Joram (ca. 849-842 B.C.E.), but King Amaziah (ca. 800-783 B.C.E.) restored Judah's sovereignty over Edom and rebuilt or repaired the refinery.[11] The abundance of metals during the reigns of David and Solomon is attested to by another mining and smelting district located in the hills near Ajlun in ancient Gilead (modern Transjordan).[12] A small installation for smelting iron was discovered at Gerar in the Negev.[13]

The Ezion-geber refinery was worked by slave labor recruited from prisoners of war, a practice known from the time of King David, who employed the labor of the vanquished Ammonites. He "put them under saws, and under harrows of iron, and under axes of iron, and made them pass through the brick kiln" (*II Samuel* 12:31).

With the availability of metals the term *harash,* generally meaning "craftsman," was qualified by the name of the particular craft, as when Tubal-cain is called "master (*horesh*) of every cutting instrument of brass and iron" (*Gen.* 4:22). It may have been used by extension to mean "forger." The collaboration of Bezalel of the tribe of Judah (*Exod.* 31:2ff) with his assistant Oholiab of the tribe of Dan (*Exod.* 31:6ff) seems to reflect a certain mobility, a situation when workmen of different localities were enlisted for some large project. Both are said to have worked in brass, stone, wood, gold, and silver, not to speak of textiles. Bezalel would have to be regarded as master supervisor of the works rather than a jack-of-all-trades.

An earlier period is evidently reflected in the reference to the "dyed garments of embroidery," the precious garments coveted by the enemy, in Deborah's song (*Judges* 5:30) which is dated ca. 1125 B.C.E.

As the conquest progressed, the breached walls and gates of Canaanite cities were repaired and re-used. King Saul built his fortress at Gibea (Tell el-Ful) using the casemate method, *i.e.*, with double walls, leaving an empty space between the outer and inner walls which was divided into storage chambers.[14] The casemate type of fortification was also used by King David in Beth Shemesh and Debir (Tell Beit Mirsim).[15]

The masonry of Solomon's time is marked by carefully dressed stone blocks laid in a system of a stretcher and one or two headers. Magnificent gateways flanked by several guardrooms on either side were found to have existed in Solomon's store cities, including those in Hazor identified by Yigael Yadin.[16] We may mention his stables for chariot horses in Megiddo and, to give an idea of the architectural design of the transitional period from the united Solomonic kingdom to the secessionist kingdom of Israel, one need only examine the proto-Aeolic (or proto-Ionic) capitals discovered at Megiddo, Ramat Rahel, Hazor, and in Samaria.[17] The further development of this plant-derived form leads through Cyprus to the Ionic order of the Erechtheon at Athens.

The construction and decoration of the Temple at Jerusalem, Solomon's most cherished project, required precious imported woods and ivories. Cedar and cypress trees from Lebanon were provided by the King of Tyre in exchange for wheat and oil delivered for a number of years (*I Kings* 5:22ff.). The wood was used not only for the revetment of the interior walls of the Temple, but also in the construction of the court enclosure made up of "three rows of hewn stone and a row of cedar beams" (*I Kings* 7:12), according to a building method found in Syria.[18] Solomon's own labor force, seasoned under King David (*II Chron.* 2:6), was insufficient for the elaborate project. Tyre supplied workers in metal, stone, and wood, even weavers and gold and silver workers. Hiram or Huram, a craftsman from Tyre, whose mother was of the tribe of Naphtali according to one tradition (*I Kings* 7:13) and of Dan according to another (*II Chron.* 2:12), is represented in the Bible as proficient in all these crafts. He was more likely the caster, a craft valued more highly than that of the stone mason.

The use of foreign workmen was a sign of the growing wealth and status of the country. We recall how Darius of Persia built his residence at Susa. (5th century B.C.E.) with "cedar wood from Lebanon" among other materials. He employed masons from Ionia and Sardis, builders from Media and Egypt, and Babylonians for brick making. In later times too, important public buildings were entrusted to foreign architects. Trajan's chief architect in Rome was a Greek from Damascus; the Hagia Sophia in Constantinople was built by architects from Asia Minor.[19] The examples can be multiplied.

The strategic and political gains made by David and Solomon over three quarters of a century, due in large part to the relative weakness of the Assyrian and Egyptian empires in that period, gave rise to new social and economic developments. Commerce branched out in various directions: toward the Mediterranean; toward the south and southeast where the Arab tribes lived; and toward Ophir, which was probably on the East African coast.

Foreign trade was mainly a royal monopoly, but domestic trade was carried on by private persons.[20] Mercantile activities favored the development of a money economy which superseded the barter economy still prevailing in the reigns of David and Solomon. Under Solomon, for instance, the Tyrian lumbermen who transported cedar trees from the Lebanon on rafts to the Israelite port and broke them up there for timber were remunerated in kind (*I Kings* 5:23-25), receiving their wages in food rations. However, the import of commodities from abroad created the demand for a medium of exchange. Consumption increased with the emergence of the upper classes and an increase of population in the tiny land, which may have reached the 900,000 mark (300,000 in Judah and 600,000 in Israel) in the pre-exilic period.[21]

In the reign of Joash of Judah (ca. 843-798 B.C.E.) considerable repair work was undertaken in the Temple. The king—not the priests—appears as the initiator of the works, which were to be paid out of the Temple treasury. The sources of the Temple revenue were an assessment upon each individual as well as voluntary contributions (*II Kings* 12:5). The workmen and the merchants who procured stone and timber were paid in cash. The wages of the workers—stone cutters, masons, joiners, and carpenters—were disbursed by those "that did the work, that had the oversight of the house of the Lord." In other words, the money was not handled by the priests. It is said, moreover, (*II Kings* 2:16) that the workers were dealt with "faithfully."

We may see in this disapproval of the management of the priests, particularly as it is pointed out (*II Kings* 12:14) that the works did not include "cups of silver, snuffers, basins, trumpets and vessels of gold, or vessels of silver," in other words, costly cult objects. Clearly, the priests were removed from the role of employers and thus prevented from spending Temple money on articles of luxury for the enhancement of the ceremonial which was evidently of greater interest to them than was the fight against idolatry. "The people still sacrificed and offered in the high places" (*II Kings* 12:4).

The Temple repair work in the reign of the reform King Josiah of Judah was recorded in similar words. The pay masters are the "workmen that have the oversight of the house of the Lord," *i.e.*, the foremen. "Howbeit there was no reckoning made with them of the money that was delivered into their hand; for they dealt faithfully" (*II Kings* 22:5-7). As representatives of the workers they could be trusted to deal with them honestly.

While the king condemns extravagance in the ritual in Judah, the prophet Amos denounces the luxury of the rich in Israel. He aims his words in particular at their "houses of ivory" (*Amos* 3:15) and the "beds of ivory" (6:4). Ivory plaques with carved figurative designs have actually been excavated in Samaria, the capital of Israel founded by Omri. These carvings were found within the enclosure of the royal palace. The ivory plaques, some set with colored glass and pastes were parts of the inlay decoration of wooden wall panellings and of furniture. Ivory carvings were imported or already produced in the country in the time of King Solomon who had an ivory throne (*I Kings* 10:18). Those in Samaria date from the time of Ahab and his Tyrian wife Jezebel, and of Jeroboam II (9th to 8th century B.C.E.) The Phoenician style, or rather the Phoenician version of the Egyptian style, of the carvings implies that they were imports from Phoenicia or Egypt (one may remember that Solomon married Pharaoh's daughter—*I Kings* 3:1). They may have been local imitations. The fact that some of the plaques are in an unfinished state and that fragments of tusks were found on the site suggests that there was a local school of ivory workers in Israel.[22]

The stern invectives of the prophet Amos against the "palaces" of the nations (*Amos,* chs. 1-3)—all nations, comprising Tyre, Edom, Moab, Ashdod, Egypt, and finally, Judah and Israel—reflect the social and political status of the divided Jewish kingdom which had attained the rank of its neighbors. King Ben-hadad of Aram enters a coalition with King Ahab of Israel against Assyria and at the Battle of Qarqar, according to Assyrian records (853 B.C.E.), Ahab confronted Salmanassar III with 2,000 war chariots.[23]

The kingdom of Judah, with which Israel was also often in coalition, had likewise developed a considerable metal industry. At the downfall of Judah in 597 B.C.E., Nebuhadnezzar deported to Babylon along with the young king Joiachin, the princes, officers, officials, soldiers and "all the craftsmen and smiths" (*II Kings* 24:12-14).

Of course, it is impossible to identify a product as the work of a native Israelite, a war captive or a hired foreign craftsman. But this consideration applies to any country in ancient times. The Bible is very candid about the use of foreign labor and exhibits a certain pride in it as a token of prosperity. We, today, place much value upon imported commodities.

Evidence of personal pride in one's handiwork appears in Greece about the sixth century B.C.E., where we find a Corinthian ceramic plaque adorned with a figured painting signed by the potter. Names of architects begin to be associated with buildings in Greece dating from the sixth century B.C.E.[24] However in Egypt, we find records of names of master-builders and sculptors dating from the period of the XVIIIth dynasty, about the sixteenth century B.C.E., and even considerably earlier.[25] It is therefore conceivable that the names of Bezalel and Hiram mentioned in the Bible may rest on an authentic tradition.

The Samaritan plaques carry on their reverse side incised letters of the Hebrew-Phoenician alphabet which must have served as guides for the workers in their assembly tasks. Since this alphabet is very close to the Aramaic alphabet, the question of the language to which they belong has been left open.[26] As mentioned above, there is some evidence pointing to the existence of a local school of ivory workers in Samaria. Although the elephant is not named in the Bible, its ivory is referred to in numerous passages.[27] Large finds of ivory carvings were made in Arslan Tash in Northern Syria and in a palace at Nimrud in Assyria. The ivories are similar in style to those of Samaria.[28] Princely gifts, war spoils and tributes mentioned in Assyrian records and elsewhere include thrones, couches and tables of ivory.

Pottery in Palestine was of the popular utilitarian variety. Until Abraham's time most of Palestine pottery was hand-made. With the introduction of the potter's wheel the shapes of the vessels became more regular and the decoration more evenly applied.[29] Canaanite ware found at Lachish (ca. 1500 B.C.E.) exhibits painted ornaments in a frieze divided into panels (metopes) depicting a bird, a fish, or a fawn.[30] Imported Mycenaean pottery (1375-1250 B.C.E.) shows horizontal and vertical decoration of parallel lines.[31] Philistine pottery (1150-1000 B.C.E.) once again displays the metope frieze with a repeated bird design, the bird usually preening itself.[32] In contrast, Israelite pottery is sparingly decorated with painted designs.

The Bible refers in many instances to the potter's work. The treading of clay is mentioned in *Is.* 41:25. The improved double wheel is implied in the dual form of the Hebrew name of the wheel, *ofnayim* (*Jer.* 18:3). The clay is thrown on the upper lighter disk while the lower heavier one gives momentum to the spinning movement. The expression the "potter's house" used in the passage in Jeremiah refers to the potter's workshop. The Hinnom valley (*Jer.* 19:2)), rich in clay, was a center of pottery manufacture. The near-by city gate in Jerusalem was called the Potsherd Gate.[33] A more recent reference to the potter's work is found in Jesus ben Sirach (Ecclesiasticus, 38:29-30). Here mention is made of the foot-powered wheel, the kiln, and a technique which may be glazing or the coating of the vessel with a superior clay, the so-called slip, intended to reduce the porosity of the ware and improve its appearance. The slip, when burnished or rubbed with a hard tool before firing the vessel, acquired a polished look. However glaze was known neither in the Canaanite nor in the Israelite period.

In the time of the divided monarchy, pottery became a mass product. Apart from household crockery, a water decanter of the bottle type, and a four-handled banquet bowl with the interior decorated by alternating burnished and unburnished spirals have been found. Large amphoras were used for water or oil, and wide-mouth jars for grain. Jugs and juglets for perfume were found in large quantities.

In the royal potteries like those mentioned in *I Chron.* 4:23, storage jars of guaranteed capacity were manufactured for commerce and for the payment of taxes in produce. These jars bear royal stamps consisting of Hebrew letters which read: "belonging to the king." Some were found to bear the name of King Jehoiachin, others the names of cities such as Hebron, Ziph, Socoh, and Memshath, which are thought to have been sites of royal potteries.[34] Trade marks are found on ordinary cooking pots. The shapes of Israelite pottery are flowing and functional, and not tectonic in the sense that Greek pottery is.

Pottery was put to manifold uses. The excavated specimens include children's toys, small household fertility idols, female figures in the form of plaques with the design in relief or of the press-mold type with parts modeled by hand, lamps and braziers, spindle whorls and writing tablets. Potsherds were ground and, added to water-proof plaster, were used for lining cisterns.

Interesting techniques of "mass production" have been noted. In making small juglets, clay was shaped on the wheel into a tall cone. On the tip of the cone a juglet was formed and pinched off while the wheel was turning. Then the next juglet was formed and so on until the clay was used up. This technique saved time.

Another technique was used in the production of large bowls of regular shape, which generally required the use of fine clay and a skillful thrower. It was commercially more advantageous to use a cheaper kind of clay and throw a thicker bowl which, when it had become leatherhard, was turned down to the desired shape and thinness. This method did not require particular skill. It meant cheaper labor and lower prices.[35]

Because of the differences in shape and decoration of ceramic wares, pottery is a valuable criterion for dating the strata in an excavation site. Ceramic chronology checked against literary history, inscriptions and other data enables the archaelogist to identify the population group to which the contents of the particular occupational stratum belonged.

Because of their fragile nature, textiles are not frequently found in excavations. Recently, some have been discovered in Israel. In the Bible references are made to weaving and to colored fabrics. *I Chron.* 4:21 mentions the manufacture of byssus or fine linen; *II Chron.* 2:17 cites purple, blue and crimson dyes; *Prov.* 31:13 refers to a woman working in wool and flax. An idea of Israelite dress may be obtained from the Black Obelisk of Salmanassar III (ninth century B.C.E.) in the British Museum, which shows Israelite prisoners wearing turban-like headgear, fringed robes over fringed long garments, and high boots. On Sennacherib's relief from Lachish (701 B.C.E.), Israelite soldiers wear a short skirt, a shirt, a girdle and a turban. The women wear long robes and a long scarf draped over the head and extending down the back to the hem of the garment.[36]

A glance into the woman's wardrobe is provided in *Isaiah* 3:16-23 which lists corselets, girdles, gauze robes, veils, aprons, mantelets, cloaks, turbans, tiaras, and articles of adornment such as anklets, fillets, crescents, pendants, bracelets, rings, nose-jewels, and amulets. Anklets, bracelets, rings and beads of gold, silver, copper, bone, ivory and colored stones abound in "the ruins of every town."[37]

The most telling evidence of weaving and dyeing activities are the loom weights and dye-vats which have been found in the excavations. In Debir (Tell Beit Mirsim) the entire city was engaged in these related industries.[38] From the small size of the vats, Albright concluded that thread rather than whole fabrics or garments was dyed there. In Lachish J. L. Starkey found the weaving machinery still in position although reduced to charcoal. Here weaving and dyeing were undertaken in the same workshops.[39] An ingenious arrangement of stone dye-vats is explained in Chester Charlton McCown's publication of the excavation at Tell en-Nasbeh.[40] These finds have been dated in the period of the late monarchy up to the early Persian period.

The arts of seal engraving, gold and silver work, gem cutting, and fashioning of glass paste were practiced in the time of the monarchy. A number of personal-name seals were found dating from the period of the kings (8th to 6th centuries B.C.E.). Some of them display pictorial representations similar in style to those found on ivory carvings.[41] Among other items found was a weaver's seal inscribed with his name.[42]

In the Bible, gilding is mentioned in *Is.* 40:19, the "furnace for gold" and the "refining pot for silver" in *Prov.* 17:3.

The Guilds

The picture drawn from literary and archaeological sources is that of a vigorous town life centered in a number of well organized cities, with a thriving population busily engaged in a variety of trades, some basic, others belonging to the luxury crafts. Certain localities were seats of special industries. Lod and Ono were centers of wood industry (*Neh.* 11:35). Netaim and Gedera (literally, plantations and hedges) were sites of royal pottery manufacture (*I Chron.* 4:23). Albright maintains that these are proper names of places in the Shephelah, now called Hirbet en-Nuweiti and Tell ej-Judeidah.[43] There was "a fullers' field near the highway" (*Is.* 7:3) and a bakers' street at Jerusalem (*Jer.* 37:21).

Workers employed in the building trades came from various districts. For large government projects, corvée labor was used. "And this is the account of a levy which King Solomon raised to build the House of the Lord, and his own house, and Millo, and the wall of Jerusalem, and Hazor, and Megiddo, and Gezer" (*I Kings* 9:15). The levy was imposed on the subjugated peoples, the Amorites, Hittites, etc. (*I Kings* 9:20). With regard to Israelite labor, the references are contradictory. *I Kings* 5:27 has it that King Solomon raised a levy "out of all Israel;" however, in *I Kings* 9:22 we read that "of the children of Israel did Solomon make no bondservants." In addition, hired labor from Tyre was employed by King Solomon. In the time of King Joash and King Josiah of Judah the situation was different. The construction workers were paid wages and they received their pay through their own representatives. This fact is strongly emphasized, implying perhaps some past labor conflicts in which the temple administration was involved.

Some expressions designating family relations have been found to indicate guild membership. Thus Hananyah ben ha-raqqahim,

Hananyah, son of the perfumes, means a member of the perfumers' guild, and by analogy Uzziel, son of Harhaiah, goldsmiths (in plural), referred to in *Neh.* 3:18, means Uzziel son of Harhaiah, member of the goldsmiths' guild. Joab, father of the craftsmen (*I Chron.* 4:14), obviously means Joab, elder of the craftsmen's guild. Similarly, "families of the house of Ashbeh" (*mishpahot bet-avodat ha-bus*) who wrought fine linen (byssus), in *I Chron.* 4:21 were a clan of weavers. Families of scribes (*mishpahot sofrim*) referred to in *I Chron.* 2:25 were associations of scribes, while the "sons of the prophets" (*II Kings* 2:3) were members of the prophets' guild.

Thus, as Mendelsohn has shown, such terms as family, house, father, son, mean in proper contexts agglomerations of guilds, a guild, an elder of a guild and a member of a guild.[44]

The nomenclature of the guilds clearly reveals their derivation from the family unit. Mendelsohn finds a prototype for the practice of designating a member of a craft association as "son" in Old- and Neo-Babylonian texts. "Son of a smith," "son of a shepherd," "son of officials," and "sons of soothsayers" (the terms are "maru" and "aplu"), can only mean "member of such-and-such an association.[45] Once the evidence of craft guilds in biblical times is admitted, it follows—and there we cite Mendelsohn again[46] —that marks found on Israelite pottery were not always trademarks of individual potters. Two categories of stamps would have to be distinguished: stamps with proper names which are ownership marks, and stamps bearing some design such as a rosette, a pentagram, a wheel, a cross, and the letter *tau* with no proper name added. Marks of this latter type would each designate a particular potters' guild. A similar view had earlier been advanced by Albright with regard to potters marks discovered at Tell Beit Mirsim. These trademarks appeared to belong to distinct, competitive groups of potters.[47] As mentioned above, some ceramic wares bear names of cities. Whether these cities were sites of pottery production or centers of delivery of taxes in kind is uncertain.

Despite all the questions still to be solved, modern research has established the existence of certain forms of social organization among Jewish craftsmen in biblical times.

Chapter II

Crafts and Guilds in Judea during the Second Jewish Commonwealth, c. 538 B.C.E.-70 C.E.

With the Edict of Liberation issued by Cyrus II of Persia (ca. 538 B.C.E.), a new chapter of Jewish history began. In the years following this momentous act, repatriates streamed back from Babylonia to their ancient home in Palestine. The area in which they started life anew was "very small . . . stretching less than twenty-five miles in a straight line along the watershed-ridge from north of Jerusalem to south of Beth-zur, with a total population which can scarcely have exceeded 20,000 in 522 B.C." [1] There were artisans among the various groups returning from exile. Carpenters and masons are expressly mentioned in the third chapter of *Ezra* dealing with the preparations for the rebuilding of the Temple. The work was begun in 520 B.C.E. and completed five years later. The carpenters and masons were paid in cash, while the Phoenician workmen who carried timber from Lebanon by sea to Jaffa were remunerated in kind (*Ezra* 3:7).

Rebuilding the Jerusalem Wall

The Temple was rebuilt, but the great wall of Jerusalem remained in ruins for nearly four-score years. This long period was one of inaction in the infant Jewish community. Only with the arrival of Nehemiah, the newly appointed governor of the province, about

440 B.C.E., was a fresh spirit infused into the life of the community. Under his vigorous leadership, the restoration of the city wall was immediately taken in hand. The story, told in detail in the third chapter of *Nehemiah,* is a triumphant record of cooperative work on the part of the whole of the community, with all lending a hand to fortify Jerusalem against its hostile neighbors, the Samaritans, Ammonites and Ashdodites. The work was divided into sectors, and the Bible records the groups of people assigned to each sector. The city gates served to mark the points of departure for the different working groups: there was a sheep gate, fish gate, dung gate, gate of the fountain, water gate, old gate, valley gate, horse gate, east gate and gate of Miphkad. The beams, doors, locks and bars of each gate had to be restored. The tower of the furnaces, of the water gate, and other towers had to be raised anew. All groups of the community were mobilized for the work—priests, Levites, merchants, goldsmiths, perfumers, the upper classes as well as ordinary folk. Many carried burdens or performed unskilled work; others were skilled carpenters, masons and smiths.

Aware of the danger of attack by enemies, Nehemiah ordered his people to be on guard and to carry swords, spears and bows: thus a people of workers was at the same time a people in arms, as it is vividly described in *Nehemiah,* 4:11: "Every one with one of his hands wrought in the work, and with the other held his weapon."

The reconstruction of the city wall with its battlements and revetments took two years and four months, according to Josephus, *Ant.* XI. 5. 8. The whole was a feat of workmanship for a population that comprised, during Nehemiah's governorship, some 42,000 free-born Jews and 7,000 slaves and menials.[2]

Sirach on Artisanship

Little is known of the life of the Jewish people in Judea during the period after Nehemiah up to the establishment of Seleucid rule in 198 B.C.E. In this long period of more than 200 years, relatively little information is available on economic developments. The two main occupations seem to have been agriculture and handicrafts, with a not inconsiderable amount of domestic and foreign trading. The manufacture of pottery was carried on, as is proved by recent finds at Tell en-Nasbeh.[3] It would seem that entire villages in Palestine were engaged in pottery making during that period. Jerusalem is described as "a city rich in crafts."[4] More concrete information about artisans' skills is given by Jesus ben Sirach (*Ecclesiasticus*), who lived at the end of the third and the beginning of the second centuries B.C.E. Sirach dwells on the work of the Jewish farmer, and, at greater length, on that of the artisan of his time. He says (38:27-32):

> Likewise the maker of carving and cunning device,
> Who by night as by day hath no rest,
> Who engraveth signet-engravings,
> And whose art it is to make variety of design;
> He is careful to make the likeness true,
> And his anxiety is to complete his work.
> So also the smith that sitteth by the furnace,
> And regardeth the weighty vessels;
> The flame of the fire cracketh his flesh,
> And with the heat of the furnace he gloweth;
> To the sound of the hammer he inclineth his ear,
> And to the pattern of the vessel directeth his eyes.
> He is careful to complete his work,
> And his anxiety is to measure it off exactly.
> Likewise the potter who sitteth at his wheel,
> And driveth the vessel with the soles of his feet;
> Who is all the time in anxiety over his work,
> And all his handiwork is by number.
> His arms are cracked by the day,
> And before old age he is bent and bowed,
> He is careful to complete the glazing,
> And his anxiety is for the heating of the furnace.
> All these are deft with their hands,
> And each is wise in his handiwork,
> Without them a city cannot be inhabited
> And wherever they dwell they hunger not.[5]

Under Hasmonean Rule

Other trades, in addition to those just mentioned, developed in ever growing number under the Hasmoneans, the dynastic rulers of the independent Jewish state proclaimed in 141 B.C.E. by Simon the Hasmonean.

The Hasmoneans attained their goal in the struggle against the Seleucids with the support of the masses of the nation. M. I. Rostovtzeff has pointed out that the Seleucids "met staunch resistance, not from the Jewish bourgeoisie, but from the peasants and artisans, who finally asserted the independence of the country."[6]

The new state was at first small in size, and numbered scarcely 200,000 inhabitants; but this territory was soon enlarged as a result of the bold expansionist policy of the Hasmoneans. They pressed hard for an avenue to the Mediterranean coast, and at the same time made considerable strategic gains in the east and southeast. Edom and the province of Medebah in Transjordania were conquered; the district of Samaria was likewise subjugated. These striking military successes, achieved in a period of some sixty years, brought into existence a Jewish state of about half the size of the kingdom of David.[7]

The population of the new state grew, as did its economic needs. It should be borne in mind that the coastal region was densely settled by Hellenized populations engaged in commerce and industry. A number of cities in the interior, such as Samaria, Philadelphia and Scythopolis, also contained considerable Hellenized groups. The Jews of the Hasmonean state, whose forbears had lived aloof and secluded for ages, now encountered a world of far greater refinement and sophistication. Jewish artisans had to learn new skills and adapt old ones to the more civilized tastes and requirements of the time.

The advancement of arts and crafts was greatly stimulated by the Hasmonean kings. As soon as the Hasmoneans had secured their position, they undertook an extensive building program. The city wall of Jerusalem and the entrance to the Temple, destroyed by the Seleucid kings, were repaired. The newly conquered cities were fortified and castles were erected. Simon, whose efforts to advance the welfare of the state are so vividly described in *I Maccabees*, 14, ordered the building of the port of Jaffa, to attract seaborne commerce. The remarkable sepulchre of the Hasmoneans, erected by Simon in Modi'in, the birthplace of the Maccabees, was also aimed at fostering the maritime trade of his realm, as may be gathered from this description of the monument: "And he set up seven pyramids, one over against another, for [his] father, and mother, and four brethren. And for these he made cunning devices, setting about them great pillars and upon the pillars he fashioned all manner of arms for a perpetual memory, and besides the arms carved ships, that they should be seen of all that sail in the sea" (*I Macc.* 13:19).[8] It goes without saying that builders, sculptors, and skilled craftsmen of all kinds were needed to erect the monument and other structures planned by Simon and the succeeding rulers of the state. The increased trade by sea was also bound to promote the development of crafts.

As the first century B.C.E. drew to a close, Palestine may have seemed a poor country to an outsider. But the numerous grain fields, vineyards and fruit orchards throughout the land bore witness to the agricultural and horticultural progress which had been achieved. Barley was exported in large quantities, in addition to figs, olives, dates and grapes. The balsam trees of Jericho were highly prized. Though Palestine was principally a land of farms with vast stretches of grassland, at the time it also had cities with comparatively large populations and a thriving commerce and industry. Jerusalem with its 100,000 residents and crowds of visitors during the High Festivals was an international center. The total population of the country increased during the first century of the Common Era, reaching an estimated 2,500,000 in 70, the year of the Roman conquest.[9]

It is obvious that such a large community was in need of a variety of manufactured goods, tools and implements, for both the peasantry and the urban population. The latter, as has been noted, was in large part Hellenized and required a better class of wares. The Jerusalem bazaars also supplied consumer goods for the crowds of visitors from abroad. Herzfeld, in his *History of Commerce among the Jews in Antiquity* (1879), listed 118 food stuffs and manufactured articles imported from abroad against 78 produced domestically,[10] conceding that he might not have exhausted all the information on the subject contained in the mishnaic and talmudic sources. Since the publication of his book, our knowledge of trades in Palestine in that period has been considerably enlarged.

Building Trades

The ambitious project of restoring the Temple, started by King

Herod in 20 B.C.E., called for skilled labor. Masons, carpenters, metal workers, hydraulic technicians, weavers and embroiderers, goldsmiths and silversmiths—all engaged in the architectural undertaking vividly described by Josephus (*Ant.* XV. 11. 2). Presumably all these workmen were Jews. Herod, though more Greek (of Idumaean origin) than Jewish, had to defer to the religious scruples of the Jewish nation in whose eyes it would have been sacrilegious to entrust heathens with the restoration of God's Temple. Herod marshalled an army of workmen. Even priests were trained as masons and carpenters for the work of the inner Temple, probably in order to make the undertaking more palatable to the population, for there were rumors that the old Temple would be pulled down and never rebuilt.

The Temple restoration was but one of the many projects undertaken by Herod. In Jerusalem, he built a palace for himself; the three towers Hippicus, Phasael, and Mariamne; the Herod mausoleum; a theater; and a hippodrome. In other cities, too, especially in Caesarea, he spent large sums on the erection of new buildings. This activity was continued by his successors. Agrippa I, a grandson of Herod, ordered the erection of the north wall in Jerusalem. His successor, Agrippa II, enlarged the palace of the Hasmonean kings and completed Herod's Temple in 62-64 C.E. When this enterprise was finished, the king was urged to extend the public works to prevent large-scale unemployment. Thereupon the paving of Jerusalem "with white stones" was ordered. Agrippa appropriated the funds required for this from the Temple's treasury. Another important project was the erection in Jerusalem of a mausoleum by Helena, queen of Adiabene (a semi-independent state interposed between the Roman and Parthian empires), who had adopted the Jewish faith, along with her son Izates. Both were buried there.[11]

Talmudic sources speak of several hundred synagogues destroyed by Titus in Jerusalem alone. The figures they mention are no doubt exaggerated; however we do know that foreign Jews visiting Jerusalem or residing there had their own synagogues. There were synagogues of the Alexandrians, the Cilicians, the Cyreneans, and others. The inscription of a synagogue on the Ophel has survived. This synagogue, dating from the first century B.C.E., had a hospice for needy strangers and a water installation.[12] The fact that the inscription is in Greek and that many technical terms of the building trades found in the Mishnah are of Greek derivation is very illuminating.[13] There were sizable contingents of Hellenized workers of various origins, in the building trades, particularly in the larger cities. Working side by side with pagan workers when different ethnic or religious groups were employed on a state project or on the construction of a public bath, created problems for the Jewish workers. Taking such a case in consideration, the rabbis ruled that Jewish artisans may accept employment on pagan buildings, but with the following provision: As soon as the arch is reached where "the pagans put up their idols," they must stop working. It was particularly forbidden to collaborate on the construction of a basilica, a *gradum* (literally, "steps," possibly a platform for executions), a stadium and a *bimah,* or *bemah,* a judge's seat. These structures were associated in the Jewish mind with martyrdom, trials and executions (Mishnah, *Ab. Zarah* I, 7 and *Ab. Zarah* 16b).[14] The mishnaic injunction reflects the political situation, particularly after the repression of the Bar Kokhba rebellion (135 C.E.).

The realities of life, however, did not always make it easy to comply scrupulously with the religious strictures. The rabbis could not overlook the needs of the Jewish artisans who had to compete with non-Jewish workers. Rabbi Eliezer (first half of the second century), for instance, resolved that, although "none may make ornaments for an idol, [such as] necklaces, earrings and finger rings, it is permitted, if for payment."[15] The design of these articles was not always strictly abstract. As time went on other relaxations were conceded.

The Food Trades

Olive oil was an important article of consumption. It was also used as an ingredient of drugs and cosmetics and for illumination. The region of Jerusalem was well suited for the cultivation of olive trees. There was a guild of olive seethers (Mishnah, *Kelim* V, 5 and VIII, 8).[16]

The tradition of home baking seems to have been maintained mostly in the households of the upper classes. The mass of the population purchased their bread from bakery shops.[17] The Talmud indicates that the commercially baked loaves of bread differed in size from home-baked bread. As a rule, the customers and not the bakers provided the flour and fuel for baking.[18] In times of crisis bakeries proved of assistance. When famine ravaged the country in the thirteenth year of Herod's reign (25 B.C.E.), the king ordered flour to be shipped from Egypt and distributed among the people of Jerusalem; the city bakers obtained enough flour to care for the sick and the elderly who were unable to bake for themselves (*Ant.* XV. 9. 2).

Bakeries were situated in streets of their own, whereas shops selling bread and other baked goods were scattered about the cities. The markets had stalls for the sale of bread; the Mishnah refers to such a stall in the market of Lydda. As a rule, bakers sold their wares to wholesale dealers, called *poterim,* who in turn sold them to retail shopkeepers, called *manupols.*[19]

Midrashic sources tell of all sorts of baked goods which the apprentices were taught by the masters to make. It is amusing to learn that pastry bakers in Caesarea produced one hundred different kinds of egg pastries.[20] They evidently could compete with Rome's bakers of whom Pliny has so much to say (*Nat. Hist.,* XVIII. 27.105-106). The food trades included cheese-makers, brewers, millers and butchers, who also sold cooked meals.

Weaving, Fulling and Laundering

In the period of the Second Commonwealth, weaving was carried on throughout the country. It is possible that the mishnaic passage (*Baba Kamma* X, 9) referring to "buying garments of wool from women in Judea and garments of flax in Galilee" reflects the situation as it then prevailed.[21] Galilee was also known for the production of woolen goods, however. The passage quoted above is interesting from another aspect. It points to the fact that women were weaving not only for the household, but also for the general market. A passage in *Ketuboth* V, 5 likewise deals with women weavers. *Ketuboth* 106a discusses whether the women weavers working on the repair of the temple curtains were paid from the Temple building funds.[22] There are references to young and unmarried women engaged in weaving, one of them in the Syriac *Apocalypse of Baruch* (10, 19):

> "And you, ye virgins; who weave fine linen
> and silk with gold of Ophir."

However, weaving was in the main a man's occupation. Josephus (*Jewish War,* V. 8. 1) mentions a market for woolen goods in the New City of Jerusalem. The synagogue of the *tarsiim* in Jerusalem belonged to the weavers of "tarsian" cloth. There was also a synagogue of weavers in Lydda.[23]

The fullers' trade, an accessory to weaving, occupied many hands. Fulleries were combined with laundries which, the Mishnah stresses, were important in the Near East for hygienic reasons. Launderers were permitted to work until midday the day before Passover to supply their patrons with fresh garments for the festival.[24] Another concession of the rabbis is interesting from the political point of view. Jewish laundrymen were permitted to wash garments of non-Jews in the interest of good neighborly relations.[25]

Tailoring

Commerical tailoring was unknown in biblical times, as garments were woven directly on the looms by the family for the use of its members. The term of *hajiyat,* or tailor, appears for the first time in the mishnaic and midrashic writings; another term was *tofer.* The tailors of this period worked not only for individual customers, but also for dealers in clothes; the tailors' market in the New City of Jerusalem was located near the woolen market. The making of priestly garments was the job of Jerusalem's master tailors.[26]

Leather Crafts

The tanners of Palestine, like those of ancient Greece, pursued their trade outside the cities. The Mishnah and Talmud classified leather dressing among the coarser trades, like pottery and mining, but its economic importance was never underestimated. Shoe-, boot- and sandal-making occupied many hands. Others produced garments of leather, and sacks for the transportation of wine and oil. There were also harness and parchment makers, and makers of leather bags. The Mishnah (*Kelim,* XVI:16) mentions a leather case, *trenetak,* which was a kit with compartments for a pen, lancet, knife and a pair of scissors; this, it would seem, was used by surgeons.[27]

Metal Work

The metal trade embraced smelters, blacksmiths, coppersmiths, goldsmiths, silversmiths, needle makers, and armorers. The smithies were located in Jerusalem. With the outbreak of the Roman-Jewish War in 66 C.E., the smiths' trade virtually became a war industry, as pointed out by Josephus (*Jewish War*. II, 22. 1).

Gold- and silversmiths produced articles for the household as well as ornaments. One ornament should be mentioned here, the "city of gold" or "Jerusalem of gold." This was a mural crown imitating a wall encircling a city and fortified by battlements. The statue of the Tyche of Antioch (Fortune of Antioch) by Eutychides, third century B.C.E., wears such a mural crown. There are also representations of the Tyche of Palmyra and of Dura, with mural crowns. Evidently, the "fortune" of Jerusalem was similarly portrayed. The custom of honoring a young bride by having her wear the "city of gold," or a mural crown, referred to in the Babylonian Talmud (*Sota* 49a; *Shab*. 59a), is reflected in the medieval usage of having the bride wear a royal crown.[28]

Glass Blowing

Glass blowing was invented in the second or first century B.C.E. Hand-made glass was produced by the Egyptians from the Eighteenth Dynasty on (ca. 1500 B.C.E.).[29] The Jews took over the new technique from the Syrians of Tyre and Sidon. Job refers to glass as an article scarcer than gold (28:17). First imported, glass was later produced in Palestine[30] and made into cups, bottles, spoons, etc. It was cheaper to make vessels from glass than from copper.[31]

Arts and Crafts and the Temple

The Temple administration, with the court of the king, was one of the largest employers of labor. Masons, carpenters, embroiderers, weavers, goldsmiths and other metalworkers were constantly engaged in repairing the buildings and utensils. Barbers and tailors were also employed. There were, finally, the Temple's scribes, musicians, singers, makers of musical instruments, bakers of the showbread and makers of incense. The latter were privileged groups.[32] Their skills were handed down from father to son and the artisans were loath to admit outsiders into their ranks. The Mishnah and Talmud record the names of such experts and families of experts. The Mishnah says (*Yoma,* III, 10-11) :

> They of the house of Garmu would not teach [any other] how to prepare the showbread. They of the house of Abtinas would not teach [any other] how to prepare the incense. Hygros ben Levi had a special art in singing, but he would not teach it [to any other]. Ben Kamtzar woud not teach [any other] in [his special] craft of writing.

The families—should one say guilds?—of Garmu and Abtinas actually monopolized their position. When they claimed higher wages, the Temple administration dismissed them and summoned showbread makers and incense makers from Alexandria to take their place.* The experiment failed, because of the inefficiency of the new craftsmen, and the houses of Garmu and Abtinas were reinstalled. The talmudic record (*Yoma* 38a) says that the members of the houses of Abtinas and Garmu agreed to resume work after they were offered double the amount of wages they received before they struck, namely 2,400 denarii per day instead of 1,200.[33]

Stone Ossuaries

Toward the close of the Second Commonwealth, the custom prevailed of removing the bones of corpses from their niches in the burial places after a certain time and placing them in chests or

* Probably those employed in the Temple of Leontopolis, in Egypt.

ossuaries made of wood, stone or clay. Several hundred ossuaries were excavated near Jerusalem, and in other parts of the country. Among the workers employed in making ossuaries were men from Galilee, to judge from names inscribed on the lids of some of the chests. The names being accompanied by figures, it has been suggested that these notations indicated the amount of work days spent on the job, or of ossuaries completed. The figures may refer to wages paid or due to the workers.[34]

Artisans' Quarters and Artisans' Badges

In ancient Jerusalem, before its destruction in 70 C.E., certain districts, markets, and streets were inhabited by artisans of the same trade. Blacksmiths, goldsmiths, leather workers, dyers, bakers, weavers, fullers, potters, cheese-makers, and other craftsmen were concentrated in their own quarters. The different trades, it has been suggested, had synagogues of their own. The synagogue of the weavers in Jerusalem has already been mentioned. In addition, the weavers possessed their own burial place.

When the artisan passed through the city or went to a nearby village, he was recognized by the distinctive badge he wore. The tailor had a needle stuck in the front of his dress; the wool carder showed a woolen thread; the dyer carried different colored threads from which patrons could select the desired shade; the carpenter displayed a ruler; the leather worker was recognized by the apron he wore; the weaver carried a small distaff behind his ear; the scribe a pen. The tannaic scholar Eleazar ben Azariah (first century C.E.) said of the wearing of badges: "There is something grand about artisanship; every artisan boasts of his trade, carrying proudly his badge in the street." [35]

Social Position of the Artisan

Rabbi Eleazar's statement is an expression of the high regard in which artisans were held at the close of and immediately following the Second Commonwealth. This attitude differed markedly from that of Jesus ben Sirach. Although, as we have seen, Sirach emphasized the important economic role of the artisan class, he denied it any part in public life, which was the exclusive domain of the learned men or *Soferim*. Sirach did not object to the *Soferim* keeping aloof from manual labor; he even ventured to say that "the wisdom of the learned men comes by opportunity of leisure; and he that has little business shall become wise." Such being the case, Sirach argued, "wisdom" cannot be the portion of "farmers or artisans absorbed in their daily round of toil." He said of farmers and artisans:

> But they shall not be inquired of for public counsel,
> And in the assembly they enjoy no precedence.
> On the seat of the judge they do not sit,
> And law and justice they understand not.
> They do not expound the instruction of wisdom,
> Nor understand the proverbs of the wise;
> But they understand the work they have wrought,
> And their thought is on the practice of their craft.

With the fall of Jerusalem and the loss of independence, the spiritual leadership of the Jewish community was taken over by men of the humbler professions. Priests and members of the upper classes had been deported or had perished. To a large extent, the new leadership consisted of farmers and artisans. Among the sages of the Mishnah (second century C.E.), we find quite a few bearing the name of the trade in which they were engaged. Hillel earned his livelihood as a woodcutter; Akiba was a shepherd; Abba Chilkia a day laborer; Nechuniah a cistern worker; Joshua ben Hananiah, one of the prominent tannaic scholars and some time head of the Academy of Yabneh (Jamnia), was a needle-maker or, according to another version, a charcoal-burner. The tannaim Isaac and Judah were smiths; Hanina and Oshaia were shoemakers; there were among them a baker, a perfumer, and a butcher by the name of Judah; Nehemiah was a potter; Judah ben Ilai was a cooper who taught his students while sitting on a cask; Judah Hayyatai was, as his name indicates, a tailor; one Johanan was a sandalmaker, and another a scribe; Joshua ben Halafta was a tanner and another Joshua a miller of grits. The New Testament mentions tentmaking as the trade of Paul, tannery of Simon, coppersmithing of Alexander of Ephesus, and silversmithing of Demetrius, who, according to *Acts* 19:24, spoke before the men of his guild.[36]

The Mishnah (*Bikkurim* III:3) records an example from the period of the Second Temple showing artisans of Jerusalem joining Temple officers in a group to welcome a procession of pilgrims from abroad. The occasion was the ceremony of the offering of the first fruits. It is evident that the aristocratic point of view was losing ground, to be superseded by an acceptance of the artisan as a man whose counsel bore weight. It remains true, however, that respect for and familiarity with the teachings of the sacred Law was a prerequisite for higher social status, which was denied the illiterate peasant (*am-haaretz*) and not always available to the artisan.

Concluding Remarks

The six hundred year period of the Second Commonwealth began with the rehabilitation of the country by those who returned from the Babylonian Captivity. Conditions were so hard that many thought of going back. The exhortations of the prophets Haggai and Zachariah and the exertions of Ezra and Nehemiah were needed to keep the people on the job of restoration. From Jerusalem and the region around it, Jewish settlements spread, in time, to other parts of Judea, forming the "tiny nucleus for a Jewish state" (Albright), to be built later by the Hasmoneans. It was a community of farmers and artisans, with a sprinkling of traders. However, Josephus' statement, "Ours is not a maritime country; neither commerce nor the intercourse which it promotes with the outside world has any attraction for us" (*Against Apion,* I, 12, 60), gives a rather conservative evaluation of the economy of his time, the first century C.E., when crafts and industry were expanding.

With the growth of population, which had reached 2,500,000, the need increased for a variety of skills—for builders, overseers, masons, plasterers, carpenters, metalworkers and painters. Weaving, dyeing and glassmaking were the most important crafts in the period, but butchers, fishermen, bakers, wine and olive oil producers, garment workers, shoemakers and others likewise were required to meet the stepped up demands of the growing economy.

In addition, armormaking had emerged under the Hasmoneans who needed weapons for their campaigns against the Seleucids and for supplying their garrisons in times of peace. The increased need for metals prompted Herod to obtain from Emperor Augustus a grant to exploit the coppermines of Cyprus.[37]

Toward the end of the era, the Second Commonwealth was remarkable not only in the religious and cultural field, but also for its social and economic advances. The relative prosperity of the country even allowed for the exportation of some manufactured products. Because of the growth of its artisan class, the Jewish state was able to attain a measure of economic self-sufficiency. If the Palestinian "masses lived in dismal poverty" (Baron), this observation does not apply to the artisans. As the saying went: "Though a famine last seven years, it does not pass the artisan's gate" (*Sanhedrin* 29a).

Even though potters, dyers, tanners and weavers were largely established in the villages, the process of urbanization began to draw them into the cities. In the last century of the Second Commonwealth a semi-capitalistic trend developed, accompanied by social unrest which was one of the causes of the Judeo-Roman war.[38]

Guilds which had existed in ancient Israel grew in importance during the Second Commonwealth. Members of the guilds were recognizable by the insignia they were proud to display. Jewish guilds originated at about the same time in the Diaspora, especially in Egypt and Asia Minor. On the whole, artisans occupied a respected place within the community.

CHAPTER III

Crafts, Guilds and Labor Legislation in Palestine, 70-636 C.E.

Conquest by the Roman legions in 70 C.E. cost the Jewish people its statehood, its capital, and its Temple. Jerusalem and other cities lay in ruins. Hundreds of thousands died in battle or from famine, or fled, or were deported. In Jerusalem 40,000 surrendered to the Romans during the siege. Some cities, such as Yabneh and Lydda, however, were spared the ravages of the war. Yabneh became a rallying center as the seat of the Sanhedrin and of the talmudic academy of Rabbi Johanan ben Zakkai who had made peace with Rome. Lydda maintained synagogues and schools; Bethar (headquarters of Bar Kokhba in 132-135) had a law court and schools. The Jewish population of Bene Brak, Bethlehem, Ben Aziz, Emmaus, Gimso, Hebron, Kefar Etam and Rimmon survived. Thousands of those who had fled from their homes in 66-70 returned after peace was restored. The recovery, says Buechler, was so rapid that "in two generations a hundred thousand Jews could again rise in several hundred places of Judea against the Roman rule."[1]

Recent archaeological discoveries also show that life was restored soon after 70 in many places not wholly destroyed by the war. In 132, on the eve of the Bar Kokhba uprising, Palestine had an estimated Jewish population of 1,300,000, which after the uprising's crushing defeat in 135 was reduced to about 700,000. Half the population resided in Galilee where Roman reprisals were less severe than in Judea and other parts of Palestine.[2] The life of the nation, after Bar Kokhba's defeat, shifted to Galilee.

Galilee became the religious, cultural, and socio-economic center of Palestinian Jewry under the Patriarchate. The first to hold the office of Patriarch was Judah Hanassi (160-200); the last, Gamaliel VI, who died without an heir in 425.

Agriculture during the Patriarchate and until the Arab conquest in 636 was the chief occupation of the people, followed by handicrafts, industry, commerce and the professions. The population lived, in the main, on what was produced within the country, imports being comparatively insignificant; there was some exporting of farm products and manufactured goods.

Textile Crafts

The textile crafts embraced a whole congeries of trades—the raising of sheep, cultivation of hemp, weaving of wool, linen and silk, fulling, dyeing, washing, sewing, etc. Palestinian textile production made marked progress in the first centuries of the Common Era. It has been rightly stressed that while fabrics such as those used for the garments of the High Priests, used to be imported from Egypt or India during the period of the Second Commonwealth, Palestine itself now produced such fabrics for export. Both talmudic and non-Jewish sources point to the excellent textiles of Beth Shean (Beisan or Scythopolis), Usha, Beth Mechusa and Arbel (or Irbid); the well known tariff ordinance of Emperor Diocletian, issued in 295, listed the Beth Shean textiles. The Jerusalem Talmud *(Kiddushin II, 5)* also refers to them. At that time Palestinian linen seems to have been preferred to Egyptian linen, and Roman writers praised the garments made in the Beth Shean workshops. Coarse cloth in demand by the common people was produced in Arbel, Navrash, Tiberias and Usha. Both Tiberias and Usha were known for their production of mats. Sepphoris, an important urban center in Galilee, had a synagogue of the weavers. According to the Mishnah, there were 300 weaving shops in Kfar Namra.

Silk weaving flourished in Upper Galilee, the township of Giscalah being renowned for it; the silk fabricated there was sold in the markets of Tyre. Long before the reign of Emperor Justinian (527-565), silk yarn from China and India reached Palestine where it was woven. It has been suggested that Jews in a number of localities in the Negev purchased the silk yarn from caravans passing through Aqaba from the East on their way to Gaza; they interwove the silk with wool and exported the finished fabrics to the West. El Majdal, in the Negev, was once the bustling scene of the Middle East's finest textile production. More precise testimony is given in a fourth century work, *Totius Orbis Descriptio,* which states that purple silk was manufactured in Zerifin (Sarepta), Caesarea, Neapolis and Lydda. Purple dye was produced from the juice of the trumpet-shell or purple-fish, found on the Mediterranean coast from Tyre to Haifa and farther south.

The inhabitants of whole villages in the Darom (south of Palestine) engaged in purple dyeing; the fingers of the menfolk were permanently stained by the dye. The name of one place, Migdal Zevaia (Dyers' Tower), otherwise known as Taricharya, is significant. The existence of numerous dyers lends weight to Avi-Yonah's suggestions that dyestuffs were exported. Like the salve makers of those days, the Palestinian dyers developed special and secret techniques which were handed down from father to son. Shopkeepers used to complain about the smell from neighboring dye works tainting their goods; the rabbis therefore forbade the opening of such installations in the vicinity of shops. While some dyers received dyestuffs from their customers, others supplied their own dyes.[3]

Pottery and Glass Blowing

Whole villages engaged in pottery making. Many jars, amphoras and oil lamps were unearthed in recent years in Lydda, Bethlehem, Kefar Sichin and Kefar Hanania in Galilee. Naaran was also known for its pottery. Gerasa, in Transjordania, was reportedly the seat of a guild of potters.[4]

As a rule, pottery was manufactured in places where suitable clay was available. The production did not require expensive tools or great outlay. Glass blowing, however, required both technical skill and considerable investment. Tiberias was a center of glass making. It is suggested that the production techniques were passed on from Palestine to the Western world.[5]

Basketry, Rope Making, and the Extraction of Oil

The palm tree, widely cultivated at the time in Palestine, was useful in a number of ways. Palm branches were used to make baskets, palm fibers for rope and string, and palm leaves for small baskets, mats, brooms and writing material. Beth Shean was a center of basket making, Damascus a market for its wares.[6]

Under the second Commonwealth, as we have seen, the production of oil was an essential element of the country's economy and foreign trade. According to Josephus, Galilee was a prominent center of oil production. During the Bar Kokhba uprising, the Romans destroyed virtually all oil producing trees, but they subsequently grew up again, as reported in the Talmud, and oil resumed its place as a lucrative item of export, though it had to compete with high quality Spanish oil and low priced African products.[7]

Armor Making

The Maccabeans needed weapons, and so did the defenders of Jerusalem in 66-70. After the war, the Romans placed orders for weapons with Jewish armorers. Ironically, these weapons were used against the Romans by Bar Kokhba's troops. Swaggering with a sword on the Sabbath seems to have been a favorite pastime until the Talmud strictly forbade carrying swords, bows, cuirasses, clubs and spears on the Sabbath day.[8]

Building Trade

With the recovery of Palestinian Jewry in the second half of the second century C.E., the building trade revived. Talmudic sources contain frequent references to builders (*kablanim*), architects (*adrichalim*), bricklayers (*banaim*), carpenters (*harashim*), etc.[9] There was a considerable demand for synagogues, which were used as places of worship and as community houses. More than forty Palestinian synagogues, dating from the third to the seventh centuries have been discovered.[10] Painters and mosaicists worked at decorating the walls and floors of synagogues and dwellings. Painters, incidentally, like dyers, had special and secret techniques for the preparation of their materials.[11] The synagogue decorations displayed human figures, animals, plants and contemporary ornamental designs. Two Jewish mosaicists who laid out the pavement of the synagogue of Beth Alpha (sixth century) inscribed their work with their names: Marianos and his son, Hanina.[12]

Social Regard for Craftsmanship

The Palestinian community valued artisans both as a productive element and as citizens worthy of full participation in the social and cultural endeavors of the community. This is not surprising if one keeps in mind that many of the rabbis made their living by manual labor. Some lectured in their workshops, while others carried their tools along to the academies. The *tanna* Simon ben Yohai, though not an artisan himself, reportedly bore a basket on his shoulders when he went to the academy, pronouncing these words: "Great is labor for it honors the worker" (*Nedarim* 49b). Of the many rabbinical statements emphasizing the economic security afforded by manual labor, the following may be cited: "Abundance derives only from manual labor." "The father that fails to teach his son a trade, teaches him to rob."[13]

Life was hard in the years immediately following the defeat of Bar Kokhba. Students of the talmudic academies were particularly affected. Some emigrated to Parthia (formerly Babylonia); others stayed on and took to handicrafts, combining work with study of the Torah. In Sepphoris, in the second half of the second century, there was an association of Torah students whose members divided their time between prayer, study and work. One of the principles of this association was: "Make thy Sabbath a workday [with regard to food and drink] and do not depend on other people" (*Pesahim* 113a). According to Buechler, "The full independence at which they were aiming could only be realized by adopting a regular handicraft." The patriach Judah Hanassi (160-200) said that "if a person has no occupation, people comment unfavorably on him and ask whence has he his food" (*Aboth de-Rabbi Nathan,* 2nd version, XXI, 22b).[14]

The vocational training of youth preoccupied the rabbis of the second century. The matter was discussed in the academy of Usha (Galilee) and the consensus was that fathers should train their sons in a craft. Judah ben Ilai, himself a cooper, staunchly supported this view. The question arose what trade to recommend to fathers who were not artisans for the training of their sons. Rabbi Meir suggested that one should choose a neat and easy craft, like tailoring, because "the stitches form neat, straight lines, like the furrows of the field" (*Berakhot* 63a). The tanna Rabbi Ishmael interpreted the biblical phrase "choose life" (*Deut.* 30:19) to mean "choose a craft."[15]

Rabbi Ishmael was also the spokesman of those who claimed that study of the Law should not absorb the sages entirely, but that they should find time to take part in communal affairs or to work with their hands. In contrast, Rabbi Simon bar Yohai, though praising the value of labor, said that the sage should give all his time to the study of the Torah. Both Ishmael and Simon discussed the problem at length, without reaching any conclusion. The issue was taken up again in one of the academies. The discussion ended with this wise pronouncement: there are many who favor the idea of Simon bar Yohai, while others adhere to the philosophy of Ishmael.[16]

The crafts were preferred to agricultural work because the latter was at the mercy of the vagaries of the elements.[17] The detailed descriptions of the crafts and their technical procedures in the Mishnah and the Talmud reflect the greater familiarity of the rabbis with artisanship.

Guilds

The concentration of a trade in one locality was, apart from other considerations, motivated by the desire "to keep an eye on one's fellow and to watch prices," as was so aptly formulated by a historian of medieval craft guilds. Some talmudic sayings convey the same concern.[18] However, the suspicious watchfulness of the competitors was, in the course of time, mitigated by the necessity of joining forces to regulate conditions. This is not to say that professional jealousy ceased altogether. Competition prevailed in one form or another. But with the emergence of common interests a *modus vivendi* had to be found. Artisans of the same calling begin to band together against external factors threatening one and all. There was the constant danger of competition from foreign artisans coming to settle and set up a new workshop. The association or guild provided an answer to this threat. This policy is briefly expressed in the following regulation: "The residents of an alley can prevent one another from bringing in a tailor, a tanner, a teacher, or any other craftsmen" (*Tosefta, Baba Mezia* XI,16; *Baba Batra* 21b). This meant that residents of an alley who pursued the same trade, by associating together in a guild could prevent the coming in of foreign craftsmen, and thus secure a monopoly in that trade.

In the absence of guild statutes dating from that early period, one must piece together such references to the organization and function of guilds as are scattered in the talmudic sources. The head of the guild was called *rabban* (*Aboda Zara* 17b), or *rosh ha-umanot* (*Midrash Tehillim* 114, 9). Wool weavers and dyers were permitted to purchase raw materials in partnership; it is safe to assume that such agreements were arranged by the weavers' and dyers' guilds. The *Tosefta* contains a reference to a bakers' strike, which presupposes a decision by an association of bakers (*Tosefta, Baba Mezia* XI,25). The term *regiah,* used in the *Tosefta,* is interpreted by some scholars to mean arrangement or combination—"bakers are allowed to form a combination." Isidor Epstein, however, in his *Social Legislation in the Talmud,*[19] insists that *regiah* means strike; A. S. Herschberg holds that it means a lockout, in which case the passage should be understood as saying that the master bakers decided to lock out their journeymen.[20] One learns from the *Tosefta* that a butchers' guild decided to assign each member a day on which he is allowed to work, punishing anyone who infringed upon that day. One of the basic functions of the guild organization was the protection of the worker in his job. Time and again artisans were warned against encroaching upon the jobs of their fellow workers.

Apparently the guilds insured their members against loss of tools or working animals. Two instances are worth mentioning. "The mariners," said the *Tosefta,* "are entitled to stipulate that one who loses his boat should be provided another boat. If this was caused by his own fault, they would not have to provide him with another boat." The same procedure applied with regard to ass-drivers. The ass-drivers "were entitled to stipulate that if one lost his ass, he should be provided with another ass. If the loss was caused by negligence [on his part], they would not have to provide him with another ass; where this was not due to negligence [on his part], he was provided with another ass."[21]

Apprenticeship

The institution of apprenticeship is frequently mentioned in the mishnaic and talmudic literature. The master was called *rav,* and the apprentice *talmid* or *shulayu.* The term of apprenticeship was agreed upon between the master and parents of the boy. The usual term was five years. In the *Midrash Ekha Rabba* (3, 6), we are told that a mother brought her son to Caesarea to apprentice him to a baker. The baker said: "Let him stay with me five years and I shall teach him to make 500 sorts of goods baked out of white flour; if he stays with me another five years, he will be able to bake 1,000 sorts." Another story concerns a boy who was brought to a pastry baker, also in Caesarea. The baker stipulated that the boy was to stay with him four years, and then another four years until he should know how to prepare a hundred kinds of egg pastries.

As a rule, the son of an artisan followed the trade of his father; he was looked at askance if reluctant to do so. The *Agada* tells an odd story illustrating this attitude. A fuller died when his son was still a youth. The widow first placed the boy with a master [of an unnamed trade], but the boy soon ran away. The mother then put the boy in a school, but he ran away from school as well. The mother then said: "Well, there is nothing more to be done. I shall have to let him learn his father's craft." She took him to a member of the guild to which her deceased husband had belonged and said: "Take the boy and teach him his father's skill." The fuller took the boy into his shop. But now the real trouble commenced. The boy would say: "I have a headache," and it would prove to be a pain in the foot. He would complain about a pain in the foot, and it would be a headache. Finally the master grew angry. He took the boy back to his mother, saying: "Here, take your son back; bury him alive, for he has abandoned his father's calling."[22] Such cases of boys refusing to follow their fathers' trade may explain the numerous exhortations of the talmudic rabbis on that score. "God," they said, "makes every calling gratifying in the eyes of those who follow it."

It is interesting to note that Jewish boys were sometimes apprenticed to Samaritan and pagan masters. Relations between masters and apprentices were reportedly good. Apprentices' salaries were as a rule deposited with their masters.[23]

Labor Legislation[24]

Wages, working hours, labor contracts, and contracts between artisans and their patrons were regulated by the guilds, communal authorities, or the rabbis.

As a rule the work day began at sunrise and ended at sunset, embracing a maximum working time of twelve hours. It included the time which the workman needed to return home from the place of his employment (*Baba Mezia* 83a); this time could not be deducted from the laborer's wages. Overtime work had to be agreed upon beforehand between employer and employee even if the former was prepared to pay for it at a higher than usual rate. Epstein suggests that this additional pay was offered, not for longer working hours, but for better work.

Wages were generally low, but so was the standard of living. The mass of the population had but one hot meal daily.[25] Skilled artisans earned the equivalent under present conditions, of a dollar a day, unskilled laborers from ten to twenty cents.[26] Wages were generally paid in cash, though in some places meals given to workers were deducted from their pay. The meals, however, were to include "dainty dishes" (*Baba Mezia* 83a, 92a). Day and night laborers were paid upon completion of their work. Workers by the week were paid every week, monthly workers every month.

Quarrels sometimes arose as to whether or not wages had been paid. In the absence of witnesses the worker's claim was validated upon his swearing an oath (*Baba Mezia* 112b). This is not the only instance of the talmudic legislators' partiality to labor. However, it would not be correct to state that the rights of employers were disregarded. Workers quitting their jobs not only had to provide substitutes, but also had to see to it that their employers suffered no material damage by their withdrawal (*Baba Mezia,* 77b). If an employer whose workers deserted him hired other workers at higher wages, he was allowed to make up the difference from the wages of those who had left. On the other hand, employers who broke their contracts with their workers not only had to pay them in full for the period which had been agreed upon, but also the difference between their wages and the higher wages of the substitutes (Mishnah *Baba Mezia* VI, 2).

Employees were enjoined to do good and faithful work and to avoid any waste of time, which the Talmud bluntly termed robbery. Except for meals, the worker was to devote every minute of his time to his task. To save the employer's time, the Talmud went so far as to exempt the worker from reciting the morning *Shema* on the ground, permitting him to pronounce it aloft on a scaffolding or in a tree. The Talmud also allowed workmen to shorten the prayer of Grace after meals in order to save time (*Berakhot* 16a).

Payment was due the artisan upon delivery of the finished work. He was entitled to insist upon immediate payment, lest he be put off indefinitely (Mishnah *Baba Mezia* IX, 12). Needless to say, the artisan was responsible for loss of or damage to the material given him by the patron. Thus, a dyer had to pay for wool he had dyed improperly. The following passages of the Mishnah (*Baba Kamma* X, 9) are worth quoting in this connection:

> Threads of wool which the washerman pulls out belong to him, but those which the woolcomber pulls out belong to the householder. If the washerman pulls out three threads they belong to him, but if more than that they belong to the householder. If there are black [threads] among the white and he takes them all out, they belong to him.
>
> If the tailor leaves over thread sufficient to sew with or a piece

of cloth three fingerbreadths square, they belong to the householder.
What a carpenter takes off with the plane belongs to him; but [what he takes off] with a hatchet belongs to the householder. But if he is working in the domain of the householder, even the sawdust belongs to the householder.

Concluding Remarks

The sages of the Mishnah minutely regulated conditions of labor and relations between craftsmen and patrons. Many of the legislators were craftsmen themselves, and had personal experience of the matters in question. Jewish guild statutes of later periods (17th and 18th centuries) have a pithiness and brevity which recall the Mishnah's labor regulations; undoubtedly there was a direct influence, as the Mishnah was widely studied, and by artisans as well.

The Palestinian craftsmen of the period of the Patriarchate had, as far as we know, no guild statutes. They were guided by the pronouncements of their spiritual leaders, the rabbis, who decided upon matters of labor. The rabbis also established the labor policies of the town councils in Palestine.

CHAPTER IV

Jewish Artisans and Guilds in the Diaspora: 323 B.C.E.-640 C.E.

The dispersion of the Jews began with their deportation by the Assyrians from the kingdom of Israel in 721 B.C.E. In 586 B.C.E. the Babylonians deported the Jews of the Kingdom of Judah. After the death of Alexander the Great in 323 B.C.E., there was a continual voluntary departure of Jews from Palestine, with the result that Jewish communities sprang up in Parthia, Syria, Egypt, Africa, and Roman Europe.

Growth of the Jewish Population in Parthia

Following the edict of the Persian King Cyrus (538 B.C.E.), some 50,000 Jews returned to Palestine. This was but a fraction of the Jewish population which had settled fifty-odd years earlier in the land along and between the Euphrates and Tigris rivers. The majority of Jews who remained grew in numbers and in social and cultural significance over the years. This fertile region was ruled from 250 B.C.E. to 226 C.E. by the powerful Parthian dynasty, which valiantly resisted the eastward march of the Romans. The Jewish population amounted to about 1,000,000 in 70 C.E., and had increased to about 2,000,000 two hundred years later under the Sassanians.

Several factors in addition to natural increase contributed to the growth. Remnants of the Ten Tribes deported from Israel in

721 B.C.E., and dispersed about the Near East, joined the Parthian communities; considerable numbers of pagans accepted the Jewish faith; finally, a steady flow of emigration from Palestine set in after the destruction of the Second Temple and the defeat of Bar Kokhba. As a result, from the 3rd to the 6th century the Sassanian Empire held the largest Jewish community of antiquity.[1]

Despite oppressive policies and bloody persecutions of some of the Parthian and Sassanian kings, Jewish life went on. Jews earned their livelihood by farming, cattle raising, cutting lumber, vine-growing, handicrafts, industry, commerce, and shipping. They set up communal institutions and promoted the study of the Law. The Babylonian Talmud was their creation. The cities of Nehardea, Pumbedita, Sura and Mahuza, famous for their talmudic academies, were also the principal seats of Jewish industrial and commercial activity.

Jewish Crafts and Industries in the Sassanian Empire

The country's industry included the weaving and dyeing of linen and wool, embroidering, tapestry making, tailoring, leather craft, pottery, brick making, carpentry, cabinet making, metal work, basketry, pearl fishing, brewing, etc.[2] Hiuen Tsiang, the Chinese Buddhist, who visited India in the course of his westward travels in 629-645 C.E., and had gathered some infomation about Persia, wrote: "They [the inhabitants of the Sassanian Empire] draw up water to irrigate the fields. The people are rich and affluent. The country produces gold, silver, copper, rock-crystal, rare pearls, and various precious substances. Their artists know how to weave fine brocaded silks, woolen stuffs, carpets, and so on."[3] To this one may add that there was a highly developed system of waterways for the transportation of commodities, which stimulated ship building and required the services of large numbers of sailors, boat haulers, and longshoremen.

Metal, Brick and Wool working

It may be recalled that King Nebuchadnezzar had deported one thousand smiths from Judah to Babylonia. Among the repatriates to Jerusalem from what was then Persia were masons and carpenters subsequently employed in the restoration of the Temple. Masonry and carpentry were thus apparently practiced by Jews in Persia in the late sixth century B.C.E. There is a gap in the record of the following centuries. The Babylonian Talmud, concluded about 500 C.E., was begun in first century C.E. It offers a wealth of information on the diffusion of arts and crafts among the Jews under Parthian rule and under the Sassanian dynasty in Persia. This information consists, however, of scattered bits of evidence that need to be pieced together. We learn, for instance, that the blacksmith (*nappach* or *pechami*) was a popular figure, that coppersmiths and gold- and silversmiths were in demand.[4] The *naggar* was both joiner and carpenter. Along with wood, brick was the main building material. Jews made and laid bricks, were plasterers, mortar mixers, lime burners and whitewashers.

Judging from the Babylonian Talmud, Jews lived in some towns and villages under their own administration with their own labor taking care of the needs of the community. Apart from the ordinary type of dwelling, there were mansions of the wealthy (*Horayot* 6a). The rabbinic academies had a considerable overflow of students, particularly in the *Kallah* months (Adar and Elul) preceding Passover and Rosh Hashanah. The academy at Pumbedita accommodated 12,000 students from all over the country on these occasions. The synagogue unearthed in the ancient caravan city of Dura-Europos on the Euphrates, was built in 245 C.E. and throws light on the synagogue design of that period. Built on the site of an older Jewish house of worship, the Dura synagogue included a main chamber for prayer, approached from a colonnaded courtyard, and several rooms in an outer precinct used by the synagogue personnel and as school rooms for children.

The Jewish community of Dura-Europos was comparatively small, however, The communities of Nehardea, Pumbedita, Sura, and Mahuza probably possessed larger synagogues. An outstanding feature of the Dura synagogue were the mural paintings displaying biblical scenes.[5] It is not known whether the artists were Jews. Judging from talmudic references to painters and painting, it can be assumed that the Dura synagogue was not the only example of its kind.

The Pearl Trade

Pearl fishing flourished on the Persian Gulf from earliest times. Pearls were perforated before being brought to market. Jews were apparently engaged in these activities for generations, though the Talmud refers to the perforating of pearls as the trade of slaves (*Ketubot* 40a; *Arakhin* 14b). Benjamin of Tudela (twelfth century) reported that Jews in the Bahrein Isles in the Persian Gulf were active in the pearl trade.[6]

Textiles

The beating of flax, spinning, cloth weaving, carpet weaving, silk weaving, laundering and dyeing occupied numbers of Jewish craftsmen. Josephus tells the story of two Jewish brothers, Asinaeus and Anilaeus, sons of a widow who had them apprenticed to a weaver at Nehardea. Having been flogged by their master for tardiness, they ran off and became leaders of a powerful band which waged war against the Parthian King Artabanus (*Ant.* XVIII, 9. 1 f.) . Later Nehardea became known for its weaving trade, mostly conducted by Jews, and its woolen goods were exported to foreign countries. Southeast of Nehardea was an exclusively Jewish locality, called Pum Nehara, which was also known for its woolen cloth, as was Be Mikhse, situated on the border between the Sassanian Empire and Arabia. Be Mikhse cloth, called Tutabe, sometimes served as currency (*Ketubot* 67a).[7]

Wool production was carried out on a large scale in the Sassanian Empire. Competition among wool traders was sharp. It often happened that local wool traders objected to the entry of foreign traders into their markets, and the disputes were brought before the Jewish judges for adjudication. Thus outside wool traders, who came to Pum Nehara to dispose of their wares were the subject of a complaint by local dealers to Rabbi Kahana, the judge. Rabbi Kahana, an *amora,* at first decided in favor of the local dealers. But when the foreign traders argued that they had come to Pum Nehara to collect outstanding debts and had to make a living in the meantime, Rabbi Kahana revised his judgment.

"If that is so," he told them, "you are permitted to sell enough in order to keep yourselves until your debts are collected, but afterwards you must leave this place" (*Baba Batra* 88a).[8]

The weavers of that time produced both cloth and garments. The Talmud humorously mentions the troubles of the customer whose woolen garments did not fit: "At what stage do [Divine] visitations commence? R. Eleazar said: If a man had, for example, a garment woven for him to wear and it does not fit him." An ill-fitting garment, we read, is one of the means by which the Lord chastises sinners (*Arakhin* 16b).[9]

Garments were produced not only for the local market but also for export. Colored garments were in particular demand.

The weaving of linen was concentrated in the cities of Borsippa and Pumbedita. The geographer Strabo singled out Borsippa, on the Euphrates, for its linen weaving.[10] Pumbedita's climatic conditions and well-watered fields favored the cultivation of flax. The local flax market, termed in the Talmud "Bi ketanah di Pumbedita" (*Gittin* 27a and *Baba Mezia* 18b), attracted visitors from other parts of the country.[11] Nehar Abba, a spot not far from Pumbedita, likewise acquired renown for its durable linen (*Sabbath* 140b).

Hemp fiber was used for the manufacture of ropes. "Rope of Sura" and "rope of Kamhunia," near Sura, was well known in Babylonia.[12] Cordage was an important article in a country with river navigation. Mats of hemp made in Mahuza were used for drying dates (*Sukkah* 20b).[13] A specialty of Rodia, a locality mentioned in the Talmud (*Ketubot* 67a), were the so-called "Rodia sacks." The sack makers who also produced the coarse garments of the herdsmen had their own guild and place in the market.[14] Money bags of leather or hemp were manufactured in Mahuza (*Ketubot* 67a). The attitude of the rabbis toward the diverse trades is interesting. The making of nets for catching birds was regarded as a great skill. However, only the makers of fish nets were permitted to work on the intermediary days of Passover and Sukkot, for fish was needed for the festival meals. The weavers of hair nets and veils were regarded as having a bad character because of their patronage consisting of women. However, one of the *amora* teachers, Levi ha-Sardi, was, as his name indicates, a hair-net weaver.[15]

The rabbis fought deception of every kind. The Babylonian Talmud (*Baba Mezia* 60a-60b) makes clear what is to be regarded as fraud. A more expensive product was not to be mixed with a cheaper one; wine was not to be mixed with lee or diluted with water; new goods might be painted to make them attractive, but an old utensil was not to be painted to improve its appearance lest it be sold as new. Nor was it permitted to dye cattle. The case of a slave with his hair dyed black to appear younger was added as a joke. The rabbis discussed the practice of underselling, or bribing the customer by giving sweets to the children. Some rabbis were not opposed to it since "it eases the market."

Carpet and Tapestry Weaving

Students of the arts and crafts of antiquity have emphasized the role of Jews in carpet weaving, an art which they continued to practice in the Near East down to modern times. Very early, Jews learned from the Assyrians or Syrians (it is not clear which because of the confusion of the names in the sources) how to weave patterns with figures of fabulous animals into fabrics, an art they later carried to other countries.[16] Pliny says that "weaving different colors into a pattern was chiefly brought into vogue by Babylon, which gave its name to the process."[17]

Embroidery

The Temple in Jerusalem, rebuilt by Herod, boasted a "Babylonian curtain" in its interior, separating the sanctuary from the cella. Josephus Flavius describes it in detail (*Jewish War,* V. 5.4). "It was embroidered with blue and fine linen and scarlet and purple, and of a contexture that was truly wonderful." He interprets the colors as symbolic of the four elements. There were some astronomical designs depicted on it, "all that was to be seen in the heavens, except for the signs of the Zodiac." It may be assumed that embroidery was used to emphasize the weaved-in patterns. It was an honorable, artistic craft. Rabbi Juda praised embroidery (*Machta Talmiuta*) as the most attractive craft because the cleanest (*Kiddushin* 82a, b).

Tailoring

The Talmud abounds in references to the tailoring trade. Tailors, like launderers and barbers, were allowed to work till noon on Passover eve. There is a characteristic story of a dealer in clothes, a Syrian, waiting impatiently on Passover eve for the delivery of a luxurious garment by a Jewish tailor.[18] Some tailors specialized in the production of an upper garment, called *sarbal,* in the Talmud though this term has been taken to refer to the wide Persian trousers. Samuel, an *amora* of the third century, granted permission for the addition of fringes to this garment (*Baba Mezia* 60b).[19] Tailors used to add the name of their trade to their own names. Thus there was a Hanan Hayyath ("the tailor") in Pumbedita.[20]

Laundering and dying

Launderers were permitted to work on the eve of Passover and on the intermediary days of Passover and Sukkot. Damaging of clothes by the launderers was not infrequent, to judge from complaints brought before the rabbinic courts. The mending of garments after washing was part of the launderer's job.[21]

Dyeing was a companion trade to weaving. A special group of artisans dyed the *tzitzit,* blue fringes which the Law required on male dress. To achieve the right shade of blue took special skill. Pumbedita was a market for *tzitzit;* Rabbi Samuel ben Judah had a workshop there for dyeing wool for this purpose.[22]

Basketry

The city of Babel, south of Sura, was known as a market for baskets (*Baba Batra* 22a). Competition, especially between local and outside basket makers, was sharp. The *amora* Rabina, who was the judge at Mata Mechasya and in whose jurisdiction Babel fell, was asked to decide whether outsiders were allowed to sell their wares in Babel. He decreed that they might sell their baskets in the market, but forbade peddling their wares from house to house in the locality (*Baba Batra* 22a).[23]

Leather Craft

Leather work was quite differentiated. There was the flayer or skinner (*shalach*) and the hide dresser or tanner (*bursi*), the belt and the harness maker, the sandal and shoemaker, and the maker of skin bottles. The skin bottlemaker (*sakak*) played a special role in the leather trade in antiquity.[24] From biblical times on, water, wine, oil, milk, and other liquids were transported in skin bottles or leather bags. Other articles included covers for mules and asses; aprons worn by wool carders, flax spinners, and surgeons; pads which porters placed under their loads; cradle covers; breastpieces for children to protect them from scratching by cats; muleteers' aprons, etc.

Food and Beverages

Slaughtering of meat and baking, particularly of matzot for Passover, were ritually supervised, as were wine and oil products.

The Talmud mentions the president of the Academy of Sura, Rav Hisda (ca.217—ca. 309) as making a fortune out of brewing. Another *amora,* Rav Papa ((300-375), grew rich from the brewing of date beer. Vinegrowing, too, was lucrative. Pumbedita had quite a number of Jews engaged in vinegrowing, some of them on a large scale. But only two vinegrowers, Rav Sakkai and Rav Hanina, possessed vine presses. Sura was renowned for its wine and beer.[25] Pumbedita was an important producer of oil, its products being sold throughout the country.[26]

Extractive Industries

In addition to the small farmers, there were Jewish owners of large farms who employed Jewish laborers, as may be inferred from talmudic regulations concerning the payment and working conditions of agricultural laborers. The management of large farms required technical personnel and the Talmud frequently mentions the land surveyor (*e.g. Baba Mezia* 107b).

Fishing has already been mentioned. The hunter, particularly the fowler (*rishba*), is a familiar figure in the Talmud (*Sabbath* 130).[27]

Shipping

Shipping was naturally important in a country through which flowed the mighty Euphrates and Tigris rivers with their numerous canals. Many groups of people were engaged in river traffic. The Talmud speaks of the seaman (*sapan*), sailor (*malach*), ferryman (*maaborah*), shiphauler (*nagad*), diver (*amodaah*), and porter or longshoreman (*shakalai*). Jewish workers were engaged in hauling of vessels by ropes in the ports of Sura and Pumbedita. Raba mentions the longshoremen of Machuza (*Baba Mezia* 77a).[28]

Jewish Guilds in the Sassanian Empire

At the bazaar of Nehardea, butchers, tanners, cobblers, and other Jewish artisans had their stands.[29] The Talmud also refers to guilds of basketmakers, weavers, sackmakers, boat-haulers, butchers, and shepherds. The boat-haulers, weavers, shepherds, and others had songs of their own which they sang while working. The *amora* Rav Huna said: "The songs of the boat-haulers and ploughmen are permitted, but those of the weavers are forbidden" (*Sotah* 48a).[30] The latter were evidently objectionable to the neighbors.

Merchants formed guilds of their own. Both artisans and merchants, fearful of the intrusion of outsiders, passed protective regulations. A rabbinical authority could, however, invalidate these regulations. The Babylonian Talmud, *Baba Batra* 9a, tells the story of two butchers who agreed that if either slaughtered on the other's day, the skin of his beast should be torn up and destroyed. One of them did, in fact, slaughter on the other's day, and the other butcher went and destroyed the skin. Summoned before Raba, he was condemned to make restitution. Rav Yemar bar Shelemiash thereupon pointed to the *Baraitha,* which actually gives townspeople the right to inflict penalties for breaches of their regulations. Rav Papa, however, qualified that right, emphasizing that it holds good unless opposed by a higher rabbinical authority in the town.

The right to settle in a town was one of the matters debated in the talmudic schools. Rav Huna ben Joshua, *amora* of the second half of the fourth century, declared as follows: "A resident of a town may prevent a resident of another town [from settling in opposition to him in his town], but if he is accounted to the *kraga* (government poll tax), he cannot be prevented" (*Baba Batra* 21b). L. Rabinowitz, in translating this passage, suggested that Rav Huna had in mind a person belonging to the same tax district. However this may be, the rabbinic decision implies that the setting up of a trade depended on the consent of the residents of the city. This was in accord with the *Tosefta* decision according to which an artisan desiring to set up shop in an alley needed the permission of the members of his craft residing in that alley. The enforcement of this rule was basic to guild policy.[31]

No guild statutes or regulations of any kind have been preserved from that remote time which would allow us to analyze the structure of the guilds. The Babylonian Talmud often refers to the *Rashei,* (heads or presidents) of the guilds or crafts (*omanot*). We do not know how the heads and other officers of the guilds were chosen. The following reference in the Midrash on the Psalms (also known as *Midrash Shoher Tov,* 115a) is worth quoting here: "When the head of the craft has been dismissed, the whole craft has been removed." We are not told by whom the head of the guild is dismissed, whether by members of the guild, by the community administration, or by anyone else.

Some light is shed in talmudic sources upon the system of apprenticeship in Babylonia. Masters were required to conclude agreements with apprentices,[32] but they could extend the term of apprenticeship up to ten years, thus taking advantage of cheap labor.[33]

Jewish Arts and Crafts in Roman Egypt

Under Ptolemaic (323-31 B.C.E.) and Roman-Byzantine rule (until ca. 640 C.E.), Egypt was, next to the Sassanian Empire, the largest Jewish center in the Diaspora. Philo (first half of the first century C.E.) estimated that the number of Jews in Egypt had reached the million mark. The bulk of Egyptian Jewry was concentrated in Alexandria, the metropolis of the country and one of the largest cities of antiquity. Jews also resided in seventeen other cities and towns, of which seven were situated in the district of Arsenoites, in northern Egypt.[34]

The economic pursuits of the Egyptian Jews included farming, handicrafts, commerce and shipping. The Mishnah contains a significant statement about the crafts exercised by the Alexandrian Jews. The *tanna* Rabbi Juda (second century), who made a visit to Alexandria, was greatly impressed by Jewish achievements there:

> Whoever has not seen the Double Stoa of Alexandria, has not seen the glory of Israel . . . And they were seated there not in mixed order, but goldsmiths apart, silversmiths apart, blacksmiths apart, coppersmiths apart, and weavers apart. So that when a poor [artisan] entered there, he recognized the members of his own craft and turned to them to find means for the maintenance of himself and his family (*Sukka* 51b).[35]

This record is interesting in two respects. It indicates the crafts which the Jews practiced in Alexandria and shows that the Jewish artisans were organized in guilds, somewhat on the model of the Roman collegia. One of the functions of these associations was looking after the welfare of members and possibly also of fellow-workers who were non-members.

The guild of Jewish weavers in Alexandria was registered as a corporation according to Roman law.[36] Alexandria was renowned for its textiles, which ranged from ordinary linen to fabrics woven from a mixture of yarns called *polymita.* The weaving of pictorial tapestries was a craft in which Jews excelled. Thus, the poet Claudian (fourth century) born in Alexandria, referred to the *vela Judaica* (curtains produced by Jewish weavers) with figures of Indian monsters woven into them (*Against Eutropius* I, 356-357).[37]

The Jewish coppersmiths of Alexandria were known throughout the land and beyond its borders. Wearing their aprons and carrying their bedding, they moved from place to place about their work. The renown of the coppersmiths reached Jerusalem, and, according to the Talmud, the Temple administration used to summon them to repair bronze and brass utensils, such as cymbals and mortars

(*Arakhin* 10b.). Alexandrian coppersmiths made, upon order from the Temple of Jerusalem, doors of Corinthian bronze which "shone like gold" (*Yoma* 38a).[38]

Two specifically Jewish trades were connected with the Temple cult: showbread baking and incense making. Mention was made in a previous chapter of the showbread bakers and incense makers summoned from Alexandria by the Jerusalem Temple following a strike of its own bakers and incense makers. The question arises as to why the Temple administration turned to Egypt. The answer is perhaps to be found in the fact that a Jewish temple (founded in 170 B.C.E.) existed in Leontopolis which must have had in its service trained showbread bakers and incense makers.[39]

A talmudic reference to Alexandrian goblets (*Baba Mezia* 28b) is an indication of the fame which that city's glassware enjoyed. The goblets were widely exported. Names of Jewish glass blowers have been found in such ancient Egyptian cities as Caranis, Oxyrhynchus, and Thebes.[40]

Other crafts practiced by the Jews in Egypt in the first centuries of the Common Era included tanning and pottery-making; the latter occupying whole families,[41] and the ritual and beverage industries.

Philo listed the maritime trade as one of the four chief occupations of Alexandrian Jewry. Jews were shipowners, captains, sailors, and longshoremen. Synesius mentions that on a voyage he made from Alexandria to Cyrene, the captain and more than half the crew were Jews.[42] There was a corporation of Jewish sailors (*navicularii*) in Alexandria—one of the few Jewish guilds (the abovementioned corporation of weavers was another) organized according to Roman law. It should be mentioned that Jewish artisans, as a rule, joined general artisan corporations, without being compelled to participate in their religious ceremonies. Such was the case in Philadelphia. On the other hand, there were Jewish artisans in Egypt who did not belong to any corporation.[43]

Sabbath was strictly observed, Jewish sailors heaving their vessels to on its eve. The Church Father Origen, born about 185 in Alexandria, mentions Jewish carpenters, masons and other workers stopping work on the Sabbath.[44]

A sixth-century geographer, the monk Cosmas Indicopleustes, a native of Alexandria and, as his name indicates, a traveler to

India, dwells in his *Christian Topography* on the Jewish arts and crafts of biblical times and of his own day. In speaking of the construction of the Tabernacle of the ancient Israelites, he decribes at length "all manner of workmanship, both of carpentry and of working in gold and silver and brass, and blue and purple, and scarlet thread, and fine twinned linen, and stone and wood work." In conclusion he adds: "And beyond question you will find that up to this very day most of those arts are most zealously cultivated among the Jews."[45]

Jewish Metal Workers in Pre-Mohammedan Arabia

Cosmas also visited southern Arabia, where he was able to observe the life and work of Jewish artisans. Since ancient times, Jews had lived in Arabia. Those residing in the oasis of Medina and Khaibar farmed, cultivated grapes and palm trees, and kept bees. There was a large concentration of artisans in Medina: 300 gold- and silversmiths reportedly lived in one quarter of the city. Many smithy tools and agricultural implements, were found in Jewish dwellings after the conquest of Medina by Mohammed. Stores of hidden weapons captured from the Jews enabled Mohammed to equip new levies of soldiers. The interesting point is that these weapons were the work of Jewish armorers. The Arabic sources tell of cuirasses, swords, spears, and projectile machines; the latter were employed by the Jews to defend settlements against hostile nomads. The so-called "David cuirasses" were famous throughout Arabia, and Arab poets praised their strength and splendor. The name did not commemorate King David, but a skilled Jewish armorer in Arabia. Dyeing should be mentioned among the trades practiced by Arabian Jews in that remote period. And in Maqna, a place near Aqaba and the present Israeli port-city of Elath, there were Jewish fishermen.[46]

Jewish Crafts in Ancient Times in Syria, Asia Minor, the Balkans, and Rome

Weaving, dyeing and glassmaking were the chief trades plied

by Jews in Syria, Asia Minor, and the western countries of the Diaspora. We know that Beyruth Jews were engaged in silk weaving. In Hierapolis, in Asia Minor, Jewish carpet weavers and dyers either had their own guild or constituted the majority of an existing guild of those trades.[47] Tyre was renowned for glass-making, and Tyrian Jews practiced that craft down to the Middle Ages. There were Jewish glassblowers in other parts of Roman Byzantium. According to a legend current in Constantinople, a Jewish glassblower, angered by his son's secret participation in a Christian communion, threw him into his furnace, but the Holy Virgin blew the fire out and saved the boy. Another story deals with the miraculous conversion of a Jewish glassblower by Saint Simon Salus. The Saint repeatedly broke his glass vessels until the artisan crossed himself. Greek glassblowers working in Marseilles in 687 are said to have used designs of Jewish masters.[48]

The Jewish community of ancient Rome, liberally estimated at some 40,000, included tent makers, tailors, and butchers. Reference is made in the Talmud to a Jewish tailor in Rome who worked for a non-Jewish master.[49]

The poet Martial, who lived at the time of the fall of Jerusalem, had a Jewish slave (*Epigrams* VII, 35, 3-4), and pointed out the poverty of the Jews in Rome.

Although there is no direct evidence that there were Jewish glass workers in Rome at that time—unless we infer from Martial's reference to a hawker from Trastevere (a city district inhabited by Jews) who peddled matches for broken glass (*Epigrams* I, 41, 3-5), that the hawker was a Jewish glass worker—one particular type of Roman glass, the *fondi d'oro,* gold glasses of the third and fourth centuries found in Rome, raises a problem. Some of these glasses are of Christian origin and portray saints; others are decorated with profane subjects; and there is a group of gold glasses which display in their decoration the ark, the seven-branched candlestick, the Sabbath fish meal, the Temple with the booths for the Feast of Tabernacles and various Jewish liturgical symbols.[50] These representations are similar to those found in Jewish catacomb paintings in Rome and in synagogue mosaics in Palestine. Pressed glass jars and plaques with Jewish symbols in raised patterns of the late Roman and Byzantine periods have been found in Palestine and Syria, the latter even in Yugoslavia and Cyprus.[51] It may be assumed that these various glass articles were made by Jewish craftsmen.

The technique employed in the manufacture of the gold glasses consisted of pressing designs etched in gold leaf between two layers of transparent glass. This technique carries us to Egypt where vessels and ornaments, such as beads and bracelets, were produced in glass interlaid with gold leaf since ancient times.[52] The superior quality of Egyptian glass was greatly valued in Rome and praised by Martial in many passages of his epigrams. The gold glass technique is described in a medieval treatise of uncertain date "De coloribus et artibus romanorum," by Heraclius (Eraclius), in a paragraph "de fialis auro decoratis" (of vessels with gold decoration). Another paragraph deals with paintings on glass. The color is made of different ingredients including powdered glass and lead, the *plumbeum vitrum, Judaeum scilicet* (crystal glass, namely Jewish glass).[53]

CHAPTER V

Jewish Arts and Crafts in the Near East: 640-1500

In 636 an Arab army marched into Syria and crushed the opposing Byzantine forces; in 640 Egypt was overrun; and upon its complete conquest by the Arabs in 641, the Sassanian Empire ceased to exist. The Omeyades, who first ruled this vast realm, established their capital in Damascus in 661. The Abbasides, who dethroned them in 750, transferred the capital to Baghdad. The caliphate of Baghdad, which in the ninth century extended as far west as Morocco and Spain, was a great empire united by a common religion and official language. The abolition of tariff boundaries within this tremendous area greatly facilitated the exchange of goods, and arts and crafts made remarkable strides. In addition to Arabs, Persians, Copts, Jews, Turks, and other groups actively engaged in crafts. Commercial relations were established with India and China in the East, the Mediterranean countries in the West, and with the interior of Africa to the southwest. Though the Baghdad caliphate was weakened by the rise of the caliphates of Cordova and Fez, the Aghlabid state of Kairuan and the Fatimid dynasty in Egypt, it continued to exist until put to an end by the Mongols in 1258.

The Jews in the Baghdad Caliphate

A large Jewish population lived in the heart of the caliphate, between the Euphrates and the Tigris. A huge procession of Jews gathered in 655 before the city of Piruz Shabur to welcome the conquering Caliph Ali. The total Jewish population of the caliphate is estimated to have been as high as 1,000,000 in the 8th century.[1] Numerous Jewish communities lived under the secular leadership of the Exilarchs, with spiritual guidance given by the *geonim,* who emerged about the time of the Moslem conquest and were active for four centuries in Sura, Pumbedita and Baghdad. The *geonim* enjoyed great authority within the caliphate and outside it. Individuals and whole communities turned to them for advice and guidance in religious, legal, educational, and economic matters. The responsa or *teshuvot* of the *geonim* to the inquiries *(she'elot),* shed light on Jewish law, life, and customs, and constitute one of the main sources of information on handicrafts in that period.

The Jews welcomed the Moslem conquerors, hoping that under their rule political, social, and economic conditions, which had deteriorated under the last Sassanians, would improve. The upward trend in commerce and trades that set in benefited Moslems, Persians, Copts, Jews, and other groups alike. By the end of the eighth century, Jews began to turn away from farming, however. Firstly, because the land tax, *haradj,* introduced by Caliph Omar, was based on the size of the estate alone and ignored the factor of income. In addition, Jewish landowners were more heavily taxed than non-Jewish. Secondly, farmers in general suffered from the political unrest, often reaching the point of uprisings against the Arab rule. Thirdly, the system of irrigation using the waters of the Tigris and Euphrates was neglected under the Omeyades, leading to a decline in agricultural output. Finally, the rise of Baghdad, the new capital, caused large numbers of farmers to desert the land and go to the city. The *gaon* Moses Kahana of Sura (825-837) referred to the fact that most of the Jews of his time did not own land.[2] The *gaon* Sherira (968-998) complained: "Most of the parents make their sons take up other occupations by which to earn a living."[3] It would be incorrect, however, to assume that farming was entirely abandoned by Jews of the Baghdad caliphate. On the contrary, records of the tenth through twelfth centuries mention Jews cultivating fields and vineyards.

Trend Toward the Cities

The big cities—Basra and Mosul, as well as Baghdad—continued to attract country people, including Jews. These three cities took the lead in commerce and industry, superseding Sura, Pumbedita, Nehardea, and Naresh which, in Sassanian times, had been bustling centers of trade. Farther east, in what had been ancient Persia, Hamadan, Isfahan, Samarkand, and Shiraz likewise emerged as populous urban communities with large Jewish concentrations. Benjamin of Tudela and Petahia of Regensburg (Ratisbon) who visited the Baghdad caliphate in the late twelfth century reported on the size of the urban Jewish populations there. Their figures differ widely. Benjamin's 40,000 people for Baghdad appears greatly exaggerated as compared with Petachia's figure of 1,000. They agree, more or less, in their estimate of the Jews at Mosul (7,000 and 6,000). We have no way of checking on Benjamin's figure for Basra, which he gives as 10,000. Those for Hamadan and Isfahan are even higher.[4] The estimate of the total Jewish population of the caliphate was between 700,000 and 1,000,000. The soberer calculations of modern historians yield a much lower figure —300,000 in all.

Jewish Crafts under the Baghdad Caliphate

Though the Jewish artisans of the caliphate were an important group, comparatively little is known about their history, social and economic structure and relations with the non-Jewish workers. As so often happens in Jewish history, the masses left few records. The Jewish sources deal with the well-to-do, the learned, the communal leaders, the favorites of the princely courts, the financiers, the physicians, etc., but give little space to the man in the street.

From occasional references it would appear that owing to the flight from the countryside, among other causes, there was a stronger trend toward the crafts and commerce.[5]

The *geonim,* following the sages of the Talmud, stressed the value and importance of artisanship. The *gaon* Yom Tov Kahana was a weaver.[6] Hai ben Sherira, the *gaon* of Pumbedita (998-1038), in a didactic poem *Mussar Haskel,* advised fathers to teach their sons a craft. In one of his responsa he quotes the will of a goldsmith who desired his sons to carry on his trade. "I leave," said the will, "a grindstone for grinding gold and silver dust . . . when the end is near and God shall decree my death . . . let the three youngest sons get eighteen portions of the inheritance . . . but the grindstone shall belong to them alone." [7]

Metal Crafts

Among the metal crafts, goldsmithing took the foremost place. Historians of the arts and crafts are agreed that, under the Baghdad caliphate, the goldsmith's craft was, by and large, a Jewish one, at least until about the year 1000.[8] A responsum of the *gaon* Natronai (second half of the ninth century) mentions that Jewish goldsmiths and silversmiths used to hire out their grindstones to non-Jewish masters,[9] and Jewish jewelers catered to non-Jewish customers. Jews were good patrons of the jewelers, especially with the custom of the marriage ring spreading among the Jews of the caliphate. The *geonim* Saadia (928-942) and Hai, both refer to it. *Gaon* Natronai mentions the wearing of rings by men, and rings and earrings by women. In answer to an inquiry, Natronai ruled that women may go abroad on the Sabbath wearing earrings; however, neither women nor men should wear rings set with engraved gems.[10] The production of amulets, much in favor among Jews in Moslem countries, of gold and silver vessels and ornaments for the scripture scrolls gave ample scope to the jeweler's craft. Baghdad alone, according to Benjamin of Tudela, had 28 synagogues and houses of prayer, which implies a large demand for ceremonial articles.[11] It was also customary to present gifts of gold and silver vessels to the Exilarch.

Jewish craftsmen produced copper bowls, candelabra and clepsydras (water-clocks). Clepsydras are described in a responsum as "copper bowls with a hole at the bottom. . . . They are placed in water, and when the water reaches a certain point it is a half hour; to this point, an hour, to this point, an hour and a half. And the points are called peaks." [12]

Jews were allowed to patronize non-Jewish blacksmiths on half-holidays in order to speed their homecoming for the festivals of Passover and Sukkot. This implies that ordinarily there were Jewish blacksmiths to do the work, but that the Jewish smiths did not work on half holidays, as was generally the rule among Jewish workers in those times.[13]

The prohibition of using knives produced by non-Jews for slaughtering or circumcision points to the existence of Jewish cutlers.[14] There were also Jewish locksmiths and ironworkers in the building trades. Nor should the armorer's craft be overlooked. Jewish armorers were famous in Arabia from pre-Mohammedan times. Throughout the Middle Ages, weapons were produced by Jewish craftsmen in the Near East.

Art Crafts

Besides the goldsmiths we must mention the seal engravers. Exilarchs and *geonim* ranked in the first place among their patrons. The signet ring of the Exilarch exhibited a fly. The seal of the Gaon Hai bore the figure of a lion.[15] Merchants, too, carried seals.

The resplendent garments of the Exilarch described by the travelers Benjamin and Petahia, were apparently the work of Baghdad weavers and embroiderers. The author of the chronicle *Seder Olam Zutta* describes the installation of the Exilarch in Baghdad: "And all the representatives of the community and their wealthy people sent him lovely garments, beautiful ornaments, and gold and silver vessels, each and every man offering according to his ability." The chronicler describes the "gorgeous silver coverings and coverings in blue, purple and scarlet red" of the wooden canopy prepared for the Sabbath of the inauguration. One gathers that embroiderers, jewelers and carpet weavers delighted to display their skills on such occasions in a city famous in the Middle Ages for its arts and crafts.[16]

Calligraphy deserves special mention. The art goes back to biblical times, when calligraphers were organized in guilds. In the Second Commonwealth, calligraphers wore distinguishing badges. Their chief employment was the copying of the books of the Torah. The passage in the talmudic tractate *Soferim* (1, 9) forbidding gold lettering in the books of the Pentateuch indicates that gold illumination was practiced by the scribes. In the period of the Baghdad caliphate, calligraphers, influenced by copyists of the Koran, began to employ ornamental designs. The Hebrew *Codex Babylonicus Petropolitanus* (916), which originated in the Baghdad caliphate, exhibits attempts at ornamental lettering. Colophons in Bible codices of that period occasionally mention the names of the calligraphers.[17] Scribes were employed in the office of the Exilarch, by the *geonim,* and by private individuals.

Textiles

Jewish spinners, weavers and dyers specialized in much-valued colored textiles. In addition to wearing apparel they produced pillows, blankets, saddle cushions, and door curtains. Some of the *geonim* permitted the mixing of flax thread with woolen thread in fabrics not intended for wearing apparel.[18]

Jewish workmen were strict in the observance of the Law. In doubtful cases, they applied to the spiritual leaders. Thus, dyers raised the question of whether it was permissible to work on the eve of the Sabbath. The *geonim* assented, in order that people might have clean garments for the Sabbath. Economic considerations also played a part. Poor artisans were at a disadvantage if forbidden to work on Friday, even if only for part of the day. As for the intermediate days of Passover and Sukkot, the *gaon* Natronai ruled that tailors may work at such time, because they were "poor people."[19]

Jewish silk production was an important industry in the Baghdad caliphate and in Egypt, Sicily, and Spain in the early Middle Ages. In the Baghdad caliphate, Jews cultivated mulberry trees for silk production, bred silk worms, and spun silk yarn. Here again a religious question arose: was it permissible to feed the worms on Saturdays and during festivals? The *gaon* Hai consulted the opinions of his predecessors and decided that it was permissible to feed the worms on festivals, but not on the Sabbath.[20] The *gaon* Matatia permitted feeding them on the Sabbath also.

Glass Making and Pottery

The wine trade required bottles, pitchers, and flasks. Wine and other liquors had to be delivered in different vessels in compliance with religious precepts.

Lamps, generally made of glass, were lit in synagogues and private homes on the Sabbath. Putting out the light on Sabbath was considered physical work. The *gaon* Natronai describes how lamps were extinguished automatically: "Water is put in the bottom and oil on the top. When the flame burns down to the water, it goes out. In this way the flame is not put out [by hand]. This is the usage wherever the sons of Israel live." [21]

Pottery shops were to be found everywhere. They were especially busy before festivals. One of the *geonim* gave a recipe for waterproofing of vessels. They were to be coated with sulphur before polishing or glazing.[22]

Leather work

Tanners generally pursued their trade on the outskirts of the cities, where the stench of the hides would not offend. The tanners' yards of Baghdad, for example, were located along the highroad behind the cemetery near the Isa Canal which skirted the city in a wide curve. Jewish sources indicate that tanners lived and worked in separate quarters on the outskirts of the cities. They were organized in guilds and had their own synagogues. This was also the case with copper smelters. "Their skin," one record reads, "absorbs a bad odor for which there is no remedy, and from the pores the bad odor is exuded which nothing can remove. And in those years it was customary for every person to separate himself from those craftsmen and not to sit with them, and they did not mix with them, and kept afar from them. Therefore these craftsmen had synagogues for themselves, which exist in our day in many places." [23] These workers were denied the privilege of making pilgrimages to Palestine. In order to protect people from contact with the malodorous crafts, owners of wells located inside towns were sued for selling their property without informing the buyers that the wells had previously been used by tanners.[24]

Makers of *tefillin* (phylacteries) were directed to blacken the leather on the outside, as required by the Law of Moses; the inside could be green or white but never red, as this would cause scurf on the scalp; or, as others suggested, might look like feminine embellishment.[25]

Parchment Manufacture

We do not know whether the Jews of the caliphate manufactured paper. Paper making, introduced in Samarkand from China (751), spread westward to Baghdad, Damascus, Tiberias, and Tripoli.[26] The *gaon* Sherira, whose responsa offer many a glimpse into artisan life, minutely describes the manufacture of parchment:

> "In this fashion they produce parchment amongst us. They bring dry skins which are shedding their hair; the skins are soaked in water until the hair falls away and they become soft. Thereupon the workmen place the skins in a lime vat, putting therein a small amount of water and dog's excrement and a bit of salt. They cover the vat over and let the skins stand, in summer one day and in winter three, but not longer than that, lest they warp. Then the workmen take the skins out of the vat and examine them for rents. If they are torn, the rents are sewn together and the skins stretched on a wooden frame prepared for that purpose, and a great deal of gallnut is brought with which to rub the skins and a third of a liter of water [a Baghdad liter contains thirteen ounces]. The skins are coated with gallnut on both sides and then sprinkled with water, the gallnut being applied more liberally to the hairy than to the fleshy side. This is done to each skin twice daily, and the third time they are coated with yet more gallnut and placed in the sun in order to become glossy. There they are left to dry, after which they are shaken out."[27]

An accessory of the mason's craft were sandals made of iron or wood, used for trampling down and smoothing out pitch or lime.[28]

Living Standards of the Jewish Artisans in the Baghdad Caliphate

Artisans on the whole earned little, as both Jewish and Arab sources testify. Benjamin of Tudela noted that the Jewish cobblers of Baghdad were among those paying the lowest taxes. The Arabic author, Abu Uthman Amr ibn Bahr al-Jahiz (died 869), while stating in his *A Reply to the Christians* that the Christians in the Baghdad caliphate occupy the more elevated positions in the economic and social sphere, pointed out that the Jews were merely "dyers, tanners, cuppers, butchers, and cobblers." On the basis of this and other Moslem witnesses, Adam Mez, in his *The Renaissance of Islam,* came to the conclusion that "in the lowest class of taxpayers (in the Abbasid Caliphate) were the Jewish money-changers, tanners, shoemakers and, particularly, dyers." But it should be pointed out that the situation was not altogether bleak. The weavers, embroiderers, silk producers, metal workers, goldsmiths and silversmiths are not mentioned in the works of the medieval Moslem authors; some artisans in these categories were surely more prosperous.[29]

Jewish Arts and Crafts in Syria

The Arabic geographer of the tenth century, al-Maqdisi or al-Muqaddasi, noted that in Syria most of "the assayers of coins, the dyers, the bankers and tanners were Jews." [30] Benjamin of Tudela who visited Antioch and Tyre in the 1160's reported that in Antioch there were ten Jewish residents, all glassmakers; in Tyre he found 400 Jews [or families], some shipowners among them, and makers of "that fine Tyrian glassware which is prized in all countries." [31]

In 1260 Syria came under the rule of the Mamelukes. The Syrian chronicler of that period, Bar Hebraeus, remarked that the position of the Jews was very low. This statement was in line with similar utterances by Moslem writers about the humble status of Jewish tanners, dyers, and tailors. Bar Hebraeus noted, however, that there were some physicians and government officials among the Jews.[32] As a Jacobite bishop of Jewish origin, he was perhaps somewhat biased. At any rate, the picture he draws is incomplete.

By the middle of the thirteenth century there were about 40,000 Jews in Syria, the largest groups in Damascus and Aleppo. There were also communities in Tripoli, Palmyra, Baalbek, and Tyre. Damascus was the center of the silk industry. Jews, both men and women, were engaged in silk weaving. Weaving designs and biblical verses into rugs was their specialty. Bookbinding and carpentry are mentioned among Jewish skills. Glassmakers were to be found in Aleppo and Jewish jewelers in Damascus.[33]

Damascene arts and crafts were dealt a hard blow by the invasion of Timur Lang (Tamerlane) in 1400. He drove the finest artisans of Syria away to Samarkand. Damascene production declined, the Jewish along with the rest.[34]

Arts and Crafts in Medieval Palestine

Under the Abbasides, Palestine was a fertile country with a florishing agriculture, according to the records of Arab geographers. Jerusalem's annual September fairs attracted merchants (who also came as pilgrims) from Pisa, Genoa, Venice, and Marseilles. These fairs continued to be held under Moslem rule. Dyeing, weaving and glassmaking were the traditional skills.[35] Economic prosperity led to increased cultural activities. The talmudic academy moved from Tiberias to Jerusalem. In the tenth century the Palestinian Gaonate was created.

Benjamin of Tudela (1160's) met dyers everywhere. He observed how the dyers and other artisans regularly visited the tribe of the Druses in the Hermon mountains to sell them their products. "The Druses," he noted, "are friendly to the Jews."

The dyers in Jerusalem, then the capital of the Latin kingdom of the same name, were granted monopoly of the trade. They had their workshops in a building purchased from King Baldwin IV.[36] In 1187, Petahia of Ratisbon encountered only one dyer there. The man had paid a high price for the monopoly he enjoyed.

Benjamin met twelve dyers in Bethlehem, two in Beth Nubi, and one each in Jaffa, Lydda, Serain, and Kiryataim. Dyers were, in all probability, the only Jewish residents left in many a Palestinian town under the Crusaders' rule, with the exception of Rama, New Askalon, and Tiberias, where Benjamin found 300, 200, and 50 Jewish residents respectively.

With the conquest of the Kingdom of Jerusalem by Sultan Saladdin in 1187, Jews began to return to Palestine, from Europe as well as from the Near East. However, parts of Palestine remained under Christian rule until the fall of Acco in 1291. In 1260 the Mongolian invasion brought disaster to Jerusalem. When Rabbi

Moses ben Nahman (Nahmanides) came there in 1267, the city was a shambles. He found among the 2,000 residents only two Jews, both dyers. Nahmanides set about to revive the community and appealed to those who had fled before the Mongols to return. Estori Farchi, a Jewish scholar from southern France who settled in Palestine in the early fourteenth century and was studying its topography and archaeology, drew attention to the fertility of the land.[37] Farchi lists communities in Jerusalem, Lydda, Ramleh, Beth-Shean, Safed, and five other localities. He mentions glassmakers in Hebron. They lived in a separate quarter as an organized group. Isaac Chelo who visited Palestine in 1334 highly praised the work of a dyer in Sarafand.[38]

Jewish Arts and Crafts in Egypt: 900-1500

Little if anything is known about the history of the Jews in Egypt during the long period embracing the last centuries of Byzantine rule and the first centuries of Moslem rule.

Alexandria had "40,000 tributary Jews" when the Arabs took the city in 641.[39] In 758, Jews are mentioned as living in Fostat, which became a suburb of Cairo in 969. Thereafter Jewish life was concentrated in Fostat-Cairo, the capital of the country under the Fatimid dynasty. Communities of Palestinian Jews, Bablyonian Jews, and Jewish groups from Mediterranean countries grew up there in the course of years. About the middle of the twelfth century, Jews were also living in a number of other cities, of which Alexandria, Bilbeis, and Mahalla deserve special mention. In the latter half of the twelfth century Benjamin of Tudela, noted 2,000 families in Fostat-Cairo, 3,000 families in Alexandria, 3,000 persons in Bilbeis, and 5,000 in Mahalla. But his figures are obviously exaggerated.

Modern scholars estimate that some 30,000 Jews lived in 29 localities in Egypt. In the thirteenth century an influx of immigrants took place, caused by the Mongolian invasion in the Near East and persecutions in Christian Europe. Jews were also attracted by the international trade then focused in Alexandria. With the city's continuing growth, foreign Jews came there on business or to settle permanently. The same was true of Cairo, which, in the first half of the fourteenth century, was seven times as large as the Paris of that time.[40]

The Arabic word *amshatti,* forming part of the names of some Jews, points to their trade of wool carding. The Arabic term *kazaz* means silk weaver; Jews with the name *al-kazaz* are mentioned in the Genizah documents of the tenth to thirteenth centuries. *Hariri,* another term for silk weaver, also appears in these sources as a Jewish surname.

Trade was concentrated in areas inhabited by Copts, but Jews, too, lived in these areas. They engaged in flax weaving in Fostat and Alexandria. To ransom Jews captured on the high seas by pirates, the Alexandrian community collected, in addition to cash, raw flax and woven fabrics.[41]

In a Geniza document we find reference to "bleaching the yarn," to "reeling it," to weaving and embroidering.[42]

Jewish women embroiderers wove gold threads into silk. Commissioned by members of the princely houses or by *pashas,* they had to work in the palaces, for the valuable stuff could not be taken off the premises. The rabbis viewed with concern this lengthy residence of the women (among whom there were wives of *kohanim*) in a Moslem environment. But rabbinical prohibitions were of no avail. The women argued that poverty compelled them to earn a living and that they had their husbands' permission to work away from home.[43]

The dyer's trade is recognizable in Jewish names followed by the term *tavag* which is a derivative of *tsava,* Hebrew for dye. Tavag is a common name among Jews of the Near East to this day.

Glassmakers' names appear in the Genizah documents accompanied by the Hebrew term for their trade, *sagag.*[44]

The Jewish jewelers of Cairo were renowned. The Fatimid rulers and the Egyptian upper class were their patrons. A story is recorded about the widow of a high official who complained about a Jewish jeweler to whom she had entrusted "a *kuba* woven with gold and pearls."[45] The Persian traveler Nasir-li-Kushran who visited Egypt in 1046-1049 tells the story of a Jewish jeweler who enjoyed the confidence of the caliph, but was murdered by the caliph's soldiers. The murder is also related in a Genizah document.[46] Some goldsmiths mentioned in Genizah documents of the eleventh and twelfth centuries bear the name of their craft: *ad-d'-havi.*[47]

Silversmiths and coppersmiths fashioned ceremonial objects for synagogues. A list of ritual articles owned by the synagogue of the Palestinians in Fostat included: four silver Torah crowns, eight pairs of pomegranates (headpieces for the Torah scroll), thirty-six Passover plates, two large copper candelabras, two small copper candelabras, and twenty-four silk Torah covers, some brocaded with gold.[48]

We find in Egypt, as in other parts of the Near East, Jewish manufacturers, such as the two brothers who operated a clothing factory in Cairo, one attending to the production of garments, and the other traveling abroad to sell.[49] Occasionally, Jewish laborers were employed by Moslems. Thus Moslem millers hired Jewish youths along with Moslems to fetch wheat from customers and return the flour to them.[50]

Later, under the Mamelukes—former court slaves who had established their rule over Egypt in 1260—paper and sugar factories were established by Jews. Sugar made from cane was an important Egyptian industry. The Arab historiographer Ibn Dakmak (died 1407) listed 50 sugar factories in Cairo. Six were owned by Jews. A few decades later, sugar became a monopoly of Sultan Barsbay (1422-1438).[51]

If we take Benjamin of Tudela's figures for the latter part of the twelfth century at their face value, Egyptian Jewry had definitely declined in numbers by the fifteenth century. In 1481 Meshullam da Volterra found only about 800 Rabbanite families in Cairo, about as many Karaites and a small group of Samaritans.[52] Fostat, which according to the Arab historian Makrisi, a native of Cairo, (1365-1442), had twelve synagogues in his time,[53] was almost deserted when Meshullam visited it. The suburb was swallowed up by the big city. Da Volterra was impressed by the huge Cairo warehouses packed with merchandise, but does not say whether Jews were among the owners. A few Jews were influential at the sultan's court and da Volterra was graciously received. He had no eye for the humbler people, it appears, and does not say anything about their condition. The Jewish community in Alexandria, he was told, had declined from 4,000 householders to about 60 families. Here too he noted large warehouses which belonged to French, Genoese, Venetian, and Arab merchants.[54]

Manuscript Illumination

In medieval Egypt as in Syria, Jews practiced the arts of calligraphy and manuscript illumination. A number of tenth and eleventh century Hebrew manuscripts of Egyptian and Syro-Palestinian provenience have been preserved and exhibit lettering and ornamentation in raised gold and colors. In the Bible codices the picture of the Temple with its vessels appears, illuminated in gold. In North African manuscripts of the thirteenth and fourteenth centuries, colors predominate. The largest collections of these manuscripts are in the Leningrad Public Library and in the British Museum. The latter owns a Karaite Hebrew Bible in Arabic script with fullpage arabesque designs. An eleventh century marriage contract from Fostat is in the Bodleian Library at Oxford and there are a few medieval Egyptian Hebrew primers at the Cambridge University Library.[55]

General Remarks

Fragmentary though our evidence is, we can draw the following conclusions about the role of the Jews in the arts and crafts and in the entire occupational structure of the medieval Near East. Jews were free to engage not only in the distribution but also in the production of goods, for they did not labor under disabilities like those imposed upon them in Christian Europe. They continued to exercise skills familiar to them since ancient times. In addition, they acquired a number of skills which Moslems and others had developed, notably in the manufacture of textiles and in jewelry work. In Baghdad, Damascus, and Cairo, three leading centers of Moslem arts and crafts, Jewish silk-weavers and gold and silversmiths excelled. Glassmaking was carried on by Jews in medieval Syria and Palestine, while Jewish dyers could be found throughout the Near East.

This was a period of migration from East to West. What the New

World was to Europeans in modern times, Europe was to Asiatics in the Middle Ages. In the wake of the Arab invasion of North Africa and southern Europe, Jews of the Baghdad caliphate moved westward to Egypt and the adjacent territories of North Africa, then to Sicily, the Balearic Islands, Spain, and the south of France. The artisans among them brought varied skills to their new homes. The Jewish handicraftsmen brought the idea of the guild from the Near East. They joined Moslem guilds or formed guilds of their own. The handing down of skills from father to son contributed to the stability of tradition in handicrafts. On the other hand the employment of women in outside jobs was a symptom of disintegration. Palestine, with its reduced Jewish population, still harbored some categories of artisanship. However, the center of Jewish life had shifted westward.

CHAPTER VI

Jewish Arts and Crafts in the Byzantine Empire

The Byzantine Empire, even after the Arab conquest in 636 of Syria and Palestine with their large Jewish populations, still contained sizable Jewish communities in Asia Minor, the Balkan peninsula, southern Italy, and such Mediterranean islands as Sicily, Crete, Corfu, Chios, Evvoia. Despite occasional waves of religious persecution accompanied by forcible conversions to the Christian faith (which caused some Byzantine Jews to flee to neighboring countries, as, for example, to the Crimea in 723), and despite the legal and social restrictions decreed by the Crown and Church, Jewish life continued more or less intact until the fall of the Empire in 1453.[1] Statistics on Jewish population are lacking, but according to estimates, in the twelfth century 12,000 persons (or families) lived in the Balkans and on adjacent islands, in the midst of a native population estimated at 15,000,000.[2]

Jews in the Byzantine Empire engaged in agriculture, navigation, commerce, moneylending, the professions, and in such crafts as weaving, sericulture and making of silk garments, dyeing, tanning, leatherwork, furriery, metal work, and glass making. Evidence from the early Middle Ages is scant. One learns of a dyer, Eliakim Caleb, at Corinth in the first half of the tenth century. In 1170 Benjamin of Tudela found one Jew, a dyer, in Corfu. In Sparta in the latter part of the tenth century a Christian employed Jewish workers for finishing woven goods.[3] More data, is available for the following centuries.

Silk Work

We know from a medieval chronicle that, in 1147, King Roger II of Sicily sent "his fleet against Byzantium, and took Corfu, Cephalonia, Thebes, Corinth and the rest of the coast as far as Malvasia. . . . He led all the Jews of that land captive to Sicily."[4] The author of another medieval chronicle, the bishop Otto of Freising, referred to the captives as "artificers who wove silk garments."[5] King Roger employed these silk workers in his royal factory in Palermo. It has been suggested that the number of craftsmen carried away by the king from Thebes alone was 2,000; most of them were Jews. This event is considered to mark the emancipation of western Europe from the Byzantine monopoly of sericulture, which now spread from Sicily to the Italian mainland and to Provence.[6]

Further research is needed to show how this concentration of Jewish silk workers in Thebes came about, and whether they were organized in guilds of their own, for the state-controlled Byzantine guilds did not admit Jews. The tenth-century *Book of the Prefect,* containing the regulations for the Byzantine guilds, makes no mention of Jewish guilds. A regulation forbidding the sale of raw silk to Jews, lest they smuggle it out of the country, is the only reference to them in the entire work. This attitude on the part of the Byzantine state-controlled guilds was in line "with the religious and racial discrimination [practiced] against Jews and other minorities." However, as pointed out by Robert S. Lopez, this policy was softened "thanks to the greater liberality (or weakness) of the Comnenian dynasty towards all kind of aliens." In 1148, Emperor Manuel Comnenus granted recognition to a Jewish guild.[7] It is not known what this guild's craft was, the nearest guess being silk weaving.

It is significant that the act of recognition came one year after King Roger raided the Byzantine coast and carried off Jewish silk weavers to Palermo, which event may have prompted the Emperor to treat the Jewish minority more tolerantly.

Byzantine sericulture was by no means destroyed by the depredation of 1147. The chronicler's remark that Roger carried away "all the Jews" (*cunctos Judaeos*) was an exaggeration; twenty-odd years later, one hears about the recovery of the silk trade in Thebes, Corinth, and Patras. Benjamin of Tudela has much to say not only about Jewish weavers of silk, gold, and purple cloth in Pera (a suburb of Constantinople) and Thessalonica (later named Salonica), but also about Thebes, where he found about 2,000 Jewish residents. Benjamin praised the Theban workers "as the most skilled artificers in silk and purple cloth throughout Greece." [8] The fabrics or garments were in great demand outside the Byzantine Empire, and Genoese shippers tried in vain to obtain the Emperor's permission to export them from Thebes.[9]

Silk production continued to flourish after 1204, when Thebes came under the rule of one of the leaders of the Fourth Crusade. The Duchy of Athens and Thebes was formed in that year. Duke Guy de la Roche tolerated the Jewish community of Thebes, and garment makers prospered.[10] Their skills were apparently handed down from father to son. This must also have been the case in other Balkan cities, for, as late as 1500, we find Jewish silk weavers in the city of Modon, on the coast of the Peloponnesus. Modon and the city of Coron were ports of embarkation for pilgrims traveling to the Holy Land. In that period both cities were thriving centers of Christian and Jewish crafts.[11]

A German pilgrim, Arnold von Harff of Cologne, stopping in Modon on his way to Palestine, made the following entry in his travel diary: "We went farther beyond the gate into the first suburb in which is a very long street inhabited solely by Jews, whose womenfolk do beautiful work in silk, making girdles, hoods, veils and face coverings, some of which I bought." [12] Coron was famous for its cochineal production.[13] It can safely be assumed that the Jews of Coron were active in that trade, which was widely carried on by Jews in the Middle Ages in the Mediterranean area.

Farther north, in the city of Durazzo, on the Albanian coast, where the Republic of Venice had established its rule in 1392, the Jews had to deliver annually to the local administration over ten yards of luxurious velvet cloth called *catasamitum*. It has been suggested that the levying of this contribution may have gone back as far as the twelfth century, "the hey-day of the Byzantine-Jewish artisans producing this type of expensive fabric." [14]

By 1047, silk and purple cloth was manufactured on the island of Chios.[15] Benjamin of Tudela found 400 Jewish families there.

Meshullam of Volterra who visited Crete in 1481 found in Moron, "a small city by the seaside," 300 Jewish householders, "all of them engaged in handicrafts and trade." [16]

Rhodes

The island of Rhodes merits considerable space in a history of Jewish trades. In 1472, an anonymous German pilgrim from Cologne to Palestine praised in his diary the beauty of the Jewish women and their skill in making articles of silk, especially exquisite, valuable silk belts ("costliche sejden gurdel").[17] At that time the Jewish population was quite large. But it suffered severely as a result of Turkish attempts to invade the island in 1480-81. Meshullam of Volterra, who visited Rhodes in 1481, reported that the Jews lived in "perfect tranquility." However, Obadiah of Bertinoro found a different picture in 1488. He spent six weeks in Rhodes. There were

> altogether 22 Jewish families, all poor, who subsist with difficulty on vegetables, not eating bread or meat, for they never slaughter nor do they buy any wine, for fear of getting into disputes with the Greeks who dwell there. When they buy in the market, they touch nothing that belongs to the Greeks. The Jews here are all very intelligent and well educated; they speak a pure dialect and they observe the law against wine just as strictly as against pork, and are very moral and polite; even the tanners are neatly dressed and speak with propriety. They all allow their hair to grow long and are beautiful in person. Nowhere are there more beautiful Jewesses than in Rhodes; they occupy themselves in doing all kinds of handiwork for the *Acomodores* [the nobles of the land], and in this way support their husbands. [18]

Tanning

Jewish tanners worked in Pera, a suburban district of Constantinople. Benjamin of Tudela records that their Greek neighbors were angered by the emptying of the foul-smelling contents of their vats into the streets. Early in the fourteenth century, Emperor Andronicus II (1282-1328) set aside a special quarter for Jews engaged in dressing furs and in tanning hides imported from the Crimea. The quarter bordered on the Venetian quarter, which was established in 1204 after the partial occupation of Constantinople by the Latins. The Emperor also formed a guild of Jewish tanners and furriers under control of the State. Jewish artisans residing in the Venetian quarter, as subjects of Venice, needed special authorization to join the guild. They were assigned to the dressing of furs, whereas those guild members who remained subjects of the Emperor did the tanning. This arrangement existed until 1319, when Andronicus ordered his subjects, the tanners, to find other occupations. The "Venetian" Jewish artisans then took over the tanning trade despite the Emperor's declaration that it was reserved to Greeks. One day Byzantine soldiers entered the shops of the "Venetian" artisans still defying the Emperor's order, confiscated the hides, and destroyed them. The Republic of Venice demanded that the losses sustained by the Jewish artisans, who had in addition been evicted from their homes, be made good. An exchange of diplomatic notes followed.[19]

Jewish tanners were also active in Modon, in the Peloponnesus. Time and again, the local authorities (*castellani*) warned them against dumping the refuse of their trade before the doors of their waterfront dwellings. Finally, in 1390, they were ordered to move away to a safe distance. A second such order, issued the following year, shows that the tanners resisted forsaking their established homes. The Jewish tanners of Modon were forbidden to work on Sundays and Christian festivals, a great hardship, for the tanners strictly observed the Sabbath and Jewish feast days. There long existed in Modon a guild of Christian tanners which apparently followed a tolerant policy toward the Jews. It is interesting to note that, in 1464, Jews were the only tanners in Modon.[20]

Jewelry

Byzantine jewelry was famous in the Middle Ages. The capital of the Empire, Constantinople, ranked next to Baghdad and Damascus as a place of skilled gold and silversmithing. We know the name of one Jewish jeweler, the silversmith Obadia (eleventh or twelfth century).[21]

Conclusion

The Byzantine Empire, stretching from Asia Minor to southern Italy and Sicily (though the latter possessions were lost in the ninth and tenth centuries), was a bridge between East and West. Such skills as silk weaving, dyeing, and jewelling were transmitted through the Byzantines to the Western World. Byzantine Jewish craftsmen were particularly instrumental in carrying the silk industry to Italy, whence it spread farther north and west. The Byzantine Jewish craftsmen formed guilds and handed down their skills to their sons. An interesting feature of Jewish occupational life was the extent to which women worked. On the whole, we know comparatively more about Jewish activities in crafts in the Byzantine Empire than in any other economic field.

CHAPTER VII

Jewish Trades in Southern Italy in the Middle Ages: 500-1500

Today southern Italy has an insignificant Jewish population.[1] The only Jewish community south of Rome is in Naples. But, in the Middle Ages, numerous Jewish communities existed in southern Italy throughout the successive periods of Byzantine, Saracen, Norman, Hohenstaufen, Angevin and Aragonese rule. Agricultural, commercial and maritime activities were developed, arts and crafts offered opportunities to many people, and Jewish lore and secular learning flourished. There was a saying current: "Out of Bari goeth forth the Law, and the word of the Lord cometh from Otranto." Jewish philosophers, astronomers, and translators of Arabic writings into Latin were also busy in Salerno, Naples, Palermo, Girgenti, and other places, lavishly supported by the rulers of that time. As the fifteenth century drew to a close, Jews reportedly resided in more than 250 localities in southern Italy from Naples to Reggio di Calabria, and on the islands of Sicily, Malta, Gozzo, and Pantelleria. Their total was perhaps 70,000 persons.[2]

The Political Setting

This numerical strength, coupled with economic stability and spiritual energy, was conditioned by the following political factors.

The coming of the Saracens to Sicily in the early part of the ninth century created a favorable atmosphere for the further development of the Jewish communities, which had been established centuries before, and prompted Jews from countries under Christian rule to migrate there. Across the sea, Jews were living in precarious conditions under Byzantine rule in the provinces of Apulia and Calabria. Their situation improved when, in 1053, Norman nobles wrested Apulia and Calabria from Byzantium. In 1091, Sicily fell to the crafty Norman rulers and, in 1101, Duke Roger II established the kingdom of Sicily, Calabria, and Apulia.

This event marked the start of an interesting era in the history of southern Italy in general and of the Jewish community in particular. The "first modern king" of the medieval world, as Roger has been called, signally adapted his rule to the composite character of his realm, which consisted of many creeds and nationalities—Latins, Lombards, Normans, Greeks, Saracens, and Jews. Sicily, in particular, was "a meeting-place of races, tongues, commercial products, religions, civilizations." Roger, as well as his successors, "pursued an enlightened policy of tolerance rare in that age. Neither Jew nor Greek nor Saracen was molested in his religion. Local rights and usages were respected." [3] The government departments issued documents in Arabic, Greek, and Latin. The municipal constitution of Palermo allowed Jews, Greeks, and Arabs their separate notaries for drafting legal deeds in their own languages. It was laid down in the city of Catania, as of 1168, that Latins, Greeks, Jews, and Saracens were to be tried according to their own laws.[4]

The Suabian (Hohenstaufen) King Henry, who assumed the rule in 1189, continued the liberal policies of his Norman predecessors. His son, King Frederick II (1208-1250), would not tolerate any discrimination against Saracens or Jews. True, he was obliged to yield to the Roman church when it introduced the Jewish badge at the Fourth Lateran Council (1215) and Sicilian Jews were ordered to wear it; but the order was not strictly adhered to.[5]

Economic Stratification

In the Norman-Hohenstaufen cosmopolitan state no person was

barred from attempts to earn a living because he belonged to a different national group or religious creed. Aware of the accomplishments of Greeks, Saracens, and Jews in farming and industry under Byzantine and Moslem rule, the Norman and Hohenstaufen kings encouraged these groups in every way to exercise their skills. Immigration was not barred; on the contrary, foreigners were encouraged to settle in the country, and were even transplanted to Apulia, Calabria, and Sicily, where they were easily integrated into the economic structure of the Norman-Hohenstaufen state. In 1147, Jews of Spain, fleeing the persecutions of the Almohades, came to Trani, which emerged as a center of silk production. Roger II, as mentioned before, brought Jewish silk weavers in 1147 from Thebes to Palermo, setting them to work in the royal silk factory. The expulsion of the Jews from France in 1182 led to the further growth of the southern Italian community. The first Hohenstaufen king, Henry, "invited many Jews" to take up residence in Corigliano and other cities of Calabria. And Frederick II, in pursuance of his colonizing projects, transplanted Jews from the island of Djerba, on the North African coast, to Sicily, allotting them land for the cultivation of henna and indigo required by the dyeing industry. The Jews of Djerba, who formed a separate congregation within the Palermo community, also planted date palms at the king's request; they were promised reduced taxes.[6]

In this general setting, the chances were favorable for the emergence of a class of Jewish craftsmen large in numbers and varied in skills. Thomas Aquinas (1227-1274) had the Jewish laborers of southern Italy in mind when he said, in his *De Regimine Judaeorum* (on the Government of Jews), addressed to the Duchess of Brabant: "The rulers of the countries would do better to compel the Jews to work for their living, as is done in parts of Italy, rather than to allow them to live in idleness and grow rich by usury."[7] Born in Aquino, in the kingdom of Naples, Aquinas had, in his youth, seen Jewish artisans ply their trades there.

Silk Weaving

The weaving of silk and cloth and dyeing were of prime importance. These trades, it will be remembered, were actively followed by Jewish artificers in late antiquity in the eastern Mediterranean area, above all in Palestine and Egypt. In the early Middle Ages, the Byzantine Empire and Sicily emerged as centers of weaving and dyeing, in which Jews took a conspicuous part.[8] The Saracens transplanted sericulture to Sicily, but it took firmer hold under the later Norman rule. The Italian silk manufacture originated in Sicily and in the southern part of the Italian Peninsula, whence it spread to central and northern Italy, France, and other parts of Europe.[9]

Jews were active in the production of silk in the period of the Norman and Hohenstaufen rulers. Mention has been made of their working in the royal factory in Palermo; the textiles produced there were glowingly described by the writer, Hugo Falcandus, in his letter of 1190.[10] But even before 1147, Jews were producing silk in Reggio di Calabria, in Catanzaro, and farther north in Amalfi, Cosenza, Gaeta and Salerno, as well as in other localities.[11] It appears that the manufacturers of silk were also engaged in selling. They bought raw silk from peasants, finished it, and sold the product.[12]

Lucca, once capital of the County of Tuscany, attained fame through its silk industry in the later Middle Ages. F. Edler de Rovere has suggested that it was introduced there in the eleventh and twelfth centuries "neither by Arabs from Sicily, nor by Greeks from the Byzantine Empire, but by Jews from Southern Italy." [13]

Dyeing

The dyeing trade was usually combined with the finishing of textiles. In Sicily, the Jews learned to use locally cultivated plants, of which the henna grown in Partinico should be mentioned. The Saracens, as noted above, had started the cultivation of dyeing plants in Sicily. In addition, African Jews from the island of Djerba introduced henna and indigo for the crimson and blue colors required by the dyeing industry.[14] As noted before, a group of Djerba Jews was prevailed upon to settle near Palermo in the early thirteenth century—an indication of the great need felt for dye stuffs in Sicily. Kermes, a dye whose sale was monopolized by the Jews of Arles, was imported from southern France.[15]

Jewish dyers are first recorded in Gaeta, north of Naples, in 1129.[16] In the late 1160's, Benjamin of Tudela met groups of dyers in Benevento and Brindisi. Cosenza, Trani and other places in the south of the Italian peninsula had Jewish dyers. They were found in Palermo and throughout Sicily. In 1245, most of the twenty-five Jewish families of Malta were engaged in the dyeing trade, as were the eight families on the tiny island of Gozzo. In many a community the dyeing shop constituted a kind of Jewish center near the synagogue. Often the dyers' group was almost identical with the community. Indicative of the large number of Jewish dyers are the entries in tax registers, where the dyers' tax is termed the "Jews' dye-tax." *Tincta Judaeorum* is recorded in Benevento, Girgenti, and elsewhere.* The dyers had a special preparation which was also used for writing. Bernardus Provincialis (twelfth century), in his commentary on the Tables of Salernus, said: *"Licium, i.e. judaycum quo Judaei tingunt pannos suos et etiam scribunt";* Licium [lithium], that is Jewish licium which the Jews use for dyeing their clothes and also for writing.[17]

The great advances of the weaving and dyeing industry in the south of Italy early in the thirteenth century may have prompted King Frederick II to monopolize these trades for the state. Though the Jews formed only three per cent of the total population, they had become intimately associated with both trades. In 1231, the king charged Jewish silk manufacturers of Trani with the administration of the state monopoly. They were ordered to buy all the raw silk of the country at a maximum rate established by the state; to supervise the finishing and dyeing; and to sell it, at a 33 per cent profit, for the benefit of the treasury.

The Crown, it has been suggested, did not wish to place the silk monopoly in the hands of officials unfamiliar with the details of production. Accordingly, the Crown kept all dye-works, including those in the domains of the barons and church dignitaries, under its control, charging Jewish experts to reorganize the industry. Zones of operation were established, one in the north of the kingdom (called *Terra di Lavoro*) and four in the Abruzzi. Dyeing was concentrated in these zones under the supervision of Jewish agents,

* One finds entries like *Cabella judaice et tinctorie,* or *Cabella judaice tinctorie et celandre; celandre* means finishing.

who employed mostly Jewish labor familiar with both silk weaving and dyeing.[18]

The political disturbances following Frederick's death (1250) put an end to these experiments in state monopoly. Private enterprise, it appears, was restored in both the silk and dyeing industries. However, Jewish weavers and dyers, to all intents and purposes, continued their activities in southern Italy and further north. Some probably went to Lucca, where silk production flourished in the later Middle Ages.

The close association of the Jews with these trades may account for the Palermo community's obligation to provide banners for the royal castles and warships; this was revoked only in 1421.[19] Messina, while opposing any further increase of its Jewish population, not only allowed a Jewish silk weaver of the city of Catanzaro to settle in the city in 1486, but conferred citizenship on him.[20]

In addition to silk weaving and dyeing, other handicrafts may be noted. In Salerno and Bari, Jews enjoyed the monopoly of "preparing and selling cloth manufactured by pressing machines." In Salerno, they also produced earthenware and skin bottles.[21] We should like to know whether Jews engaged in glassmaking, which in Palermo "exceeded even the skill of Venetian craftsmen." [22]

Scribes and Illuminators

The production of books was an important craft. The Jews were literate people and there was always need for copies of Bibles, prayer books, ancient and contemporary rabbinical writings, poetical works, grammatical and medical treatises, travelogues and others. The Hebrew script developed in Italy is a mixture of the Spanish and German type of Hebrew penmanship, characterized by a sense of balance and harmony. A list of about 490 scribes has been compiled for Italy alone in the period up to 1500. Some of the manuscripts written on fine vellum were beautifully illuminated and illustrated with figurative scenes. The colophons of the scribes do not usually mention the illuminations, an omission also typical of Christian scribes. The craft of the scribe and the illuminator was closely connected with the preparation of parchment, inks and colors. Judging from the places of origin of the copyists mentioned in the colophons, they were frequently itinerant artists and therefore hardly able to develop any kind of fraternal associations. However, their calling was hereditary, handed over from father to son and involving a rigorous training in the traditional rules of their craft.[23]

Religious Intolerance

In the second half of the thirteenth century, the political and social situation of the non-Catholic population—Jews and Saracens—in the south of Italy began to deteriorate. The Hohenstaufen King Frederick II—that fascinating liberal monarch, "the amazement of the world," as he was called—fought the Roman church, but eventually Rome won the battle. The Angevin Kings of Naples, who also ruled over Sicily, depended on the good will of the Popes. The Inquisition took advantage of the situation and forced conversions of Jews were initiated in the kingdom of Naples in 1282.[24] This development wrote *finis* to the long period of religious tolerance. Sicilian Jewry was, for the moment, spared such trials. But there, too, conditions worsened under Aragonese rule during the fourteenth and fifteenth centuries. The militant monastic orders set religious zeal aflame, with its concomitant of persecution of the Jews. However, some of the rulers of Naples and Sicily, with an eye to government finance, maintained a more lenient attitude.

The Period 1250 to 1492

After 1250, the economic stratification of southern Italian Jewry remained virtually what it had been in the Norman-Hohenstaufen period. We have evidence of Jews in various places of southern Italy engaging in a variety of handicrafts: tailoring, embroidery, dyeing, tanning, saddlery, cobbling, jewelry making, blacksmithing, joinery, and butchering.[25] In Palermo, womenfolk worked at weaving. Jews were busy in the ports as longshoremen, stevedores, porters, etc.[26] Obadia of Bertinoro, on his trip to Palestine, spent the months of July to September 1487 in Palermo. He noted that 850 Jewish families lived in one street situated "in the best part of the town." "They are," he says tersely, "artisans, such as iron-smiths and coppersmiths, porters and peasants." On his eastward path from Palermo, he stopped in Messina, a city with 400 Jewish families which were "richer than those in Palermo, almost all of them artisans; there are only a few merchants among them." On the ship leaving Messina for Rhodes, Obadia was joined by other travelers, among whom were three Jewish leather workers from the city of Syracuse.[27]

The role of Jewish artisans in Sicily was stressed in a memorandum of the Sicilian Privy Council to King Ferdinand of Aragon dated June 20, 1492—two days after promulgation of the decree of expulsion. The monarch's attention was called to the adverse effects of that act on the economic and strategic position of the island. Vital industries would be ruined, above all the metal industry. The authors of the memorandum declared: "Another difficulty lies in the circumstance that all artisans of this realm are Jews. If they leave the country forthwith, the Christian population will experience a lack of laborers able to provide the mechanical implements and especially iron work indispensable for blacksmithing, the manufacture of agricultural tools, and equipment of ships, galleys and other vehicles. For it is impossible to find enough Christians to manufacture these necessities. As a result of the shortage of all these commodities, the few [Christian] craftsmen able to produce them will raise prices to an exorbitant level." [28]

However, these arguments of the Privy Council and intervention by other bodies were not heeded by the king. The municipality of Palermo emphasized in its petitions that expulsion would be a breach of the privileges granted to the Jews. The city elders requested time to dispatch a delegation to the king to explain their fears of the losses the city and the kingdom would suffer following the expulsion of the Jews. This intercession of the Sicilian capital's citizenry was of no avail. The expulsion decree was carried out on January 12, 1493. The craftsmen's request for permission to take their tools with them was refused.[29]

Guilds

The Jewish handicraftsmen in Sicily did their work in shops or stands in the markets. Some were engaged as homeworkers by entrepreneurs, especially in silk manufacture. Dyers were organized in associations or guilds. A guild of Jewish carpenters in Palermo is mentioned in official documents dated May 1451. The master carpenter, Joseph Caschisi, was appointed warden of the guild by the Sicilian Viceroy on May 18, 1451, in recognition of his skillful work in the construction of the royal palace in Palermo.[30]

Jewish Handicrafts in Sardinia

The Jewish population of Sardinia, whose settlement went back to antiquity, was enlarged considerably in the fourteenth century when it came under Aragonese rule. Jewish immigrants arrived from Aragon, the Balearic Islands, Provence, and even from German lands. However, the estimated number of 5,000 Jewish residents in Sardinia is probably exaggerated.

Economic stratification was much like that of the Sicilian Jews. Among the handicraftsmen, in addition to weavers, there were blacksmiths, coppersmiths, and tinkers. The constant hammering of the metalworkers so annoyed their Christian neighbors on Sundays and Christian holidays that Ferdinand of Aragon, in 1488, forbade such work on those days. It has been suggested that Jews may have worked in the silver mines around the cities of Iglesias and Alghero. It is known that Jews were banned from residence in Iglesias and around the silver mines in 1327, "owing to suspected malpractices," but the decree was soon revoked. Early in the fifteenth century, the community of Alghero, after payment of a considerable sum of money, obtained the exclusive right of prospecting, excavating, and mining in the vicinity of the town. There is later evidence of licenses granted to Jews to prospect for metals.[31]

In 1492 the Inquisition was established in Sardinia, followed by the expulsion of the Jews from the island early in 1493.

Conclusion

In medieval Sicily, southern Italy and Sardinia, the pattern of Jewish crafts was much the same as in the Byzantine Empire. Owing to their friendly relations with the Christian population over a period of centuries, evidenced by the lack of intransigence on the part of the Christian guilds, Jews and Moslems were free to pursue their economic activities. They were protected and even encouraged by the Norman and Hohenstaufen rulers. Under the rule of Spain the era of tolerance came to an end.

Chapter VIII

Jewish Trades in Southern France in the Middle Ages

Two Jewish cultural centers existed in medieval France. The northern center comprised the communities in the provinces of Champagne, Burgundy, Ile-de-France, Normandy, Anjou, and Poitou. In rabbinical sources, it was called the land of "Zorfat." The southern center embraced the provinces of Languedoc and Provence, and was called in rabbinical literature, "Provinzia." The river Loire separated the two centers. The French language north of the Loire was the *langue d'oïl,* while that of the south of the river was known as the *langue d'oc.* The Jews of the north were exclusively devoted to talmudic studies, while those in the south, like the Jews of Spain, showed an interest in philosophy and the sciences as well. The economics of the two Jewries also differed. In the north, the Jews engaged only in commerce and credit operations, whereas south of the Loire Jewish occupations included agriculture, viticulture, commerce, and arts and crafts.

The anti-Jewish efforts of fanatical church dignitaries met with little success in the Provence. In the early Middle Ages, Jews of Narbonne and other places owned rural estates. The Arab invasion from Spain, in the first half of the eighth century, left its mark on social conditions in southern France, creating a measure of understanding between the different races and religions. The tolerant policy of the Carolingian monarchs (751-987) toward the Jews was continued by the Counts of Toulouse and Provence, who were virtually independent rulers until the Capetian monarchy brought them under its sway in the later Middle Ages. In such a political climate, Jewish economic activities could develop freely. The notion of shutting the Jews out of the economic system of the

Christian world had not yet entered the minds of the rulers of southern France. Jewish artisans plied their trades without any serious interference on the part of the Christian craft guilds.

The historian G. B. Depping, in his book on the Jews in the Middle Ages, draws attention to the Jewish gold- and silversmiths of Trévoux, north of Lyons. After their expulsion from the latter city, in the late fourteenth century, Jews settled in Trévoux, carrying with them a craft which they continued to practice in the first half of the nineteenth century. It consisted of refining gold and silver and drawing out threads "as thin as hair." The Jewish masters of Trévoux did not, however, enjoy a monopoly; Paris and Lyons gave them competition.[1]

There were Jewish dyers in many places in the south of France. Notary registers of Montpellier for the years 1293 and 1294 contain several names of Jewish dyers.[2] Avignon, it seems, had the largest group of Jewish artisans. There were weavers, fullers, cloth-shearers, washers, and other workers in the textile trades. Tailors were numerous in Avignon, as well as in Marseilles, Montpellier, and Perpignan. The Jewish tailors of Avignon produced ready-made clothes for the market.[3] Those of Perpignan formed a guild which maintained a hospital of its own.[4]

A bookbinder, Mossé Alment, is mentioned in the records of the University of Avignon of 1456 and 1457 (fols. 83 and 90).[5] He may have been a refugee from Germany, judging from his name. Jews did leather work in Montpellier.[6] A *"magister lapidis"* is mentioned in Marseilles records.[7] There were soap makers in Arles,[8] and a Crescas Davin set up a soap factory in Marseilles (fourteenth century).[9] Marseilles also employed Jewish porters.[10]

Avignon, residence of the Popes from 1309 to 1376, was capital of the ancient county of Venaissin, which was part of Provence. The Jewish artisans of Avignon and Venaissin encountered some opposition from Christian artisans, but on the whole continued their trades with little molestation, under the protection of the Popes. When the Popes left Avignon for Rome, the Christian guilds complained about the Jewish artisans to the municipality, which time and again passed measures to restrict their activities.[11]

In 1500, the history of the Jews in Provence came to an end. They were expelled, most of them going to Turkey, where the family name of Provençal is frequently encountered. The Provençal artisans practiced their crafts in Salonica, Constantinople, and elsewhere in the Ottoman Empire in the early modern period. The tiny Jewish community of Venaissin (in the Department of Vaucluse), survived until the twentieth century.

Chapter IX

Jewish Crafts in Germany, Northern France, and England in the Middle Ages

The bulk of the Jews of Germany and northern France consisted in the early Middle Ages of merchants carrying on international commerce and, in the later Middle Ages, of moneylenders and petty traders. Here and there, individual Jews owned land, particularly vineyards. It seems that non-Jewish labor was employed on the larger estates.[1] To be sure, there were a few Jewish artisans in German and northern French cities, such as butchers, bakers, distillers, tailors, and barbers, who catered to the needs of their co-religionists. But any attempt by these artisans to secure a market for their products among the non-Jewish populace was frustrated by the Christian guilds, the butchers' and tailors' guilds being particularly vigilant in this respect. The privileges granted to the Jewish communities by emperors, dukes, and bishops in the eleventh to the thirteenth centuries make no mention of craftsmen at all.[2]

Barred from Craft Guilds

The Christian guilds explicitly barred Jews from membership,[3] which would imply that occasional efforts had been made by Jews to secure admission. In the later Middle Ages, Jewish goldsmiths, dyers, glaziers, blacksmiths, and millers were active in some German cities, as evidenced in rabbinical writings and municipal records.[4] More information exists about the tailoring trade: Jewish tailors in Wiener-Neustadt, in Austria, were working in the early fourteenth century for Christian patrons. In Hildesheim, Germany, the tailor, Isaac, was registered in the town's book in 1442. And in Duderstadt, in Lower Saxony, two Jewish tailors were permitted, in 1457, to employ Christian journeymen. On the other hand, the municipal council of Fuerth permitted a maximum of two or three Jewish tailors to ply their trade, but for Jewish patrons only. At the same time, the council forbade Jewish barbers and musicians to sell their services to Christians. One learns of Jewish boatmen who worked for Jewish shipowners carrying cargo up and down the Rhine and Main rivers.[5]

Bookbinding

According to the *Sefer Chasidim* by Judah ben Samuel of Regensburg (thirteenth century), German Jews learned bookbinding from the monks.[6] In the fourteenth and fifteenth centuries they seem to have specialized in *cuir ciselé,* a leather tooling technique of carving free-hand slightly raised figures and ornamental designs into the moistened leather, without the use of blind stamps. One of these bindings bears the Hebrew inscription "Pentateuch for the Nuremberg Council to whom life may be granted—Meir Jaffe, the designer." The designer is identified as "Meierlein Jude von Ulm" who was given temporary residence at Nuremberg in 1468 while binding some books for the City Council. In 1490, another Jewish master bound the city records of Noerdlingen. An Isaac ben Zecharia made a tooled leather case for a double goblet for the Archbishop of Mainz, Diether von Erbach (first half of the fifteenth century).[7]

Illumination of Manuscripts and Playing Cards

The use of gold lettering in Hebrew manuscripts goes back to an old tradition. The Letter of Aristeas, (second century B.C.E.), verse 176, mentions a Pentateuch scroll written in Hebrew on parchment with gold letters. In illuminated Bible codices of the tenth and eleventh centuries from the Cairo Geniza, gold was used in the lettering, in the ornamental designs, and in the illustrations depicting the vessels of the Temple. In the Hebrew manuscripts of the thirteenth to fifteenth centuries in European countries a variety of colors and designs in the current styles were introduced. The *Mishneh Torah of* Maimonides (in the Academy of Science at Budapest) executed in Cologne, in 1296, is a typical illuminated manuscript with figure illustrations in the High Gothic style. The scribe Nathan ben Simeon ha-Levi states in the colophon that he worked on the manuscript from April 22, 1295 to September 9, 1296, and that he provided it with painted pictures. He also names his patron. This is one of the few colophons that mention the work of illumination explicitly. In view of their close adherence to the trends in European art it has been doubted that the ornamental designs and the illustrations in Hebrew manuscripts were the work of Jewish illuminators. In some manuscripts, however, the script and the pictures are so closely interwoven that the possibility of collaboration with a Gentile artist must be excluded. It is evident that the designs were derived from Christian Bible illustrations and from pattern books, duly adapted to their purpose.[8] The art of hand illumination was not entirely given up with the invention of printing and the introduction of woodcut illustrations, and a few types of writings continued to be executed by hand. Jews apparently were also engaged in painting playing cards. The town book of the city of Landau, in the Palatinate, for 1520 deals with the complaint of the card-painter Meyer Hayyim whose trade suffered because of the importation of playing cards from other cities. The Council decided to stop the sale of imported cards.[9]

Minters

Jewish minters worked for secular and church rulers in the early Middle Ages. A Jew named Priscus minted coins for the Frankish king, Chilperic I (561-584). David Haccohen was a minter in Hesse, Germany, in 1180. The minter, Shlom, was in the service of the Austrian duke Leopold V (1177-1194). Jechiel, who worked for the Bishop Otto of Wuerzburg (1202-1223), made coins bearing his own name. Jewish minters were also active in

Hungary and Poland, whither Jews began to migrate as the result of persecutions which accompanied the Crusades.

Silver coins struck in the reign of the Hungarian king, Bela IV (1235-1270), were marked with the Hebrew letter *aleph*. The mintmasters of the Polish kings of the Piast Dynasty struck the names of the rulers in Hebrew, followed by the term *berakha*, (benediction) on the coins. Other coins bear the names of the minters, Abraham son of Isaac Nagid, Joseph Kalish, etc.[10]

Medieval England

The economic stratification of the Jews in medieval England, where they settled after 1066, was much the same as in northern France, but with greater emphasis on moneylending. Moneylenders were protected by the kings. J. M. Rigg mentions a goldsmith, Leo, who obtained a charter from King John. He believes that other crafts may have been open to them, for the craft-guild system was not very developed as yet. On the other hand, he points out that the sphere of their trading operations was seriously restricted by the merchant guilds.[11] At any rate, moneylending remained the outstanding occupation of the Jews in England.

A striking change was announced by the English Crown in 1275. In his *Statutum de judaismo* King Edward I forbade Jews to lend money, but permitted them instead to ply crafts, carry on commerce, and lease landed property for ten-year periods. This law, which is considered a bold effort to change the socio-economic structure of medieval British Jewry, was bound to remain a dead letter, however, for neither the merchant nor the craft guilds would admit Jews, and the clergy strongly protested against leasing land to them. Even without these obstacles, the English Jews, who had been engaged in moneylending for about two centuries, could hardly have emerged overnight as farmers or artisans.[12] They remained enmeshed in the antagonisms which accompany the money trade. In 1290, fifteen years after the issuance of the *Statutum de judaismo*, they were expelled from England.

Chapter X

Jewish Arts and Crafts in the Iberian Peninsula Until 1391: Spain, Navarre, Portugal

Nowhere in medieval Europe did Jews develop arts and crafts to such a degree as in the Iberian Peninsula, particularly in Spain.

Jews emerged in Spain at the beginning of the Common Era, when it was a province of the Roman Empire. Under the Visigothic rule (409-711), Jews lived in the city of Toledo, in the southern region, later called Andalusia, and in the northeast, in Catalonia. They engaged in handicrafts, farming and commerce. "An agricultural and military people like the Visigoths, in an age of war, could not be expected to do much to develop industry and commerce. Such as there was of both was carried on by some Hispano-Romans, and by Greeks and Jews." [1]

In 586, King Reccared adopted Catholicism and proclaimed it the religion of the state. This event markedly affected the status of the Jews. The Catholic clergy now launched, with the support of the Crown, an anti-Jewish campaign. Reccared's successor ordered Jews either to accept the Catholic faith or leave the country. Some, particularly those possessing landed property, were converted, others found asylum with friendly Visigothic landowners; and many emigrated to France and North Africa. The Arab invasion of Spain in 711, however, with the decisive defeat of the Visigoths at Jerez de la Frontera, brought about Moorish rule and the end of the persecutions.[2]

Under Moslem Rule

The swift Arab conquest of most of the Iberian Peninsula ushered in a period of physical security and religious and economic freedom. Crypto-Jews openly reverted to Judaism, and those who had fled to North Africa returned.[3]

The caliphate of Cordova, established in 755, grew into one of the richest and most populous states of western Europe. Except for the Christian kingdoms of Leon, Castile, and Navarre in the north, the Islamic caliphate ruled the whole peninsula. Agriculture flourished, rice, sugar, and other useful plants hitherto unknown in Spain were cultivated, and industrial arts were developed on a remarkable scale. Factories and smaller workshops were set up throughout the country, from Saragossa and Calatayud in the northeast to Cordova, Almeria, Malaga, and Granada in the south. The manufacture of textiles, such as silk, cloth, and linen of fine quality, occupied a prominent place in the economy. Tapestry weaving centered in Baza, in the province of Granada. Furriery was a thriving trade. Ceramics and glass were produced. Metal ware and ivory carvings were among the best in Europe. Cordovan jewelry rivalled the Byzantine, and the city's leather goods were highly prized. Toledo was famous for its weapons; Jativa was the site of paper mills.[4]

It is a fair guess that, in this period, the Jews learned many of the skills we find them exercising centuries after the downfall of the Cordovan caliphate in the eleventh century. Moslem artificers were their teachers, we can be sure, although consideration must be given to the fact that Jewish arrivals from the Near East, who came in the wake of the Moslem conquest, probably included craftsmen. In the tenth century, representatives of the Jewish artisans and merchants met in the synagogue at Cordova to welcome back the statesman Hasdai ibn Shaprut from a diplomatic mission to Pamplona in Navarre, which he had undertaken on behalf of the Caliph Abd-ar-Rahman III; this would seem to indicate that a Jewish artisan class existed at the height of the Cordovan caliphate.[5]

The streets of tanners, furriers, shoemakers, and other artisans, which we find in the Jewish district of Saragossa in the thirteenth century, in all probability originated during the Cordovan caliphate. Similar busy Jewish districts no doubt existed in other cities. Evidence is scarce, for almost all of the official records of the Moslem period have been destroyed. Besides, Arab chroniclers devoted most of their attention to political and dynastic matters while Christian writers were interested chiefly in the success of the *Reconquista.* The Hebrew chronicles describe persecutions, the achievements of Jewish scholars, and the careers of Jewish statesmen in the service of Moslem rulers, but seldom deal with workaday matters. The responsa of Rabbi Moses ben Hanok of Cordova (tenth century), Alfassi (1013-1103), and his disciple, Joseph ha-Levi ibn Migash (1077-1141), while shedding some light on farming and commerce, contain little information on handicrafts. As Abraham A. Neuman puts it: "Altogether the fund of information derived from these works is not of sufficient volume to form an adequate picture of Jewish life in Moorish Spain." [6]

One gets a passing glimpse into the role of Jews in the silk industry from Abraham ibn Daud (1110-1180), author of the chronicle, *Sefer ha-Kabbalah.* He notes that Jacob ibn Gau, who had been appointed prince and supreme judge of the whole Jewish community of the Cordovan caliphate in 985, was engaged with his brother, Joseph, in silk manufacture. The Court commissioned them to weave precious silk fabrics and banners interwoven with Arabic slogans, emblems, and various decorations.[7] There is reason to believe that Jewish workers were employed by the Ibn Gau brothers who, as Ibn Daud states, were themselves skilled craftsmen.

In Cordova, the Jews lived in a quarter north of the caliph's palace, but their number is not known. The city's entire population must have been large, although the reports of Arab travelers that in the tenth century it numbered 130,000 dwellings were no doubt exaggerated.[8] The city of Lucena, south of Cordova, was entirely inhabited by Jews. Gaon Natronai of Sura, in the Baghdad caliphate, referred to Lucena as a "Jewish place" already in 853.

Later, the Arab geographer, Edrisi (1099-1164), in his "Description of Africa and Spain," likewise called Lucena "the city of Jews." Edrisi's whole passage about Lucena is worth quoting: "The suburb is inhabited by Moslems and a few Jews. There stands the mosque; but the suburb is not encircled by walls. The city, on the contrary, is girded by solid walls and is surrounded on all sides by a deep fosse and channels. . . . The Jews inhabit the inner part of the city, whither they permit no Moslem to enter. They are wealthier than those of any other country under Moslem rule, and are on the watch against any enterprises of their rivals." [9] Granada and Tarragona, southwest of Barcelona, were also "Jewish cities," according to Arab geographers of the tenth, eleventh, and twelfth centuries.[10]

The Rise of the Christian Kingdoms

The caliphate of Cordova fell apart after 1031 into a number of smaller states which were attacked, one by one, by the rulers of the Christian kingdoms. Alfonso VI, King of Leon and Castile (1065-1109), occupied Toledo in 1085, where a large Jewish community existed, superseding the one of Cordova. Saragossa, a Moslem stronghold in the north, was conquered by Alfonso I, King of Aragon, in 1118. Meanwhile, however, Berbers from North Africa invaded Spain and established their rule, as the dynasty of the Almoravides. The Almoravides at first persecuted the Jews, but later mitigated their hostile attitude, as the remission of a large contribution demanded from the Jewry of Lucena makes apparent.[11]

Things took a turn for the worse when other and more fanatical Berbers, the Almohades, poured into Moslem Spain. They absorbed the rest of the Spanish Moslems, fought the Christian kings, and ruthlessly persecuted the Jews. In a panic, the latter fled to the north or emigrated overseas, that is, across the Mediterranean. Refugees from Cordova, Seville, and Granada settled in Toledo and other cities within the Christian part of Spain. The Almohades were defeated by the combined armies of Leon and Castile, Navarre and Aragon, under the leadership of Alfonso VIII of Castile, at Naval de Tolosa in 1212. Jews fought alongside the Christian armies, rejoicing at the victory which marked the end of the bloody rule of the Almohades.

Alfonso's son, Ferdinand III, proceeded to conquer Cordova and other Moslem strongholds in the south of the peninsula. As a result, Arab rule came to an end in all of Spain and Portugal, except for the kingdom of Granada where it endured until 1492. Ferdinand III united Leon and Castile into the kingdom of Castile in 1230.

By that time, the king of Aragon, James I, the Conqueror, had rounded out his possessions with the addition of the Balearic Islands. Thereafter, Christian Spain consisted of three kingdoms: Castile, Aragon, and Navarre; Portugal had emerged earlier as a separate kingdom. But Navarre was small in size and fell under the control of Aragon, respectively France. Jewish life in the main became concentrated in Castile and Aragon.

Castile: 1000-1400

Early in this period, Castile was a preponderantly agricultural and pastoral country, with little commerce or manufacture. It developed more slowly than other European countries; its cities were few, and industries slow to develop. Had it not been for the Moors, and Jews who had acquired their knowledge of arts and crafts alongside the Moors, Castile's economic backwardness would have been even greater. Though Moors and Jews were confined to separate quarters, they were an economic factor of considerable importance in Christian Spain.[12]

The earliest mention of Jewish craftsmen in Castile concerns the ancient city of Leon, where the family name of *Ashkafa* (meaning shoemaking) appears in 1053, shortly after Leon was first united with Castile; a Jewish goldsmith of Leon is mentioned in 1110. We have more evidence from the second half of the thirteenth century concerning the southern and northern districts of Castile. In a register of Jewish house owners in Jerez de la Frontera for 1266, a tailor, two armorers, a lace maker, cobbler, butcher, and other artisans are listed. About the same time, a Jewish blacksmith was living in the city of Valladolid. And in Soria, the local Christian weavers' guild, which originated in 1283, enacted regulations governing Jewish weavers.[13] As the thirteenth century came to its end, the scope of Jewish crafts in Castile enlarged.

The size of the Jewish population of Castile as of 1290 was about 3,600 families. Toledo with its 360 families or householders had the largest community.[14] The Jews of Toledo plied various trades. The city was already the Jewish garment center of Castile. Shoemakers lived and worked here in their own street. Of the 65 Jewish householders of Segovia, a third were engaged in such trades as weaving, dyeing, furriery, saddlery, shoemaking, pottery, blacksmithing. There were also smiths and dyers in Avila; a rabbi, Juda, is listed as dyer. In the small village of Valdeolivas, in the district of Cuenca, east of Madrid, in 1388, there lived twenty Jews, of whom six were shoemakers, three tailors, one a weaver, one a smith, and one an itinerant artisan. These figures reflect the general distribution of Spanish Jewish labor among the principal crafts.[15]

As the foregoing indicates, a good part of Castilian Jewry made their living as artisans. In view of the relatively small Jewish population, the Jewish artisans would seem to have counted many customers among the non-Jews. Frequently, Jews were the only people possessing a certain skill. For example, Jewish coppersmiths had to be called in at the end of the fourteenth century to repair the municipal copper fountain in Burgos.[16]

Rabbinical Labor Regulations in Castile

The growth of a Jewish artisan class in Castile is also reflected in the responsa of Asher ben Yehiel, chief rabbi of Castilian Jewry in the period 1305-1327;[17] many of the questions submitted to the rabbi bore on trades. Weavers, tailors, tanners, bridle makers, blacksmiths, shoemakers, and others sought his advice about difficulties which they had with patrons, fellow workmen, or with the elders of the community. Since, as far as we know, no Jewish craft guilds existed at that time in Castile, Rabbi Asher's decisions effectively regulated conditions of labor, relations with customers, relations between partners, and apprenticeship. A few cases will illustrate the nature of these regulations.

A weaver received an order from a patron. When the latter supplied him with the material for the job, the weaver noticed that it was of poor quality and asked to be relieved of the task. The patron, however, persuaded him to continue his work by promising him a larger payment. When the job was finished, the customer refused to pay the higher amount which he had promised, arguing before Rabbi Asher that the weaver had left him no alternative but to make a promise which he felt that he was not bound to fulfill.

Rabbi Asher decided that the weaver had no right to walk out on a job he had undertaken; having entered into an agreement, he was obliged to keep it.

In another case, a Gentile sent a messenger to place an order for a garment with a Jewish tailor. The tailor was about to cut the material when another tailor entered the shop and he too was commissioned by the messenger to make a garment. When the two garments were being delivered, the first tailor demanded a higher amount maintaining that the other tailor was entitled only to a workman's pay having learned his craft from him. Rabbi Asher ruled that both were to be paid the same amount since the patron had considered them master tailors of equal competence.

The following dispute was brought to Rabbi Asher for a decision. Three shoemakers who had worked in partnership decided to dissolve their association. They agreed, however, that should an occasional job offer itself to one of them, the proceeds would be divided among all three. Now, it happened that one of them received an order from a Gentile client to dress a skin for him, and the other two claimed a share in the payment. Rabbi Asher found that the partnership had ceased to exist with regard to shoemaking, but not with regard to other kinds of work.

Another interesting case involved a master tailor who obtained a loan from a fellow Jew. It was agreed that the latter would in lieu of repayment, be taught the trade and accepted as the tailor's partner. Both swore to keep the agreement. When the tailor's wife learned about the agreement, she objected, for she was afraid that her husband would not be able to support her if he was to share his earnings with a partner. Rabbi Asher held that the wife's objection was invalid.

In Castile, in the early part of the fourteenth century and later on in Aragon as well, complaints of violations of contracts of apprenticeship were brought before the rabbis for hearing. One such contract contained a clause requiring the father of the apprentice to make good any damage caused by his son. A dispute arose on this point and the question was raised whether the agreement had "legal force without a formal obligation." Rabbi Asher ruled that labor contracts were binding even in the absence of a formal obligation. The agreement between father and master was a labor contract; if the boy had in fact caused the damage, the father must make good for it.[18]

Aragon: 1100-1400

We know more about the history of Jewish crafts in the kingdom of Aragon. Originally, Aragon was a small territory on the southern slope of the Pyrenees belonging to Navarre. It became an independent kingdom in 1035, and grew in size and importance following its conquest of a number of Moorish cities and union with Catalonia in 1137. In 1232, the Balearic Islands and, in 1238, the province of Valencia were subjugated by King James I. Barcelona, capital of Catalonia, and Valencia, capital of the province of the same name, were important western Mediterranean ports and provided outlets for the agricultural produce of the Aragonese hinterland. Commerce expanded at an increasing rate, especially after the annexation of the Balearic Islands, and Catalonia became an area of considerable industrial activity.

Jews are first reported in Aragon as inhabitants of the city of Saragossa, where a community emerged immediately after the Arab conquest of 713. The first mention of Jews in Jaca, the original capital of the kingdom of Aragon, is in 1062; Huesca, 1096; Montclus, 1099; Calatayud, 1120; and Lerida, 1158. Later, as a result of the flight from the persecutions of the Almohades, the number of towns with Jewish inhabitants steadily mounted. Before 1391, Aragon, apart from the Balearic Islands, had between 3,500 to 4,000 Jewish families, or just about as large a Jewish population as Castile. Saragossa contained 200 families. In 1340, Huesca had 340 male Jews over the age of 15, about the same number as Calatayud. Barcelona contained about 200 Jewish families; Valencia, about 250; Perpignan, from 200 to 250; and sixteen other cities about 50 Jewish families each. In Catalonia, Jews lived in the villages; in Aragon, though they were city dwellers, many owned land in the adjacent countryside and engaged in agriculture, stockbreeding, and vine growing on the side.[19]

Aragon developed industries more rapidly than Castile, and greater opportunities offered themselves to craftsmen. The *juderia* of Saragossa included, as already indicated, a number of streets named after the trades of their inhabitants. There was a cutlers' street, jewelers' street, tanners' street, furriers' street, saddlers' street, shoemakers' street, etc.[20] Saragossa's Jewish craftsmen had Gentiles among their customers. The royal court employed quite a number of tailors, shoemakers, armorers, jewelers, and pearl workers. The court craftsmen were often granted privileges by the king entitling them to special honors in the Jewish community and also exempting them from community taxes. In 1347, the pearl worker, Gadella Avenarama, obtained through king Pedro IV two seats for himself and his descendants in the synagogue at Calatayud, thus circumventing the synagogue board. In 1324 he had already obtained lifetime exemption from all taxes. The community elders appealed to the Crown, pointing to the loss of income to the community. The only way the elders could exert pressure on the court craftsmen was to threaten them with excommunication.[21]

The clergy also patronized Jewish artisans. Lope Fernandez de Luna, the archbishop of Saragossa, had a Jewish tailor (1373). There were tailors, weavers, tanners, blacksmiths in Huesca, Lerida, Perpignan and other towns. These trades were traditional among Jews in Spain and could be traced back to about the middle of the twelfth century.[22] By the end of the fourteenth century Jewish artisanship had become, according to Baer, "the most vital part" of the Jewish population in Spain; in Aragon, perhaps more so than in Castile.

The notary files of Barcelona tell the impressive story of the spread of the arts and crafts among the Jews not only in that city, but in the country at large, for many of the artisans who applied to the Barcelona notaries for registry of their documents came from other places. In the files we find mention of weavers of silk covers and curtains, dyers of various woven fabrics, clothmakers, workers in coral, turners, diemakers, buttonmakers, lace makers, goldsmiths, silversmiths, coppersmiths, embroiderers in gold and silk, makers of musical instruments, tailors, shoemakers, furriers, bookbinders, etc. The bookbinder Mahir Salamo was engaged, in 1367-1389, by the royal treasury at Barcelona to bind its account books. Frequently, the Jewish person registered in the files is termed a *managerius,* that is an artisan of no defined trade. Several persons are listed as porters; they were presumably employed in the port of Barcelona.[23]

The Jewish communities of Aragon were autonomous bodies, and their councils, called *aljamas,* regulated religious, judicial, educational, fiscal, economic, and welfare matters. They exercised police functions within the *juderias;* were responsible for the security of the community, ordering the erection of the walls around the *juderias* or their repair; built roads; administered institutions; and regulated weights and measures. Thus, the councils gave employment to masons, carpenters, smiths, and other craftsmen. Community engineers, or builders, were appointed by the councils to superintend the workmen.[24]

Attitude of Rabbinate and Aragonese Court toward the Artisans

The importance of crafts in the economy of Aragonese Jewry is reflected in the responsa of two outstanding rabbinical authorities, Solomon ben Adret, chief rabbi of Barcelona (1280-1310), and Isaac bar Sheshet, rabbi at Saragossa (1370-1374) and later head of a yeshiva in Valencia (until he finally emigrated to North Africa). Isaac bar Sheshet was a champion of the artisans and of the humble classes in general. His spirited defense of the poor Jews of Saragossa against the oligarchic clique controlling the *aljama* led to his resignation from his rabbinical post. Though otherwise rigorous in his interpretation of rabbinic law, he was ready to stretch a point for the workingman. Thus, he permitted the poorer artisans of Murviedro, a city in the district of Valencia, to work on half holidays,[25] pointing to a precedent established in the talmudic and gaonic periods.

The royal court markedly favored Jewish artisans and appointed some of them as master craftsmen of the court. Further, the court would seem to have been interested in raising the social standing of the craftsmen within the Jewish community. King John I, in 1390, ordered that two of the five judges (called *barurim*) of the Jewish community, who were artisans and thus unable to sit regularly with their colleagues on the cases coming before the court, should be allowed, with the concurrence of the parties to the action, to conduct their own examination in the facts of cases, with all the judges assembling together only for the pronouncing of the judgment.[26] This decree shows that the *aljamas* of Aragon elected artisans as judges.

Jewish Artisans in the Balearic Islands

Jews were living in the Balearic Islands as early as the fifth century. Under Moslem rule, which lasted from the eighth to the early thirteenth century, the islands were, according to the Arab chronicler, Ask-sha Kanti, "one of the most fertile and best cultivated countries that God ever made and the most abundant in provisions of all kinds." [27] In addition to vinegrowing and commerce, Balearic Jews were engaged in handicrafts, as were those in Sicily and the other Mediterranean lands under Moslem rule.

In the twelfth century, the persecution of Spanish Jewry by the fanatical Almohades caused an influx of refugees from the mainland into the Balearic Islands. Jews continued in their traditional pursuits when the Balearics came under Aragonese rule in 1232. The commercial and industrial importance of the Balearic Islands increased when Sicily became an Aragonese possession because of the strategic situation of the Balearics between Sicily and Catalonia. Jews from the south of France and from North Africa were also attracted to the Balearic Islands. In this way the Jewish community grew in numbers and importance.[28]

In the fourteenth century, the city of Majorca had between two hundred and three hundred Jewish families.[29] To protect the local Jewish artisans against competitors arriving from the outside, the *aljama* of Majorca, in 1315, imposed a weekly tax on all such persons.[30] Soap making, a trade commonly plied by Mediterranean Jews, engaged many Majorcan Jews. The soap maker Solomon Benallel, in 1381, was granted a monopoly of the trade for ten years, because of his services to the royal court and to the community.[31]

Lace making was another Jewish craft in the Balearics. Lace interwoven with gold and silver, called *redecillas* or *tellilas,* was exported to the Spanish mainland where it fetched fancy prices. It is interesting to note that this lace was condemned in various sumptuary edicts of Castile, Aragon, and Navarre.[32] Majorcan Jews also wove woolens and manufactured clothes and covers. We learn something about these occupations in connection with the persecution of 1391, which compelled many Jews to accept Christianity outwardly, living thereafter as crypto-Jews or *Marranos.* In that year, the governor of Majorca, Francisco Saggariga, issued a decree which said: "The converts to the Christian faith of the lineage of the Jews, are admitted to exercise the trade of weaving, which will be taught to them, even though they may be of the lineage of infidels." [33] However, not all the Jews of Majorca became converts. Thus, we learn that Jewish barbers were prohibited in 1413 from serving Christian patrons and that tailors were forbidden to accept orders from any Christian woman "whatever her rank may be." [34]

The descendants of the Balearic Marranos, called *chuetas,* whose number was recently estimated at about 300 families, are still engaged in goldsmithing, a craft plied by their ancestors in the Middle Ages. However, as late as 1782, they were barred from the goldsmiths' guild of Majorca.[35] To this day, although most of them are devout Catholics, their Jewish descent is a matter of common knowledge.

The Jewish Cartographers of Majorca

The Jews of Majorca made outstanding contributions to cartography and the development of nautical instruments. Two brothers, Isaac Nafuci and Ephraim Bellshom, attained fame as makers of astronomical and nautical instruments. Nafuci was ordered by King Pedro IV, in 1359, to come to Barcelona "to make the clocks and sextants that we desire." In 1365, he produced a silver quadrant for the king and, together with his brother Ephraim, astrolabes for the Infante John, later King John I. Members of the Cresques family of Majorca became widely known as cartographers. Abraham Cresques, called "magister de mapamundi," drew up a map of the world in 1381. King Pedro was fond of him, as well as of Nafuci; in 1387, Cresques was given 150 gold florins, while Nafuci obtained the position of *shohet* (ritual butcher) in Majorca, a post which because of its ritual implications entailed considerable prerogatives. The map which Abraham Cresques compiled in collaboration with his son Jaffuda was presented by the Infante John of Aragon to Charles VI of France. Later, John I of Aragon ordered Jaffuda Cresques to make a new map of the world. Jaffuda continued to work in Majorca, where he was known as the "Jew of the compasses," in the service of Kings John and Martin. He was converted to Christianity in 1391, taking the name of Jaime (Jacob) Ribes. The two Cresques, father and son, contributed to contemporary knowledge of the geography of northwest Africa, mapping the continent as far down as Timbuktoo, on the Niger River. Flourishing Jewish settlements existed throughout the Middle Ages in the oasis of Tuat, in the central Sahara, and even in the Sudan. Jewish merchants of the Mediterranean area knew of the trans-Saharan route leading from Tuggourt and other places in the *Maghreb* to Timbuktoo. Obviously, Abraham Cresques drew upon their knowledge.[36]

Jewish Handicrafts in Navarre

In the Middle Ages, the kingdom of Navarre straddled both sides of the Pyrenees. Jews lived there as far back at the tenth century and Jewish communities developed in Pamplona, the capital of the kingdom, Tudela, Estelle, Olite, and elsewhere. However, the total number of Jewish families in Navarre at the end of the thirteenth century amounted at the most to 500. The heads of these families were chiefly engaged in commerce. Only when Navarre came under French rule in 1276 did Jews become moneylenders after the fashion prevailing in French lands.

Though commerce dominated in Navarre, there were such artisans as tanners, gold and silversmiths, silk weavers, cobblers, furriers, tailors, and dyers. In 1389, the tanners of Tudela paid the Crown thirty-five sueldos for the use of a tannery on the Ebro River. In larger cities, like Tudela and Pamplona, Jewish goldsmiths, silk embroiderers, and shoemakers occupied their own rows of shops.[37] The royal household employed Jewish seamsters, tailors, and goldsmiths. We know of Jewish laborers, and also that women were "often employed" as workers in the building trade—a unique occurrence in medieval Jewry. The wages of Jewish female workers were less than those of male Christian workers, averaging about three-quarters of the latters' wages.[38]

Jewish Artisans in Portugal

Portugal was established as an independent kingdom in 1143,

and the history of its Jewry dates back to the reign of its first king, Alfonso Henriques, who died in 1183. The Jewish population grew to the point where Lisbon harbored three "Jewish" streets. Coimbra, Santarem, and Evora likewise had large Jewish communities, and Jews were scattered throughout the countryside. The Jewish artisan class was large. In addition to tailors and shoemakers, there were masons, carpenters, and smiths. We know of a blacksmith, Santo Samay, who tended his forge in Coimbra in 1431.[39] Two categories of artisans need to be distinguished: the settled urban and the itinerant rural artisans. The latter went from village to village, and even to the laborers in the fields, to mend shoes and clothing. The matter of these itinerant Jewish repairmen was brought up at the Cortes in Evora in 1482. The "representatives of the kingdom laid before the king that Jewish workmen, as cobblers, repairmen, and so forth travel through the country in search of work, and while the laborers are employed in the fields, they are in contact with their wives and daughters," which, added the complainants, is highly injurious to good morals and the Catholic faith; and, in consequence, they demanded that "Jewish workmen should not be permitted to travel throughout the country, but be confined to their Jewries, where those who require their work will be sure to find them." To this complaint of the Cortes, King John II answered that "it was for the convenience of the country folk that he had permitted Jewish workmen to offer their services to the laborers and that if those workmen committed any crime they could be brought to justice.[40]

King John II of Portugal, like John II of Castile and Alfonso V of Aragon before him, understood the country's need for skilled artisans, even if they were Jews or Moors. In the wake of the Spanish expulsion of 1492, he enticed artisans to settle in Portugal. After 1495, his successor, Manuel I, followed in this path with even more unscrupulous ingenuity. Although, upon his marriage to Isabella of Spain, daughter of Ferdinand and Isabella, he had promised to cleanse Portugal of the presence of the accursed Jews, he would not let economic considerations be entirely overridden by religious and dynastic zeal. In 1497, the Jews living in Portugal were given the choice of conversion or exile, but Manuel imprisoned those who had chosen exile until the time set for their departure had passed. Thereupon they were declared slaves and forcibly baptized.[41] In that way, he saved his soul and served his mundane interests at one stroke. In Portugal as in Spain, the Jewish and Moorish minorities were eliminated in the interest of religious and national homogeneity.

Chapter XI

Jewish Craft Guilds in Spain

Craft Guilds in Spain

The origins of the craft guilds in Christian Spain go back to the end of the twelfth or beginning of the thirteenth century. Even before that time, however, Moorish Spain had had associations of craftsmen whose purpose it was to lay down working conditions, control output, and represent the common interests of the members. The Christian kings, on entering cities conquered from the Moors, were surprised to find well-organized groups of artisans, each residing in its own quarter. In Valencia, for instance, more than twenty sections of the town were each allocated to a different craft.

The Christian guilds in Spain, like guilds in other European countries, were religious fraternities. They had their churches or chapels dedicated to their patron saints. The *confradia* or *cofradia* (fraternity) attended church and civic ceremonies *in corpore.* It provided welfare benefits to its members. In the course of time, economic objectives were adopted, if, indeed, they had not been present from the start. The *cofradia* became a full-fledged guild, generally called *gremio,* although the older name *cofradia* was often retained.[1]

The guilds set up rules concerning the control of raw materials and their distribution among members, the inspection of working conditions, and standardization of output. Relations between masters, journeymen and apprentices were closely regulated and certain political tasks were undertaken. At first, guild membership was voluntary, but, about the close of the fourteenth century, it was required of all artisans.[2] The institution of apprenticeship was dealt with in the famous code of law, *Las Siete Partidas* (Seven Codes), of the Castilian King Alfonso X (1252-1284). It stipulated that masters may ask payment for the training of apprentices. The contract was to be concluded between the boy's father and the master. As a rule, the term of apprenticeship varied between four and five years.[3]

Jewish Guilds

It has been suggested that Jewish and Moorish artisans were free to join the Christian guilds. Thus Chapman says that "many of the guild members were foreigners, or Jews, or Mudejares." [4] Klein, in his "Medieval Spanish Guilds," asserts that Jews were permitted to enter the guilds. But these statements are not corroborated by documentary evidence. We must conclude, on the contrary, that the Spanish Christian guilds were usually barred to Jewish and Moorish artisans. We know this to have been the case in the fifteenth century. Whether matters had been different in the fourteenth century can only be conjectured. The religious function of the Christian guild must not be overlooked in any discussion of this problem. Jews and other non-Christians could not easily join guilds simply because so many of the activities of the guild were religious in nature. It must therefore be assumed that Jews and Moors were excluded from the guilds. Later, after the establishment of a racial criterion for admission to the guilds, not even Jewish or Moorish converts to Christianity could join. In 1474, Queen Isabella of Castile issued an ordinance whereby apprentices applying for admission to a guild, in addition to a baptismal certificate, had to provide full proof of *limpieza de sangre,* purity of blood.[5]

However, the Christian guilds, though inaccessible to Jews, could not effectively bar Jewish artisans from plying their trades. Indeed, Jews and Moors retained their dominant position in the arts and crafts down to the expulsions of 1492, 1501, and 1609. The artisan character of the medieval Jewries of Spain, Sicily and Provence, distinguished them from those of Germany, northern France and England, where only an insignificant number of Jews lived by manual labor. It must be borne in mind that the Spanish guilds lacked the power and public authority of the German and French guilds and were dependent on the Crown, which often protected the Jewish and Moorish workmen in consideration of their contribution to the industry of the country and to the treasury. Efforts made by the Spanish guilds to prohibit certain trades to Jews, or to control their activities, failed. Two examples illustrate the situation in Aragon. In 1391, King John I ordered the authorities of the city of Albarrazin, southwest of Teruel, to stop the town council from attempting to impose its rules on Jewish tailors and other artisans. The council was undoubtedly acting for the local Christian guild. Even more drastic was John II's order, in 1461, to the authorities of the city of Monzon to quash the local Christian tailors' decision to expel the Jew Ganto of Briviesca who had settled in Monzon with the intention of opening up a tailor shop.[6] Actually, attempts to oust Jewish practitioners from the trades were not general in Aragon. We will see how the town council of Saragossa made important concessions to Jewish craftsmen in spite of the opposition of the Christian guilds.

Things were much the same in Castile. King John II (not to be confused with John II of Aragon) decreed, in 1443, that Jewish and Moorish craftsmen were to pursue their trades without interference from city councils, guilds, or private persons. It would seem that the Castilian Crown kept to this policy in the second half of the fifteenth century. As late as 1489, when the municipality of Burgos forbade Jewish tailors and other craftsmen to ply their trades outside the Jewish quarter, the royal couple, Ferdinand and Isabella, acting upon Jewish complaints, annulled these prohibitions.[7]

Christian attacks on Jewish craftsmen and merchants were not always prevented.[8] The Jews fully realized that to protect their economic position they had to establish organizations of their own. When, how, and to what extent such organizations were formed and functioned, is a matter as yet little explored. But it can be safely assumed that the number of Jewish guilds in Spain, particularly in Aragon, was not inconsiderable, even though we have evidence only of a few. On the basis of extensive research into the social and economic history of Aragonese Jewry, Manuel Serrano y Sanz asserts that the Jews had a considerable number of *"gremios* and *cofradias."* He pointed out in particular the shoemakers' and skindressers' guilds in Saragossa.[9]

The Articles of the Jewish Shoemakers Guild of Saragossa (1336)

On March 15, 1336, King Pedro IV approved the guild articles submitted to him by the Jewish shoemakers of Saragossa. The preamble of the document is in Latin, the text of the articles in Spanish. In conclusion the king states, in Latin, that he is acting at the request of the shoemakers, and that the articles shall remain in force for generations to come. Among the witnesses listed at the end of the document are the Infante Jaime and the Archbishop of Saragossa.[10] This statute deserves special attention as it is the only complete code which we possess of a medieval Jewish guild.[11]

Like the by-laws of Christian *cofradias* of that period, the Saragossa articles deal with matters of religion and welfare. Care of ailing members was an important concern. Guild wardens were required to visit their sick twice a week, on Mondays and Thursdays. Members destitute as the result of illness received two dineros daily from the guild treasury. On Saturdays, it was the duty of every member to visit ailing members. When a member died, the entire guild remained with the body until burial, conducting religious services in the house of the deceased. Eight days after burial, a service was held in the synagogue and a sermon was preached in praise of the deceased. Guild members absent from this service were fined a dinero. The guild helped members celebrate such family events as a wedding, a *brit mila,* etc. Personal offenses were punished by fines, as well as by exclusion from the *cofradia* for one month, which bespeaks the high sense of honor of the Spanish Jews. Members gathered twice yearly to listen to a reading of the guild articles—"so that everyone may know how to conduct himself."[12]

The Saragossa shoemakers' guild is mentioned in a notary document dated June 5, 1414, where it is called the *confradia* of the *"hasguafim,"* meaning *capateros* or shoemakers. The guild representatives, Acach Gallur and Solomon Paci, are mentioned by name.[13]

Agreement between the Christian and Jewish Guilds of Skindressers in Saragossa (1440)

In 1440, the Jewish skindressers' guild of Saragossa concluded an agreement with the Christian guild in the presence of the municipal authorities. Both parties agreed that inspectors for the Christian skindressers were not to be allowed to enter Jewish workshops unless accompanied by a Jewish inspector. The Jewish inspectors were to receive a third of the fines imposed on skindressers who had violated the rules of workmanship. Unsatisfactory work by Jewish skindressers was to be examined by inspectors of both groups. The Jewish inspector was authorized to hold a key to the yard of the Christian skindressers. If a new workshop was opened in the neighborhood of the Jewish skindressers, the latter were to receive a fee of ten sueldos. Upon concluding a contract with a master, an apprentice paid a fee of five sueldos to the guild.[14]

This agreement is interesting in two respects. First, it shows the good working relations between Christian and Jewish artisans in Saragossa. Secondly, it shows that Saragossa, as a thriving industrial center, was anxious to foster harmony among its various ethnic and religious groups. The city authorities were careful to preserve a benevolently neutral attitude in these matters.

Other Jewish Guilds in Aragon

One of the four synagogues at Saragossa belonged to the turners, which implies that the turners had a guild. The synagogue served the entire community.[15]

In Barcelona, capital of Catalonia, there apparently existed Jewish butchers', dyers', and sailors' guilds. The dyers enjoyed a more than local fame, and fabrics from abroad were sent to them to be processed.[16] As already remarked, Jewish porters were working in the port of Barcelona.

The weavers' guild at Calatayud had their own synagogue. Another Jewish guild, perhaps of weavers, seems to have existed in Huesca. The Jewish tailors of Perpignan, which belonged to Aragon in the later Middle Ages, had their own hospital.[17]

Apprenticeship

The statute of Saragossa's Jewish shoemakers' guild makes no mention of certain vital elements of guild organization, especially regulation of the conditions of work, economic policy, and relations between masters and journeymen as well as between masters and apprentices. We know from the rabbinical *responsa* of this period that, in Castile and Aragon, agreements were concluded between the master and the apprentice or the apprentice's father. The Castilian chief rabbi, Asher ben Yehiel, as we have seen, dealt with matters of this sort. His Aragonese counterpart, Rabbi Solomon ibn Adret, in a case where a boy was not satisfied with the conditions agreed upon between his father and the master, decided that the youngster might withdraw from the agreement provided he was not supported by his father, and thus was an independent person according to talmudic law.[18]

Later, articles of apprenticeship were agreed to between masters and apprentices directly; the agreement was signed before a Christian notary and filed in his register. The first documented instance of such an agreement between master and boy, concluded before a Christian notary, occurred in 1386, when a Jewish youngster of the village of San Martino in Catalonia was articled to a tailor of the village of Verdus. The boy promised to serve his master faithfully for one year, the master undertaking in return to feed, clothe, and teach him the trade. Both took an oath on the Torah. The articles were drawn up in Latin and deposited with the notary.[19] Another contract signed before a notary "in accordance with the usage of the city" states that the tailor, Struch Ananell of Barcelona, agrees to provide the apprentice, Samuel Baruch of Barcelona, with food, clothing, shoes, and shirts.[20]

The term of apprenticeship was five years as a rule; in Catalonia, three to four years. The master undertook to provide the boy with "good and sufficient food, drink, clothing and shoes, in sickness and in health," and to teach the boy the trade.[21]

Guild Autonomy and the Rabbis

Rabbi Solomon ibn Adret was for many years the spiritual leader of the community in Barcelona. He took an active interest in guild matters. Asked for his opinion on the legality of the guild regulations of the Jewish butchers, dyers and sailors, he declared:

> If these guilds pass a rule concerning their trades, it is binding upon the individual tradesman as are the laws of the Torah, for every trade organization is a city unto itself and does not require the consent of the outer community for its enactments . . . The members of a guild are as autonomous in their own affairs as are the citizens of the city. Therefore, each group or community is permitted to conduct its affairs and to prescribe fines and punishments which may not be found in the laws of the Torah. This is the practice of all the holy congregations and no one has ever questioned its legality.[22]

This statement is remarkable for the complete backing it gives to the regulatory practices of the guilds, whose enactments Rabbi Solomon ibn Adret likens to the laws of the Torah. Later on in the same statement, he expresses his concurrence with the talmudic regulations concerning labor, and quotes the *Tosefta* (*Baba Mezia* XI, 16) on the artisans' right to prohibit outsiders from setting up competing shops.

Rabbi Adret's pronouncement attests the autonomy of the guilds within the Jewish community. The guilds watched any attempt on the part of the *aljama,* the community council, to infringe upon their powers. Similarly, the non-Jewish guilds jealously guarded their rights and powers against the interference of the city councils.[23]

Chapter XII

Decline and Expulsion of the Jews of Spain and Portugal

The Persecutions of 1391

The year 1391 was a turning point in the history of Spanish Jewry. Less than 200 years had passed since the victory of the Christians over the Almohades, and the restriction of Moslem rule in the Iberian Peninsula to the small kingdom of Granada. The victorious rulers of Castile and Aragon showed every consideration to the Moors and Jews, who promoted commerce and trades. The Christian owners of large estates emulated the kings in employing Jews in their colonizing projects. The Jews were also used as agents of the treasury, judges, diplomatic agents, and medical experts. They practiced diversified trades. There were the familiar weavers, silk mercers and dyers, tailors, button makers, curtain makers and embroiderers, and the more unusual painter—not dyer—of panels in wool (*pictor pannorum lane*). Baer lists anchor-, instrument-, lantern-, scale-, and dice-makers, cutlers, turners, workers in coral, apothecaries and soap makers, bookbinders, and silversmiths, and female Jewish dirge-singers at Christian funerals.[1] Evidently, as Américo Castro remarks, "the Jew did everything there was to be done."[2] Because of their ubiquity, animosity against Jews—and also against Moors—spread among the townspeople, but it did not become articulate before the second half of the fourteenth century.

The Spanish church, boastful of its achievement in the *Reconquista* and suspicious of Jews and Moors, led the campaign. Both were considered a menace to the faith and hence to the homogeneity of the nation. Hatred of Jews was preached from the pulpits; the Jewish religion was attacked in pamphlets, some of which were compiled by Jewish apostates. Prominent rabbis and lay leaders were forced to participate in public religious disputations with Catholic clergymen, chiefly monks. The church found allies in the townspeople—merchants and artisans—and in the mob, especially in the port cities.

By 1370 things reached such a pass in the kingdom of Castile that, at the Cortes convened by Henry de Trastamara in the city of Toro, the representatives of the towns demanded the expulsion of the Jews. Henry refused to consider this drastic measure. However, a regulation was enacted requiring Jews to live in separate quarters and wear a distinctive badge. They were to refrain from riding horses or mules and from ostentation in dress.[3] The agitation did not abate. Particularly violent were the preachings of Ferrant Martinez, the archdeacon of Ecija, who was active in Seville in the 1370's and the 1380's. He was deprived of his post, but was later reinstated and renewed his campaign.[4] Jews lived in dread of physical attack.

Representatives of the Jewish communities meeting at Madrid in January, 1391, learned that pogroms were in the making in Seville and Cordova. On June 6 of that year, the mob attacked the Jews' quarter in Seville and a terrible carnage ensued. For three months, there were bloody massacres of Jews in Cordova, Toledo, and many other Castilian cities, and all along the coast, from Valencia to Barcelona. The pogroms were organized by agents who visited the various towns. Ten such emissaries were sent from Seville to Valencia and later to Barcelona.[5] The persecutions even leaped across the water and reached the Balearic Islands.

The Aftermath of 1391: Emigration and Mass Conversion

The survivors of the slaughter fled to Portugal, North Africa, and Turkey. Many others accepted baptism. The mass conversion of 1391 has been attributed to the high degree of assimilation of the Jews into Spanish culture, but fear was obviously the main motive. Some Jews found temporary refuge with members of the nobility or went into hiding in the cities.

Spanish Jewry's recovery from this hard blow was painful and slow. It took more than two decades to reestablish Jewish life, whereupon new troubles arose in 1411-1414 when the Dominican friar, Vincente Ferrer, visiting Castile and Aragon, incited rulers, upper classes, and populace against the Jews.

Solomon Alami, author of the pamphlet, *Iggeret Mussar* ("Letter of Moral Instruction"), who witnessed both the catastrophe of 1391 and the agitation of Ferrer in 1411-1414, wrote: "And the calamity befell us in recent years in the districts of Castile in their length and breadth, and also in the kingdom of Catalonia, in the year of 5151 (1391), when numerous small and large communities were annihilated. And in the twenty-second year after the calamity (1412) the remnants of Jewry in Castile were exposed to disgrace and ridicule." The last sentence is a reference to the preachings of Ferrer.

Alami expressed high regard for the artisans, pointing out that they formed the bulk of Spanish Jewry. Like the teachers of the talmudic times, he said: "Learn a trade and be able to make a living from thy labor." In a most significant passage of his pamphlet he attacked the members of the Jewish upper class who were to blame for "the ruin of their people" and who were the first to embrace Christianity.

The Castilian Edict of 1412

An edict of Catalina, the queen-mother of Castile,, promulgated in Valladolid in 1412 was intended to cut Jewish economic activities drastically. Jews (and Moors, for that matter) were to be barred from all administrative positions; doctors forbidden to treat Christian patients; apothecaries to sell medicines to Christians; artisans and farmers to employ Christian labor. Jews and Moors willing to accept the Christian faith were not to be hindered by friends and relatives from doing so; Jews seeking to emigrate were to become serfs of the king.

The categories of artisans mentioned in the ordinance included smiths, carpenters, tailors, doublet makers, clothiers, shoemakers, furriers and butchers. Working for Christian customers was to be strictly forbidden.[6]

Alami conceded in his pamphlet that the well-to-do were the first to accept baptism, partly because they had no trade to fall back on. He noted that there were also handicraftsmen among those who deserted the faith.

If enforced to the letter, the edict would have meant the ruin of the Jewish farmer, merchant, artisan, laborer, and professional. In the meantime, Vincente Ferrer had moved his headquarters to Aragon, and the Crown came to realize that it was impossible to carry out the edict. Already in June 1412, a new edict was issued in Cifuentes. Some of the strictures were relaxed, Jews were granted freedom of movement and allowed to hire Christian labor. The concession with regard to freedom of movement was made at the instance of the nobility interested in attracting Jewish workers to their estates.[7]

Deposition of the Schismatic Pope Benedict XIII and Installation of Pope Martin V

Still other factors accounted for the Castilian government's abandonment of its uncompromising attitude toward the Jews and the Moors. A new Pope, Martin V, was elected by the Council in Basel in 1417. Simultaneously, the schismatic Pope Benedict XIII was deposed for the second time, though he claimed the title until 1423. Benedict XIII, called Pedro de Luna before he became Pope in 1394, was a Spaniard, and had his entire following in Spain. To strengthen his authority, he had conceived the idea of a mass conversion of the Spanish Jews. He sponsored the violent anti-Jewish campaign of Vincente Ferrer and demanded the economic destruction of the Jews. Pope Martin V, however, was more tolerant. He renewed old Papal bulls favorable to the Jews, forbade forced conversions, condemned preachers who incited the population with tales about Jewish ritual murders, and pointed out that economic contacts between Jews and Christians could only be advantageous to the latter.

Another factor mitigating the lot of Castilian and Aragonese

Jewry was the attitude of Kings John II of Castile (1406-1454) and Alfonso V of Aragon (1416-1458). Both kings were far removed from religious fanaticism and their interest in secular culture justifies our ranking them among the humanist kings of that epoch. But what mattered most was that both rulers aimed at rehabilitating the shattered Jewish communities in the interest of their treasuries and of the economic development of their countries.[8] Consequently, the Castilian and Aragonese Jewries were able to recover from the disasters of 1391 and 1412, though conditions were never again as favorable as they had been before. It was a period of respite, lasting until Castile and Aragon were united in one realm in 1474.

Developments in Castile to 1474

The economic rehabilitation of Castilian Jewry was beset with serious obstacles, chief of which was the townspeople's hostility to Jewish competition in the trades and in commerce. During the political disturbances of the regency, ended by John II's assumption of his duties in 1419, many Castilian cities issued laws against Jews and Moors on their own authority.[9] However, King John II was determined to stop the towns' usurpation of his prerogatives. Fearing a loss of revenue might result from a policy of discrimination, the king issued an ordinance at Arevalo in 1443, regulating the property rights and economic pursuits of both Jews and Moors. The king stipulated that Jews and Moors should in no way be hindered in their dealings with Christians. "Nor are trades and useful handicrafts forbidden to them, as clothesmen, silversmiths, carpenters, barbers, shoemakers, tailors, clothiers, milliners, braziers, bridle makers, saddlers, rope makers, potters, curriers, basket makers, money changers, and all similar trades, mechanical arts, and useful handicrafts, in which they use manual labor and work. Christians may serve them in such trades and handicrafts for just wages and hire, as no authority is thereby derived by them; nor are they in any way honored thereby; nor can they assume power from such trades; nor can they thereby injure, molest, or condemn Christians; nor would it cause too much familiarity, nor constant company and association, provided the said Jews and Moors do not form partnerships with the Christians in the said arts and trades, or become too familiar, or keep constant companionship with them."[10]

This ordinance is noteworthy in many respects. It offers a list of trades plied by Jews and Moors and recognizes their freedom to employ Christian journeymen. At the same time it seeks to allay any apprehensions in the Christian population concerning the dominating role the Jewish and Moorish masters might acquire. The matter of partnerships between Jewish and Christian masters, will be discussed later, in connection with the guilds.

To the trades, listed in the ordinance, we may add on other evidence pearl dressing, parchment making, manufacture of stamped leather and leather bottles, dyeing, shearing of cloth, and weaving.[11] The fine wool derived from the merino sheep grazing in the Castilian highlands was a staple of the Spanish economy. Cattle and goats yielded hides for the leather industry in which Jews and Moors were extensively engaged.[12]

Aragon: 1400-1474

Compared with Castile, the attitude of the urban population of Aragon toward the Jews was less rabidly hostile. This is reflected in the rules concerning Jewish commerce and handicrafts of March 7, 1390, confirmed on December 27, 1401, by the municipal council of Saragossa. These regulations authorized Jewish artisans and merchants to establish shops or stands in the Jewish quarter and in the city, and to sell their goods without interference from Christian guilds. The list of artisans enumerated in these regulations includes weavers, tailors, embroiderers, furriers, tanners, leather workers, shoemakers, pack saddle makers, bridle makers, blacksmiths, braziers, turners and silversmiths.[13] Some other crafts, such as knitting, are mentioned in the fifteenth century files of the public notaries of Saragossa.[14]

Relations between individual Jewish and Christian craftsmen were correct and even friendly, despite the generally hostile attitude of the Christian guilds. Thus, a Christian dyer of Saragossa undertook, in 1406, to teach a Jewish rug weaver the entire art of dyeing, excepting only the secret of obtaining certain hues. In 1457, a Christian embroiderer in gold and silver and a Jewish gold beater agreed to work in partnership and to teach each other their skills.[15] At the same time, Jewish artisans succeeded in enlarging their Christian patronage, among whom were members of the court of Aragon, noblemen, church dignitaries, burghers, and peasants. It should be emphasized that Aragonese Jews, and craftsmen in particular, often lived in the smaller towns and villages. The growth of Christian patronage after the anti-Jewish campaign of 1411-1414 is especially noteworthy; it tends to support the contention of various historians that Jews and Moors provided the bulk of Aragon's artisan class. Thompson points out that the Jews were mainly engaged "in the fulling mills, tanneries, forges, and iron works," in addition to pottery and jewelry making. According to Thompson, in the reign of John II, of Aragon, (1458-1479), Jews or *conversos,* were "practically the only persons who had been able to keep up any industry and commerce."[16]

The activities of Jewish bookbinders and jewelers were opposed by the church authorities. King Alfonso V permitted Jewish masters to bind books for Christians, but excepted missals, breviaries, and other religious books. Christians who ordered the binding of such books with Jewish masters were subject to a fine.[17] It is questionable whether the ordinance was strictly enforced, for many Christian bibliophiles, among them monks, had a high regard for the work of Jewish bookbinders. It has been suggested that the Moors introduced the art of leather tooling and that the Jews acquired it from them.[18]

Jewish goldsmiths and silversmiths fashioned crucifixes, reliquaries, goblets, and other Christian ceremonial objects. Thus, in 1399, we find the silversmith Solomon Barbut, who had been working for King John I of Aragon, making a reliquary for the prior of the Augustinian order in Barcelona. A bull of the schismatic Pope Benedict XIII of 1415 forbade the making of crucifixes and goblets by Jewish masters.[19] Jewelers also repaired clocks. The silversmith Moses Jacob of Perpignan was ordered, in 1341, to repair the clocks in the royal palace at Barcelona.[20]

Calligraphers and illuminators of parchment manuscripts must have been fully occupied in the Jewish communities in Spain, judging from the quite considerable number of surviving specimens. The famous Hebrew Bible of the Bodleian Library (Kennicott I) carries the names of the copyist Moses ben Jacob ibn Zabarra and the illuminator Joseph ibn Hayyim. The work was completed at La Coruna in 1476. Joshua ben Abraham ibn Gaon of Soria copied two Bible codices in 1305 and in 1306. The latter is Codex Kennicott II of the Bodleian Library. The Farchi Bible was produced by Elisha Crescas who worked on it for seventeen years, from 1366 to 1383.[21]

Depredation of the Jewish Community

As a result of Ferrer's campaign in 1411-1414, conversions, chiefly in the upper strata of the Jewish community in Aragon, took place and the *aljama* of Saragossa lost many of its leaders. Under these circumstances, artisans assumed the duties of community officers and judges. On order of King Alfonso V, on March 29, 1417, the governor of Saragossa and Vidal de la Cavalleria, a former Jewish leader, now a *converso,* set out to investigate the management of the *aljama* and to remove the artisans who "ought to be the governed and not the governors" from the administration. The Jewish poet Solomon Bonafed contributed to the clamor against the "tailors [who] have become judges and the strapmakers [who] have become *dayyans* (religious judges)" in a satirical poem which he sent to Vidal de la Cavalleria.[22]

To the defense of the artisans it may be said that they were not as uncouth and ignorant as they were represented by the members of the upper classes. Although the following example may be an exception, it is interesting to note, according to an entry in a notary's file, that a shoemaker, Jacob Eli, bought from a Moor, Muca el Calbo, on January 27, 1427, two Hebrew books, *Macephet Yuamot* (apparently *Massekhet Yebamot*) and *Perus del Rabenu Shlomo* (Commentary of Rabbi Shlomo) on Genesis. The books were written on parchment and bound in red leather. The price was four Aragon gold florins.[23]

The Eve of Expulsion

The years 1474 and 1479 marked the beginning of the end of Spanish Jewry. In 1474, Isabella, daughter of Henry IV, ascended to the Castilian throne and, in 1479, Ferdinand became king of Aragon. Ferdinand and Isabella had been secretly married in 1469, with the help of a clique of courtiers to which belonged Don Abraham Senior, tax collector under Henry IV and later chief rabbi of Castile, and Pedro de Cabalera, of the famous Aragonese Marrano family. Jews and *conversos* both had wanted a strong government which might reestablish order and security out of the political chaos then reigning in Castile and Aragon.[24]

At first, the position of the Jews did not noticeably change under the rule of the royal pair. Jews plied their trades with very little interference.

On the eve of the expulsion, Talavera de la Reina, a city west of Toledo, had a small Jewish community with 168 tax payers. Thirty seven possessed more than 10,000 maravedi, 70 from 1,000 to 10,000, and 60 possessed only from 100 to 500 maravedi. Of the "wealthy" taxpayers (the maravedi had greatly declined in value) thirteen were basket makers, three were goldsmiths, two shopkeepers, and there were several physicians and tax farmers. The rest were blacksmiths, strap makers, tailors, cobblers. In Haro, not far from the border of the kingdom of Navarre, most of the forty-eight Jewish taxpayers were potters.[25]

In Baer's estimate, the artisans were a large and significant part of the 30,000 Jewish families in Castile and the 6,000 families in Aragon.[26]

The anonymous author of an account of the expulsion, probably written in April or May, 1495, points out that most of those banished were artisans.[27]

Marrano Artisans

From the conversions of 1391 and up to the expulsion, the Jews formed two groups in Spain: those professing the Jewish faith and the *conversos* or Marranos. Economic historians of medieval Spain, when speaking of the contribution of the Jews to the industrial life of the country, often have both Jews and Marranos in mind. The documents of the tribunals of the Inquisition reveal the high proportion of artisans among those tried for lack of zeal for the faith.

Relations between Jews and converted Jews remained close. Some of the Marrano artisans confessed before the tribunals to having learned their trades with Jewish masters.[28] After Isabella's edict of 1474, Marrano masters, journeymen and apprentices ceased to be admitted to the Christian guilds. With the institution of the Inquisition, in 1487, wholesale expulsions from the guilds "of many skilled artisans, industrialists, and merchants among the Jewish and Moslem converts" began to take place.[29]

Expulsion

The Expulsion Edict of Ferdinand and Isabella, signed on March 31, 1492, and made public between April 29 and May 1, compelled approximately 250,000 Jews to leave Spain. Three months were allowed them to settle their affairs. This proved too short a period to dispose of tools, merchandise, and property, and those expelled suffered huge material losses.[30] The summer months of 1492 witnessed public auctions of tools, looms, wool, cloth, manufactured goods, and other property of the Jewish textile establishments in the Aragonese cities of Barcelona, Valencia, Saragossa, Huesca, Lerida, Manresa, Hijar, and Barbastro. Most of the Jewish property went at a price which represented only a fraction of its value, and some had to be abandoned entirely.[31]

Some 100,000 of the exiled went to neighboring Portugal, gathering in the border cities of Benavento, Zamora, Ciudad Rodrigo, Badajoz, and Merida. Others set out for the Spanish ports with the intention of sailing to Italy, North Africa, the Balkans, and the Near East. John II of Portugal was willing to allow the exiles to remain eight months in Portugal, and undertook to furnish them with ships on moderate terms to carry them where they wished to go. The king had an eye out, however, for certain types of artisans whom he wished to retain in Portugal. Armorers, smiths, and braziers declaring their intention to remain, were required to pay only four cruzados on entering the country, instead of the eight cruzados exacted from all but infants.[32]

But, under John's successor, Manuel, who married a daughter of Isabella of Spain, all Jews were ordered to leave by decree of December 4, 1496. Many chose Catholicism in preference to exile, forming a new group of New Christians. But the rigors of the Inquisition subsequently forced many of this group into exile, too, where they joined the Jews who had gone before. Among them were more than a few craftsmen, mechanics, and especially armorers.

Economic Consequence of the Expulsion

The expulsion cost Spain the skill and industry of thousands of artisans. Sultan Bayazid II of the Ottoman Empire, whither many of the exiled migrated, is reported to have exclaimed, referring to Ferdinand of Aragon: "Is this a politic king who impoverishes his own country and enriches ours?" [33]

Ferdinand himself, three years after the expulsion, "complained bitterly at a meeting of the Cortes at Tarazona in 1495 of the collapse of craft integrity and industrial zeal in the kingdom." [34] When Suleiman the Magnificent's Grand Vizier, Ibrahim, in 1533, asked the Spanish ambassador to the Porte why Spain had not advanced economically, the reason given was the expulsion of the Jews and Moors.[35] French and Italian travelers and geographers who visited Turkey in the sixteenth and seventeenth centuries emphasized the contributions of the skilled Spanish exiles to the Turkish economy. As late as 1795, the French consul in Salonica, Félix Beaujour, wrote:

> The Jewish nation, driven from Spain by Ferdinand and Isabella, sought in Salonica under Sultan Bayazid II, an asylum, new rulers and the free exercise of its religion. The Castilian (textile) factories were then the most renowned in Europe; the Jews who managed them were thoroughly acquainted with their operations. They offered their industries to the Sultan.[36]

The verdict of modern historians supports this account. Thus, Mojeron, author of a *History of Medieval Spain,* writes that the banishment of the Jews "must be considered a crime."[37] James W. Thompson states: "The most skilled workmen in Spain had not been Christians, but Moors and Jews," and, he continues, "in skilled industry as in skilled agriculture the expulsion of the Jews and Moors was detrimental." [38] But religious unity was considered more important than prosperity.

Chapter XIII

Jewish Crafts in the Ottoman Empire: 1500-1800

The exodus from Spain, Portugal, Sicily, and Provence in the later Middle Ages was directed toward the east. Turkey was the country in which the Jewish exiles found asylum without conditions or reservations. Sultan Bayazid II (1481-1512), like his father Mohammed II, favored Jewish immigration. Both sultans were men of intellectual tastes, and tolerant in their attitude toward non-Turks. "They cared more for the economic development of the newly conquered territories than for religious controversies." The anonymous chronicler of the expulsion from Spain, already mentioned, pointed out that the refugees were kindly received by Bayazid because they brought skills to the country.[1]

Earlier Jewish Migrations to Turkey

Jewish groups had immigrated to Turkey since the middle of the fourteenth century. They came from Bavaria, Austria, Hungary, France, and, after the pogroms of 1391, from Spain. New Jewish communities arose in Adrianople, the modern Edirne, Sofia, Plevna, Salonica, and other Balkan localities following their conquest by the Turks. A rabbinical leader among the immigrants, Isaac Zarfati (the name points to his French origin), made a moving appeal in 1428 to Jews in the Rhineland, Suabia, Styria, and Moravia to come to Turkey, "the country of abundance." When Constantinople fell in 1453, Jews all over Europe looked toward the new Turkish capital as a goal for settlement. Under the last Byzantine rulers, Constantinople had had a very small Jewish population; but now the foundations of a large center were laid. The chronicler, Elijah Capsali (1490-1555), wrote: "'Sultan Mohammed sent this message throughout the Empire: Listen, descendants of the Judeans in my realm! Everyone of you who wishes to come to Constantinople may do so. The remnants of your people will find a haven here.' And large hosts of Jews came from every quarter, and the Sultan assigned them dwellings; and the Jews established themselves there. . . . The Sultan permitted the erection of houses of prayer and of learning, and ordered three chairs to be set up in the Divan [Crown Council], one for the Mufti, another for the Greek Patriarch, and a third for the Chief Rabbi." [2]

Salonica

After 1492, boatloads of Jewish immigrants arrived in the Turkish ports. Salonica (ancient Thessalonica) was a focal point of immigration. Jews had been living there since ancient times. Among the 500 Jewish families recorded in the 1160's were makers of silk garments and metal workers.[3] After the capture of the city in 1430 by the Turks, Jews began to come from Central European countries. They established an Ashkenazic community, different in ritual, habits, and economic stratification from the native Greek-Byzantine, or Romaniote Jews. With the influx of Spanish, Sicilian and Provençal Jews after 1492, Salonica became a populous city, with the newest immigrants emerging as the dominant element. At first, accommodations were lacking and houses were built with the assistance of masons, carpenters, and smiths among the immigrants themselves.[4] The new quarters took their names from the immigrants' places of origin: Aragon, Catalonia, Castile, Majorca, Sicily, Apulia, Calabria, Lisbon, Evora, etc. Altogether, there were more than thirty Jewish communities, each forming a congregation with its own synagogue, school and welfare institutions.

Textile Industry

The textile industry was foremost among the trades practiced by the immigrants. It seems to have been well established as early as the first half of the sixteenth century.[5] The Salonican hinterland, an important sheep-raising area, produced wool. We learn from rabbinical sources that Salonican Jews paid the peasants in advance for their wool, the latter making delivery after accumulating the wool of two or three shearings. Meanwhile, however, it frequently happened that other weavers went to the peasants and bought up their stocks of wool, so that the original buyers were seriously damaged. To prevent this, the rabbis issued ordinances confirming original buyers of wool in their priority right (*hazakah*), a right that was also accorded to tenants of shops and dwellings, regular patrons of merchants, and artisans.

The making of cloth was described in the responsa of Rabbi Samuel di Medina of Salonica (1540-1590), known as *Mahrashdam,* and by other rabbis of the period.

The wool yarn was washed, cleaned, and dyed, two colors being habitually used: red (made with urine) and blue (made of indigo); in the responsa, the blue yarn was called *d'agnire.* Then the wool was woven into cloth and the cloth fulled, the fuller bearing the Spanish name of *batanero.* After the fuller came the carder (*betaldar*), followed by the shearer (*tondetor*). Then the cloth was carefully inspected to see if it was clean, oily spots especially being watched for. Such spots were removed and the material cleaned by expert workers (*desterdar*), after which it again went to the carder and shearer.

Upon completion of this procedure, some textiles needed additional treatment to make them either finer or more durable. For this, special workers were employed. The so-called *escabechar* steeped the cloth in a sour liquid to strengthen it, while the *afenar* improved its fineness. Rabbi Hayyim Shabetai of Salonica (1556-1647) said that forty vital trades—he used the mishnaic term *abot hamelahot*—were involved in the production of cloth.[6]

There was a marked division of labor in the textile industry of Salonica, where the entire process of cloth manufacture was concentrated. This contrasts, for example, with England's medieval textile industry, which sent its undyed cloth to Holland to be "finished and sold by the Dutch." Later, in 1614-16, an effort was made to finish the cloth in England, but it failed because the art of dyeing "could not be learned overnight."[7] In Salonica, expert dyers who had come from Spain, Sicily, and Provence were available.

The craftsmen worked at home, the entire family lending a hand. The wool washers, however, had a special spot in the city market. Dyeing was done in yards behind the workers' homes, the stench arising from the preparation of the red dyestuff often involving the dyers in litigation with their neighbors. The fulling mill, or *batan,* was located in the northwestern part of the city, near the sea, where the cloth could be dried better and the townspeople spared the smell of the dyes. Porters brought the cloth to the fulling mill; water carriers (*aguadores*) provided water for washing and dyeing.

The textiles varied in quality. The standard cloth of Salonica, called *aba* and sold widely over Turkey, was of a heavy texture. There were others of a lighter weave and lower price. *Sobremano,* also made in Plevna, was a cloth covered with thin hair; *cuenta* was of a better quality; *carisea* was a fine fabric; *armintines* and *turpines* were coarser weaves and sold at cheaper prices.[8]

Hans Dernschwam, a representative of the Fuggers of Augsburg, who traveled in Turkey in 1553-1555, noted in his diary that there were many Jewish weavers in Salonica, and that their "products are sold throughout Turkey."[9] The Turkish army was a big buyer of Salonica cloth. The Turkish traveler Evliya reports how "the blue cloth which comes from Salonica" was stored in warehouses in Istanbul. The janissaries, an elite corps of 80,000, received ten yards each and a piece for the turban. This was a rather coarse cloth, and according to another passage in Evliya's travelogue, on one occasion the janissaries were promised "fine scarlet cloth."[10]

The Jewish community of Salonica paid a yearly tax of 1200 bolts of cloth to the Sultan (1567). The demand for cloth increased in times of war when the army needed material for uniforms. In peacetime, unsold goods would often accumulate and would have to be disposed of in nearby cities or even as far away as Belgrade, Sofia, Bucharest, Constantinople, Smyrna and Alexandria.[11]

Artisan and Capitalist

The Salonican textile industry went through the same process of development as those of other European countries. After a time, the individual craftsman stopped dealing directly with the consumer, who began to get his wares through middlemen. When the craftsman needed cash to purchase his raw material, he was compelled to borrow from the capitalist.[12] The latter began to buy the wool from the Macedonian peasants, in turn selling it to the craftsman on credit. At a later stage, people with money at their disposal set up shops and began to compete with the small craftsmen. The bigger manufacturers of cloth sought to monopolize the provisioning of the Turkish army, contending that the smaller producers' cloth was of poorer quality. Both parties appealed to the central government in Constantinople. The artisans addressed a petition to Mose Hamon, physician and counselor to Sultan Suleiman. They complained of the unfair competition of the wealthy manufacturers, pointing out that if they were unable to sell cloth to the army, life would become "like Sodom and Gomorra, each would devour his companion." The petition concluded on a pathetic note: "All that we are, we owe to the making of cloth which occupies men, women and children."[13] This is one of the earliest references to Jewish child labor.

It appears that Hamon's intervention with the Sultan on behalf of the craftsmen was not without success. The Salonican authorities were ordered to buy cloth for the army from both the factories and the artisans.[14] But it was a losing battle. In a *haskamah* (decision) the rabbis forbade the big manufacturers to exploit the weavers. On the other hand they enjoined the workers to faithfully account to the employers for the wool handed out to them. A *haskamah* of March 10, 1564, issued jointly by several rabbis, prohibited textile workers from borrowing money from the factory owners, to protect them from exploitation and eventual ruin.[15] But the worker had no choice, as he was entirely dependent on the industrialist. Labor conditions deteriorated further in the seventeenth and eighteenth centuries. Salonican textile workers looking for job opportunities were found in Verria, Escopia, and even as far away as the island of Rhodes.[16]

Synagogue Workshops

In his history of the Jews of Salonica, Joseph Nehama suggests that the Jewish textile workers had a guild and that the appeal to Mose Hamon was an organized action of the guild.[17] While there is no reference to any such association in the rabbinic responsa, it does appear that some synagogues at Salonica operated textile workshops as a source of funds for their welfare work. According to a Turkish geographer and traveler, Mustafa ben Abdalla Hadshi Halfa, who visited Salonica in the seventeenth century, during Hanukkah, the synagogues distributed cloth from their shops to needy students of the Talmud Torahs. The day of the distribution was a "festival for the entire city." [18]

Decline of Salonican Textile Industry

The chief reason for the decline of the textile industry in Salonica was the competition of Venice and Ancona, the modestly priced Ancona wares being particularly damaging. In 1606, English wollen cloth, the so-called "londres," appeared in Turkey, followed at the end of the seventeenth century by French textiles. The Salonican market was swamped in the eighteenth century by foreign cloth—Austrian, Dutch, Italian, English and French. In 1785, "Leipzig cloth" was widely sold in Macedonia. The Salonican textile industry was also damaged by the devaluation of the Turkish currency, which started under Sultan Ahmed III (1705-1730) and continued throughout the eighteenth century. Prevented from raising their prices, Salonica's manufacturers began to use wool of an inferior quality.[19]

The Turkish government did nothing to protect Salonican manufactures and permitted foreign goods to be imported freely. An attempt by the Minister of State, Rami Effendi, early in the eighteenth century, to open a textile factory in Constantinople with the help of Salonican Jewish weavers was not successful.[20]

Jewish Salonica in 1685

M. V. Coronelli, geographer to the Republic of Venice, described the life and work of the Jews of Salonica in his historical study published in 1687.

> There are in this place numerous people, and the great number of habitations that are built in the plain are but low and base, and not sufficient to contain the great number of Jews that dwell in them. Besides, they are not a little inconvenienced by the horrid stink that is in the streets, especially since they are so narrow. There is a considerable trade, as well as from commodiousness of the situation as for the great quantity of silk, wool, skins of all sorts, wax, gunpowder, corn, cotton, and iron. The Jews mostly busy themselves with trades and have to themselves the manufacture of stuffs with which to clothe the Janizaries; and by this means they find a way to pay the tribute to the Grand Seigniour. There are in it forty-eight mosques, thirty Greek churches, thirty-six great synagogues, and many other small ones.[21]

Carpet weaving

Carpet weaving was an important craft in Salonica. The carpet weavers were called *manteros,* from the Spanish *manta,* meaning blanket, in contrast to the *draperos,* the cloth makers.[22] The carpets apparently found a wide market. Two statements, one from the middle of the seventeenth century, the other from the second half of the eighteenth, bear witness to this. The above-cited Mustafa ben Abdalla Hadshi Halfa said of the Salonican weavers, that "they produce the world-famous multicolored carpets which nowhere are made so well." The French scholar, Cousinéry, who visited Macedonia in 1785, had the following to say: "The Salonican Jews . . . produce carpets of all sizes and ranging in quality from the best to ordinary. Their sale throughout all of European Turkey seriously hurts that of the Smyrna carpets, which are velveted and more expensive, whereas the Salonican produce is cheaper and less durable." [23]

Silk Work

The silk of Salonica compared favorably with that of Patras, then known as the best in the country. Silk thread produced by Jewish craftsmen was exported to Ancona and Venice.[24]

Metal Work

Jewish metal workers from Spain and Sicily brought their skills to Turkey. Foreign observers noted that the Turks learned from them how to make the modern weapons needed by their army in that period of continuous warfare. The Italian, Benedetto Ramberti,[25] and the Frenchman, Nicolas de Nicolay, dealt with this matter in their travel accounts. De Nicolay, who accompanied the French ambassador to Turkey in 1551, had occasion to observe matters at close range. He noted the "excellent workers in all crafts and manufactures among the recently arrived Spanish and Portuguese refugees, especially Marranos who, to the great detriment and damage of Christianity, have conveyed to the Turks many inventions, arts and machines of war, namely, how to produce artillery, guns, gunpowder, cannon balls and other weapons." [26]

Marrano blacksmiths, coppersmiths, and tinsmiths were to be found not only in Salonica, but also in Constantinople and other cities. Gold and silver founders, refiners and wire drawers worked in close cooperation with jewelers, filigree workers from Provence, and pearl setters.[27]

In Sidrocapso, near Salonica, a small Romaniote community survived from the Middle Ages. In the middle of the fifteenth century Ashkenasic and Sephardic Jews settled there.[28] The silver mine in Sidrocapso was exploited by Salonican Jews. The French naturalist, Pierre Belon du Mans, who studied the resources of Turkey and neighboring countries in the 1540's, visited the Sidrocapso mine in 1547 and described it at length in his remarkable travel reports. The workers of the mine included Jews, Albanians, Greeks, Serbs, Turks, Circassians, and others. There were also Jewish employers and foremen. Spanish was the dominant language among this motley crew. Belon noted that work stopped on Friday evenings and was resumed Monday mornings, to give both Christians and Jews an opportunity to enjoy their respective Sabbath days.

The annual output of the mine was worth between one to two million ducats. The Sultan received a monthly sum of 18,000-30,000 ducats.[29]

The Craftsmen from Sicily

An entire street in Salonica was inhabited by Jewish potters from Sicily, the *cantareros*. They varnished pots, pitchers and water containers just as they had done in their native Messina. There were sailors and fishermen from Sicily. As late as the 1930's, there was a synagogue of fishermen (*Cal' de pescadores*) in Salonica.[30]

Soap Making

Fine soaps were made from olive oil, but when olive oil was not available tallow or lard had to be substituted. The rabbinate of Salonica did not object to the use of lard for making soap.[31]

Other trades

Coronelli noted tanners and leather workers among the Spanish and Sicilian Jewish immigrants in Salonica. There were also bookbinders. Salonica became a Jewish center for the printing of books in the sixteenth century. In concluding we must mention Salonica's Jewish longshoremen and porters, famed for their sturdy physique and tough spirits.[32] They could be found there up until World War II. On Saturdays, the port was idle because the dock workers, porters and longshoremen would not work on that day.

The Textile Industry in Other Balkan Cities

Textiles were also manufactured by Jews in the Balkan cities of Plevna, Escopia, Edirne (Adrianople), Verria, Larissa, and Tricala. Three Jewish communities—Greek, Sephardic, and Sicilian —existed in Tricala. The Sephardim brought their knowledge of weaving and dyeing to Tricala, and a marked division of labor developed there, as in Salonica. It took two and one half months to produce finished goods for the market. Three fulling mills were in operation.[33]

Arts and Crafts in Constantinople (Istanbul) in the Sixteenth and Seventeenth Centuries

Constantinople's Jewish population was larger than that of Salonica—15,035 males in 1553 and 30,000 in 1574. Both figures are the conservative estimates of foreign visitors. The economy of Constantinople's Jewry was very much like that of the Jews of Salonica, only the mercantile element was stronger. Evidence for this is the testimony of travelers who visited Constantinople in the 1530's-1550's. Ramberti, de Nicolay, Belon du Mans, and Dernschwam, all pointed to the commercial activities of Jewish merchants of Constantinople, and to the crafts practiced by Jewish artisans. Ramberti wrote in 1534 that "the countless Jews, or Marrani, are those who have taught and are teaching every useful art to the Turks; and the greater part of the shops and arts are kept and exercised by the Marrani." [34] Nicolas de Nicolay, as we have already indicated, called attention to the role of the Jewish armorers in equipping the Turkish army. Hans Dernschwam gives a more detailed account of the crafts plied by the Jews of Constantinople. "There are," he says,

> all sorts of artisans among the Jews who make a living selling their products publicly, for in Turkey every man is free to carry on his trade at home, in a shop or on the street. Whether he is skilled or not, knows little or much, no one has a word to say if he only pays his tax to the Sultan and his rent for the shop. There are no cloth shearers among the Turks. There are two cloth shearers among the Jews and some among the Greeks. The Jews of Constantinople also have a printing press and they publish many rare books. They have goldsmiths, lapidaries, painters, tailors, butchers, druggists, physicians, surgeons, cloth weavers, barbers, wound surgeons, mirror makers, dyers, silk workers, goldwashers, refiners, essayers and engravers . . .[35]

In his description of the gorgeous pageant held in the capital in 1539, on the occasion of the circumcision of the princes, the Austrian historian Hammer-Purgstall mentions the seven-limbed dragons made by Jewish artificers and carried by them in the procession.[36]

Jewish Guilds in Constantinople (Istanbul)

In his travelogue Evliya has devoted considerable space to the description of the *alai,* a pageant of the guilds in Constantinople which took place in 1638, in the reign of the Sultan Murad IV. Evliya based his compilation on an official description of the city, its buildings and its working population. It would appear that Jews, Greeks and other national groups marched in the procession along with Moslems in the respective guild units. Apart from these guilds, some crafts were represented entirely by one ethnic group. Thus the 100 tin melters (I. ii, p. 165) were all Jews and apparently belonged to a Jewish guild. This would also be the case regarding the "aqua fortis makers, the alchemists" (gold and silver refiners) (I. ii, p. 191), the parchment makers (I. ii, p. 207), and the pearl merchants (I. ii, p. 189).

On the other hand, the Jewish smiths, nail smiths, locksmiths and borers, evidently belonged to general guilds, or a general joint guild. The goldsmith's art was regarded as a noble calling, and Evliya, a courtier, son and grandson of courtiers, states that he was a goldsmith himself. It is not clear whether Jews were only gold and silver refiners, or also goldsmiths. The Customs in the port of Istanbul employed 40 Jewish inspectors. An important Jewish group were the musicians, comics, tumblers and all sort of performers (I. ii, pp. 240, 241) whom we will meet in Prague and other places as experts in Turkish music. Among the twelve companies of boys in the entertainment business one company consisted of Jewish boys.[37]

The Turkish guilds reflected the ethnically heterogeneous character of the population. It is most likely that the foreign element even played a preponderant role. Material published by Georges Vajda shows that in the Turkish guilds the Christian element predominated in the seventeenth century.[38] This observation would account for the emergence of separate Jewish guilds.

Jewish Crafts in Rhodes

The Jews of Rhodes manufactured swords and daggers for the Knights of St. John, the rulers of the island until 1522 when it was conquered by the Turks.[39] It is interesting to note that the Jews had helped the Knights of St. John defend Rhodes when it was first attacked by the Turks, in 1481. The Knights of St. John were generally tolerant toward the Jews. However, in 1502, the Grand Master of the Knights, Pierre d'Aubusson, decreed that all the Jews of Rhodes must accept the Christian faith on pain of banishment from the island.[40] Many Jews followed the order. A Jewish smith named Abraham, who lived to see the Turkish siege of 1522, appealed to Sultan Suleiman to allow these crypto-Jews to profess their old faith openly. The Sultan agreed, and gave his approval to the immigration into Rhodes of Spanish refugees living in Salonica, Smyrna, and Constantinople.[41] Spanish soon became the dominant language in the Rhodesian Jewish community. The French pilgrim, Carlier de Pinon, who visited the island in 1579, found that most of the residents were Jews.[42]

The list of crafts practiced by the Jews of Rhodes included carpentry, blacksmithing, tinsmithing, jewelry, tanning, making of wooden shoes, tailoring, bookbinding, butchering, and barbering. There were also Jewish chimneysweeps, as well as workers with sulphur.[43]

In the sixteenth century, Rhodes had a busy textile industry, although it did not approach the scope and importance of the textile trade of Salonica. In fact, artisans from Salonica helped to establish it. There were two textile mills on the island which belonged to Sultan Suleiman and,, after his death in 1566, to Sultan Selim II. These mills were leased to Jewish entrepreneurs.[44]

Much wearing apparel made of linen, cotton, and silk was manufactured in Rhodes. Shirts, drawers, cloaks, silk wrappers, and buttons were exported to Anatolia, Egypt, and elsewhere. Men and women worked in their homes. The wages earned by the women were not insignificant, amounting to from fifteen to thirty piasters a week. We learn from communal and rabbinical sources that this money was spent on jewelry and fine garments.[45]

The rabbinate of Rhodes intervened when competition among manufacturers became too sharp. Chief Rabbi Ezra Malki, who held office in the second half of the eighteenth century, pronounced this *haskamah*: "Having learned that some Jews have gone to the villages to buy raw silk at prices higher than is customary, and having ascertained that this may affect the livelihood of their fellow Jews, we have decided and ordered that no person may buy silk at more than the customary price on pain of being excluded from the community. Silk of first quality must be bought at forty piasters the *oka,* and that of lesser quality at thirty-five." [46]

Printing

The Ottoman Empire was a center of Hebrew book printing in the sixteenth century, with Sephardic and later Ashkenazic Jews operating a number of printing presses. Not only Hebrew but also Latin, Greek, Italian, and Spanish books were printed in these establishments. Constantinople, Salonica, and Safed were the chief centers for printing. Gerson Soncino, the famous typographer, opened a large printing establishment in Constantinople in 1530. Among the Salonican firms that of the expert printer Juda Gedalia should be mentioned. In spite of great difficulties, he managed to transport the presses of his former partner, Eliezer Toledano, from Lisbon to Salonica. In 1653, two Ashkenazic Jews opened a printing shop in Safed. The demand for printed books was so great at times that Christians were hired and taught the Hebrew types. Jews also engaged in casting type.[47]

Moldavia and Wallachia

The Danubian principalities of Moldavia and Wallachia, under Turkish suzerainty until 1878, were, in this earlier period, a bridge between Poland and Turkey over which a lively traffic passed. Polish and Turkish Jews figured among the merchants of varied nationalities who carried on this trade. Moldavia and Wallachia were agricultural; the peasants were serfs of a landed nobility (*boyars*), and there was no native middle class. Armenians, Greeks, Hungarians, Jews, and others filled this gap in Rumanian economy, functioning as middlemen in the exchange of goods. Polish Jews for the most part settled in Moldavia, whereas Sephardic Jews crossed over into Wallachia from Turkey. As a rule, these middle-class merchants were foreigners who were brought in by the "*boyars*" and settled on their estates, permission for this having been obtained from the ruling princes (*hospodars*). Jews founded entire towns as, for instance, Folticeni and Mihaileni, or peopled urban districts as in the city of Focsani. Jassy, the capital of Moldavia, and Bucharest, the capital of Wallachia, absorbed a considerable number of Jews. As they came from countries possessing highly developed Jewish crafts, it is only natural that we should find many earning a living as artisans in their new home, too. Jewish artisans and manufacturers were an essential element in Moldavian and Wallachian industry in the eighteenth century.

Bucharest harbored Jewish tailors, shoemakers, tinsmiths, lacemakers, bookbinders, silversmiths and jewelers, as well as engravers. Jews also made pipes and playing balls and started the manufacture of paper, potash, and glassware.

Jewish artisans in Bucharest, as was generally the case in the Ottoman Empire in this period, were admitted into the Moslem guilds. Turkish influence was strong in the Danubian principalities, which may explain the fact that Jewish masters were appointed by the princes of Wallachia as wardens of the guild of silversmiths. A Jewish jeweler, Eleazar, was appointed warden of the Bucharest jewelers' guild in 1792. Jewish craftsmen working for the princes and nobles were occasionally exempted from paying taxes.

Moldavia had a larger Jewish population than Wallachia. In addition to the artisans listed for Wallachia, Moldavia possessed Jewish tanners, furriers, cap and hat makers, watchmakers, coppersmiths, masons, carpenters, and house painters. Tailors and furriers were engaged in the mass production of clothing for the peasantry. The Jewish artisans of Moldavia, unlike those of Wallachia, formed guilds of their own.[48]*

Arts and Crafts in the Near East

Turning to the Turkish dominions in Asia, we find Jews manufacturing silk in Bursa (Brussa), capital of the district of the same name. With the arrival of Sephardic immigrants at the end of the fifteenth century, commercial and industrial activities advanced. Silk was imported from Persia by Jewish merchants who traveled as far as Hormuz, on the Persian Gulf. They also brought the silk worm back with them and introduced sericulture in Brussa.

* At the end of the nineteenth century, over 75 per cent of all bookbinders, watchmakers, engravers and cap makers in Rumania, as well as a large percentage of tailors and furriers, were Jews. Most of them resided in Moldavia.

A guild of Jewish weavers existed there as late as the nineteenth century.[49]

The large Jewish community of Smyrna (Izmir) had a number of guilds, foremost of which was the weavers' guild. Each guild had its own house of prayer and study, and a rabbi (Hakham) who, on the Sabbath, studied portions of the Bible, Midrash, ethics, and the cabbalistic book of the *Zohar* with guild members. Smyrna's rabbis insisted upon strict religious observance. To be admitted as an apprentice, a boy had to pass an examination by the rabbi. He had to know the three daily prayers and the benedictions.[50]

In Aleppo, the goldsmith's craft was the most important. The Jewish butchers and shoemakers there had their own guilds. A certain type of shoes was made only by Moslems, another only by Christians. There were Jewish dyers and weavers in Baghdad, and coppersmiths in Damascus. Jean-Baptiste Tavernier (1605-1689) found in Lar, a city in Persia, workers in silk, most of them Jews, making exquisite belts.[51] In Yemen there were Jewish masons, armorers, repairmen of all sorts and silversmiths, also distillers of alcoholic beverages. The trade was barred to Moslems.[52]

In the eighteenth century, Christians and Jews in the Near East seem to have been admitted to Moslem guilds without any obligations of a religious character. Bernard Lewis maintains that the Islamic guilds were not only open to "Jew, Christian and Muslim alike," but were often predominantly non-Muslim.

In Egypt, which came under Turkish rule in 1517, Jewish artisanship was traditional. Raw silk, imported from Syria, was worked into different articles which were exported back to Syria. Most of the silk workers in Cairo and towns in the Delta were Jews. Jewish women embroiderers worked in the palaces of Egyptian nobles. Rabbi David ben Simra (*Radbaz*) declared such employment permissible, provided that the women were over forty, were accompanied by two other women and did not work at one table with men.

The leading gold and silversmiths in Cairo in the eighteenth century were Copts, but Jews, Syrians, and Armenians also practiced the craft.[53]

Revival of Crafts in Palestine in the Sixteenth Century

At the close of the fifteenth century there was an immigration of Jews from Central Europe, Italy, and the Iberian Peninsula to Palestine. Jerusalem, with about seventy Jewish families in 1488, had grown to some four thousand Jews in 1522. Safed, Hebron, Tiberias, and other localities were also settled by newcomers. One of the new arrivals wrote in 1495 to his people in Italy: "Those skilled in such crafts as the goldsmith's, blacksmith's, weaver's, or tailor's can make a living here."[54] An Italian-Jewish author who visited Palestine in 1522, wrote: "Who does not possess capital to go into business must become an artisan. There are four good trades in Israel: weaving, goldsmith work, leather work, and tanning. Gilders are also needed. Strong people can work for a daily wage in the building trade and make a good living. A tailor will also support himself."[55]

Safed was a bustling industrial and spiritual center. In 1550, it numbered 10,000 to 14,000 residents, the largest urban population in Palestine. Fifty years later, it was estimated to harbour 6,000 householders, or about 30,000 persons, which is probably exaggerated. Safed's economic importance stemmed from its wine and olive oil, textiles, and export trade. Economic prosperity enabled the Jewish community of Safed to play a role in the religious and spiritual life of Palestine. The Jerusalem rabbi, Levi ben Habib, opponent of his ambitious Safed colleague, Jacob Berab, sarcastically asked "whether it was because of the large quantity of clothes made there that Safed arrogated to itself the leadership of Judaism."[56]

Moses di Rossi, a merchant from the Italian city of Cesena who visited Safed in 1535, pointed out in a letter the growing importance of that city. In his estimate, better quality textiles produced in Safed could compete with Venetian wares. The production of a certain cloth, called *carisea,* reached 15,000 bolts a year. Clothing and silk articles were manufactured for export.[57]

In the sixteenth century, Safed's textile industry was second only to Salonica's. Other trades profited from its growth.[58] However, the revival of trades and crafts in Palestine turned out to be of brief duration and was followed by decay and ruin in the seventeenth and eighteenth centuries. Jewish craftsmanship was revived in Palestine only in the late nineteenth century.*

* We know that a numerous class of Jewish craftsmen existed in the countries of the *Maghreb,* that is, in Libya, Tunisia, Algeria and Morocco. There were textile and garment workers, embroiderers, rug weavers, cobblers, leather workers, metal workers, gold and silversmiths, butchers, distillers, and repair workers of many kinds. Some of these trades were native to the Berber Jews, others probably were introduced by refugees from Spain. Unfortunately, however, no reliable data antedating the nineteenth century are available.

Chapter XIV

Jewish Trades in Italy in the Early Modern Period

Following the wholesale expulsion of Jews from Sicily and Sardinia in 1493, and from the kingdom of Naples in 1540, Jewish life in Italy shifted to the central and northern regions, where only a few communities had previously existed. In the early modern period, more Jews established themselves in Tuscany, the Republic of Venice, the Duchy of Savoy, the Grand Duchy of Ferrara, the Margravate of Mantua, and some parts of the Papal States. Larger communities emerged in Rome, Venice, Padua, Mantua, Bologna, Ferrara, Florence, Pisa, Siena, Ancona, and Turin; and, later in the seventeenth century, in Leghorn as well. In addition, Jews lived in numerous smaller towns, but rarely in villages. In almost all places, they were confined to segregated quarters, called ghettos.[1] At the end of the Renaissance, about 1600, an estimated total of 35,000 Jews were living in Italy. Political conditions were unstable, with periods of religious tolerance and economic prosperity alternating with years of discrimination, persecution, and expulsion.[2]

Economic Stratification

As usual in a situation of political insecurity, the Jews were driven to commerce, petty trade and money lending. There seem to have been some craftsmen among the Jewish population in Rome, according to a report of the Bavarian diplomatic agent, Henry Kalteisen of June 29, 1449.[3] A tailor in Florence, Benedetto or Baruch, a recent convert to Christianity, is mentioned in 1488.[4]

In 1492 Jewish refugees from Spain began to arrive in Italy. Pope Alexander VI (1492-1503) granted them asylum, to the dismay of the Spanish ambassador who expressed his sovereign's surprise that the enemies of Christ should be welcomed in the Eternal City. The Pope also admitted Jewish exiles from Sicily. Jews banished from Provence arrived in 1508.[5] Duke Ercole I d'Este allowed Jews to live in Ferrara in 1493.[6]

The Jews who manufactured saltpeter to make gunpowder for Lorenzo de Medici probably hailed from Spain.[7] A group of Jewish silk manufacturers in Bologna in 1537 are likely to have come from Spain, or from Sicily. This group maintained a printing press for the publication of Hebrew religious books.[8]

Jewish Artisans in Rome in the Sixteenth Century

A census of Rome's population in 1526 showed a total of 55,000 residents, among whom 3.1 per cent or 1,758 were Jews. The occupations of 91 of the 385 Jewish householders were listed in the census. Among them were 22 tailors, 7 shoemakers, 4 weavers, one worker in wool, one furrier, one dyer, one mattress maker, one sword maker and one fisherman. The tailors, Ammon and Abraham, are listed as "hyspanus" (from Spain), the tailor, Isaac, as "catalanus" (from Catalonia).[9]

A Jewish tailors' guild apparently existed in Rome as early as the fifteenth century. In 1541, the Christian tailors of Rome proposed to their Jewish colleagues to agree on a common policy for the purchase of cloth. The Jewish tailors authorized Judah ben Yehiel and Joshua ben Solomon Corcos, the latter a communal leader, not a tailor, to negotiate for them. The agreement was signed by Judah ben Shabbetai, secretary of the Jewish community. Both parties pledged themselves to buy black cloth only. White cloth might be bought if the tailor declared his intention to dye it black. The price of black cloth was fixed at 14 scudi in cash and 16½ scudi on credit. The price of floss-silk was fixed at

16 scudi paid in cash. It too had to be black. To buy cloth with holes or defects of any kind was forbidden, unless the defects had been removed.[10]

The last item implies repair work and dealing in second hand clothes. An interesting reference to dealing in second hand furniture is to be found in Vasari's "Life" of Michelangelo. While working on the monument for Pope Julius II, Michelangelo, exasperated by the intrigues at the papal court which hampered his work, ordered his servants to sell his furniture "to the Jews" and left Rome. This episode took place some time after 1516.[11]

The archives of the city of Rome preserve contracts of apprenticeship drawn in Hebrew. Apprentices were articled to tailors for a period of three years. One such contract, dated 1544, was made by the tailor Samuel with a Jewish woman named Caracoso, mother of the youth Michael. The master undertook to board and lodge the boy, the mother to take care of his clothing. Should the master leave Rome, the apprentice was to accompany him. Each party was to pay a fine of three scudi to the treasury of the papal *Vicario* in case of violation of the agreement.[12]

There were Jewish guilds of apothecaries and of bakers of *matzot*. In 1539, the head of the bakers' guild was a certain Yehiel.[13]

Metal Work

Sword making was one of the skills plied by Jewish workers. The armorer, Salomone da Sesso, named after his conversion to Christianity, Ercole de' Fideli (c. 1465-1519), worked for the court of Ferrara. Most famous was the so-called "Queen of Swords" which he made for Cesare Borgia. The Metropolitan Museum in New York, The Kensington Museum in London, the Musée des Invalides in Paris and other public collections possess swords with etched figure decorations made by Ercole.[14]

A silversmith, Isaac of Bologna, was employed by the royal court in Naples in 1474. Mantua had a street of Jewish goldsmiths. Members of the jeweler's family of Formiggini worked for two centuries for the dukes of the house of d'Este. Farther north, there were Jewish goldsmiths in the Duchy of Savoy; in 1623, the

Christian guild succeeded in halting their activities, but for a brief period only.[15] Venice was the chief place of manufacture of Jewish engagement rings; these were exported to many lands.[16] Jewelers also produced Jewish ceremonial objects, such as crowns and mounts for the Torah scroll, pointers, candelabra, cups and amulets. Abraham ben Moses Tzoref was plying this trade in Venice in 1712.[17]

Ceramics, Glassmaking, Engraving, etc.

Italian-Jewish master potters produced majolica ware, most of it Passover plates with figurative and floral designs. It has been noted that these masters were influenced by "the great potters of the Renaissance employed by the Italian courts." In 1626, Lazzaro Levi received permission to produce majolica ware in Mantua. Some of the Seder plates preserved in various museums bear the signature of the potter and the date and place of production: Jacob Azulai, Padua, 1532; Isaac Azulai, Faenza, 1575; Mose Fano, Urbino, 1556; Jacob Azulai, Pesaro, 1652; a second Jacob Azulai, Pesaro, 1730.[18] The Azulai, a family specializing in ceramics, may have come to Italy from Spain at the time of the expulsion.

Meir Magino of Venice discovered a vegetable oil polish for mirrors and crystal, and, in 1588, obtained from Pope Sixtus V a monopoly for its exploitation. Jewish craftsmen in Venice and other cities produced the ingredients for artists' colors. In the seventeenth century, there was a Jewish workshop in Rome for the production of colored glass.

Mose dal Castellazzo of Venice, son of Rabbi Abraham Sachs, an immigrant from Germany, obtained from the "Council of Ten" in Venice, on July 27, 1521, the privilege to print and sell woodcuts illustrating the Pentateuch from blocks made by his sons. From his application we learn that the designs were made by himself, that he had acquired some reputation as a portrait painter and that the woodcuts were to be accompanied by comments in several languages. The privilege, valid for ten years, was granted to him. In the sixteenth century, David of Lodi engaged in copper engraving. He engraved the city map of Cremona for a book of Antonio Campi.[19]

Jewish musicians played in Rome and at the courts of Italian rulers. We also find numerous Jews who taught dancing. Anna the Hebrew, was famous for her skill in preparing facial creams and lotions. Among her patrons was Catherine Sforza, the Countess of Imola. Anna's letter to Catherine (1508), explaining the use of her creams, has been preserved. Anna was by no means the only Jewish female "beautician" of that time.[20]

Silk Weaving

In the early modern period, Italian silk weaving entered the stage of industrial production and we find Jewish entrepreneurs in the manufacture of silk fabrics. Mention has been made of a group of Jewish silk manufacturers in Bologna in 1537. In 1587, Pope Sixtus V gave Meir Magino of Venice, the oil polish inventor, a charter to establish a silk factory in Rome for a fifteen year period. Magino is also known for a book he wrote on silk manufacture. He was authorized to reside outside the ghetto.[21]

Padua was another center of Jewish silk manufacture. Moses Mantica (fifteenth century) established the first workshop for silk production in that city. In 1645, a Jewish manufacturer named Trieste established a silk industry employing several thousand workers, local non-Jews, who worked in their homes. In 1614, Jews introduced silk manufacture in Rovigo and were instrumental in reviving its woolen mills. The Jewish manufacturers of both Padua and Rovigo were ultimately driven out of business. Attempts by Florentine Jews to enter the production and sale of fabrics met with stubborn resistance from the Christian drapers and had to be given up. Jewish manufacture in Mantua, Siena, and Leghorn had better luck, and in Savoy Jews were able to get a footing in handicrafts and industry; in the eighteenth century, Jews of Savoy were running silk and cotton mills.[22]

Craft Restrictions in the Republic of Venice

The Venetian guilds barred Jews from practicing crafts. When, in the seventeenth century, Jewish turners and carpenters of the city of Padua extended their activities to Venice, the city council requested the Venetian Senate to put a stop to it, lest the local craftsmen be ruined. The Senate acted accordingly. Because of the Venetian restrictions, Jewish artisans turned to petty trade. Jewish tailors became dealers in second hand clothes which they mended before selling. Venice was only one of the Italian states to drive Jews out of the crafts. However, there were other states where Jewish artisans were allowed, Rome being the outstanding example.

'Diseases of Jewish Artisans'

Bernardino Ramazzini, Professor of Medicine at the University of Padua, in his book *De morbis artificum* (On the Diseases of Artisans) (1700), devoted a chapter to the diseases of Jewish artisans. Ramazzini pointed out that Jews were afflicted by "various diseases which result from the trades which they pursue, and not, as is commonly believed, from some infirmity of the race, and from their unwholesome diet." He continued:

> Nearly all Jews, especially the lower classes, to which most of them belong, are employed in work at which they must sit or stand. They are mostly given to sewing and furbishing up old clothes; the women, above all, whether married or single, make their living by needlework. . . . At this they excel and are so expert that they can join and mend garments made of wool, silk, or any other material so that the seam is quite invisible; at Rome the word for this is *rinaciare*. They impose on the populace these pieced garments made of many fragments cleverly put together . . .
>
> This work compels them to apply the eyes closely, also all Jewish women keep at their sewing the whole day and far into the night, using a small lamp with the merest thread of wick and a feeble light, like that of lamp in the tombs. Hence they incur all the disorders due to a sedentary life and moreover, in the course of time, they suffer from serious weakness of vision; by the time they are forty they are purblind or very short-sighted. Besides, in most cities the Jews live miserably, shut up in narrow alleys, and their women at all seasons stand during their work by open windows to get what light there is; this causes them to incur various afflictions of the head,

> such as headache, earache, toothache, cold, sore throats, and sore eyes. Many of them, especially of the poorer class, are hard of hearing and blear-eyed. . . . As for the men: all day long in their booths they sit, patching clothes, or they stand on the lookout for customers to whom they can sell their old patchwork; they are mostly cachectic, melancholic, morose; and as a rule they have the itch. . . .

Farther along, Ramazzini deals with the diseases of the workers who make wool mattresses:

> It is the custom, in Italy at least, for Jews to remake wool mattresses in which the wool has become packed by several years of daily use on beds, so that they are too hard. They lay the wool on hurdles of wicker-work, beat it with sticks, and shake it thoroughly; thus they make the mattresses softer and more comfortable to lie on. They go from house to house through the city and pick up a good deal of money here and there for this service. But that old wool has been wetted through with urine many a time and otherwise polluted and, in shaking and combing it, they take in by mouth a great deal of foul dust. This causes serious ailments, a harassing cough, and a disordered stomach. I have known many men who paid dearly for working in this way and were finally reduced to incurable consumption; they admitted that this was the cause and cursed the occupation that had brought about their sad end.

We know from other sources that Italian Jews worked in the needle trades and renovated wool mattresses, but Ramazzini's reference to a Jewish girl engaged in tobacco work is new. In discussing the diseases afflicting tobacco workers, he said of this girl that "while she worked the whole day at unwinding those rolls of tobacco, she used to feel a strong desire to vomit and often suffered from diarrhea."[23] Ramazzini, it should be remarked, presents detailed instructions for the treatment and cure of these diseases.

Jewish Trades and Industry in Eighteenth-Century Rome

In 1699, there were 10,000 Jews in Rome; in 1732, 12,000. The historian Basnage spoke of 15,000 Roman Jews in 1716. Private estimates are higher, but it would seem that 12,000 was the upper limit.[24] In any case, about one third of the Jewish population of Italy was living in Rome in the eighteenth century, virtually confined to a ghetto scarcely one square kilometer in extent. The ghetto was located on low ground on the banks of the Tiber and exposed to frequent inundations. Two main streets and six side streets traversed the area. Living conditions were appalling, with several families packed into one room. Abraham Levi, from Horn, Lippe, who resided in Amsterdam, visited Italy in the 1720's and wrote an interesting account of his travels in Yiddish. Levi describes the life he saw in the Rome ghetto in the summer of 1724: "Hundreds of tailors are in the streets, each before his stand. The women are busy making buttons and buttonholes. So famous are they for their skill that tailors of other nationalities about the city commission these women to make buttons and buttonholes for them." According to Levi, "three-quarters of the Jews of Rome are artisans."[25]

A list of the occupations of the Jews of Rome of 1726, in the Vatican Library (Bibl. Vat. Cod. 8634), includes merchants dealing with the Levant and Western Europe in rugs, precious clothes, and corals; hardware dealers; petty traders selling drugs, love potions, amulets, and bric-à-brac; fishmongers; a large number of tailors, button makers, weavers, goldsmiths, blacksmiths, carpenters, tanners, saddlers and sieve makers.[26] The Jewish tailors had cardinals among their patrons and supplied uniforms to the Papal soldiery.[27]

Efforts of Christian artisans to restrict Jewish competition were not always successful. Early in the seventeenth century, for example, Christian tailors complained to the Papal Court that the "Hebrews" of the city were making clothes out of new and not second-hand material, and asked the authorities to forbid this. But the court decided in favor of the Jewish tailors. An attempt by the Christian saddlers' guild, in 1652, to curb the activities of Jewish saddlers also failed when the Papal Court supported the Jewish saddlers' protest.[28]

In the textile trade, spinning was a special province of women. Weavers and spinners were enjoined to observe the rabbinical prohibition of mixing wool and linen.[29] In 1784, some Jewish silk manufacturers were active in Rome. When the Christian silk merchants planned to organize a guild excluding Jews, the latter submitted a petition to the Pope asking not for admittance to the guild, but simply to be allowed to go on manufacturing and selling silk as before. The petitioners emphasized the advantages which their activities brought to the city of Rome and to the general public.[30]

Leghorn

Originally a village of fishermen, Leghorn became a free port toward the end of the sixteenth century, thanks to the efforts of the Grand Duke Ferdinand of Tuscany. The city played an increasingly important role in Mediterranean commerce, with the nearby city of Pisa included in Leghorn's free port zone. On July 10, 1593, Grand Duke Ferdinand issued a charter promising extensive rights to foreigners who would settle in Leghorn. Addressed "to men of the East and West, Spaniards and Portuguese, Greeks, Germans, Italians, Hebrews, Turks, Moors, Armenians, Persians and others," the charter declared, among other things, that "none shall be able to make an inquisition, examination or accusal against you or your families, although living in the past outside our Dominion and in the guise of Christians."[31] This flat promise of religious and economic freedom to the Marranos of Spain and Portugal was unusual in a period of mounting Catholic intolerance. As a consequence, Leghorn's Jewish population grew steadily, so that it numbered about 4,500 persons at the end of the eighteenth century. The tolerant policy followed by Grand Duke Ferdinand and his successors resulted in the expansion of Leghorn's commerce as far as Egypt, Turkey, and the countries beyond. Jews established silk, cloth, and paper industries, soap factories, and, most important of all, the coral industry. Leghorn's coral ware found a market in countries as far off as Russia, India, and China.

Two Jews, Efraim Cassuto of Florence and David Teglia of Leghorn, were given the right to operate workshops for processing diamonds and other gems (not including inlay work) in Leghorn and Pisa in 1663. According to the ten years' privilege of June 17, 1663, granted by Ferdinand II, Grand Duke of Tuscany, the men or their employees were to apply for recertification of their qualifications by the governmental drafting bureau every year. It may be assumed that there were Jewish workers in these shops.[32]

Printing

Italy was one of the great centers of Hebrew printing. Jews were owners of printing shops, proofreaders, type founders and compositors. The Italian Jewish printing presses were set up in the second half of the fifteenth century and after, at a time when many Jewish printers were migrating to Italy from Germany and the Iberian Peninsula. The first two dated Hebrew books were published in 1475, one in Reggio di Calabria, on the Straits of Messina, the other in Pieve di Sacco, near Padua. In the following decade, Hebrew printing presses were set up by itinerant craftsmen in many places on the peninsula. The most famous is the Soncino Press set up in 1483 by Israel Nathan, an immigrant from Germany, who took his family name from the town of Soncino in Lombardy, where he settled.[33] Apprentices were in great demand by the printing trade, and were even sought for among the students of Jewish religious schools. The statutes of the Talmud Torah at Ferrara, adopted on May 24, 1787, contained a rule requiring less gifted students to be sent daily to the master printer, Salvador Serri, for a few hours instruction in the trade of printing. They were to learn how to set type, both with and without Hebrew vocalization marks. The trustees of the Talmud Torah paid for the students' instruction. At least four students were required to undergo training as printers, in order that the Talmud Torah might become a "perfect institution wherein such things are learned as are necessary to the community and the individual."[34]

CHAPTER XV

Jewish Artisans in Bohemia and Moravia from the Early Middle Ages to the End of the Thirty Years' War

Bohemia and Moravia, the two westernmost Slavic lands, attracted merchants, artisans, farmers, and clergymen from the neighboring German duchies of Saxony and Bavaria from the eleventh century on. The thirteenth century marked the beginning of a German mass migration which deeply affected Bohemian-Moravian political, social and cultural developments, legal institutions, municipal organization, and craft guilds. Another influential factor was the long rule of the Hapsburg dynasty over the two provinces, from 1526 to 1918. After the battle at the White Mountain (1620), the centralized Austrian bureaucracy in Vienna ruled the countries of the Bohemian crown in a harsh and at times ruthless manner, with no regard for the national feelings and cultural aspirations of the native Slavs.

Economic Developments

Trade and crafts emerged in Bohemia and Moravia in the early Middle Ages, when the other Slavic nations were still exclusively agricultural. Prague, the capital of Bohemia, played a significant part in the domestic and international trade of the tenth century. "Built of stone and lime," it was regarded by Ibrahim ibn Yakub, a noted Jewish merchant traveler who visited Prague in 965, as "the richest town in wares." It lay on the vital trade route leading from Mayence and Ratisbon to Cracow and Kiev, and then southeast to Itil (Astrakhan) at the mouth of the Volga. Prague's commercial importance also stemmed from its location on the water route along the rivers Elbe and Moldau which connected northern Germany with the Danube area. Bohemia, at that time, produced saddles, bridles, shields, and fine-textured kerchiefs.[1]

In the thirteenth century, Bohemia's mines were an important economic factor. Under King Charles of the Luxemburg dynasty (1347-1376), notable strides were made in the crafts and in industry. Foreign weavers were invited to the country. Bohemian cloth, glass and paper were in wide demand. Prague became one of the busiest markets in central Europe. After a setback caused by the Hussite Wars (1420-1437), trade and industry revived, particularly under the rule of King George of Podebrad (1458-1471). In the sixteenth century, Bohemian cloth was exported to Poland and Russia. Under Rudolf II (1576-1612), watchmaking, jewelry work, and gem-cutting became leading crafts. The Bohemian craft guilds reached their peak in the period from 1450 to 1600.

Then came a second calamity. The Thirty Years' War (1618-1648) made of once-rich Bohemia one of the poorest of countries. Handicrafts declined and cities decayed. Military requisitions, pillage, and rapine disrupted commerce and transportation. The recovery was slow. But, as the seventeenth century drew to its close, conditions improved. Attempts were made to revive the guilds. The Viennese government encouraged loyal Bohemian nobles, such as the Waldsteins and Liechtensteins, to experiment with the manufacture of silk and other textiles. The government's mercantilist policy protected domestic commerce and industry. At the end of the eighteenth century, Bohemia and Moravia were advancing swiftly toward industrialization; commerce was expanding and guild rules were relaxed. In the nineteenth century, both provinces emerged as the most advanced economic areas of the Austrian monarchy.[2]

Settlement of the Jews in Bohemia and Moravia

Jews settled in Prague in the eleventh century, but Jewish merchants had traveled widely through Bohemia and Moravia in the tenth century and even earlier. In the tariff regulations of Raffelstetten, on the Danube River in Upper Austria, issued by the Margrave Aribo, 903-905, Jews are mentioned among the merchants trafficking in goods and slaves.[3] The Jewish traveler, Ibrahim ibn Yakub, states that among the merchants of various nationalities he met in Prague in 965 were Russians and other Slavs bringing wares from Cracow, and Mohammedans, Jews, and Turks with wares from the "land of the Turks." These merchants, he noted, returned home with slaves, tin, all kinds of furs, and flour. It has been suggested that by "Turks" and "land of the Turks," Ibrahim ibn Yakub may have meant Hungarians and Hungary.[4]

The first Jewish settlers were perhaps merchant travelers from the East or, what is more likely, merchants from Germany who passed with their wagons from Mayence (Mainz) and Ratisbon through Prague on the way to Kiev and farther east to the Caspian Sea, and took the same route back. It is conceivable that some of these German Jewish merchants, having made Prague's acquaintance, remained there. During the Crusades, Jews fleeing persecution came to Prague in great numbers, mostly from Ratisbon.[5]

The Jews of Prague and of other Bohemian-Moravian towns are believed to have traded in meat and other commodities. In the thirteenth century, moneylending emerged as their main occupation. The charter of 1254, granted to the Jews of his realm by King Ottokar II of the dynasty of the Premyslides, while regulating money and credit matters in great detail, omitted all reference to commerce. However, by stipulating freedom of movement for the Jews throughout the country, the charter facilitated trade.[6] The transition in the thirteenth century from a barter to a money economy created a growing demand for loan capital in every section of the population—nobility, clergy, middle class, and artisans. There were both Christian and Jewish moneylenders. The former, as a rule, lent money for long terms to the upper classes, whereas the bulk of the Jewish moneylenders made short-term loans to petty traders and artisans. Those with larger means, however, had among their clients owners of estates, officials, clergymen, and middle-class people as well. Hussite pamphleteers dealt with the practices of the moneylenders, both Jewish and non-Jewish. Thus the noted Hussite theologian, Jacobellus of Mies, in his treatise "On the Usury of Jews and Christians," castigated the latter for exacting larger interest than was demanded by Jewish moneylenders.[7] Moneylending was by no means the only Jewish occupation; Jews traded in cattle, food, and other commodities.

Origin of Jewish Handicrafts in Bohemia and Moravia

In medieval Bohemia and Moravia, Jewish butchers, bakers, liquor makers, tailors and barbers cared mainly for the needs of their coreligionists. We cannot safely assume that Jewish artisans had Christian clientele in the medieval period, for the guilds strictly forbade Jews to work for non-Jewish patrons. The membership of the Bohemian-Moravian guilds consisted largely of German immigrant craftsmen. Guilds in Germany did not admit Jews, and in this point the guilds in Bohemia and Moravia were patterned on those of Germany. When in 1347 the Jewish butchers in Brno (Bruenn), in Moravia, disposed of ritually unsatisfactory meat to Christians, this was a very exceptional case.[8]

Before the sixteenth century the Jewish population in the country was insignificant, and the artisan group very small. In 1457 there was only a handful of towns with Jewish residents. In 1500, however, some 25 towns and 2 villages were reported to have Jewish inhabitants. In Prague 600 of the city's Jews gathered in a procession in 1522 to greet the Jagiellon King Ludwig II.[9]

With numerical growth of the Jewish population and the decrease of the opportunities offered by moneylending, Jews began to turn toward the crafts, a trend which entailed growing hostility toward them.

By the middle of the fifteenth century Jews were expelled from Brno, Olomouc (Olmuetz), Ihlava (Iglau), Uncov (Maehrisch-Neustadt) and Znoimo (Znaim). The Moravian Diet of 1525 forbade Jews to work at crafts.[10] In moving to smaller towns and villages owned by the gentry, however, they found some protection against the antagonistic guilds.

In Bohemia the situation varied from town to town. In Strakonicy, the tailors' guild passed a resolution in 1482 forbidding its members to teach Jews the trade. In Chomutov (Komotau) Jewish artisans are recorded in the municipal files for 1477-1514; there were Jewish sword makers and glaziers; glove makers are recorded for the year 1477 and the following years. In Nachod in the early sixteenth century Jews were engaged in basketry, bag making, cutlery, strap making and glazing. A sword maker is recorded in Kolin; the municipal council of Litomevrice reported in 1515 some Jewish artisans earning a modest living.[11] Zikmund Winter, an authority on the history of craftsmanship in Bohemia, summarized the situation in these words: "They penetrated into the trades."[12]

Prague Guilds and the Jews

The spread of Jewish artisanship and its scope may be inferred from the numerous complaints of the guilds and their spokesmen, the city councils. In 1509, the sword maker guild in the "Old City" district of Prague warned Jewish artificers against making and selling swords.[13] In 1515, the municipal council of the "Old City" published a list of articles—garments, furs, hunting knives, swords, daggers, bags, purses, etc.—which Jews were forbidden "to dispose of or to produce," the penalty for doing so being confiscation.[14] Similar warnings were issued time and again. Their ineffectuality caused some to cry out for wholesale expulsion of the Jews from Prague. Such a demand was made by a furrier, Kardinal by name, in a meeting of the town council, but the councillors rejected the proposal. In the meantime, Jews branched out into new trades. In 1525, a Jewish glazier, Jacob Koplman, is recorded in Prague; in 1534, the pewterers' guild confiscated vessels made by the Jewish pewterer, Vlach, charging inferior quality. Acts of violence occurred, with Christian artisans stoning Jewish artisans. The guilds requested the authorities to forbid the employment of Christian journeymen by Jews. Numerous decrees were issued to that end, but seemingly to no avail.[15]

Banishment Decrees

The question of the legal admission of Jews to trades was deliberated by the Bohemian government in Prague, in the 1530's.

The highest executive officer (*Oberstlandhofmeister*) of Bohemia suggested to King Ferdinand I that it would do no harm if the practice of some crafts were permitted the Jews. The king replied, on May 20, 1536, that such a measure required the consent of the Diet; the matter would have to await his coming to Prague.[16] Nothing followed, probably because the king was then deliberating whether or not to banish the Jews from Bohemia altogether. In 1528, Ferdinand had confirmed the privileges granted to the Jews by his predecessors and had promised that they would never be driven out of Bohemia. Notwithstanding this pledge, Ferdinand, who had been reared in Spain, carried out two expulsions, in 1542 and in 1557. Both acts of banishment were soon revoked, however, with most of the exiles returning and resuming their old pursuits.

First Occupational Census of Prague Jewry

A census of 1,000 Jewish men, women and children present in Prague on June 8 and 10, 1546, disclosed eight glaziers, eight butchers, six dice-makers, three musicians or makers of musical instruments, and a turner, a sword-maker, a bookbinder, a printer, an assayer, a grinder, a maker of mouse traps, a barber, and a surgeon.[17] This list is hardly an adequate picture of the crafts practiced by the Jews of Prague at that time. The tailors, furriers, bag makers, strap makers, pewterers, goldsmiths, cutlers, and others we know to have existed up to 1546 are not mentioned, evidently because not all the Jews exiled from Prague in 1542 had as yet returned. However, the census is significant considering that, some fifty years earlier, most of the listed trades had not been practiced by the Jews of Prague.

The Guilds' Struggle against Unaffiliated Artisans

The guilds, in the meantime, had their privileges confirmed by the king in 1558-1564. Their members were recognized as the only lawful artisans; workmen unaffiliated with the guilds were forbidden to ply their trades and condemned as "interlopers." The products of the interlopers, Jew and non-Jew alike, were branded as inferior by the guilds. But since non-guild articles were cheaper, they commanded a larger market. Moreover, the poorer classes of Prague could obtain cheap wares at the *Taendelmarkt* (flea market) in the ghetto, where second-hand clothes, furs, shoes, bags, etc. were offered for sale. The second-hand dealers knew how to clean and mend an old suit or pair of shoes, trim old fur coats with new fox or marten pelts, or embellish old bags with new rings or strings so as to make them look like new. In this way, a class of second-hand tailors, shoemakers, furriers, and bag makers emerged. They employed Christian journeymen clandestinely, learned their skills and, with their help, began to produce new goods, all of which naturally provoked the guilds to greater wrath. Irritation was also caused by the practice of some Jewish pawnbrokers to refurbish unredeemed articles and sell them as new wares.[18]

Jewry's Improved Position in the Second Half of the Sixteenth Century

Ferdinand's successor, King Maximilian II (1564-1576), followed a more lenient policy with regard to Protestants and Jews. At the request of the leaders of Prague Jewry, he issued a charter on April 4, 1567 which recognized the right of Jews to reside in Bohemia. He also promised to protect them against interference in their businesses and trades. Though Maximilian's policies lacked consistency—in 1571, he yielded to a demand of the furriers' guild for restricting the activities of Jewish furriers, and also banned Jews from Kutna Hora (Kuttenberg) and other cities in the mining district—the Jewish community's situation became more stable during his reign. The Jewish population grew and, in 1570, Jews were living in at least 75 towns and 19 villages.[19] Under Maximilian's successors, Rudolf II (1576-1611) and Matthias (1612-1619), the position of the Jews steadily improved. The comparatively favorable political climate benefited the economic position of the Jews, including that of the Jewish craftsmen.

Glaziery and Glassblowing

Glaziery was a trade vigorously plied by Bohemian Jews in the second half of the sixteenth century. Gentile patrons in Prague and the provinces included townspeople, the Catholic church and the nobility. The Prague Archbishop Zbynek Barka (1592-1606) engaged the Jewish glaziers of Liben (Lieben), a nearby town, to put window panes in the churches of his diocese. There is abundant evidence of Jewish glaziers working in the castles of the nobility in 1547, 1552, and later years. Adam Glas of Jindrichuv Hradec (Neuhaus) was a busy glazier in the 1570's and 1580's, skillful in mounting small glass panes in lead. He worked for the castle of the lord of the city (1581).[20] A Jewish glass blower operated a glassworks in Krumlev (Krumlau) in Bohemia in 1550.[21] In Prague, in the *Kleinseite* (Mensi Mesto) district, the painters and glaziers complained that a Jewish master, David, encroached on their work (1577). He said in his defense that Jews "may practice any trade except the dishonest ones."[22] Winter believes that the success and efficiency of the Jewish glaziers in Bohemia was due to an ability to obtain their materials from the glassworks on easier terms than their Christian competitors. It may be also assumed that they were satisfied with lower profits.

Goldsmiths and Silversmiths

Jewish goldsmiths were patronized by the upper class. Jacob Goldscheider, the son of Isaac Goldscheider, "the refiner" of Prague, was granted in 1586 a privilege by Rudolf II (noted for his patronage of arts and crafts) to practice his craft in Prague and in the royal cities open to Jewish residence. He was permitted to employ as many journeymen as he wished. This point is noteworthy because Jewish masters were prohibited from engaging Christian journeymen altogether.

A goldsmith, Joseph de Cerui, possibly a foreign Jew, had in 1577 obtained from the king the privilege of practicing his craft at Hradcany, the royal castle in Prague, and in some city districts without fear of interference on the part of Christian or Jewish masters.[23]

The Hebrew term for goldsmith, *tzoref,* and the Czech term *zlatnik* are to be found in a number of funerary inscriptions in the Old Jewish cemetery in Prague. Jewish gold and silversmiths undoubtedly made ceremonial objects for the synagogues and the home, many of which survived owing to some obscure plan of the Nazis to set up a Jewish museum. Signed objects are very rare. A relatively late Torah shield of 1753, in embossed and engraved silver, now in the Prague Jewish Museum, bears the signature of Joshua Zlatnik.[24]

Sword Making

Prague, Chomutov (Komotau), Louny (Laun), and Nachod in Bohemia, and Mikulov (Nikolsburg), Moravske-Budejovice (Maehrisch Budwitz), and Sumberk (Maehrisch Schoenberg) in Moravia, recorded a number of Jewish sword makers. The city archives of Moravske-Budejovice, inhabited almost exclusively by Czechs, has records up to 1562 of six Jewish sword makers (termed *mecir* in Czech).[25]

In 1607, Rudolf II appointed Jacob Isaac Michael, who was skilled in making and gilding rapiers, to work in the Prague royal castle at a monthly salary of ten gulden. Michael's Jewish origin, however, is not certain.[26]

A Synagogue Architect

An epitaph of 1625 on the tombstone of Juda Tzoref de Herz in the Old Jewish cemetery in Prague says that he "lived by the work of his hands and that from his plans all of the Pinkas Synagogue and part of the Meisel Synagogue were built." The name *Tzoref* indicates that Juda de Herz came from a family of goldsmiths. The contemporary chronicler David Gans (1541-1613), who died in Prague, mentions Juda as the architect of the Meisel Synagogue along with Joseph Wal or Wol, of whom nothing else is known.

The Pinkas Synagogue, still standing, is a medieval building. It was remodeled, enlarged and provided with a gallery in the seventeenth century. The reconstruction was evidently Juda de Herz' work.[27]

Embroiderers

No less familiar than the name of *Tzoref,* was that of Perlsticker (bead embroiderer) or Perlhefter (bead stitcher) among Jews in

Bohemia and Moravia. Solomon Perlsticker, along with his wife Golda, embroidered a velvet Torah curtain decorated "with colored silk appliqué." He presented it in 1590 to the Altneu Synagogue in Prague. In 1592 his son Pinhas with his wife Gautel added some embellishments to the curtain in *passementerie* (braid work). This ark curtain is the oldest preserved. The names of the embroiderers and the dates are embroidered on it. The Jewish embroiderers of Prague seem to have had their own guild.[28]

Tailors

Despite the opposition of the Christian tailors' guild, the Jewish tailors of Prague succeeded over the years in finding patrons among the Christian population. Early in the seventeenth century, their position had been strengthened to such a degree that the guild began to think of coming to terms with them. Preliminary talks were officially held between the guild and the Jewish tailors in 1610. The latter demanded admission to the guild, declaring their willingness to pay the guild dues and to recognize the guild regulations. In return they were prepared to reject slipshod workers in the Prague ghetto, to proclaim in the synagogues that no bungling artisans need look for shelter in a Jewish house, and to denounce poor workers to the guild. The proposal was debated before a full assembly of the guild. Two members, the German master Lucas Tanczer and the Czech master Kral, argued in favor of accepting the Jewish tailors as members of the guild. It was probably the first instance of Christian guild members pleading for the admission of Jews on an equal footing. After the two had spoken, the Czech master Vaclav Shindler arose and spoke in sharp protest: "Shall pagans enter in our midst and become members of the guild? By God, I implore you, gentlemen brothers, to refuse your consent to this proposal, for what will the other guilds say? It is unheard of that Jews should belong to guilds." And he added that he would rather his mother had drowned him in his first bath than that he should live to assent to the Jewish demand. Master Shindler's harangue impressed the audience—the assembly voted against the proposal.[29] A few decades later, the Jewish tailors formed a guild of their own.

Furriers

The Prague furriers' guild directed its attacks against Jewish dealers in fur who employed Christian journeymen to refurbish skins. Both parties to this dispute appealed to the Crown. A joint petition of the guilds of Christian furriers, tailors, and other artisans of Prague and the provincial towns was submitted to the Diet in 1593. However owing to negotiations between Mordecai Meisel, leader of Bohemian Jewry, and members of the Diet no action was taken.[30]

In 1595, King Rudolf II sought to settle the quarrel of the Christian and Jewish furriers by a compromise. The Jews were ordered to desist from employing bungling journeymen, and to apply to the furriers' and tailors' guilds whenever they needed lining and tailoring work to be done. The Christian furriers were commanded not to interfere in the sale by Jewish dealers of skins and furs, including cheap Polish furs, leather aprons and caps. But the royal document also contained a paragraph forbidding Jews to offer aprons and caps of their own manufacture on the market. As was to be expected, the compromise satisfied neither party and the struggle continued unabated for some time. One day in 1595, the guild masters locked up the shops of the Jewish furriers, who instantly protested to the authorities against this violation of the rights of free trade granted them by the Crown. The guild was ordered by the city council to remove the locks.[31] Ultimately, the Jewish furriers set up a guild of their own.

Butchers

The Jewish butchers in Prague had the usual conflicts with the Christian guild which objected to their selling to Christian customers.

In 1616, the Christian guild got an ordinance passed forbidding Jewish butchers to keep their shops open on Sundays and Christian holidays, when the peasants would come to Prague and shop in the ghetto. On November 20, 1639, St. Thomas' Day, the magistrate of the "Old City" accompanied by members of the butchers' guild, marched into the ghetto to see whether the ordinance was being complied with. The butchers at once closed their shops. Their outcries attracted a crowd of Jews who, according to the official report, were on the point of attacking the Christian party. The latter nevertheless managed to confiscate six legs of mutton. The municipal council of the "Old City" ordered the arrest of three elders of the Jewish community. The governors of Prague decided to keep the elders in prison until the community had paid a penalty. The conflict continued through the Thirty Years' War, but as the Bohemian treasury needed Jewish financial support, the Jewish butcher shops kept open on Sundays and Christian holidays.[32]

The Jewish butchers of Prague were the first to organize a guild of their own. The exact year of its foundation is not known, but the guild's key bears the date of 1620. Engraved on the key are names of the two guild wardens, Solomon Wilhartitz and Elias Nefele, and those of thirteen guild members. At the base of the key is a representation of a lion rampant, the emblem of the city of Prague, holding between its forepaws a butcher's ax inscribed with the Hebrew word *kosher.*[33]

Printers and Bookbinders

The printing of Hebrew books was begun in Prague in the early sixteenth century. Gerson ben Samuel Cohen (called Hermann in official documents) established a Hebrew press there in 1512. In 1527, the king granted Gerson a monopoly for the printing of Hebrew books, which was renewed for his son Moses in 1545 and for his grandson in 1590. In time, however, other printing presses were established in Prague in addition to that of the Gersonides, and Hebrew presses were also established in Mlade Boleslav (Jung Bunzlau) and Prostejovice (Prossnitz) in the seventeenth century. How many Jewish compositors, printers, proofreaders, and bookbinders were employed in the trade we do not know. The Prague municipal archives record the names of the bookbinders Enoch (1527), Adam (1538), and the brothers Markvart and Juda (1553). Jewish bookbinders practiced their skills in other cities as well. Winter's statement that it is not certain whether the Prague Jewish bookbinders actually engaged in that work, or simply dealt in books, is gainsaid by the bitter complaints of Christian masters about the mounting number of Jewish bookbinders.

Judah ben Samuel, author of the "Book of the Pious" (*Sefer Hasidim*), who lived in Regensburg in the early part of the thirteenth century, states, as has been mentioned, that the Jews had learned the art of bookbinding from the monks. It is possible that this craft was brought to Prague from Regensburg, many of the first Jewish settlers having come from Regensburg. The relationship between the two Jewries was close and is attested, among other things, by the common features in the design of the Altneu Synagogue and the medieval synagogue at Regensburg.[34]

Developments in Moravia in the Period from 1500 to 1648

Moravia possessed a smaller Jewish population and therefore fewer Jewish artisans than Bohemia; however their number grew steadily. Two factors account for this. First, in this period Jews lived side by side with Christians in the Moravian towns—prevalently Jewish localities emerged in Moravia only in the eighteenth century—and this helped Jewish artisans to gain non-Jewish patronage. Secondly, successive waves of Jewish immigrants arrived from neighboring Poland, where manual workers were very numerous in the Jewish community.

Tailoring, a leading Jewish trade in Moravia in later centuries, was virtually non-existent in this period. In the town of Prostejovice, there were three cutlers, two bag makers, two tanners, two glaziers, and one turner in 1550-1564. Mikulov (Nikolsburg) listed bookbinders, cutlers, sword makers, and shoemakers; Slavkov (Austerlitz), tanners, Uhersky Ostra, stocking knitters; Strassnitz and Trebic, tailors; Kounice (Kanitz), goldsmiths and glaziers.[35]

The Thirty Years' War

In the Thirty Years' War (1618-1648), Prague Jewry was loyal to the Hapsburg monarchy against the Protestant Czech Estates, who elected Frederick, Prince Elector of the Palatinate and head of the German Calvinists, king of Bohemia. The Battle at the White Mountain, fought on November 8, 1620, ended with the defeat of the Bohemian Estates and the flight from the country of the "Winter King," as Frederick came to be known because of his brief reign. The victorious Hapsburg monarch, Ferdinand II, executed many of the Czech Protestant nobles and confiscated about half of their estates, allotting them to loyal noblemen and to Catholic churches and monasteries. Protestantism in the urban population was likewise persecuted. Many Czechs emigrated, and those who remained were restricted in their rights.

The Jews, on the whole, were not affected by these events. They were spared the ravages of the army of the Catholic League, which, following its victory at White Mountain, marched triumphantly into Prague. The commander, Prince Elector Maximilian of Bavaria, acting upon a letter of Ferdinand, ordered that the ghetto be protected in case of disturbances. The elders of the Jewish community chose the anniversary of the Battle of the White Mountain to celebrate its preservation. This was the so-called Purim of Prague. Prince Karl Liechtenstein, the governor of Bohemia, permitted the dwellers of the crowded ghetto to buy houses in the peripheral Christian sections of Prague.[36]

Royal Charter of 1628

Ferdinand II, though a fervent Catholic and a disciple of the Jesuits, relaxed the economic restrictions under which Jews labored. His policy was motivated by the financial necessities of the war. The Bohemian Jews declared their readiness to pay an annual contribution of 40,000 gulden to the Crown in return for freedom in commerce and the crafts, and on August 28, 1627, the monarch granted Jewish merchants equal rights with non-Jews at the fairs, and equality in the payment of custom duties on their merchandise. Jews were now permitted to learn and practice crafts freely, without interference "by Christian artisans or others." The charter was confirmed once again by the monarch, in 1628. The section of the charter granting freedom in the exercise of crafts marked a radical departure from the traditional restrictions.

Thoroughly alarmed, the Prague guilds appealed to the Crown.

They demanded that Jewish artisans be restricted to sell their wares on the *Taendelmarkt* only and work for Jewish customers only. Ferdinand yielded to the guilds, and in June 1636, issued a provisional order embodying their demands. Just a month before, the king had ordered the Bohemian High Court of Justice to investigate ways of permitting Jews the exercise of crafts without injuring the interests of the Christian guilds. In 1637, however, the king died, and his son and successor, Ferdinand III (1637-1657), inherited the war with all its staggering costs. Not disdaining the annual contribution of the Bohemian Jews, he granted Jewish artisans permission to accept commissions from Christians. At the same time, he requested the High Court to elaborate an opinion on the rights of Jewish craftsmen, according to the charter of 1628.[37]

The Opinion of the Bohemian High Court Concerning Jewish Manual Work

First, the jurists considered the guilds' argument that the words *unter ihnen treiben,* as used in the charter of 1628, meant that Jewish artisans were allowed to work only for Jewish patrons. This interpretation was rejected by the Court. It pointed out that Jews never had been forbidden to serve Jewish patrons, so that the granting of such permission by the charter would have been entirely supererogatory. The Court was emphatic in stating that the charter clearly gave Jewish craftsmen the right to work for Christian patrons.

Most important for the student of the economic history of seventeenth century Bohemia is the Court's opinion concerning the guilds' charges about Jewish underselling. The jurists remarked that the majority of Prague's consumers were only too glad to buy goods at reasonable prices, which they knew where to find. Christians coming from outside the city limits also knew where cheaper wares could be had. The poorer classes especially were unable to pay the high prices set by the guilds, and therefore increasingly turned to the cheaper-selling Jewish artisans.[38]

Royal Charter of 1648

The opinion of the High Court was submitted to Ferdinand III at the end of 1647, near the close of the war. Jews were then participating in the defense of Prague, which was besieged by the Swedes. Whether in recognition of this exercise of patriotism, or because he had been convinced by the High Court's conclusions, the monarch issued a new and on the whole favorable charter to the Prague Jews, on April 6, 1648. All crafts were declared open to Jewish workmen, with the exclusion of the armorer's craft, the making of gunpowder, swords, and related wares. The charter declared that Jewish craftsmen were free to work for non-Jewish patrons and to sell their goods to Christians in Prague and other cities, at annual fairs, weekly markets, and in shops. In order to curb Jewish competition and reduce the opportunities to approach Christian patrons, Jewish masters might receive commissions from Christian patrons only in their homes.[39]

Expansion of Jewish Trades

Though some restrictions remained in force, the charter of 1648 paved the way for a further expansion of Jewish trades. Prague's Jewish population had grown during the war as the result of immigration from stricken areas. In 1636, it was 7,815 and must have risen higher by the end of the war. Few cities in Europe at that time could count so large a Jewish population. Jewish artisans had a large market among their own people; the number of non-Jewish patrons also grew, owing to the rising demands of the lower classes and the army.

This explains why, during and after the Thirty Years' War, new trades became open to the Jews of Prague. Besides the button, candle, soap and hat makers, the shoemakers, cobblers, dyers, and potters, we find now cabinet makers, house painters, nail smiths, plate gilders, plumbers, makers of musical instruments, and file cutters.[40]

Conclusion

In the Middle Ages, the small Jewish population of Bohemia

and Moravia was concentrated in some ten cities and towns, with Prague the largest community. The Jews were mainly engaged in commerce and moneylending, with but few in manual labor. Jewish artisans catered almost exclusively to Jewish patrons because of the guilds' opposition to their dealings with Christians.

As the Jewish population of Bohemia and Moravia grew by natural increase and immigration, changes occurred in its socioeconomic structure. In the second half of the fifteenth century, Jewish artisans began to appear here and there. In the early sixteenth century the drive to crafts became stronger. By the middle of the seventeenth century Jews had acquired new skills and an ability to satisfy the consumer needs of the different classes. The Christian master, bound by the rigidly fixed guild tariffs, lacked the flexibility of the unaffiliated artisan. Here lay a continual source of conflict.

The Crown was involved in religious wars and was torn by its own conflicting interests. Controversies and antagonisms were on the increase, and there were no foreseeable solutions.

Chapter XVI

Expansion of Jewish Artisanship in Bohemia and Moravia: 1650-1780

Growth of the Jewish Population

The number of Jews in Bohemia in the early seventeenth century was, as recorded, about 4,000. We do not know whether women, children under ten years of age, and servants were included in this figure, however.[1] Moravia's Jewish population at this time was smaller than Bohemia's.

The Thirty Years' War ushered in a period of Jewish population growth in both provinces. A census of Prague's Jewish residents of 1636, as we have seen, listed 7,815 persons. Undoubtedly, the number of Jews throughout the country likewise grew. In 1648, Jewish refugees from the Ukraine and adjacent Polish provinces—where Hetman Bogdan Chmielnicky had risen against the Polish crown and was slaughtering the Jewish population—began to arrive in Bohemia and Moravia. More refugees followed, in the troubled 1650's from Poland and Lithuania. In addition, some Jewish families settled in Bohemia and Moravia following their expulsion from Vienna in 1670. As a result of this, in 1703, Prague had a Jewish population of 11,517, which was a third of the city's total population. In 1724, approximately 30,000 Jews were registered in all other Bohemian cities, towns and villages. In Moravia, there were, at the time, more than 5,000 Jewish families or about 25,000 persons. Altogether some 65,000 Jews were living in Bohemia and Moravia in the first half of the eighteenth century.[2] This increase in the size of the Jewish population was fraught with political and economic consequences.

Reverting to Discrimination

In 1650, two years after the end of the Thirty Years' War, Ferdinand III abruptly changed the conciliatory policy which wartime financial necessity had caused him to follow toward the Jews. On April 2, he ordered an investigation of the number of Jews residing in the country. In particular, he wished to know on what grounds private proprietors of cities, towns, and villages had admitted Jews to residence in 1618. The monarch had heard that Jews leasing customs, tools, and country inns, were reaping excessive profits and employing Christians as servants; he was disturbed by reports of sexual intercourse between Jews and Christian women. The results of the investigation were presented to the Bohemian Diet in October 1650. The Diet decreed that Jews were to be removed from all localities in which they had not resided on or before October 1, 1618; it also adopted a number of anti-Jewish measures in conformity with the royal order.

Economic Implications

The reduction of Bohemian Jewry to its 1618 size became the government's policy for many decades to come. The main stress was laid, of course, on blocking the immigration of foreign Jews. Plans for reducing the growing Jewish population of Prague were discussed time and again in the 1670's and 1680's. When, in 1689, fire destroyed most of the ghetto and a plan of reconstruction was being considered by the authorities, the Christian artisans pressed for the transfer of Prague's Jews to the neighboring town of Liben.[3] The matter dragged on into the eighteenth century. In 1705 the government created a Commerce Commission (*Commerz Collegium*) to consider measures for the improvement of commerce and industry in Bohemia. The Commission recommended drastic measures against the Jews. Jews, stated the Commission, are "the born enemies of industrial growth." Their expulsion from Bohemia was the only solution of the problem; the government should have no scruples against taking this step, just as it had not hesitated in the past to confiscate the property of non-Catholics and to carry out their expulsion or extermination.

A more moderate attitude was adopted by one member of the Commission who thought that restricting Jewish artisans, the shoemakers, the tailors, and the others to selling their wares at the *Taendelmarkt* twice a week only would markedly reduce their competition. It was also suggested that Jewish merchants be prohibited from importing foreign cloth which was injuring domestic production.

These, and other proposals by the Commission, were vigorously opposed by the Bohemian treasury (*Kammer*), which emphasized the fiscal loss that would result from the curtailment of the activities of Jewish merchants and craftsmen. Among other things, the treasury pointed to custom revenues of 36,172 gulden received in the period 1720-1726 on imported foreign cloth.[4]

Fiscal reasons proved stronger than mercantilist, or protectionist, considerations. A new commission, set up in 1714 to discover ways to reduce the number of Prague's Jews, labored for several years without result. It is noteworthy that representatives of the Prague Jewish community were given an opportunity to state their case to the authorities. They invoked the royal charters which had repeatedly pledged to the Jews rights of residence and free exercise of commerce and the trades. Moreover, they answered at great length the complaints of the guilds directed against Jewish goldsmiths, watchmakers, tanners, glove makers, hat makers, saddlers, strap makers, clothiers, tailors, glaziers, belt makers, furriers, tawers, metal dealers, shoemakers, and butchers.[5]

In one point the effort of the Commission to reduce the number of Jews did succeed, however. A decree of September 25, 1726 stated that henceforth only the eldest son in each Jewish family was permitted to remain in Bohemia and Moravia after marriage; all other sons were to leave the country as soon as they took a wife. This decree effectually limited the increase of the Jewish population, which now became stabilized.[6] It was at this time that younger sons of Bohemian and Moravian Jews settled in Hungary in considerable numbers.

Expulsion Averted

Bohemian Jewry was more seriously hit when in an edict of December 18, 1744, Empress Maria Theresa ordered the Jews of Prague to leave the country by the end of January 1745, and those outside of Prague by June 1745. The principal reason given for the expulsion was the alleged disloyalty of the Jews in the First Silesian War (1740-1742). But it is likely, as has been suggested, that the hostility of the Prague guilds was a factor carrying considerable weight. The news caused a stir in many European countries, particularly in Amsterdam and London. Diplomatic intervention was undertaken by Great Britain, the Netherlands, and several other continental powers. The empress refused to revoke the expulsion edict. She finally yielded, not so much to foreign pressure as to the Bohemian bureaucracy which warned that the expulsion of 40,000 Jews would seriously injure the economy of the country. The Bohemian Diet declared that "the Jewish exodus would cause losses in the millions." Some of the sixty-one Prague guilds reported a falling off in business as a result of the Jews temporarily removing to other cities of Bohemia. Other guilds insisted on the Jews remaining where they had gone. Most of the exiles returned to the Bohemian capital in 1748 and 1749.[7]

Campaign of the Prague Guilds against Expansion of Jewish Trades

The steady expansion of Jewish trades in Prague was the subject of several memoranda submitted by the Prague guilds to Emperor Leopold I in 1670-1680, in the expectation that he would deal with Prague's Jews as he had done with Vienna's. The guilds pointed to the losses Jewish competition had caused them. The number of Christian shoemakers had fallen from 500 in 1650 to 150; tailors from 400 to 150; furriers from 100 to 29; hat makers from 40 to 9; glaziers from 30 to 6; coppersmiths from 15 to 6; tawers from 30 to 5; harness makers from 20 to 4; lace makers from 18 to 2; hat trimmers from 28 to 2. The total number of Christian masters shrank from 1,245 in 1650 to 355 in the 1670's. The number of journeymen fell accordingly. Meanwhile, the guilds maintained, the number of Jewish artisans had risen five to six times.

The guilds brought forward a host of grievances against the Jewish artisans in their memoranda. Though for the most part inept workers—one in a thousand had been properly trained—the Jews were driving Christian craftsmen from the market place. Strangers visiting Prague, army officers, and university students no longer patronized Christian masters, for the Jews were busy attracting clients around the city gates, in the streets, and in inns, manor houses, and even monasteries.

Jewish workmen made harnesses for entire regiments. They sewed mourning dresses, wedding dresses, and liveries. Jewish barber-surgeons owned fourteen shops, each barber employing from eight to ten journeymen, while Christian barbers owned eighteen shops, only four of which employed journeymen. There were sixty Jewish goldsmiths against fifteen Christian ones. Jewish shoemakers opened shops in Christian buildings and sold their wares all over Prague, hiring bungling Christian journeymen and furloughed soldiers to help them. One Jewish shoemaker manufactured 5,000 pairs of shoes in twenty days, offering them to the public at half a kreutzer less than the customary price; but the shoes only lasted from eight to fourteen days. Jewish tallow chandlers and soapmakers out-rivaled Christian masters; this was also the case with cord makers, stocking knitters, embroiderers, cartwrights, cutlers, tinsmiths, and braziers. Jewish bookbinders, employing inept workmen, sent out canvassing agents in every direction. They bound both secular works and missals and breviaries. The Jews were invading the cloth and linen trades.

According to the memoranda, the Christian guilds had been so beggared by Jewish competition that they were no longer able to make donations to churches and hospitals. The Jews, however, prospered. They bought costly objects for their synagogues; sent funds abroad for Jewish charities; and put up a magnificent display at the pageant held in Prague on the occasion of the birth of the royal heir on July 26, 1678.

In addition, the Jews were accused of "theft, sacrilege, usury, adultery, pimping, murder, poisoning, and the blaspheming of Christ, Mary, all the saints in Heaven and all Christians on earth."

Using the fire in the ghetto as a pretext, the guilds, on December

14, 1689, submitted a petition to the emperor asking for the banishment of all the Jews from Prague. The emperor proceeded cautiously, ordering the governors of the three districts to ascertain the reactions of the treasury and the Jewish community elders to the grievances of the guilds. The governors were infuriated to learn that the guilds had approached the emperor directly without their knowledge. An investigation was begun which had no result.[8]

The guilds renewed their attack in the eighteenth century. They complained of Jewish competition in house painting, upholstering, mattress and button making.[9]

Jewish Artisan Statistics

What was the actual number of Prague's Jewish workmen? We can safely assume that the figures given by the Prague guilds were exaggerated. It was only in 1729, when a census of the ghetto population was taken that some statistics were compiled. Of a total of 10,517 persons listed in the census, which included family heads, women, children, servants, student boarders, and strangers visiting Prague, 2,335 were gainfully occupied. Of the latter, 711 or thirty per cent were independent artisans. The following table is a breakdown of the artisan class by trades:[10]

TABLE I

Jewish Artisans of Prague, 1729

Tailors	158	Makers of fur-lined dressing gowns	3
Trouser makers (1 woman)	3		
Patcher	1		
Tailors (women)	17	Button makers	18
Seamstresses	36	Button makers (women)	9
Quilters	3		
		Cord makers (7 women)	37
Shoemakers	100	Lace makers	12
Shoemakers (women)	5	Embroiderers	5
Heel makers	11	Pearl embroiderer	1
		Pearl borer	1
Furriers	33	Silk reelers	7
Furriers (women)	3	Hat and cap makers	39

Milliners (women)	2	Mat maker	1
Hat dyers	3	Calico printers	3
Hat quilter	1	Collar washers	2
		Veil washers (women)	4
Goldsmiths	20	Dyer	1
Seal engravers	2		
Diamond cutter	1	Printers	7
		Compositor	1
Butchers (men)	37	Bookbinders	5
Butchers (women)	7		
Glaziers	8	Barbers and bath attendants (men)	28
Painters	5	Physician	1
Chair maker	1	Physician (woman)	1
Makers of belts for guns and swords	4	Apothecary	1
		Midwives	2
Glovers (1 woman)	2	Nurses	29
Upholsterers	4	Musicians (one termed a "jester")	15
Mattress makers	7		711
Tent maker	1		
Caparison makers	3		

The list is not complete. Carpentry, for instance, is not mentioned, although we know from other sources that Jews plied that trade in the Prague ghetto. There were also dance teachers and makers of musical instruments. Schudt (1717) mentions the organ maker, rabbi Maier Mahler.[11] The list says nothing about the journeymen and apprentices employed by masters.

Some Jews had more than one occupation. Petty traders engaged in crafts on the side, and artisans sold uncommissioned goods without the help of middlemen.[12] This was the general practice among Bohemian craftsmen. Sixteenth-century records show that they found it more profitable to quit their shops temporarily and bring their wares to market themselves than to sell to middlemen.[13]

The food and beverage trades employed many persons, but the census did not always distinguish between producers and dealers. In addition to the independent butchers listed in Table I, there were eleven male and eleven female cooks, liquor makers, and only one baker.

Other manual laborers listed by the census were: 2 carters, 27 porters of goods of all sorts, 10 water carriers (one of whom was a woman), and one lumber carrier.[14]

The census of 1729 was the first attempt in modern times by one of the larger European cities to gather statistics on the occupations of its Jewish residents. Twenty years later, in 1749, when most of the Jews temporarily in exile as a result of Empress Maria Theresa's expulsion edict had returned to Prague, a new census was taken. This time 6,000 persons were registered—as against 10,517 in 1729—of whom about 500 practiced crafts, against 711 in 1729.[15]

Epitaphs in the Old Cemetery of Prague

The epitaphs in the old cemetery of Prague tell us much about the occupations of the people buried there. Of the more than 10,000 funerary inscriptions deciphered and copied down in the second half of the nineteenth century, some 1,200 were published in 1893. These epitaphs mention the professions and communal activities of the deceased. Artisans frequently carried on their fathers' skills. However, the goldsmith Abraham was the son of a maker of niter; the shoemaker Loeb Buber was the son of a tailor; the tailor Michl was the son of the doctor Isaac; also, the cook Lieberl was the son of the doctor Isaac; the tailor Henschl was the son of a goldsmith; the goldsmith Jacob Joseph was the son of the cabbalist Moses Nash. The epitaph of the butcher David says that he was the son of the butcher Mordecai Simon, and a descendant of the author of the chronicle, *Tzemah David,* David Gans (1541-1617). Some of the artisans' epitaphs rival those of rabbis and other people of the upper classes, giving the impression that the artisan was a respected member of the community.[16]

Artisans Outside Prague: Facts and Figures

The Bohemian Diet's decision of 1650 to reduce the Jewish population in the cities and villages to the level of 1618 was completely forgotten after a while. However, the government was aware of the continued growth of the provincial Jewish population and in 1724 ordered a registration of Jews throughout the country.

Registration forms, including questions about occupations, were sent to the head offices of the fourteen provinces of Bohemia. The completed forms for all but two of the provinces have been preserved; they reveal that in 1724 a total of 3,467 Jewish families were living in the twelve provinces. The occupational statistics cover only 3,097 family heads, as the Jews of the province of Koeniggraetz did not answer the question concerning their occupations. Four main groups of occupations were distinguished:

1. Commerce: 1,623, or 52.3%. Only five persons were moneylenders or moneychangers.
2. Artisans: 586, or 19.2%.
3. Owners or lessees of distilleries, tanneries, and potasheries, and innkeepers: 417, or 13.2%.
4. Communal functionaries, teachers, musicians, book dealers, beggars, and people without definite occupations: 471, or 15.3%.

The artisans were distributed as follows:

TABLE II

Jewish Artisans of Provincial Bohemia, 1724

Tailors, seamstresses	182
Butchers	179
Furriers, leather workers	80
Shoemakers, saddlers, and belt makers	62
Corselet, strap and hat makers	31
Glaziers, plasterers	26
Stocking knitters	14
Goldsmiths	6
Potters	6
Total	586

Eighty of the tailors, 112 butchers, and most of the shoemakers, lived in villages. The Jewish village tailors worked for peasants, as indeed did some of the Jewish tailors in the cities. Christian townspeople did not dare to order garments from Jewish masters, as the Christian guilds kept a careful watch. However, the guilds in the provinces were unable to halt the spread of Jewish artisanship, mainly because of the cheaper prices asked by Jewish workmen. Thus, the Christian butchers of the town of Libochovice complained, in 1699, to Prince Charles Dietrichstein, proprietor of the place, that their Jewish confrères sold meat at 3 kreutzer 3 denars a pound while their price was 4 kreutzer 4 denars. To this, Dietrichstein tersely replied that it was to the public's benefit if meat cost a kreutzer less.[17]

Jewish artisanship expanded in many fields. In Libochovice, thirteen Jewish tailors were recorded in 1740 as against two in a previous period; the thirty-two non-Jewish tailors were organized in a guild. In the seventeenth century, most Jewish artisans were tailors and butchers; one hundred years later, we also find Jewish tanners, furriers, shoemakers, and distillers in Libochovice; a Moses Elias manufactured "Egyptian" bricks.[18] Similar growth was apparent in Mlade Boleslav, Kolin, and other towns and villages.

Arts and Crafts in Moravia

The percentage of Jews in the arts and crafts in Moravia was perhaps greater than in Bohemia, if one excludes Prague. They lived, as we have said, in private towns and townlets whose proprietors opposed the monopolistic ambitions of the Christian guilds. A reason for the spread of handicrafts among Moravian Jews was the continued immigration of skilled Jewish workers from Poland. It is safe to say that from twenty to twenty-five per cent of Moravia's Jews practiced crafts in the eighteenth century. In 1748 Christian masters of Lipnik complained that owing to the competition of the Jewish craftsmen, only a few of them were able to employ a journeyman.[19] In this town, as in others, a third of the Jewish breadwinners lived by handicrafts. Tailors constituted 48 per cent of all Jewish artisans, as against 42 per cent in the seventeenth century.[20]

The largest number of Jews lived in Mikulov (Nikolsburg), then the social and spiritual center of Moravian Jewry. About one-fifth of the Jews of Mikulov were engaged in arts and crafts. The following is a list of 1777 Jewish artisans in Mikulov.[21] (We find more or less the same distribution among the trades in other Moravian ghettos, and also such crafts as leather work, glove making, stocking knitting, soap making, weaving, the making of potash, and especially tanning. Jewish tanners frequently leased tanneries owned by noblemen and ran them with the help of Jewish and non-Jewish workers.[22])

TABLE III

Jewish Artisans in Mikulov, 1777

Tailors	20	Seal Engraver	1
Trouser-makers	8	Painter	1
Patcher	1	Tallow chandlers	2
Shoemakers (1 cobbler)	13	Butchers	7
Furriers	2	Bakers	3
Button makers	5	Barbers	6
Silk reeler	1	Cord makers	6
Goldsmiths	3	Makers and washers of quilted pea jackets	11
Bookbinders	2		
Glaziers	6		

Jewish stone cutters carved tombstones and did work for synagogues. A synagogue porch in Meseric was constructed before 1768 by Jacob ben Meir Halevy; a stone washing-basin in a synagogue in Trebic is the work of an unnamed Jewish master.[23]

Official records for the period 1699-1775 contain many names of Jewish goldsmiths. The Mikulov master Isaac Ber, listed in the records for 1732, belonged to a family of goldsmiths who had practiced the trade for a hundred years. Of the 39 goldsmiths in Moravia in 1732, eight were Jews. In 1769 the number of Jewish masters had risen to fourteen, and that of the Christians fell to thirteen. In 1769 a Jewish master of Trebic was the first to sign his work, a practice previously forbidden to Jews by Maria Theresa. Solomon Joachim of Bucovice, Moravia, did filigree work for the proprietors of that town, signing his creations "S. J." The term *professionierte* following the names of Jewish goldsmiths showed that they had satisfied the professional requirements of their craft.[24]

Calligraphers and Illustrators

The craft of the scribe, limited by the printing press, was kept alive owing to the needs of the synagogue for handwritten scrolls of the Pentateuch. There originated in Moravia about the first half of the eighteenth century a group of scribes who produced both unadorned scrolls for the synagogue and Hebrew devotional books with handpainted illustrations in color for individual patrons. One such book, a Haggadah for Passover, contains a dedication to Lazarus von Geldern, the great-grandfather of Heinrich Heine. The scribes, or *soferim* as they called themselves in their colophons, hailed mostly from Lipnik, Trebitch, and Gewitch. A number of these illustrated books, although the work of self-taught artists, are of considerable merit and are preserved in the British Museum, the Rosenthaliana in Amsterdam, the Hebrew Union College in Cincinnati, and in private collections.[25]

Social Standing of Artisans

Bernard Goldschmied was elected elder of the Mikulov community council in 1715; being an artisan did not bar him from this position of honor. On the other hand, the Council of Moravian Jewish Communities, at a meeting in 1709 at Bucovice, decreed that persons working as butchers, or tanners, or at "any of the more contemptible trades," might not be elected to the council unless they had previously held the post of community judge (*dayyan*) or received the title of *haver* (a man learned in rabbinical lore).[26] The humbler class of artisans, then, unless they were judges or scholars, were looked down upon. Manual labor by itself brought little honor. This haughty attitude, which is so much at variance with talmudic and medieval Spanish traditions, reflects the disdain for manual labor which began to be felt generally in the early modern period.

Artisans' Earnings and Taxes

We have little precise knowledge about the earnings of the Jewish artisans in Bohemia and Moravia. Most of the records indicate, however, that they led a hand-to-mouth existence. There were tailors in Prague and elsewhere unable to buy cloth. On the forms for the registration of Bohemian Jews in 1724, officials occasionally noted the economic condition of the registrants. One such note referred to "wretched tailors" (*muehselige Schneider*). On some registration lists, the artisans figured at the very bottom, following merchants, lessees, and small traders. It has been pointed out that in the district of Elbogen, where the Jews were fairly well circumstanced, there was not one artisan. Earnings were meager indeed and fell below those in many of the other occupations.

In Pacov, in the district of Bechyne, a tailor and a shoemaker earned 30 gulden annually, whereas a grain dealer earned 75 gulden, and a clothier, 110. The Christian artisans were no better off. A Christian tailor in Stupcitz, in the same district of Bechyne, earned only 20 gulden as against the 45 gulden earned by a Jewish tailor; however, the former possessed a plot of land which gave him an additional source of income. In the town of Svihov, with seventeen Jewish families, there were six merchants earning from 50 to 100 gulden per annum and two earning 40 gulden each. The tailor Lebel also earned 40 gulden annually. The teacher of the elementary school earned much less; the widow Hindele made 24 gulden by knitting stockings.[27]

Under these circumstances artisans paid very little in taxes. The tax rolls of Lipnik, Moravia, for the year 1760, show Jewish tailors paying 6, 8 and 14 gulden; butchers, 7 and 19 gulden; and an elementary school teacher, 6 gulden. There were no artisans among the taxpayers paying 100, 50, or even 20 gulden.[28]

Still, there were Jewish masters who prospered. In Prague, some members of the Jewish guilds were in a position to give out work and materials to less successful colleagues who delivered the finished products at reduced rates.[29] The same thing was done by Christian masters. This was the putting-out system (*Verlagssystem*) which made its appearance in various parts of Europe in the late Middle Ages. It led to the development of home industries and, ultimately, to the emergence of the modern factory.[30]

Chapter XVII

Survey of Jewish Craft Guilds in Bohemia and Moravia: 1600-1780

The struggle waged by the Bohemian and Moravian guilds against Jewish artisans in the sixteenth century and the early decades of the seventeenth century was resumed with greater bitterness at the end of the Thirty Years' War (1648). To defend themselves against these attacks, the Jewish artisans set up guilds of their own. The statutes and regulations of these guilds were preserved in Bohemian and Moravian archives.

Jewish Guild Statutes

Jewish guild statutes were patterned upon those of the non-Jewish guilds of Bohemia and Moravia. The Christian guilds originated in the later Middle Ages and developed greatly in the sixteenth century; in Prague alone they numbered ninety-seven at the beginning of the seventeenth century.[1] The membership of a guild was limited to artisans who had gone through the required period of training as apprentices and journeymen and had satisfied the other conditions laid down for masters, such as good behavior, citizenship, and so forth. Relations with fellow members, with members of other guilds, with non-guild artisans, with patrons, with municipal and governmental authorities, and with the church were regulated in considerable detail. Ways and means were devised to curb unfair competition among members and to restrain non-members from working at the trade. Funds were set up for assisting fellow members and their families in case of sickness or death. Religious ceremonies and various festivities were observed with pomp and display to strengthen the solidarity within the guild and its prestige without.[2]

Prague Jewish Guilds

There were ten or eleven Jewish guilds in Prague in this period. The butchers' guild was founded before 1620. The by-laws of the tailors' guild of 1690 were a paraphrase of older by-laws of unknown date, destroyed in the great Prague ghetto fire of 1689.[3] The tailor Mordecai Kaz who died in 1678, had been a warden of the guild for many years.[4] The barbers' guild was organized in 1688.[5] There were also guilds of lace, braid, cord, and button makers, shoemakers, furriers, druggists, musicians, embroiderers, and goldsmiths. A guild of keepers of beer shops is also mentioned.[6]

Guild Banners and Emblems

The Prague Jewish guilds, like the Christian guilds, carried their flags and emblems in the festivals and pageants which were held on special occasions, such as the birth of an heir to the throne. When Prince Leopold of Hapsburg was born in 1716, and Prince Joseph on April 24, 1741, the Jewish guilds put in a splendid appearance in the pageants arranged in Prague. In J. J. Schudt's description of the pageant of 1716, it is noted that the physician Salman was followed by the druggist David, behind whom marched the barber-surgeons and their journeymen, each with his basin for letting blood. The butchers carried two banners and their "key that shone beautifully." [7] In the 1741 pageant, the tailors' guild flew its banner made of odds and ends of cloth, upon which scissors were embroidered in gold. The members of the furriers' guild were clad in Persian furs; they carried two banners and a stretcher on which stuffed animals were displayed. The emblem of the shoemakers' guild was a goblet shaped like a large boot. The musicians also had a goblet for their emblem. The guild of lace, braid, cord, and button makers displayed an artisan's stool or work bench *(Hand-*

werks-Stuhl) as their emblem. The barbers' emblem was a razor, the druggists' a mortar. Each group of artisans was preceded by its band.[8] The emblems of the trades are also found engraved on tombstones in the Jewish cemetery of Prague; scissors for tailors, mortars and pestles for apothecaries, a balsam jar for physicians (or apothecaries), harps for makers of musical instruments and for musicians, books for printers, and so forth.[9]

Prague Jewish Guild Statutes: Membership

The statutes of three Jewish guilds of Prague have thus far been published: the barbers' guild of 1688, the tailors' guild of 1690, and the shoemakers' guild of 1730. The statutes are written in characteristic Austro-German bureaucratic style.[10]

The barbers' statutes begin with a list of the members' names; the tailors' with the signatures of its six guild wardens. The shoemakers' guild had twelve masters at its founding and had a provision prohibiting the admittance of new members. In contrast, the tailors' guild admitted anyone who was making new clothes, and after 1750 trouser makers as well. Jobbing tailors and butchers were strictly barred, as they were in the Christian guilds. The shoemakers' guild included master shoemakers, cobblers, and heel makers. Applicants for membership had to prove that they were not only residents but also natives of Prague. This stipulation evidently mirrored political considerations—we know that the Prague authorities were anxious to reduce the city's growing Jewish population, or at least to keep it constant. It should be noted that the Christian guilds in the provinces also required members to be of local origin; but the Prague Christian guilds merely required members to be Bohemian subjects. As in any other guild, a candidate had to furnish proof of good character. Only married artisans could enter the guild.

A new member received the title of master and was registered in the guild's book. The act of registration was witnessed by the signatures of the guild wardens, and a fee of three thaler was paid in: one, going to the guild treasury and two, to the wardens. As this last requirement was not strictly observed, it was decided, in 1732, that all new guild members who had been registered without the wardens' witnessing the signatures were to re-register and pay the fee. Another reason for re-registration was the fact that bachelor artisans had been taken into the guilds in defiance of the by-laws.

Bachelors were prohibited from becoming guild members for fear that they would enjoy a competitive advantage over masters who had to support a family. An exception, however, was made if a journeyman was the son of a deceased master. Though a bachelor, he was permitted to carry on his father's trade and to engage a journeyman and an apprentice, since he was now the breadwinner of the family. Similarly, the widow of a deceased master was permitted by the guild to carry on his work with the help of a journeyman so long as she did not re-marry; profits were to be shared between her and the journeyman.

New guild members were permitted to employ one journeyman or one apprentice in the first year after their marriage. In the following year, they might have both a journeyman and an apprentice. As a rule, only one apprentice was allowed each master, although we find masters frequently having two or more. There was a twofold reason for this. The guild wished, first, to equalize output, and, second, to keep down the size of an artisan class whose already swollen numbers had brought it into economic straits.

Apprenticeship

A boy, applying either directly or through his father or a relative to a master for apprenticing to a trade, was accepted after eight days' probation, the master registering him in the record book of the guild. Each party paid one half of the registration fee of forty-eight kreutzer. The master was paid a fee upon his agreeing to train the youth for two to three years, after which period the apprentice became a journeyman with an initial daily wage of six kreutzer. The board and lodging of the apprentice were the master's responsibility. If an apprentice was not properly trained, his master was required to refund the fee he had received and was barred from accepting new apprentices for three years. If the master of an apprentice died during the first two years of apprenticeship, his heirs were required to return the apprenticeship fee to the father or relative of the youth. If the apprentice proved satisfactory as journeyman, his master was not to apprentice another boy before the lapse of one year.

Journeymen

A journeyman, seeking employment with a master, underwent a three days' trial. If he proved satisfactory, he was registered in the guild's book. Payment of the registration fee of forty-eight kreutzer was divided between master and journeyman, the latter pledging to the guild secretary to do good and honest work. As a rule, a journeyman hired himself out for half a year. He was to give four weeks' notice if he wanted to leave. If, however, he had been with a master an entire year, the latter could require him to continue working for him, provided he paid the journeyman the same wages he could get from another master.

Three years as a journeyman was considered the minimum for acquiring experience in a skill. After completing this term, a journeyman might marry and apply for a master's title. Permission to marry was obtained from the elders of the Prague community, upon the guild wardens' testifying to the journeyman's good conduct. This rule may have resulted from Christian artisans' complaining about Jewish workmen who married early and then set up shop as masters to compete with them.

Journeymen frequently sought to work for two masters. The guild administration forbade this, except where the second master had no patrons for half a year and hoped to secure some with the help of journeymen working for other masters. The initial daily wage of six kreutzer might be raised after a time. Wages were paid daily or weekly; payment by the piece was also allowed. Needless to say, journeymen were forbidden to work on their own account; tailors might not make their own clothing, not even their wedding clothes; they were obliged to order them from the master. On a journeyman's wedding day, however, his guild would present him with a gift. If a master was in arrears with his wages, a journeyman might not take any of the master's property in pawn, even if he intended to deposit it with the guild wardens. On the other hand, journeymen were protected against masters who claimed any of the formers' work as their own; such a contingency could possibly arise if a journeyman was paid by the piece.

Both journeymen and apprentices were warned against leaving their masters without giving notice. Thus, barbers' journeymen or apprentices who deserted their masters might not be employed by other members of the guild and were forbidden to appear "in the street where they had been employed" for a period of three years.

Hours of Work

The medieval guilds fixed working hours from 4 or 5 A.M. to 7 or 8 P.M. in summer, and from dawn to dusk in winter. Jewish journeymen and apprentices in Prague worked from 6 A.M. to 8 P.M., except on Fridays and the eve of holidays. They were free for half an hour daily to improve their reading and writing ability—in which language, German, Czech, or Hebrew, is not said. It is known that boys seeking to apprentice themselves to the barbers' trade had to know German.

Guild Policies regarding Competition, Workmanship, and Outsiders

The guild, as guardian of the welfare of all, set up rules to prevent one member from obtaining commissions at the expense of another. Point four of the statutes of the Prague tailors' guild of 1690 required a master to leave the place, be it in or outside the ghetto, as soon as another guild member had secured a job and was about to take the patron's measurements for a garment. The penalty for transgressing the rule was two ducats to be paid into the community treasury. Fines were also imposed on masters who entered the shops of colleagues and belittled their work in the presence of prospective patrons. The barbers' guild forbade its members to solicit people passing in the street, or to open shops in the vicinity of other members' shops. Shoemakers were warned by their guild against selling their products in more than one shop.

Time and again, guild members were enjoined to maintain solidarity and brotherhood, to respect each other, and to avoid quarrels. Disputants reported their cases to the guild wardens for arbitration. Point two of the shoemakers' guild statutes emphasized that litigant members were to go only to their wardens, and "not to other officers, such as the inspectors of the ghetto streets or of the *Taendelmarkt.*"

Guild members were prohibited from accepting orders from dealers in second-hand clothes, or from non-guild artisans producing second-hand goods, because both of these sold at less than the guild prices. This was the same policy that the Christian guilds followed in their fight against Jewish labor and second-hand dealers.

The medieval guild, as we know, protected the interests of the consumers along with the interests of its members. Members were warned against defective workmanship and the sale of poor or fraudulent products. This was also true of Prague's Jewish guilds. Thus, the shoemakers strictly prohibited dishonest work, threatening with severe penalities those who would cheat their patrons. Consumers who complained of being overcharged were heard by the guild warden in the presence of an assistant judge of the Prague Jewish Court.

The Jewish guilds prosecuted non-guild artisans, even if they were Jews, as strictly as Christian guilds prosecuted non-guild artisans of their own faith. Non-members were considered inferior workers, bunglers, and botchers. The barbers' guild of Prague denounced as inept all those workmen who solicited barber's work on the streets. The membership increased rather slowly. In 1729 the guild numbered thirty members (twenty-eight male and two female), as against twelve in 1688.[11]

Guild Administration

The guild wardens, called "elders," managed the affairs of the guild. They enforced guild regulations, administered justice in guild matters, transacted the daily business of the guild, and imposed fines upon offending members. Prague also had super-wardens—higher officers overseeing the activities of the guild wardens—appointed from among the elders of the Prague community. The super-wardens kept the moneys handed to them every three months by the guild treasuries. Thus the guilds were not entirely autonomous bodies.

The guild wardens, numbering four to six, were elected by the membership every three years, on which occasion the guild by-laws, as a rule, were revised. The dates of forthcoming elections were announced in all synagogues. Masters married no less than two years acted as secretaries of the election meetings. The right to vote was enjoyed only by those who had served as secretaries at previous elections. Only masters married no less than ten years were eligible to serve as wardens. Each month one warden was charged with the full responsibility for administering the affairs of the guild; all the wardens met together each Sunday to advise him. At the end of the month, he turned over to his successor the guild's record book, all accountings, and the cash in the guild treasury. His fellow wardens and the guild controllers served as witnesses to the fact that everything was in order. The retiring monthly warden then reported on the proposed expenditures of the guild. Before every new election of the guild administration, the monthly warden, assisted by two members of the guild, drew up a preliminary estimate of the costs of the election and submitted it to the super-warden.

The wardens received two-thirds of the registration fees as salary; we do not know whether this was enough to free them from the necessity of working at their trade. In addition to wardens, the guilds employed a staff of secretaries and minor officials. Each guild maintained an office where the statutes, record books, banners, emblems, and money box were kept; the guild wardens held their meetings there.

Contributions and Fines

Master tailors and journeymen contributed one kreutzer each week to their guild; shoemakers, three kreutzer; and master barbers and journeymen, fifteen kreutzer every three months. Registration fees were another source of income for the guilds, as were fines for infractions of guild regulations, though some of the latter went into the community treasury or to charitable institutions.

Religion and Welfare

The churches usually encouraged the formation of guilds which supported them by regular attendance at services and generous donations. Many guilds had their patron saints, maintained their own chapels, and erected church buildings. Similarly, Jewish guilds in Spain, Poland and Lithuania supported the synagogues, had their own chapels or guild chambers, and contributed to the improvement and embellishment of synagogue buildings. Members of the Jewish guilds in Bohemia had various religious duties. Journeymen and apprentices were required to attend the morning services, particularly on Mondays and Thursdays. On Fridays and the eve of holidays, work stopped in the shops at 1 P.M. in the winter and at 3 P.M. in the summer. Masters, journeymen, and apprentices all left the shops in order to prepare for the coming of the Sabbath or holiday. No work was permitted on the intermediate days of Passover and Sukkot. Members of the shoemakers' guild were requested to attend Sabbath lectures on Jewish law held by a rabbinical scholar engaged for that purpose by the guild. Absentees had to deliver half a pound of candles to the school for needy children which was maintained in the ghetto. In the tailors' guild even the journeymen and the apprentices were required to attend Sabbath lectures; absentees furnished candles to the synagogue.

Members who fell ill were cared for as follows. A master in straitened circumstances received one gulden and thirty kreutzer monthly from the guild treasury if his illness was a prolonged one. A journeyman received thirty kreutzer immediately after he took sick and thereafter twenty kreutzer monthly for as long as he was incapacitated. When an apprentice fell ill, his parents or relatives took care of him. If he had no parents or relatives, the guild contributed at least half a thaler to the cost of his nursing.

Abuses and Corruption

The history of guilds records many violations of guild rules not only by the rank and file of the membership, but also by guild officers charged with their faithful execution. Time and again, guild regulations were defied despite threats of heavy fines. Guild wardens in western Europe and also in Bohemia not infrequently abused their power and embezzled guild funds. For instance, Jan Lankas, warden of the Christian Prague painters' guild, was found guilty of embezzlement in 1502, and a warden of the Augsburg Christian tailors' guild was hanged in 1513 for the same crime.[12]

Guild wardens were often elected by fraudulent means. Jewish wardens were not exempt from the charge of corruption and mismanagement, as the records of the Prague Jewish tailors' guild reveal. In 1733 the entire membership submitted a complaint to the Bohemian Treasury (*Kammer*), the highest government office for Jewish affairs, contesting the election of the wardens. It was pointed out that some were not residents of Prague, others had been convicted of offenses, and still others could not read or write. Moreover, a warden had kept an apprentice a half year without registering him; two wardens employed twelve and fifteen journeymen each, whereas other masters were short of help. The newly-elected wardens were accused of embezzling guild funds and of unlawfully fining for absenteeism from the Sabbath lectures. The truth, it seems, was that members had been turned away for lack of room. The guild totaled 250 men, including masters, journeymen and apprentices.[13]

Barber-surgeons

In those days, barbers often performed minor surgical operations, including bloodletting, the lancing of wounds and abscesses, the removal of warts, and the pulling of teeth. The medical faculty of the University of Prague insisted that barber-surgeons should undergo tests, and in 1701 the Prague authorities empowered it to conduct such examinations. They must have been quite rigorous, for of the seventeen candidates in 1718, only three passed. The men received their certificates with the warning not to encroach upon the physician's sphere.[14] Jewish barber-surgeons were restricted to treating Jewish patients only; however, we know that Christians in Prague and in the provinces not infrequently resorted to Jewish surgeons.

Later in the eighteenth century, in 1778, a sort of Jewish chirurgical academy, called the *Gremium,* was established by the government. It was directed by a physician and two elder barber-surgeons. The membership included the Jewish surgeons of Prague and of three neighboring districts. The purpose of the *Gremium* was to provide more efficient training in the surgeon's craft.[15]

Musicians

The Jewish musicians' guild of Prague was formed in the seventeenth century in consequence of clashes with Christian musicians, who protested against Jewish bands playing at Catholic baptisms and weddings, and at parties given by Christians on Sundays and holidays. It appears that the Prague Jewish band played, in 1580, at the wedding of the Czech nobleman Peter Vok Rozemberk and that the band's playing was "very pretty." The Christian musicians' guild repeatedly lodged complaints with the Archbishop of Prague in 1642; but the prelate decided in favor of the Jewish musicians.[16]

A Merchants' Guild

The Jewish clothes dealers of Prague organized a guild of their own in the latter decades of the seventeenth century. These dealers used to purchase cloth manufactured in Liberec (Reichenberg), in northern Bohemia, and export it from Prague to places in and outside of Bohemia. In 1682, Hirshl Jonas Pohlin was the spokesman of the Jewish clothes merchants in negotiations with the Liberec manufacturers.[17]

Craft Guilds in Moravia

Jewish craft guilds also grew up in a number of Moravian towns during the seventeenth and eighteenth centuries. These guilds were established by the noblemen, proprietors of the towns, in order to supervise the relationships between the Christian and Jewish workmen and arbitrate their feuds. These Jewish guilds were not autonomous organizations like those in Bohemia, but rather organs of the lords and their policies.

Tailors' Guild in Uhersky Brod (Ungarisch Brod)

This Jewish guild, dating back to the 1630's according to some records, was probably the oldest in Moravia. Uhersky Brod was a lively commercial and industrial center. The town belonged to the

Counts von Kaunitz. The statutes of the guild were drawn up in German, but the word for "guild" used there was the Czech term, *cech,* spelled the German way as *Zech.* According to the by-laws, the elections of wardens were held yearly and not triennially, as in Prague. This practice may be attributed to the influence of immigrants from Poland where annual elections in Jewish guilds were customary. Another Polish feature was the requirement that besides the judges *(dayyanim)*, the rabbi witness the guild elections.

In Poland, the rabbi played an important role in guild affairs; in similar fashion, the rabbi of Uhersky Brod arbitrated disputes among guild members and heard the complaints of customers about defective work. At election time, a decision was taken concerning the guild's contribution to the lord of the town.

The Uhersky Brod guild established three categories of members: those born there; foreigners intending to become subjects of the lord of the town; foreigners who preferred to remain such. The admission fee was two gulden, three gulden, and three thaler respectively. All members, however, seem to have enjoyed the same rights as guild members. At least we find nothing indicating the contrary.

Non-resident tailors were barred from becoming partners of guild members. If an outsider appeared in Uhersky Brod and tried to win trade away from local tailors, the beadle of the synagogue went to warn him. If he persisted, the guild wardens might fine him as much as three thaler. Orders placed with one guild member by the lord of the town or the military authorities were shared by all, the reason being that such commissions were more profitable than the regular run of work. Just as Jewish masters were forbidden to seek Christian patronage, so were the Christian masters of Uhersky Brod forbidden to accept orders from Jews.

The rules concerning apprenticeship merit attention. The fee for training an apprentice was fixed at fifteen gulden. If an apprentice completed his training and sought employment as a journeyman with another master, his old master might keep him for at least half a year more, provided he matched whatever offer of wages was made to his former apprentice. Similarly, journeymen were required to go on working for a master even after their term had ended if the old master paid them the same wages offered by other masters.[18]

The Tailors' guild in Mikulov (Nikolsburg)

In Mikulov (Nikolsburg), in southern Moravia, a tailors' guild was already in existence in 1647. The original statutes are lost, but the statutes issued in 1697 by the lord of Mikulov, Prince Leopold Ignaz von Dietrichstein, are available. They fixed the number of masters, which was not to exceed eight, each with one journeyman and one apprentice. The Jewish masters were forbidden to open shops in the houses of Gentiles and to sell clothes to other than Jewish customers. An exception was made on fair days. Hawking ready-made clothes and entering Christian dwellings to sell them was also prohibited.

The Christian tailors' guild of Mikulov had to be furnished the names of the eight Jewish masters and their journeymen. Furthermore, Jewish tailors receiving commissions for making military uniforms had to share the work with their Christian confrères.[19] This placed the Jews in a position somewhat subordinate to the Christian guild.

Prince Dietrichstein regularly received a handsome sum from his Jewish tailors. To become a master, a Jewish tailor had to pay 150 gulden into the prince's treasury. An apprentice, advanced to the position of journeyman, paid 40 gulden. In addition, each of the eight masters made an annual payment of 11 gulden and 15 kreutzer for the right to work, and 5 gulden for his journeyman. If a master died, his widow might continue his business with the help of the journeyman employed in the shop. When she remarried, or died, the eldest of the eight journeymen became a master.

Masters and journeymen had to be natives of Mikulov. Journeymen did not work for wages, but on their own account. They contributed a certain amount daily to the dues paid by the master into Prince von Dietrichstein's treasury. This system seems to have been profitable to both master and journeyman. However, the journeyman was tied to his master; if he deserted him he was expelled from Mikulov forever.[20]

Masters and journeymen formed two distinct groups within the guild. They had their own seals; the master's seal showed a large pair of scissors, the journeyman's a smaller one, with the circumscription "Jewish masters" and "Jewish journeymen" in Hebrew.[21]

Tailors' Associations in Bucovice, Prostejovice, and Lipnik

After tireless negotiations with the respective feudal lords and the Christian guilds of Bucovice, Prostejovice, and Lipnik, in Moravia, the associations of Jewish tailors (*Judenschneider*) of those places succeeded in securing a recognized place for themselves. For the right to work, however, they paid a fee to the lords of the towns and to the Christian guilds. An agreement was concluded in 1775 between the Jewish tailors' association and the Christian guild of Bucovice. The Jews were allowed to sew uniforms for army officers but were barred from working for the urban population. An outside Jewish tailor, wishing to settle in Bucovice, paid three gulden to the Christian guild and three gulden to the Jewish tailors' association.

To take an apprentice, a Jewish master had to get the permission of the proprietor of the town and to contribute one gulden to the guild and to the association. The tailors' association was obliged to contribute to the guild on Corpus Christi Day. It is interesting to find the Jewish tailors complaining to the authorities, in 1782, that the payments which they made with so much effort were being "used for guild dinners and excessive drinking"; but this protest received no reply.[22]

The Jewish tailors' association of Prostejovice (Prossnitz), a town famous for the excellent clothes manufactured there, won the right, in 1677, to make garments for the peasant population throughout the district. It appears that townspeople, wishing garments made of superior foreign fabrics imported by Jewish dealers, ordered them from Jewish tailors. But, as a rule, the Prostejovice Jewish tailors were forbidden to work for Christian townspeople.[23]

The town of Lipnik, like Mikulov and Prostejovice, was owned by the Dietrichstein family. Prince Ferdinand Dietrichstein's charter to the Lipnik community (1656) granted the right to sell ready-made garments to Christians, townspeople and peasants alike, at the fairs of the three Dietrichstein towns of Lipnik, Weisskirchen, and Drahotice. This favor had to be paid for by an additional thaler over and above the seven thaler which the tailors contributed to the treasury of the lord for the right to work. Dietrichstein justified his concession to the Jews by pointing out that it was in line with the "practice throughout the whole country."[24]

The Jewish Master

Official recognition of the Jewish master came only in 1753. In an ordinance concerning Moravian Jewish artisans and trades, issued on February 10, 1753, Empress Maria Theresa stipulated, among other things, that Jewish artisans must undergo an examination for the title of master.[25] The Empress was anxious to prevent a decline in the quality of workmanship.The examination was to take place in the presence of several Christian masters and the warden of the Jewish guild. The Jewish candidate was required to show a piece of work which was neither too heavy nor too costly, so that it could be sold thereafter without too much difficulty. The new master received a certificate, for which he paid no fee, and permission from the town council to practice his trade, likewise without fee. He was allowed to employ journeymen and apprentices. This last-mentioned privilege, however, was no innovation, for we have seen that Jewish artisans employed journeymen and apprentices long before 1753. The ordinance contained nothing to enlarge the sphere of activities open to the Jewish craftsman. Officially he was still limited to Jewish patronage.

Conclusion

Looking back over the three hundred years' struggle of the Bohemian and Moravian Jews for the right to practice crafts, we must recognize that no one ordinance or charter was decisive, but rather the economic reality. The urban, as well as the peasant population, needed goods, especially goods sold more cheaply than the guild products. This provided an entering wedge for the Jewish craftsman. If they had been compelled to work for Jewish patrons only, many of them would have had to give up their trade.

CHAPTER XVIII

Jewish Trades in Western Europe in the Early Modern Period

Turning from eastern to western Europe, one finds there few Jewish artisans in the early modern period. Farming and crafts, as in the Middle Ages, were barred to Jews. "The guilds were closed to the Jews; they were kept back by the crucifix which hung in each guild-hall, and round which members assembled. Accordingly, if they wished to engage in any industry or trade monopolized by a guild, they were forced to do so as outsiders, interlopers of free trades." This is the judgment of Werner Sombart, the famous historian of capitalism.[1]

Holland: Diamond Cutting, Tobacco Dressing, Printing, Silk Work

Such was the case even in Holland where Sephardic Jews fleeing the Inquisition in Spain and Portugal found asylum at the beginning of the seventeenth century. Later, Ashkenazic Jews from Germany and Poland came to Holland and were also hospitably received.* Both Jewish groups enjoyed religious liberty and freedom of movement in the tolerant country. The Dutch guilds, however, stubbornly refused to admit Jews. This meant

* Sephardic means "from Spain" and Ashkenazic means "from Germany." Spain and Germany stand for a variety of Mediterranean, and northern and eastern European countries, respectively.

the exclusion of Jewish artisans from most of the trades. Jews were able to ply only those crafts which were not organized in guilds, or where the guilds were less stringent. Dutch Jews were engaged chiefly in commerce, banking, some industries, and petty trade.

Amsterdam was the chief center of Dutch Jewry and of the Dutch Jewish crafts. In 1674, 2,500 Sephardic and 5,000 Ashkenazic Jews lived there, in a total population of 180,000. In 1796, the number of the Sephardim was about the same, whereas the number of Ashkenazim had risen to 20,749 (the total population of the city being 200,560 in that year).

Diamond cutting and polishing was the most important craft exercised by the Jews in Holland. This skill had been introduced into Amsterdam by Flemish artisans from Antwerp in the course of the struggle of the Low Countries against Spanish rule in the second half of the sixteenth century. Between 1610 and 1615, Sephardic Jews, refugees from Spain and Portugal, took up diamond polishing, one of them, Solomon France, having been apprenticed to a Christian master; subsequently it became a specifically Jewish trade and developed steadily as such through the eighteenth and nineteenth centuries. This was essentially a home industry, with wives working at turning the grindstones. Later, workshops were established. Sephardic and Ashkenazic masters were at first employed by wealthy Sephardic diamond dealers; later, Ashkenazic Jews also became diamond merchants. The term of apprenticeship for diamond polishers was from fifteen months to four and a half years. Some masters received from 60 to 250 guilders for training apprentices.

Though apparently some diamond cutters were economically fairly well off, the majority worked under strained conditions. Among the latter was the famous philosopher, Baruch Spinoza, who eked out a living grinding lenses. In 1750, as many as 600 Jewish families were engaged in the diamond-cutting trade. A decrease in the supply of rough diamonds which began to be felt about then led to unemployment, particularly among the Christian diamond cutters, who were not inclined to accept the lower wages with which the Jewish cutters contented themselves. As a result, the Christian cutters, in 1748, began a campaign against the Jews. They requested permission from the Amsterdam municipal council to establish a diamond cutters' guild; Jews already engaged in the trade would be compelled to undergo an examination, after which they were to contribute to the guild without enjoying the benefits of membership; no new Jewish masters or apprentices would be permitted; and Jews would be forbidden to work on Sundays. In a memorandum to the council, the Christian cutters declared that they could not, like their Jewish competitors, be satisfied with a low living standard nor would they complement their earnings, as the Jews did, by cleaning shoes and selling combs, spectacles, and old clothes. Hence, they said, the very presence of the Jewish cutters undermined their existence. However, the municipal council rejected the petition.

Tobacco dressing was another trade of the Jews of Amsterdam and other Dutch cities. Of a total of twenty-four Jewish persons married in Amsterdam in 1649-1653, fourteen were tobacco dressers. A notary's entry of 1656 mentions Ashkenazic dressers in a tobacco workshop in Vlooyenburg, a part of the Jewish quarter. Ashkenazic Jews were in the majority in the tobacco-dressing trade, and continued so into the nineteenth century.

In the seventeenth and eighteenth centuries, Amsterdam was famous for the Hebrew books which were printed there. Manasseh ben Israel, the renowned rabbi, scholar and communal leader, was a pioneer in the trade, and set up a printing shop in 1626. From that date until 1732, there were 318 Jewish printers in Amsterdam, some of whom printed books in languages other than Hebrew or Yiddish. We know that Manasseh ben Israel employed Jewish as well as Christian printers and illustrators. Salom Italia, a Jewish engraver, and Rembrandt did some work for him. David de Castro Tartas, who later acquired his own press, learned the trade in Manasseh's printing shop. Emanuel Benveniste, who operated a press in 1641-1659, hired Christian and Jewish "master-printers" and printers' apprentices. Christian and Jewish bookbinders were also employed by Jewish press owners. The number of Jewish workers increased, after 1650, with the influx of refugees from Poland, among whom were typesetters, proofreaders, and bookbinders. Christian press owners also hired them. Some of the refugees became owners of presses as, for instance, Joseph Proops of Poznan.

Amsterdam had both a printers' guild and a booksellers' guild. Manasseh ben Israel was refused membership in the printers' guild in 1648, but later a number of Jewish printers were admitted.

A group of Sephardic settlers in Amsterdam received permission to establish workshops for producing silk. The City Council provided them with rent-free space in municipal buildings for a period of five years, on condition that they would train apprentices in the trade. We know of a Christian, Hans Petersz de Jonghe, who was apprenticed to a Jewish silk master, Isaac Buenes, in 1610, for a term of six years.

The Jewish silk trade, however, came to an end in the early 1650's, when the Amsterdam silk workers set up a guild barring the admission of Jews.

The brothers Abraham and Isaac Pereira, "Portuguese merchants of the Jewish nation," received the right, in 1655, to open a sugar refinery in Amsterdam. In their petition, they pointed out that such activity was not forbidden to Jews. Jewish and Christian workers were engaged. Similar enterprises were established in later years.

Amsterdam Jewry, numbering 23,000 toward the close of the eighteenth century, was probably the largest in the world, surpassing the large urban Jewish communities of eastern Europe. Various artisans, in addition to those described above, catered to the needs of this Jewish population. Among them were watchmakers, engravers, portrait painters (among the Sephardim), saddle makers, tailors (officially termed "repairers of old clothes"), cobblers, bakers, and brewers. Jews were also in the medical, legal and pharmaceutical professions, though the professional guilds often put obstacles in their path.

In the provincial towns, even more than in Amsterdam, the guilds were on the watch to keep Jews out of the trades, professions and commerce. It should be borne in mind that not only craftsmen but also grocers, hardware dealers, clothing merchants and others were organized in guilds. Some guilds combined crafts and mercantile activities, as, for instance, the goldsmiths' and silversmiths' guild in Haarlem, whose members bought and sold gold and silver. Beginning in 1664, the membership sought to prevent Jews and other non-guild members from trading in these metals. But, early in the eighteenth century, Israel Isaacs and his son Miguel Israel were admitted to the guild as *meesters*. In the town of Zwolle, the Jews had to persevere for many years before they were admitted into the furriers', shoemakers', tanners', and other guilds.[2]

The Dutch Christian guilds continued to harass and obstruct Jewish artisans until 1796, when, under the influence of the French Revolution, the Jews of Holland obtained civil rights.

England

When Jews were readmitted to England in the 1650's, the economy they evolved partially resembled that of the Jews of Holland. The Sephardic Jews of England were, for the most part, merchants, brokers, and manufacturers. However, there were also Sephardic engravers; in the 1730's, a silversmith, Abraham Lopez de Oliveira, was making ceremonial objects for synagogues. The Ashkenazic Jews, except for a small group of prosperous business people, were small shopkeepers, peddlers, itinerant fruit vendors, fishmongers, and domestic servants in the households of the Sephardim. There were only few artisans. London, had, from the latter part of the seventeenth century on, Jewish tailors, butchers, gold and silversmiths, diamond polishers, watchmakers, sugar bakers, cravat washers, tallow chandlers and a "penny barber opposite the synagogue."[3] They were too few to arouse the opposition of the London guilds.

France

On the eve of the Revolution of 1789, there were 19,624 Jews in France living chiefly in Alsace, which had become a part of France some hundred-odd years earlier. A little more than 400 families of Sephardic Jews lived in Bordeaux and its environs, and smaller Jewish groups were in Nîmes and in the formerly papal territories of Avignon and Venaissin, in the south of France. The Alsatian Jews were petty traders, cattle dealers, and moneylenders. Jewish artisans worked exclusively for their fellow Jews. Efforts to obtain Christian patrons were frustrated by the guilds. The Sephardim of Bordeaux were engaged in commerce and industry. Some of them had large undertakings in the French colonies of the West Indies. In the city of Nîmes, Jewish cap makers met with the resistance of the local guilds which prohibited the employment of Jewish journeymen by Christian masters.[4] The guilds were backed by the authorities until the revolution put an end to discrimination.

Germany

More information is available on Jewish trades in the many German principalities of the eighteenth century. In Prussia, the largest German state, the guilds had the backing of the government for their policy of rigidly barring Jews from any trade protected by an established guild. King Frederick II, in his charter for the Prussian Jews, dated April 17, 1750, decreed "that in the future no Jew shall presume to engage in any manual trade, nor venture upon any except seal-engraving, painting (art), the grinding of optical glasses, diamond and gem cutting, gold and silver embroidery, fine cloth needle work, the collecting of gold by a sieving process, and other similar trades in which vocational associations and privileged guilds are not found."

The charter laid down no new regulations, merely making official the position of Jews in the crafts as it had evolved since their re-admission to the country in 1673. We possess records of such Jewish craft activities in Berlin, Koenigsberg (where Polish and Lithuanian Jews skilled in braid trimming, lace making, dyeing of sable furs, and quality tailoring were permitted to work), Frankfurt on the Oder (where button making was a prominent Jewish trade), Halberstadt (gold and silver refining), Oschersleben (hair-sieve making), Zuelz in Silesia, and Hildesheim. Embroidery was one of the outstanding manual trades among Jews; the municipality of Duisburg asked the government to permit a Jewish embroiderer from Bohemia to settle there and cater to the students of the university. Similar efforts were made on behalf of embroiderers in the university city of Jena, in Saxe-Weimar, though the members of the Jena faculty were divided as to whether Jewish embroiderers should be admitted. In Silesia, annexed by Prussia in 1744, Jewish goldsmiths and braziers continued to work at their occupations. In the duchy of Cleve, on the western border of Prussia, Jews did glazing, since this trade had no guild. Similarly, the successful eighteenth-century parchment maker, Marcus

Frank (1731) of Hildburghausen in the duchy of Saxe-Meiningen, had no guild of Christian parchment makers to oppose him.[5]

In the South German region of Franconia, with its fractured sovereignties, the Jewish community of Fuerth occupied a prominent place. From a tiny community in the first half of the sixteenth century, Fuerth's Jewry grew to the relatively imposing number of 2,600 by the end of the eighteenth century. Their success in commerce and banking was made possible by the liberal attitude of the municipal authorities and the Margraves of Ansbach and Bayreuth, who were the rulers of the city. Nevertheless, the Fuerth craft guilds excluded Jews from the trades. The Jewish tailors, embroiderers, bookbinders, barbers, bakers, butchers, and other craftsmen were forbidden to have Christian patronage. They worked exclusively for a Jewish clientele.[6]

The cantor of the Fuerth synagogue, Elkan Naumburg, was a skilled embroiderer of Torah curtains; two of these, still extant, bear the dates 1714 and 1723. Though embroidering was only an avocation for him, Elkan's artistry is rated highly. Elkan got commissions from outside Fuerth—from Kriegshaber, near Augsburg in Bavaria, from Amsterdam, and even from the Hambro synagogue in London. Jacob Koppel Gans, another embroiderer of ark curtains, worked in Hoechstadt in what was later Bavaria. One of Gans' curtains is in the possession of the Jewish Museum of New York. A third south German Jewish artist, Gerson Mayer, was credited with making, in 1738-1739 the embroidered covering for the tomb of Emperor Henry and Empress Kunigunde in the cathedral of Bamberg.[7] A Bohemian Jew in early eighteenth century Fulda, skilled in embroidering with gold, made "missal robes and other Roman Catholic vestments."[8]

Eliezer Sussman of Brody, in Galicia, decorated in the 1730's a number of small synagogues in Franconia, in Bechhofen, Kirchheim, Horb and Unterlimburg, with wall paintings in the folk art style of synagogues in Poland.[9]

In November 1768, the municipal council of Erfurt, where Jews were forbidden to settle, considered the petition of a certain Nathan, *Schutzjude* of the city of Bamberg, who sought permission for temporary residence in order to ply his trade of dyeing cloth. The man pointed out that he was "not a Jew who buys or sells merchandise whereby injury can be done to the country or city."

He went on: "I am on the contrary an artist skilled in various kinds of dyeing, particularly of silk, and am able with little effort and at small cost to dye garments in half an hour so that they look like new. I am also in a position to teach people these skills, which are hardly known in Germany, in a short time." The council agreed to admit him. He was to pay four gulden a week, plus the regular *Leibzoll* for entering and leaving the city.[10]

Engraving

Engraving was one of the specifically Jewish crafts to which the guilds made no objection. Jewish engravers were active in the eighteenth century in western and central Europe and farther east. They practiced their craft at fairs and markets, and had patrons among the upper classes of Jewish and non-Jewish society, and notably at the princely courts. Court patronage was owed to a considerable degree to the influence of the court Jews, who served the German princes as financial agents, purveyors to their armies, and mintmasters. Some of the engravers were sons or relatives of court Jews. Thus, the well-known seal and medal engraver Jacob Abraham (1723-1800), was the son of the court Jew of the Duke of Mecklenburg-Strelitz. The seal engraver Philipp was the brother of the court agent, Nathan of Mecklenburg-Schwerin.

German Jewish engravers carried their skills abroad. Aron Isaac seal engraver from Brandenburg, who migrated in 1774 to Stockholm, was a pioneer in the establishment of the modern Jewish community of Sweden. At first, he was denied admittance unless he renounced his faith. This Isaac refused to do, but eventually he was permitted to settle in Stockholm with his family. Other Jewish engravers worked in Denmark and Italy. The engraver Solomon Bennet from Polotzk, White Russia, was active in Berlin and London. He engraved portraits after contemporary paintings. Father and son Judah and Solomon Pinehas were court painters at Bayreuth and Dresden, respectively. They specialized in miniature portrait painting.[11] But these activities belong rather to the history of art.

Austrian and Prussian Policies

The Edict of Tolerance promulgated by Emperor Joseph II on January 2, 1782, for the Jews of the Austrian possessions, was the first step toward the abolition of the medieval restrictions imposed upon the Jews of the capital city of Vienna. They were permitted, from then on, to learn all kinds of crafts or trades from Christian masters in Vienna as well as elsewhere and, to this end, to apprentice themselves to Christian masters or to work as their journeymen.[12] However, it was pointed out, the Emperor did not wish to exercise any compulsion on Christians and Jews and hoped they would come to an understanding among themselves. In fact, very few Christian masters were ready to accept Jewish apprentices.

Thirty-two years earlier, Frederick II of Prussia, another enlightened, if absolute, monarch had endorsed the restrictive medieval policies of the guilds with respect to the Jewish artisans in Prussia. These restrictive policies remained in force in other German principalities until the nineteenth century, when the way was opened for western European Jewry to engage freely in arts and crafts.

This new freedom was one of the results of the French Revolution of 1789 which caused the guilds to disappear, along with other medieval institutions, privileges, and distinctions.

CHAPTER XIX

Jewish Artisans in Poland and Lithuania: 1350-1648

In 1386, Poland and Lithuania were united by the marriage of the Polish Princess Jadwiga to the Lithuanian Grand Duke Jagiello. It was a major historical event, for it saved both countries from conquest by the powerful Teutonic Order.

The battle of Tannenberg, or Grunwald, on July 15, 1410, in which the knights were defeated by the Polish-Lithuanian armies, changed the political balance against the Order. Its *Drang nach Osten* was now checked. The menace hanging over Poland-Lithuania and the neighboring Slavonic principalities was eliminated. Poles and Lithuanians could now develop their own states and their economic and cultural life in peace. The knights waged war once again in 1454-1466, but were again beaten and compelled to cede to Poland an outlet to the Baltic. The independent history of the Teutonic knights came to an end and the Slavonic and Lithuanian peoples of Eastern Europe were able to breathe freely.

Origin of the Jewish Center in Poland-Lithuania

The few Jews of Poland and Lithuania in 1410 rejoiced at the news of the defeat of the Teutonic knights. From the twelfth century on they had fled from persecution and massacre in the Germanic lands and it was clear that a victory of the knights would have spelled death, destruction and further flight for them. A united Poland and Lithuania was emerging as a great power between the Baltic and the Black Seas. Its rulers wanted the barren lands to be settled and permitted hosts of foreigners to immigrate. Jews established themselves within the Polish-Lithuanian territory in ever-growing numbers. In time the new Jewish center rivaled the Jewries of the Sassanian Empire of late antiquity, the Baghdad caliphate of the early Middle Ages, and Spain of the late Middle Ages.

Beginning of the Jewish Migration to Poland and Lithuania

In the early Middle Ages, Jews migrating from the Near East to Europe by-passed the area later known as Poland-Lithuania. Their goals were Italy, Spain, France, Germany, and England, the centers of western civilization and of advanced economy. As a result of this westward drive, which ended in the second half of the eleventh century, numerous Jewish communities were established along the trade routes from the Near East to western Europe. Thanks to their connections with fellow Jews in the Near East, Jewish merchants carried on an international trade along these routes.

However, the Crusades put an end to this. The Crusades were as much an economic as a religious enterprise. One of their chief aims was to bring Christian Europe into closer contact with the markets of the Near East. This aim, as we know, was achieved. As a result, Jews were ousted from their crucial role in international trade and were forced into petty local trade and into moneylending. Such was the case in England, France, and Germany.

The Crusades also revealed how insecure the Jewish situation was in western and central Europe. They ushered in an era of persecutions and expulsions, accompanied by confiscation of property, forced cancellation of debts owed to Jewish creditors, religious outbreaks, and accusations of Jewish crimes against the Church. Life became unbearable for the Jews of western Europe, and they began to leave their homes for the underpopulated and economically underdeveloped regions of eastern Europe. Thus, for a period of four centuries—1100-1500—Jews migrated from their homes along the Seine, Rhine, Main, and Danube to new abodes along the Vistula, Nieman, Bug and Dniester.

At the same time, or even a little earlier, a trickle of Jewish immigrants reached Poland-Lithuania from southeastern Europe and the nearby Asiatic areas. Descendants of the Khazar converts to Judaism figured among these latter immigrants. However, the immigrants from central and western Europe far outnumbered those from the East. By the end of the fourteenth century, Jewish communities were found in a west-east chain of cities crossing the Polish-Lithuanian state: Poznan, Kalish, Cracow, Przemysl, Lwow (Lemberg), Lutzk, Brest-Litovsk, Grodno, and Troki, to name only the most important cities. In 1500, the number of communities had reached sixty, clear evidence of the sustained character of the immigration.

The Political Status of the Newcomers

Parallel with this stream of Jewish immigrants, Gentile Germans in even larger numbers streamed into Poland and Lithuania to colonize the rural areas and to settle in the towns as merchants and artisans. The Polish principalities were especially in need of colonists after the Mongol invasion of 1237-1240 had laid waste to large areas; whole towns and hamlets were destroyed, and commerce and handicrafts disrupted. Boleslav the Pious, Prince of the Duchy of Great Poland (1247-1279), promised the Germans special privileges in return for their coming to colonize the country. Under the Magdeburg Law, urban settlers received the privilege of self-government; it authorized the German burghers of the Polish, and later also the Lithuanian, cities to organize their own municipal councils and guilds. From the beginning, Jews were excluded from these bodies and treated with hostility by them. The German settlers brought to Poland attitudes and policies which made conditions very difficult for Jewish traders and artisans. The German burghers would have eliminated the Jews from the economic life of Poland altogether had it not been for the rights and privileges also granted the latter group by the Polish rulers.

In 1264, Prince Boleslaw, after deliberating with his highest officers and the representatives of the estates, bestowed a charter on the Jews "who had established themselves over the length and breadth of our country." This charter defined their status, rights, duties, and economic activities. The charter guaranteed the Jews freedom of religion, freedom of movement, freedom of economic activity, personal security, and the right of communal self-government. Because his country needed financial resources for its development, Boleslav encouraged moneylending by the Jews. The Boleslaw charter, patterned upon similar charters issued by the Austrian Duke Frederick the Warlike (1244), and Ottokar II, King of Bohemia-Moravia (1258), has been called the *Magna Carta* of Polish Jewry. In 1344 and on later occasions, King Casimir III, called the Great (1333-1370), issued three additional charters to the Jews which, together with the statute of Boleslaw, were successively confirmed by the Polish kings as their "general privileges." These privileges formed, as it were, the constitution of the Jews of Poland; they were the counterpart to the German settlers' Magdeburg Law.

Developments in Lithuania

The founder of the powerful medieval Lithuanian state, the pagan Grand Duke Gedymin (1316-1341), displayed a tolerance rare in that era of European history. He called upon foreign merchants and artisans to come and settle in the country, pledging full freedom of religion. "The Russians," he once declared, "may pray according to their usage, the Poles according to theirs, and we Lithuanians shall worship according to our custom. Have we not all one God?"

Lithuania remained a pagan country until the end of the fourteenth century, when Catholicism was adopted. But fanaticism, such as was found in Spain, was resisted for a long time, and the Tartar, Russian, Jewish and other settlers were not discriminated against. In this climate of tolerance, the Jews were able, over the centuries, to develop a great economic and cultural center. In the fourteenth century, and even earlier, Jews came into Lithuania by three routes: from the west, through Poland, to the region around Grodno; from the west and southwest, through Poland, to Volhynia, then belonging to Lithuania; and from the southeast to Troki and localities as far north as the shores of the Baltic Sea.

Lithuania, was even more of an agricultural country than Poland. Its people lived by farming, cattle raising, horticulture, apiculture, fishing, and logging. Trades and commerce were in their infancy. The towns were scarcely more than large villages, most of the people living dispersed about the countryside, in lonely huts in the forests, or near rivers and lakes. The Jewish and other immigrants developed internal and external trade and handicrafts.[1]

The French diplomat and traveler, Gilbert de Lannoy, who visited Troki in 1414, at the time an important city, noted that there were "Germans, Lithuanians, Russians and a great number of Jews" among the residents, "and that they spoke their own languages."

Grand Duke Vitovt, to whom his half-brother Jagiello (1386-1430) had handed over the actual rule, granted charters to the Jews of Troki, Brest-Litovsk (both in 1388), and Grodno (1389). The first two charters are very similar to the charter of the Jews in Poland. They show that the Jews of Troki and Brest-Litovsk were chiefly engaged in commerce and moneylending. The Grodno charter paints a somewhat different picture.

The Grodno charter makes no mention of moneylending. Jews were free to farm the land they possessed or might acquire. Merchants were entitled to dispose of their merchandise at the Grodno fairs, in their shops, or in the streets. Artisans could ply their trades without restriction. This article of the charter is particularly important. It is the earliest reference to Jewish craftsmanship in eastern Europe, and it was frequently invoked by Jewish artisans in their struggle with Christian guilds for their right to practice crafts. The Grodno charter also authorized Jews to buy cattle, and to slaughter and sell meat "at the fairs, in streets and in their shops" in any quantity.[2]

Jewish Artisanship in Fifteenth-century Poland

With the growth of the Jewish population in Poland in the fifteenth century and increasing competition from non-Jewish merchants and moneylenders, Jews began to take to the crafts. In

Lwow (Lemberg), an important seat of commerce and industry, there were twenty-five craft guilds which admitted only Catholics. Armenians and Jews were barred from membership and restricted in the practice of crafts. Jewish butchers and tailors, catering to their co-religionists, had existed in Lwow since the establishment of the Jewish community in the thirteenth century. Now they began to acquire non-Jewish patronage. There were also tanners, weavers, and glaziers among the Jews.

In Cracow, the Jewish community concluded an agreement with the Christian merchants in 1485 providing that "Jews and Jewesses are permitted daily to sell garments and collars made by them." These articles of wearing apparel were not made to order for individuals but were manufactured for sale on the market, as the word "daily" would imply. The tailors and furriers engaged in this work were called "paupers," or the poor. They did not own their materials and tools; these were supplied by the entrepreneurs for whom they worked. We have a very early instance here of the putting-out system (*Verlagssystem*).

In this period in Cracow, we find among Jews a carpenter, distillers of alcoholic beverages, and butchers who had an agreement with the Christian butchers' guild (1494). It is interesting to note that the board of elders of the Jewish community which consisted of merchants and bankers, also included an artisan (1465). In Warsaw, then the capital of the Duchy of Mazovia, there were Jewish furriers and cord makers. They lived in the suburb called Blonie, being barred by the guilds from carrying on trade in the city. They worked chiefly for non-Jewish patrons, the Jewish population of Warsaw being insignificant.[3]

The Jews in Poland-Lithuania: Some Figures

By 1500 the Jewish communities numbered about 60; by 1570 there were over 160. I. Schipper estimates that there were 100,000 Jews in Poland, including Lithuania, in 1578.[4] Anti-Jewish pamphlets of the early seventeenth century spoke of over half a million. However, modern historians believe that the figure of 300,000 would be more correct. Even if this figure appears somewhat too high, Poland-Lithuania had the largest Jewish population of any country in that period, except perhaps Turkey.

As the Jewish population grew and the municipalities refused permits for the renting of new houses, Jews began to settle in the economically less developed east and southeast provinces—in Volhynia, Podolia, and the Ukraine.

Expansion of Jewish Crafts, 1500-1648

The eastward drive had other causes. The Polish nobility and a rising Christian middle class began to push Jewish merchants out of the commerce in grain and other commodities. The leasing of customs, tolls, and domains in which Jews had been engaged was forbidden by the Crown upon a resolution of the Polish Diet of 1505. This meant loss of employment for a whole group of managers, cashiers, and clerks. This shift in the economic structure of Poland compelled the Jews to look for new outlets: in new places and in new jobs. Crafts offered opportunities; both the usual peasant crafts, and others requiring more special skills and a degree of industrial organization. We now find Jewish shoemakers, saddlers, harness makers, soap makers, and tallow chandlers, sword and gun makers, workers in brass and iron, locksmiths, watchmakers, joiners and carpenters, embroiderers in gold braid and beads, button and glove manufacturers, and bookbinders.[5]

Jewish Artisans and the Guilds

The relationships of the guilds with the Jewish artisans took various forms. The chief grievance of the guilds was that non-organized labor did not share their financial burdens. However, there was no question of admitting non-Catholics into the guilds. This large group included Armenians, Tartars, Greek Orthodox, Jews, and others. This is not the place to discuss the treatment of the various religious and ethnic units by the guilds. Arrangements and mutual concessions were made, but the Jews no doubt had to fight harder than other groups for their right to work.

In Lutzk (Luck) in the sixteenth century we find Jewish tailors and furriers selling coats and furs to peasants at the town's fairs and in the neighboring places of Klevan, Olyka, and Torchyn, in exchange for their cattle. The Lutzk Christian guilds of tailors and furriers protested to the authorities against the encroachment on their rights. The case was brought before the royal court in Cracow and King Sigismund I, in a decision of August 4, 1539, conceded to the guilds the right to require dues from the unaffiliated artisans (five kop of groszy per year to be paid each guild). By the same token the king confirmed the right of the Jewish tailors and furriers to ply their trades and to sell their wares to peasants for cattle.

In Grodno the Christian guild complained to the local authorities in 1704 that the Jewish artisans refused to pay them dues. The Jews pointed out that the royal privileges of Sigismund III of 1629, Wladislaw IV of 1633, and Jan Kasimir of 1649, granted them the right to carry on trades freely. The *starosta* (Lithuanian term for Governor) offered to appeal to the king on behalf of the litigants. In order to save expenses, both parties agreed to compromise (1706).

The Jewish tailors, furriers and cap makers from then on were permitted to work and sell their goods in shops and on the market unmolested, nor was their right to hire Christian journeymen and train Christian apprentices to be contested. The Christian guild was to promote the trainees of the Jewish artisans to journeymen and masters, which implies that the guild recognized the training by Jewish masters as adequate. In return, the Jews were to contribute six zloty and two pounds of gunpowder to the guild on Corpus Christi Day. The vexing obligations of providing candles for the guild's altar, of rallying under the guild's standards on festivals, and attending funerals of guild members were waived. Furthermore, the Jews were exempted from the jurisdiction of the guild's court, except in cases where damage was caused to goods belonging to Christian masters. At the trials of such cases, elders of the Jewish tailors were to be present.[6]

The developments in Lutzk and Grodno were not typical, however. In other large cities—Poznan, Przemysl, Lwow, Lublin, Brest-Litovsk, Minsk, and Vilna—there were endless frictions between the guilds (which were supported by the municipal councils) and the Jewish workers. The Jewish community councils, the Kahals, supported their artisans by petitioning to the kings and invoking their solemn pledges. Onslaughts by the guilds, which included harassment of every kind up to confiscation and destruction of Jewish wares as well as physical attacks, were no exception.[7] That Jewish artisanship, nevertheless, survived was due to several factors which will be indicated here briefly.

The guilds were anxious to control the crafts and to uphold their monopolistic prices. However, there were vast areas in the country where the guilds' jurisdiction was limited or non-existent. In the towns privately owned by the nobility, such as Berdichev, Brody, Bialystok, Czortkow, and many others, the lord of the town was the ruler. In the royal cities, too, there were the estates of the nobles and the clergy which were not subject to the jurisdiction of the municipal councils, the supporters of the guilds. In fact, neither the population at large, the peasantry, nor the nobility was willing to pay the high prices imposed by the guilds. It must be added that contrary to the propaganda spread by the guilds about the inferiority of Jewish workmanship, there must have been among the Jewish artisans some excellent workers who possessed not only the technical skills but possibly also the latest models from abroad to attract a more discriminating clientele. We hear of the Jewish lace makers in Cracow who worked for the nobles and the monastic orders. Prince Lubomirski, the *voyevoda* (wojewoda, the Polish term for Governor) of Cracow, employed the lace maker Abraham for a number of years. Pinkas Zislovich, a jeweler, worked for the court of Prince Chetvertynski. In Przemysl Jewish tailors were patronized by Polish noblewomen and the clergy.[8]

The First Jewish Guilds in Poland

Jewish guilds originated in the first half of the seventeenth century in Cracow, Lwow, and Przemysl. The statutes of the guild of the furriers in Cracow of 1613, published in the original Hebrew, show that these furriers were dealers rather than workers in furs. The next in date are the statutes of the barbers' guild in Cracow of 1639.

The Statutes of the Cracow Jewish Barbers' Guild

Seven barbers, one of whom was also the community's physician for the needy, gathered in Cracow on December 18, 1639 to draw up guild statutes for the regulation of working conditions and relations with fellow artisans and apprentices.

Membership. "Brotherliness and friendship among themselves" was adopted as the guiding principle of the guild. The founders agreed that a new member might be admitted only with the consent of all. This applied not only to barbers from the outside coming to settle in Cracow, but also to resident barbers absent temporarily from the city at the time of the establishment of the guild. As to non-members, even if competent masters, the guild decided "to employ every possible means to prevent them from doing their work." Sons-in-law of members could become members.

Regulation of Work. If a patron, dissatisfied with a barber's work, engaged another barber, the second barber might not begin to work before the first had been paid. If a patient called two barber-surgeons simultaneously, they shared the fee and all expenses equally as long as the wound was open. But if one came first and closed the wound, the second was obliged to "turn around and depart at once."

Fees. The barbers, "having bound together not to raise prices and thus impose a burden upon the people of our community, will accept the fees that people have been accustomed of old to pay for bloodletting, cupping, haircutting, and the healing of bruises and wounds."

Apprenticeship. A master barber may have only one apprentice at a time; apprenticeship was for three years, which was considered to be the minimum term for learning the trade. In the first two years, an apprentice was under no circumstances permitted to bleed a patient. In the third year, he might do so only when the master was "at his side." A master, with the consent of the other guild members, might take a second apprentice, but the second apprentice was to have the status of a partner and to receive a third of the fees. Apprentices, both those who were being trained in the trade and those working as partners, were forbidden "to marry a local girl in order not to cast additional burdens on the people of the community," a rather unusual provision.

Fines. Violations of guild by-laws were punishable by fines, the money to be given to charity. Officers and judges of the community—not the guild—imposed the fines.[9]

The statutes of the barbers' guild concluded on a cheerful note by stating that "during the three festivals they [the members] will have a good time, enjoy themselves to the full, and be glad and merry of heart."[10] Not a word about the apprentice here, however.

The Cracow barbers' statutes of 1639 were an early product of Jewish guild organization. Compared with the guild statutes of later periods, they lack essential provisions concerning the economic, social, religious, cultural, and welfare aspects of guild life.

Concluding Remarks

After 1650 the spread of handicrafts among the Jews of eastern Europe gained momentum. It is estimated that at the end of the eighteenth century, at least a third of the Jewish population was engaged in manual work. The organization of guilds likewise advanced. They must have numbered in the hundreds. Cities like Cracow, Lwow, Brody, Lublin, Poznan, Leszno (Lissa), Vilna, and many others possessed several Jewish guilds each, and in some cases, more than ten. The history of these guilds, their structure, their policies, their relations with non-Jewish guilds, and their place in the larger Jewish community, will be treated in more detail in the concluding chapters.

CHAPTER XX

The Spread of Jewish Handicrafts in Poland-Lithuania After 1648

In the period of 1500-1648 Poland-Lithuania, stretching from the shores of the Baltic Sea to the Ukrainian steppes, reached the zenith of its political and military power. It was a period of economic prosperity based on the rich agricultural output of the country. The Baltic ports assumed importance in the exportation of Polish grain, timber and potash. In 1648, 300,000 tons of grain passed through Gdansk (Danzig) for shipment abroad—the highest annual export figure of that commodity ever reached in the history of the kingdom of Poland-Lithuania.

Foreign trade, moreover, fanned out in other directions: first, through the city of Lwow, along the so-called Tartar route in a southern direction to the Ottoman Empire; second, westward to Germany and the Netherlands, and, third, eastward to the Muscovite Czardom. Of the Polish fairs of that time, Lublin's stood out as the famous meeting place of merchants coming from different countries. Arts and crafts flourished in the cities and smaller urban places. The guilds' production attained the peak of efficiency. Literature and the sciences received fresh impulses from the European movement of the Renaissance.

The Jewish community, which had grown from a comparatively small number at the close of the Middle Ages to approximately 300,000 souls in the first half of the seventeenth century, benefited by the upward political and economic trend. The Jewish merchant class and the various artisans' groups maintained their positions despite the jealousy and the aggressive policies of the non-Jewish merchants and craftsmen. This was due to a number of factors: the protection of the Crown; the favorable attitude of the nobility, eager to attract Jewish traders (especially for the export of grain) and artisans into the towns and villages that were owned by them; and the inner cohesion and solidarity of the Jews who defended their rights to engage in commerce and the crafts.

The Jewish community councils (*Kahals*) and the central council (*Vaad*) of the four constituent parts of the Kingdom of Poland remained alert to prevent the curtailment of these rights and interceded to that end with the Crown, the members of the Diet (*Sejm*), and the central and local organs of the administration.[1] The councils frequently acted as the spokesmen of the Jewish merchants and handicraftsmen in their conflicts with the Christians.

The Jewish councils were also concerned with the setting up of communal welfare agencies and educational institutions. The talmudic academies (*yeshivot*) became widely known within and beyond the borders of Poland. In 1638, Simone Luzzatto of Venice, a keen observer of Jewish life, described with satisfaction the peaceful development of Polish Jewry, its achievements in the field of learning, and its communal self-government. Several decades earlier, Rabbi Moses Isserles of Cracow (1520-1572) wrote to a colleague who had left Poland to accept a rabbinical position in Germany that he thought it was better to subsist modestly on dry bread in Poland and to enjoy the serene life there than to seek one's fortune in other countries where the hatred of the Jews was more prevalent.[2]

Historians have called the years 1500-1648 the "golden age" in the history of Polish Jewry. This is an overstatement. One must keep in mind that some areas, such as the province of Mazovia and its capital city of Warsaw, were restricted for Jews and that vicious anti-Semitic agitation and even riots were not infrequent, especially in the early seventeenth century. But, compared with later developments, conditions of Jewish life in Poland-Lithuania prior to 1648, on the whole, were favorable.

A Decade of Distress: 1648-1658

This calm state of affairs was suddenly disrupted in April 1648 by the uprising of the Ukrainian Cossacks and peasants, under the leadership of the Hetman Bogdan Chmielnicky, against the Polish crown, the Polish nobility, which owned vast latifundia on both banks of the Dnieper, and the Roman Catholic clergy. The Jews, who, as lessees of the revenues of the landowners, were disliked by the peasant serfs, became involved in the uprising. Chmielnicky allied himself with the Crimean Tartars and was thus enabled to defeat the Polish armies. In a short time, he overran the Ukraine, Volhynia, Podolia, and the Polish provinces westward. His troops and irregular bands spread terror and killed great numbers of Poles and Jews. Panic-stricken crowds of Jews who escaped the ordeal fled to Lithuania and the western districts of Poland, or crossed the borders to reach safe havens in Austria, Germany, Italy and Holland. This flight marked the beginning of the migration of Jews from eastern Europe back to the west where the ancestors of the refugees had originated.

However, Chmielnicky was soon deserted by the Tartars, who made peace with Poland (1649). In the battle of Berestechko (1651), he was defeated by the Polish army; a Jewish unit took part in the battle on the Polish side. Chmielnicky was forced to conclude a treaty with Poland by which, among other conditions, the Jews were restored the right to settle in the Ukraine. Polish Jewry relaxed, at least temporarily. But more upheavals were in store for the Polish state and its Jewish population.

Chmielnicky now turned to Czar Alexei Mikhailovich for support, offering the incorporation into the Muscovite Empire of that part of the Ukraine which was inhabited by people of the Greek Orthodox faith. The country was to become an autonomous province. Moscow accepted the offer and, in 1654, Russian troops and Cossack bands invaded Lithuania and White Russia and brought disaster to the Jewish population. Jews who survived the massacres were deported as prisoners to Russia, as far as the city of Kazan on the Volga; others managed to flee to the western parts of Poland and abroad.

In 1655 Sweden declared war on Poland. Swedish armies invaded the western and central provinces of Poland and besieged many cities. The civilian population suffered grievously. However, the Poles rallied for a counterstroke. Hetman Stephen Czarnecki defeated the Swedes, who soon evacuated the conquered Polish territory. In liberating the country from the enemy, Czarnecki accused the Jews of high treason for alleged help to the Swedes. Polish units attacked the Jewish population and killed many. It has been asserted by modern historians that the atrocities perpetrated in the province of Great Poland were committed against the wish of Czarnecki, but the Jewish chroniclers of the massacres, some of whom were eye-witnesses of the gruesome events, termed the Polish commander-in-chief "hangman," and likened him to the "villain Chmielnicky" (Hebrew: *chmel harashah*).[3]

Polish authors called the years of foreign invasions the period of the "deluge" (Polish: *potop*). The Jewish chroniclers compared it with the misfortunes that befell the Jewish people in the time of the destruction of the First and Second Temples in Jerusalem; in fact, they spoke of the "Third Destruction." Manasseh ben Israel, in his petition to Oliver Cromwell to re-admit the Jews to England in 1655, gives the figure of the Jewish victims of the Ukrainian pogroms as 180,000.

The bloodletting was staggering and the material losses were likewise enormous. If credit is to be given to reports by contemporary writers, a total of 700 Jewish communities, large and small, were affected by the disaster.[4]

The Aftermath of the Castastrophe

In 1657, the threat of expulsion was added to all this. When King Jan Kasimir was informed by his generals and counsellors that Jews had allegedly helped the Swedes during their invasion, he decided to banish them from the country and to refuse re-entry to those who had found refuge in neighboring states.

Having learned of the king's plan, the Jews made known to him, through "various persons" interceding on their behalf, that they were prepared to make financial sacrifices if the expulsion plan would be abandoned. The offer made the king change his mind. An edict of March 28, 1657 ordered the Jews to pay 100,000 zloty to the treasury before Pentecost (May 20), which amount was to be deducted from future payments of the poll tax. The alternative was confiscation of Jewish property and total expulsion.[5]

It is interesting to read in the light of the allegations of Jewish disloyalty, the king's own declaration of March 18, 1658:

> Part of the Jews were robbed and killed by our soldiers, another part of them was ransacked or massacred by foreign troops; many lost their lives under tortures. Those who survived cannot find peace in the towns and at the marts; they cannot expect security for their existence. Those who sought refuge outside the Polish boundaries are afraid to return. I know that many of the belongings of the Jews who had been plundered by the burghers of the cities are still hidden by them, and that the Jews are as yet unable to recover their losses.[6]

However, no governmental action was taken to redress the damages caused to private or communal Jewish property. Poland was then in such a state of anarchy that the authorities, even if they so wanted, would have been unable to help the Jews to recuperate their losses. How impoverished the bulk of Polish Jewry was, the treasury knew best. Tax payments were obtained only with the greatest difficulty. The Jews had to be exempted from various kinds of taxes and dues.

The Polish population as a whole was gravely hit by the foreign invasions, sieges, diseases, famine and concomitant afflictions. Exact figures are not known but estimates have it that between 1648 and 1659 Poland-Lithuania lost about one-half of its population of 4,000,000.[7]

The recovery of the Jewish merchant class was hampered by discriminatory legislation enacted by the Polish Diet back in 1643. While the Polish merchant was allowed to earn seven per cent on imported goods and a foreigner five per cent, the Jew was permitted only three per cent. Catholics also received preferential treatment with regard to import and export duties as compared to Christian dissidents and Jews.

The Polish economist, W. Surowiecki, in his study on the decline of industry and the cities in Poland, pointed out that this legislation was intended to demoralize the Jewish merchant class and to bring about its bankruptcy. The historian, T. Korzon, believed that whatever its purpose, this economic policy was self-defeating, since it compelled the Jewish merchant to undersell his competitors.[8] The fact was, as the treasurer Marcin Matczynski had stated in the 1680's, that Jewish merchants were greatly impoverished and unable to pay their debts.[9]

The Jewish Supreme Council (*Vaad*) of the Polish communities issued a proclamation in 1676 lamenting the disastrous situation: "We have sinned heavily before God," it stated. The people were urged to avoid causes of friction with non-Jews, to abstain from such jobs as leasing state revenues, and to consult the elders of their local communities concerning their dealings with non-Jews.[10] The *Vaad* did not, and could not, point to the political and economic disintegration of the Polish state as the main cause of the calamity that befell them.

It was a national calamity as well. At the cessation of military operations in 1660, half of the arable land was out of cultivation. Poland needed a long period of peace and stability. Instead, a war with Turkey engaged the country in 1672-1676. The Great Northern War followed in 1700-1721. As a result, grain exports through the port of Danzig fell to 7,000 tons in 1713 and to 4,782 tons in 1737, as against 300,000 tons in 1648. The decline of the export trade caused the depreciation of Polish currency. The once famous fairs of Cracow, Lublin, and Lwow decayed, looking like "phantoms of themselves." Many other urban places sank to the level of barely vegetating provincial towns.

Under the kings of the Saxon dynasty (1697-1763), Poland ceased to play a decisive role in international politics and became an object of foreign diplomatic intrigues.

The country was weakened from within as well, by the constant bickerings of factions headed by ambitious magnates. "Domestic fury convulsed the state." The sessions of the Diet were frequently disrupted. A deputy of the Diet, opposed to a bill under deliberation, had only to shout his *Liberum veto* to have the Diet adjourned. A new Diet then had to be convened. This practice amounted to a complete sabotage of the legislative machinery. The authority of the Crown dwindled rapidly; the administrative apparatus deteriorated. A saying became current: "Poland exists by disorder." Ultimately, the state of anarchy and lawlessness, coupled with civil strife and the interference of foreign powers, particularly Russia, led to the liquidation of the Polish Commonwealth (1772-1795).[11]

Internal Migration

Under the impact of the political events and the devastation of the cities, the Jewish population spread over countless rural localities. According to the Polish census of 1764-65, there were 430,009 Jews in Poland and 157,649 in Lithuania. If one adds 6.35 per cent for infants under one year of age, the total would be 624,973. Rafael Mahler arrives at a total of 750,000, assuming that about twenty per cent failed to register.[12]

At the first partition of Poland in 1772, when Austria, Prussia, and Russia annexed Galicia, the valley of the lower Vistula, parts of Great Poland and of White Russia, the Jewish population that remained within the borders of the amputated Polish state was reduced to 500,000, or at most to 570,000. During the following twenty years, however, the number grew considerably, partly owing to a surplus of births over deaths and to immigration from the annexed territories.

The Polish statesman, Thaddeusz Czacki, estimated the number of Jews in Poland after 1772 at about 900,000, amounting to roughly ten per cent of the total population.[13] Even if we assume that 800,000 would be a more correct figure, it clearly shows that the Jews had emerged from a small minority and became a substantial part of the population of Poland. The Jewish question of the nineteenth and twentieth centuries was in the making.

Economic Stratification

Spread over the villages, the Jews became the "arendars," "randars," or "arendators," a designation derived from the medieval Latin term "renta," or "renda." They were the lessees of the flour and lumber mills, dairies, breweries, alcohol distilleries, country taverns and inns. More than one-third of all gainfully occupied Jews derived their income from these manorial sources.

The rest of the Jewish village householders were petty traders and artisans. Artisans were to be found chiefly in the urban places. Thus, in the provinces of Great Poland, almost one-half of the Jewish urban population engaged in crafts; in the central provinces the proportion of artisans amounted to twenty-five per cent. Higher figures are reported for the eastern provinces. In Vilna in 1765, out of 743 Jewish breadwinners, 324 were artisans. In Rzeszow the respective figures were 292 and 111 for the same year.[14]

The boundaries between occupations were not sharply drawn, however. Many people held more than one job in order to make ends meet. Artisans traded their goods or those of others and engaged in lessees' activities; traders engaged in repair work. Storekeepers did manual work in off-hours, and so forth.

Merchants formed the third category, followed by small professional groups, the religious functionaries, doctors, and teachers; associated with these were clerks and servants. At the bottom of the social ladder were persons without definite occupations, and beggars, that is, persons who depended on charity or engaged in occasional work as it came their way, the so-called *luftmenshen* or *shnorrers.*

Distribution of the Crafts

In compiling a list of the trades in which the Jews were active in eighteenth century Poland, we see a shift of emphasis. To be sure, we find them in the familiar occupations, as metal workers, wood workers, soap and candle makers, surgeons, barbers, brush and comb makers, and in other crafts; however, the wearing apparel industry with all its related jobs, and food and beverage production predominate.[15]

Tailoring

More than one-half of the Jewish artisans in Poland were engaged in the different branches of the wearing apparel industry, especially as tailors, furriers, hat and cap makers, and lace workers. Tailors formed about one-third of the Jewish artisans in the cities and two-fifths in the smaller towns. The predominance of the needle trades among the Jews in the early modern period has been observed in Italy, Bohemia, and Moravia as well.

Tailoring was one of the oldest Jewish trades, originating in the ritual observance of the prohibition against mixing wool and linen in garments. (*Lev.* 19:19; *Deut.* 22:11). Lithuanian and Polish Jews were strict about this observance. The basis of the biblical prohibition of mixtures, which in ancient times extended to sowing with different kinds of seeds, cross-breeding of animals, etc., was that one should not change the normal order of things. The central Jewish councils of Poland and Lithuania issued warnings against the violation of the prohibition. The *Vaad* of Lithuania resolved in 1639:

> with regard to tailors who are not careful about the prohibition of mixing wool and linen: they must use only threads that they buy from local Jews who can testify that they were present at the weaving of the threads. If the threads are brought in from other places, the rabbis of those places must issue written statements to the effect that the law prohibiting mixing wool and linen has not been transgressed.

In 1676, the *Vaad* of Lithuania appointed experts who were to check the yarns used by the tailors and to see to it that no canvas was used for the lining of woolen garments.[16]

The tailors did not depend on Jewish patronage alone; they had customers among all classes of the population. In Vilna, for instance, out of 88 Jewish tailors registered in 1765, only eight worked for Jewish customers. The Polish army employed Jewish tailors and quartered them in army barracks. They worked for the nobility, the high officialdom, the clergy, the students, the womenfolk, and the peasantry.

The Jews had started the manufacture of ready-made clothes. Jewish tailors in Cracow had made clothes for the markets of that city as far back as the latter half of the fifteenth century. In the second half of the sixteenth century clothes manufactured by Jews were exported abroad, especially to Russia. The itinerant Jewish tailor, visiting markets and looking out for customers, was a familiar figure of the Polish scene. Foreign travelers amusedly reported about the flocks of Jewish tailors who surrounded prospective patrons at the fairs.

The Jewish tailor guilds tried to combat unfair competition and prevent the turbulent scenes which frequently ended in fights over customers. But the rules which they set up were more often than not honored in the breach.

Furriery

In a country where rich and poor wore furs during the long winter months, the fur trade was quite important. In contrast to the tailor trade, the fur trade required considerable capital investment. The poorer fur workers were provided by merchants with raw felts, hides, and equipment. The latter also sold the finished product. Independent furriers formed their own guilds. Jewish patronage was presumably rather limited, if we consider the sumptuary laws that the Jewish councils issued from time to time. Marten, sable, beaver, and fox were not permitted for personal use. Actually, any fur more expensive than a wolf's hide was outlawed. One such self-imposed restriction was promulgated by the Jewish Council of Lithuania in 1761.

The Jewish fur trade considerably expanded in the nineteenth century and was ultimately carried to western Europe and overseas to the United States and Canada.

Leather Work

Data on leather workers, particularly shoemakers, are scarce.[17] It was suggested that because of the discriminatory policies of the Polish shoemakers' guilds, Jewish shoemakers were careful not to disclose their trade to the census authorities. However this may be, there is some evidence of Jewish shoemakers in the eighteenth century. The sumptuary laws of the Lithuanian *Vaad of* 1639, frequently repeated, prohibited Jewish men and women from wearing "fancy shoe work." [18] Jewish shoemakers are mentioned in 1765 in Lwow and Lublin. A combined guild of shoemakers and tanners appears in Mikolaiow, Podolia. Its statutes date from 1810 but refer to earlier by-laws. In nineteenth century Russia, Jews are found also in saddlery, strap and glove making.

Conclusion

The wars that ravaged Poland from 1648 through the first quarter of the eighteenth century, and their repercussions in the Jewish part of the civil population, brought about considerable changes in the distribution and the economic stratification of the Jews. As one result of these changes, the trades in which the Jews were active diminished in number and variety. The dominant position the Jews acquired in the wearing apparel industry was not due to under-selling, or the general decline of a craft abandoned by the guilds and left to bunglers, but to the advanced production methods the Jews introduced, their organizational skill, and their ability to turn out superior work. Their contribution lay in starting mass production, which was to revolutionize one of the basic industries, and in doing this in an economically backward country.

Chapter XXI

Jewish Art Crafts, Particularly in Poland and Lithuania

A Definition of Folk Art

A prerequisite of folk art is the absence of a strong professional art. Bernard Berenson once said that Italy had no popular art because of its numerous centers, its churches, municipalities and courts which employed professional artists, thus maintaining a high standard of proficiency. Folk art flourished in the vastnesses of Russia, in Poland, and, to a lesser degree, in Bohemia and Moravia, but not in Germany, France, and England, at least according to Berenson.

We may not quite agree with regard to Germany. The crafts of the Pennsylvania Dutch, which were carried to America by German immigrants, are only one evidence of German folk art. Folk art, then, is untutored art, an art relying on tradition, on local and regional practices and techniques rather than on experimentation with new ideas and trends which originate in the large centers. The stimulating new concepts reach the peripheral areas with some delay, resulting in the overlapping of styles.

W. R. Zaloziecki,[1] in his study "Gotische and Barocke Holzkirchen in den Karpatenlaendern," points out the simultaneous use of Byzantine, Gothic, and Baroque forms in the churches of the seventeenth and eighteenth centuries in the mountain region extending from western Galicia to eastern Slovakia. The dependence of this timber architecture on masonry architecture is likewise notable. However, the building inscriptions giving the dates of construction and remodelings only rarely carried the names of the builders. It was an anonymous art.

With these observations in mind, we find that Jewish art, including architecture, in Poland in the seventeenth and eighteenth centuries shares some characteristics with Carpathian folk art. It is provincial, derivative, and, to some degree, anonymous. And yet, because the Jewish population lived not only in rural places but also in municipalities, such as Cracow, Lwow, and Lublin, and in the private domains of the landed nobility which maintained a relatively high standard of living, the Jewish artists were not as isolated and out of touch with the ideas of their time as were the builders of the Ruthenian churches.

Synagogue Architecture

Synagogue architecture attracted the attention of Polish artists and art lovers as early as the eighteenth century. Later, scholarly investigations were conducted and published by members of the Commission on the History of Fine Arts under the auspices of the Cracow Academy of Sciences, by Ludwik Wierzbicki in 1891 and by Wladyslaw Luszczkiewicz in 1896. Other studies followed, to be interrupted only by the Nazi invasion. The architectural historian, Szymon Zajczyk of Warsaw, and the architect, Mozes Blochas of Kaunas (Kovno), to whom we owe some of the most recent explorations, perished in the holocaust.

However, the materials accumulated through the years in the Polish archives were removed from Warsaw and have been preserved. A team of architects, Kazimierz and Maria Piechotka, published a comprehensive study of the timber synagogues in 1957; the English translation appeared in 1959. In my book on European synagogue architecture (1964), I have discussed masonry and timber synagogues in Poland and Russia.[2]

In contrast to eastern European peasant art, which was primarily concerned with beautifying the home and objects of everyday use, Jewish folk art was dedicated to the beautification of the house of worship. Work for the synagogue was called "holy work." This means that much of the production of the Jewish popular artist was confined to use by the Jewish community. The sacred character of Jewish art probably accounts for its toleration by the Christian artisan guilds, which fiercely fought Jewish competition in the production of wares for the general consumer. The concessions made by the guilds chiefly concerned butchers selling kosher meat and tailors observing the biblical regulation about the mixed use of textiles. The absence of complaints about synagogue builders and decorators is thus understandable.

Another aspect of Jewish folk art is the fact that it was produced by itinerant artists. This was particularly true of the building trades. Jewish guilds could take care of the interests of craftsmen living and working in a definite area, such as a town and the surrounding villages. They could protect their members from the inroads of Jewish artisans not belonging to the district over which they had jurisdiction in such matters as right to work, to sell, and so forth. But it is difficult to see what a guild could do for itinerant workers. One must assume that they formed only loose associations, if they were organized at all.

Synagogue Inscriptions

Our best information about Jewish synagogue builders and decorators is derived from synagogue inscriptions. They often provide the date and name of the artist. For example, the inscription in the timber synagogue at Mogilev on the Dnieper in White Russia (Bielorussia), dated 1740, reads: "I have traveled many days in the lands of life. I have felt it my duty to carry out this decoration donated by pious hearts. By the master skilled in the holy work, Hayyim, son of Eisik Segal from the holy community of Sluck."[3] The artist executed a very similar decoration in the neighboring town of Kopys, and one—different in subject matter—at Dolginov in the district of Minsk.[4] Sluck, his home town, is likewise in the Minsk district.

This artist traveled about the region in search of work; he also seems to have been abroad, as the reference to "traveling many days in the lands of life" would imply. A possible evidence of his travels is to be found in one of his decorations in the dome of the synagogue at Mogilev. It is the view of a walled city inscribed

"Wirms," a medieval form of the name of the city of Worms. Worms was the seat of one of the oldest Jewish communities in central Europe with a twelfth century synagogue (destroyed by the Nazis in 1938 but now rebuilt by the German authorities). The view of Worms was used as an allusion to some Jewish and German legendary material which the artist may have known from hearsay, or even from visiting the German city, as some details in the painting would suggest. It may be noted that the artist was remunerated by private patrons, "pious hearts," who donated the decoration. He did not receive a fee from the synagogue, or the *Kahal,* which shows the voluntary character of his relationship with his employers.

In the case of Gwozdziec in Galicia, we have two artists working in the same synagogue at different periods, according to inscriptions in the synagogue. Israel, son of Mordecai was working on the decoration of the synagogue in 1652, while Isaac son of Yehudah Loeb was active in 1729. Both were from the nearby town of Jaryczow, in the Lwow district.[5] It would seem that Jaryczow was a center of synagogue painters, a place where men were taught their skills, where stencils, sample books, and other materials needed by the artisans for their work were available.

It is not always clear from the inscriptions whether the worker mentioned was merely the decorator, or also the builder of the synagogue. However, the wording of the inscription in the masonry synagogue at Maciejow implies that its decorator was also its builder. It reads: "1781, year of completion of the construction and of the decoration. Work of Ezekiel, son of Moses from Sokal."[6] Born in Galicia, this man migrated to the province of Volhynia in search of work.

The carvers in wood and stone, whose work has won the particular admiration of modern artists, were probably more settled. Almost every synagogue, particularly in Lithuania and White Russia, boasted an elaborately carved Ark, which—under the influence of Baroque frames of altarpieces and of the Russian iconostasis—occasionally assumed considerable dimensions. Whether we take the one in the synagogue at Uzliany, in the district of Minsk, whose carver was Beer, son of Israel,[7] or any other in that vast area, the style—featuring scrolls, floral and animal decoration—is the same everywhere.

Tombstone and Ark Decorations

More restrained, but equally attractive, were the relief decorations of tombstones. The tombstone carvers were probably members of the Jewish burial brotherhoods and, as such, permanent residents of the localities where they worked. A variety of ornamental and symbolic motifs were found on tombstones at the old cemetery at Lublin. Those at Cernauti (Chernovitz) and Sereth in the Bukovina were richer in invention. Max Diamant,[8] in his study of Jewish tombstones in the Bukovina, mentions the names of two families in Cernauti—Picker and Steinmetz—who worked as tombstone carvers (*matseve-schlaeger*). The craft was hereditary in these families. However, they regarded this as a sideline and their principal activities were connected with their functions at the local burial society.

The carved tombstones in the old cemetery at Prague exhibit the same popular style as the ones in the Bukovina, while those in the old cemetery in Vienna reveal a more formal skill.[9] However, for all the differences in execution, the decorative and the symbolic vocabulary was much the same in the vast territory which extended from the Danube toward the Ukrainian steppes.

By the end of the eighteenth century, the ancient folk art relaxes its hold, as the impact of neo-classicism becomes more pronounced. Hillel Benjamin of Lask, near Lodz, the builder of the timber synagogue in nearby Lutomiersk—we find his name in the community records in Lutomiersk—uses a more sober formal style and fronts his synagogue with a six-column porch.[10]

The area around Warsaw and Lodz was particularly exposed to western influences. David Friedlander, who may have come from Bohemia, used some of the traditional patterns of folk art in the masonry synagogue of Wyszogrod (1810), particularly in his overelaborate carved Ark.[11] He no longer has the innocence, as it were, of the popular artist, yet he still lacks a thorough formal training.

In the area west of Warsaw and around Poznan, we find a number of synagogues with Arks carved in the same semi-popular style. The Ark in Kempen, Poznan district, carried the names of the master carver, his journeyman, and two apprentices on two tablets. On the main inscription tablet the master, "the humble" Jonah, son of Samuel Zanwel, expresses his thanks to the Lord for having granted him the skill to execute and set up the holy Ark. He gives the date of the completion, 5576 (1816). Following on the same tablet are the words: "Likewise, I, the artisan, have signed my name, Meir, son of Isaac." The inscription on the second tablet reads: "Also, we, the artisans, came to express our thanks in the House of the Lord for having had the honor of executing this holy Ark. The humble Zanwel, son of Solomon. The humble Baruch Mordecai, son of Rabbi Pinkhas of Piotrokow." Jonah had also carved the Ark at the synagogue of Staszow, Kielce district. In this inscription, dated 1825, he gives his residence as Warsaw. Jonah's father, Samuel Zanwel, also a carver, had made the Ark for the synagogue at Konin, Kalisz district, before 1816. Around 1830 we find the name of the carver Samuel Goldbaum, who made the Ark of the synagogue at Fordon, district of Bromberg, now Bydoszcz.[12]

Westward Spread of Folk Art

Indirect evidence of the role which Jewish builders and decorators played in synagogue architecture in Poland is the spread of a certain type of synagogue (with built-in central tabernacle for the reader's stand) and painted decorations to Bohemia and Moravia and even farther west, a trend which coincided with the Jewish emigration to the west following the Chmielnicky pogroms.

It is most likely that refugees from the East were the carriers of this building and decoration style. Only one name of a refugee artisan has come down to us, that of Elieser Sussman, son of Solomon, cantor of Brod,[13] who decorated and possibly built, in the 1730's, the plain, barn-type synagogues at Horb on the Main, Bechhofen, near Ansbach, and Kirchheim, near Wuerzburg. The painted decoration of these synagogues is closely related to that of the Galician timber synagogues.

To sum up, while synagogues in the large cities were built by trained architects, some of them of Italian origin, the synagogues in the smaller towns and villages were the work of Jewish builders, carvers, and painters, whose contribution is well documented.

Metal Work

The synagogues of Poland-Lithuania used a considerable amount of metal work. The silver appurtenances for the decoration of the Scripture scrolls were mostly imported from Germany and Austria and later, after the annexation in 1795, from Russia as well. However, lamps, chandeliers, candelabra, sconces made of brass, which were found in large quantities in the synagogues and in domestic use, were produced in the country. Only one name of a brazier, Baruch (eighteenth century), has survived, as well as photographs of some of his candelabra in the synagogue at Pogrebishche in the Ukraine.[14] The Ark of the "High Synagogue" at Cracow (seventeenth century) bears an inscription saying that Zelman and Hayyim, sons of Aaron, made the iron doors for it.[15]

The Work of Scribes

An eminently Jewish profession was that of the scribe, who copied by hand the parchment scrolls of the Pentateuch for the use of the synagogue. Also, certain books for individual patrons were still written by hand in the eighteenth century. Copied from printed texts, they were occasionally embellished with vignettes and colored figure illustrations. The synagogue of Pogrebishche possessed a daily prayer book (*siddur*) of this type copied by Aryeh Yehudah Leib, son of Baruch, and dated 1735. The synagogue at Wolpa owned a holiday prayer book (*mahzor*) produced by Hayyim Meerowich in 1781.[16] An anonymous work was the parchment *siddur* of 1712 with figure illustrations in color, dedicated to Abraham, son of Moses, in Rzeszow, Galicia.[17] These scribes and draftsmen probably were also the designers of the curtains of the holy Ark which were decorated with symbolic motifs embroidered in silver and gold thread on silk or velvet. A number of Ark curtains, signed by the embroiderers who made them, have been discovered in various synagogues. They date from the seventeenth and eighteenth centuries.[18]

Here, we touch upon a craft which was not exclusively dedicated to the synagogue. The embroiderers produced articles of wearing apparel for men and women, Jew and non-Jew, in particular the *pasy,* silver and gold interwoven belts worn by the noblemen.

Similarly, the Jewish bookbinders seem to have been much in demand by Gentile employers. In the reign of Sigismund III (1586-1632) there were "no bookbinders besides the Jewish ones," except in Cracow and Warsaw, according to F. Siarczynski.[19] The Christian bookbinder guild in Cracow (1610), faced with strong Jewish competition, instructed its members to search the Jewish shops for books bound by Jews and to confiscate them.[20]

Craftsmen and Quality Standards

The policies of the guilds are discussed elsewhere. We are concerned here with the Jewish craftsmen as such, with their work, and the problem of whether the demand for their work was motivated by its superior quality. This is of particular interest, for the Christian guilds called the Jewish competitors bunglers (*Partacze*). New light has been cast on this problem in connection with King Jan III Sobieski's efforts to develop the town of Zolkiev. Zolkiev, near Lwow, was the king's estate and his favorite residence.

To attract skilled workers to the place, and to induce them to settle there, they were given loans for the purpose of building their houses. We learn about an embroiderer named Israel receiving a loan from the royal treasury. In 1687 a goldsmith, Hirsz Ickowicz, arrived, and in 1688 a goldsmith, Lewko Moszkowicz. In 1684 Hirsz Jelemowicz received the official title of goldsmith of his royal majesty. Another goldsmith, Sobolnik, received the title of "goldsmith and jeweler" in 1690. Moszko, a tentmaker (Polish: *namiotnik*), received a loan from the treasury, as well as the title "royal tentmaker," in 1688. Another name mentioned is the one of a certain Marek Lewkowicz, maker of strong-boxes and mirror framer. In 1689, the *Kahal* received 6,000 zloty as a loan for building or completing the building of a masonry synagogue in Zolkiev.

When the king wanted to get two "Turkish" curtains, or drapes (*zaslona*) and an embroidered cushion, the court agent, Bezalel, son of Nathan, received the order. The amount of 3,605 zloty for the purchase seems to be rather high in comparison with the loan for the synagogue building. Karaites (Jewish sectarians) and Armenians were also encouraged to settle in Zolkiev.[21]

On another magnate's estate, at the castle of Prince Radziwill at Nieswierz, in Lithuania, a Jewish engraver, Herszko Lejbowicz,[22] was commissioned to make copper engravings of 160 family portraits, dating from 1346 to 1758, in the Radziwill collection. The publication which contained these reproductions was brought out by the printing office at Nieswierz.

The style of these eighteenth-century engravings is rather dry, but it must be assumed that they were expected to render meticulously every detail of the paintings. The minute execution of details in the works of early Jewish artists may have been due also to their training as scribes. Even the work of the goldsmith Baruch Dornhelm (1858-1928) of Lwow shows this shortcoming, but it was highly admired at the time. Wladislaw Lozinski, the well-known authority on the history of Polish crafts, regarded him as superior to his rival, Hakowski, the most prominent Polish goldsmith in Cracow.[23] Baruch's father, an engraver, owned the only antique shop in Lwow. He used to travel to Berlin, Vienna, and Paris to sell Baruch's work, which could be found in the collections of Crown Prince Frederick of Prussia and Czar Alexander III. He worked from German engravings, did embossed work, and even produced small figures in the round. And yet, according to Lozinski, Dornhelm had hardly received any professional training. The Jewish artist only slowly overcame the shortcomings of the artisan. Mark Antokolski (1843-1902), the first Jewish sculptor in Russia, began as an apprentice carver in Vilna. Studies at the Academy in St. Petersburg and travels abroad widened his outlook, gave a direction to his ambitions, and loosened up his treatment of form.[24] With all this, he could not achieve the rank of a leading sculptor in Europe. But, in the following generation, the Jewish artist overcame his inhibitions. There is no trace of the artisan in the work of Chagall, even though his art has been inspired by the Jewish folk art of White Russia, where he was born and raised.

Music and Musicians

The Jewish musician was a familiar figure in the Polish-Lithuanian scene. In the synagogue the Bible was read in a kind of melody, known as cantillation; the psalms were sung according to traditional tunes. The horn (*shofar*), an instrument found in every synagogue, was used at certain occasions in the liturgy. There is no evidence of an organ in the old East European synagogues. According to Schudt (early 18th century),[25] an organ was played in the Alt-Neu Synagogue at Prague at the Sabbath Eve services. While the cantor was in charge of the synagogue singing, secular music was performed by the "klezmorim," the community musicians.

A band in Lwow, in the 1620's consisted of thirteen members. They played the fiddle, the zither, the lute, cymbals, bass and drum. The names of these musicians are of interest. Two of them, Abus Cymbalista and Eizik Bass, denote their profession, whereas some of the other names—Pasamannik, Szmuklerz, and Czapnik, which signify braid (or passementerie) maker, embroiderer, maker of buttons, button holes, etc., and hat maker—may indicate that these men were only part-time musicians, or belonged to families working in these trades. The band in Lwow had an arrangement with the local Christian musicians' guild (1629) permitting it to play at Catholic weddings and banquets, upon paying ten zloty to the guild and two zloty to the municipal treasury. In commenting on this arrangement, Balaban believes that the playing at weddings by the guild, a religious association employed by the church, was frowned upon by the ecclesiastical authorities.[26]

Be that as it may, the tolerant attitude toward Jewish musicians dates not earlier than the seventeenth century. In the sixteenth century, persons not belonging to the Christian musicians' guild were forbidden to perform.[27] Jews were not admitted to the guild. Jewish bands found particularly favorable conditions in the towns owned by the nobility. In the city of Leszno they were protected by the Count Boguslaw Leszczynski, Bishop of Lutzk (d. 1691). The charter he granted them was renewed in 1702 by Count Rafael Leszczynski. The latter forwarned the town musicians not to molest the Jews and enjoined the municipal authorities to prevent any interference on their part. King Stanislaw Leszczynski again confirmed the privilege (March 24, 1710) allowing the Jews to play for Gentiles. However, they were not to perform at baptisms and Christian weddings. In 1795 there were nine Jewish musicians in Leszno.[28]

Compared with the sources on the history of Jewish music in central and western Europe, the eastern European records are scant and of rather late date. In his standard work on Jewish music, the musicologist, A. Z. Idelson, cites the terms of payment of a cantor in Hildesheim, Germany, in 1760. The poor man had to keep one singer at his own expense and to pay the bass half a thaler per week, which amounted to half of his salary. The householders provided the food. Similar conditions prevailed, Idelson holds, in eastern Europe until late in the nineteenth century.[29]

It is mostly from nineteenth-century reminiscences that we get our information. Thus, we learn that playing dance music at weddings was the chief source of income of the musicians. They were paid by the father of the bride, and a collection plate was passed around among the wedding guests to bolster their wages. A Yiddish proverb illustrates the worries of the musician. "When two beggars go to dance, the *klezmer's* strings crack."[30]

The jester, or juggler (*marszalek, badhen*), was a popular figure at family festivities, including the celebration of the feast of Purim, which featured an Esther-play in the style of the *commedia dell'arte.*

The cantor, the band, and the juggler find their counterparts in the Jewish communities in western Europe. The Jewish exiles from Spain (the Marranos), those from Germany, the refugees from Bohemia and Turkey, carried to Poland and to Lithuania their musical traditions influenced by their environments. The juggler had his prototype in the medieval minstrel. The poems of the Jewish minstrel, Suesskind of Trimberg, in Bavaria, and his likeness, have come down to us in the German illuminated Manesse manuscript produced in the late thirteenth or early fourteenth century.[31] About that time there usually was a *spilhus* (playhouse) or a *tanzhus* (dance house) in the Jewish quarters of the German towns, besides the synagogue and the bath house.[32]

The Performing Arts

In the fifteenth century the "Morisco dancers," skillful acrobats who amused the courts and the villagers, appeared in many places. They must also have entertained in the ghettos and there were possibly Jews, perhaps Jewish refugees from Spain, among them, for we find a picture of these dynamic performers in a Hebrew Passover Haggadah manuscript of the fifteenth century, produced in Germany and illustrated in a humorous, folksy style.[33]

The popularity of the Jewish itinerant *spielleute, fahrende leute,* must be attributed to the up-to-date foreign fashions they introduced. A group of Jewish musicians who entertained at the court in Cracow in 1556 went under the name of *welsch,* an old German designation of foreigners, particularly Italians.[34]

Italy witnessed, in the Renaissance, a flowering of the performing arts in which Jewish musicians, actors, dancers, composers, and even theoreticians of music, played an active part. There were two Jewish musicians at the court of Pope Leo X.[35] At the court of the Gonzaga in Mantua we find Salomone Rossi, Il Ebreo, who produced a collection of songs for the synagogue, published in Venice in 1623. Rossi was known for his madrigals, composed in the contemporary taste.[36]

Musicians in Prague

The Jewish musicians in Prague had a well-organized guild. They were wont to appear *in corpore* at solemn occasions. They are seen in engravings illustrating the parades of 1716 and 1741 which were arranged to celebrate happy events of the imperial court. The Jewish musicians marched along with the other guilds carrying their banners, trumpets, fiddles, French horns, kettle drums, and their new organ.[37]

The Jewish guild did not permit its members to approach patrons. These—in the case of a wedding, it was the bridegroom—would come to the Jewish quarter and make the arrangements.[38]

In 1791 the *Judenstadt,* as the Jewish section in Prague was called, was ordered to supply a band of "Turkish music" for the coronation of the emperor Leopold II as king of Bohemia.[39]

The Jewish musicians of Prague were a well-trained group, although perhaps not quite in the traditional sense, as may be judged from the usual complaints on the part of the Christian guild. When, in 1641, the Christian musicians objected to the Archbishop's permission for the Jews to play at baptisms and Christian weddings, the Jews pointed out in their defense that they had been trained in the profession, possessed no other skills, and would have to starve if denied the right to accept work from the townspeople.[40]

With this background in mind, it is evident that new ideas, forms, instruments, and techniques in the field of music came from the west. It is self-evident also that in the stimulating climate of the west, the Jews were inexorably drawn into the powerful cultural stream, actively taking part in the development of music.

The fact that a modern musicologist could term the first half of the nineteenth century the "age of Mendelssohn, Schumann, Berlioz," giving equal credit to a Jew, a German, and a Frenchman, shows how rapid their progress was.[41]

The Arts and Nationalism

Eastern Europe was, in the nineteenth century, under the spell of the idea of the revival of national resources in the arts. The "Mighty Five" in Russian music—Borodin, Cui, Mussorgsky, Balakirev, and Rimsky-Korsakov—lay emphasis on the national spirit in their works.[42]

Turning to their own heritage, the Jewish composers, Joel Engel, Lazare Saminsky, Solomon Rosovsky, and Joseph Achron, set out to build up a national Jewish music.[43] Their efforts were continued in Russia in the 1930's by the folklore section of the Academy of Sciences, and resulted in building up a collection of recordings of Jewish folk music.[44]

Compared with the tendencies in the visual arts, which have outgrown the nationalistic phase, the traditionalist efforts in the field of music may hold more promise because of the emotional association with modes of religious chanting, on one hand, and hasidic song, on the other, still practiced in many Jewish communities in Europe and America. Here, more than in any other area, folk art appears to be a creative factor.

Chapter XXII

The Struggle for the Right to Work

Rise of an Artisan Class

The Polish municipal councils and artisans' guilds were based on medieval patterns transplanted to Poland by the German immigrants. In medieval Germany, Jews were excluded from the municipal councils and the merchants' and artisans' guilds. They were restricted in the exercise of commerce and barred from the trades.

These discriminatory policies did not succeed in Poland. Particularly noteworthy was the survival of the Jewish artisan class which, by the end of the eighteenth century, comprised from one-quarter to one-third of the Jewish population in Poland.

A number of factors account for these economic developments: (a) the protection of the Jewish workingman by the Crown; (b) the opposition of the Polish gentry (*szlachta*) to the guild monopolies; (c) the multi-ethnic composition of the working class in Poland; (d) the existence of sizable numbers of non-organized labor among the various ethnic groups in Poland; and (e) the resistance of the Jewish artisans to hostile acts of the Polish guilds.

Protection of the Jewish Workingman by the Crown

The medieval charters granted to the Jewish immigrants by the

Polish kings and Lithuanian grand dukes (thirteenth to fifteenth centuries) guaranteed them various rights, freedom of movement, and unrestricted exercise of commerce and trades. These charters formed the basis of the legal status of the Jews, and were confirmed in the sixteenth to eighteenth centuries by the successive rulers of Poland-Lithuania on the occasion of their accession to the throne. In addition, certain Jewish communities and individuals were accorded special privileges by the king.

The guilds, backed by the municipal councils, objected to such benevolent acts of the Crown, for they considered them as a serious threat to their rights. Their protests frequently led to the revocation of the royal charters guaranteeing Jewish rights.

However, this was usually not the end of the story. Students of Polish history know that royal edicts were not carried out immediately. The spokesmen of the Jewish artisans intervened with the Crown to obtain a reconsideration of the edict involving the basic rights of Polish Jewry as laid down in the charters. As a result, new decrees would follow, reaffirming the old rights.

As a matter of fact, the Polish guilds did not exert as powerful an impact on the economic life of the country as did the guilds in medieval Germany, France, Flanders, and Italy. In the early fifteenth century, the monopolistic policies of the Polish guilds aroused dissatisfaction among the gentry. The rural population, too, complained about the high prices maintained by the city guilds. As a result, in 1423 King Wladislaw Jagiello decreed the abolition of the guilds. However, it is not known whether this and similar decrees were carried out.[1] W. Surowiecki believes that the kings, while yielding to pressure, still were convinced that the guilds were beneficial to the country. The Constitutions of 1611, 1659, 1768, and 1776 recognized the necessity of preserving the rights of the guilds. The same kings who were condemning the guilds, were confirming the statutes of some of them.[2] In the town of Sochaczow alone twenty-two guilds received recognition by the acts of 1476 and 1521. One reason for the toleration of the guilds, not envisaged by Surowiecki, was their service in the militia, particularly important for the defense of the eastern provinces of Poland.

In any event, the nobility's opposition to the guilds, the wavering attitude of the Crown, and the protection the kings lent to non-organized labor, including Jews, weakened the position of the guilds in the long run.

The Szlachta and the Guilds

Public opinion voiced strong opposition to the guilds. The statesman and publicist, John Ostrorog (1436-1507), sharply criticized the guilds for fleecing the customers by selling them poor wares at high prices. Other political writers expressed similar dissatisfaction. The gentry attacked the price tariffs of the merchants' and crafts' guilds in the Diet (1565), and demanded the opening of Polish markets to foreigners, especially to Scots merchants.[3] On the other hand, the gentry was eager to obtain higher prices for agricultural products.

In their efforts to promote trade and industry in the towns and villages they owned, the nobles, paraticularly those in the higher ranks, favored the settlement of Jews and the granting to them of liberal charters and loans to encourage their mercantile activities in foreign markets. Thus, we see Count Joseph Potocki advancing to the Jewish merchants of Brody in Galicia 1,000,000 zloty in 1742 to help them resume business transactions abroad after a fire had ruined the city.[4] Similar conditions prevailed in other private towns, such as Leszno, Bialystok, Berdichev, Tysmienica, Czortkow, Kejdany, and others.

We have previously noted the enclaves in the royal cities, owned by the monastic orders, the upper Catholic hierarchy, high officials and the nobility. Whole blocks and city districts were exempted from municipal jurisdiction and the control of the guilds, thus offering outlets for Jewish artisanship.

The Multi-Ethnic Composition of the Working Class in Poland-Lithuania

With the multi-ethnic composition of the working population in Poland, the Roman-Catholic Polish craft guilds were facing the competition of the Dissidents, the Protestant Germans, the Greek-Catholic Ruthenians or Unitarians, the Greek-Orthodox

Russians and White Russians, the Armenians, the Moslem Tartars, and the Jews. All these groups were restricted in the exercise of trades.

In Vilna, Jews and Tartars were barred from the guilds entirely. Protestants, Unitarians, and Orthodox Russians were admitted but were not permitted full membership rights. One half of the guild wardens were Roman Catholics; the other half was elected by the Protestants, Unitarians, and Greek-Orthodox together. In some guilds Protestants and Orthodox were denied higher posts in the guild hierarchy. At guild meetings the Roman-Catholics sat in the right-hand section of the hall, while the others occupied the left-hand section. In the guilds in Vilna, a Lithuanian city, the official language was Polish. Non-Catholic members were frequently compelled to attend Catholic services. The admission of non-Catholic masters as guild members was sometimes restricted. The shoemakers' guild in Vilna, with eighty Roman-Catholic members, limited the Unitarians to forty and the Protestants to twenty.

In Lwow, Unitarians and Armenians were discriminated against by the Roman-Catholic guilds in about the same manner as were the Jews. In places where non-Catholics were admitted, they formed a group of second-class members, *i.e.* they were not eligible as guild officers. On the other hand, Protestant guilds in the western provinces of Poland, for instance at Torun (Thorn), discriminated against Roman-Catholic artisans.[5]

And yet, as time went on, religious and ethnic animosities lessened and some kind of coexistence was established. The guilds in Vilna, Lwow, Lublin, and other places ultimately adopted a more conciliatory attitude toward non-Catholics, especially Jews. Of this, more is said later.

Non-Organized Labor

In Lithuania and the eastern provinces of Poland inhabited by large groups of Russians and Ruthenians, artisans' associations had come into existence under rights based upon local custom. In many cases these associations had been founded by the lords of the towns. Apart from these organized groups, there were non-

Jewish and Jewish artisans who had obtained special royal privileges to ply their trades as the king's servants, or *servitores,* as they were called in the Polish official language of the time. Frequently their status was pure fiction, for these masters worked for any patron who asked for their services. The guilds, however, made it difficult for them to obtain raw materials and journeymen.

Another group whose size it is impossible to assess, was formed by artisans who had not joined the guilds because of their disinclination to pay dues or who were not admitted because of lack of professional training. These outsiders were the so-called "bunglers" *(partacze).*[6] The non-organized workers were a serious threat to the guilds. They sometimes managed to bring about the dissolution of a guild although they were not the only factor in the decline of the guilds.

Jewish Resistance to the Guilds

Despite the internal migration of Jews from the royal cities to the privately owned towns and villages where free commerce and trades were protected by the local lords, sizable groups of Jewish craftsmen had been formed in the royal cities—in Brest-Litovsk, Cracow, Grodno, Lwow, Lublin, Vilna, and elsewhere—cities which had recovered their position in the post-war period.

Vilna 1600-1800

The ancient Lithuanian capital had been an important commercial and industrial center for centuries. The charter of the Lithuanian Grand Duke Vitovt of 1389 had guaranteed the Jews free exercise of the trades. It was confirmed in 1629 by King Sigismund III in a charter to the Lithuanian Jews. The decree of King Wladislaw IV of 1633 specified that in Vilna trades not organized in guilds were open to Jews. Since the Christian tailors had a guild, Jewish tailors were restricted to Jewish clientele. No restrictions obtained in furriery, cap making, glaziery, goldsmith work, plumbing, and bookbinding. However, whenever a new Christian guild was established, Jews were barred from work. In 1664 Jewish and Tartar fishermen were forbidden to sell their catch on more than two days a week. In the same year Jewish glaziers were warned not to have their apprentices repair broken windows in Christian houses and not to take Christian apprentices. In 1669 the furriers' guild encouraged its members to attack Jewish furriers in the street and snatch away furs which they carried for sale. Christian journeymen, working secretly for Jewish masters, were threatened with loss of jobs and imprisonment.

While this fight flared up time and again, some guilds in Vilna came to an agreement with their Jewish competitors. Agreements were concluded with the Jewish butchers (1667), plumbers (1673), needlemakers (1673), cap makers and furriers (1741), and barber-surgeons (1786). The terms of the agreement with the cap makers and furriers stipulated payments for the maintenance of the guild's altar for ten years, restriction of manufacture to a certain kind of furs, prohibition for the cap makers to hang their emblem—a cap—in windows or outside, prohibition of hawking, except in certain areas. The number of journeymen and apprentices was not to exceed fifteen.

It was a losing fight for the guilds, however. Thirteen Christian guilds in Vilna collapsed in 1776. They included belt makers, cap makers, carpenters, glaziers, nailsmiths, plumbers, needlemakers, cutlers, lace makers, bookbinders, and jewelers. Documentary evidence on the exact dates and circumstances under which the guilds were closed is lacking. Their collapse was due to the general decline of handicrafts in the eighteenth century, a decline which was already apparent in western and central Europe in the seventeenth century.

Helena Wolczacka has shown in her study of the glazier's craft in Vilna in the late eighteenth century how the lack of demand for highly skilled craftsmanship killed the work of the glazier. Stained glass windows, the glory of medieval churches, were no longer in fashion in the period of the classical revival. The glaziers' guild, disregarding the changes in taste, still required from a candidate for the master title a highly elaborate masterpiece, such as a monstrance with sunburst, or a lantern with turrets. The glaziers' guild in Cracow refused membership to glaziers who merely knew how to set window panes (1650), with the result that the glazier's job became the lot of the *partacz,* usually the Jew. The hardest blow to handicrafts was dealt by the glass manufactory at Urzecz, a foundation of the Radziwills, which brought to the market cheap, mass-produced wares.[7]

The collapse of the thirteen Christian guilds in Vilna is known from a complaint filed with the district court of Vilna on November 2, 1776, in the name of the local guilds and the Christian residents of the city. The complaint was directed against the city council which, allegedly, in collusion with the *Kahal* (Council of the Jewish community), had brought about the ruin of the townspeople. The city council was accused of imposing high taxes and spending the money privately. The still-functioning guilds were said to be unable to compete with the flood of articles imported from abroad and from other cities in Poland. The remedy suggested was the removal of the Jews to the outskirts of Vilna.[8]

Nothing is known about the court's action. The Jews remained in Vilna as long as Polish rule lasted, nor were they removed by the Russians who occupied the city in 1795.

The indictment of the city council for collusion with the Jewish community council is a new phenomenon, for they were usually at loggerheads. Evidently the commercial interests represented in the city council at Vilna aligned themselves with those of the Jews rather than with the decaying craft guilds.

Lublin, 1616-1789

In Lublin the situation was similar to that in Vilna. Organized and non-organized labor sustained an unremitting battle. By a court decision on May 27, 1615, Jewish tailors had been forbidden to work unless they belonged to Lublin's tailors' guild. The guild did not admit Jewish members, however, nor did it allow Christian masters to accept Jewish apprentices. When, in 1656, the Jewish quarter in Lublin was destroyed by Russian Cossacks who at that time occupied the city, and the Jews moved to the center of the town, the competition between Jewish and Christian masters reached its peak. The courts were busy arbitrating between the litigants. A Jewish tailor Heysyck Rubinovich, fined by court decision (1659) for working without the guild's permission, was put in the prison of the Jewish community for refusing to pay the fine. The community administration let him free, disregarding complaints of the guild to the court. Finally, Rubinovich and a master, Rubin Moshkovich, on behalf of the Jewish tailors of Lublin, managed to obtain an agreement with the guild on September 17, 1660, stipulating that twenty-four Jewish tailors residing in the town were to be permitted to exercise their trade.

In another case, the liberal attitude of a Christian guild was due to particular circumstances. In the Lublin suburb of Podzamcze a new Christian tailor's guild was formed by members seceding from the established guild. Jews were admitted as members, probably in order to break the monopoly of the old guild. In any case, the experiment did not succeed, for the authorities closed down the guild in 1660 on legal grounds.

At an unknown date, the Jewish tailors of Lublin formed their own guild. Its statutes have not survived, but it appears that the guild had its own rabbi. By agreement with the Christian guild, Jewish masters were permitted to make men's and women's clothes against yearly dues to the Christian guild. The number of Jewish tailors was, as before, not to exceed twenty-four. Those in surplus were advised to leave the city under threat of *herem* (religious ban) by the rabbi.

The situation was evidently not alleviated, for in 1767 there was an outbreak of hostilities. Two masters of the Christian guild, along with their journeymen and apprentices, attacked the Jewish tailors and beat several of them until blood ran. The event provoked a public scandal and caused the city council to intervene. The ringleaders were arrested. The matter dragged on until 1789, when a new arrangement was made with the Christian guild. The number of approved tailors was raised to forty-four against an annual payment of nine zloty from each to the guild's treasury. One apprentice and one journeyman were allowed a master. Should a tailor leave the city for good, another one could take his place with the consent of the Christian guild and upon an entrance fee of twenty zloty.

In return for these concessions, Jews were forbidden to give out work to strangers and transient journeymen, to hawk ready-made clothes in the monasteries of Lublin and in the houses of the nobles and other city residents, and to solicit orders in houses where Christian tailors lived.

Similar arrangements were made with other Christian guilds.

However, they could not eliminate the conflicts or alleviate the tension due to the pressure of cheap labor.

Toward the end of the eighteenth century, the Jews comprised about one-half of the total population in Lublin. In 1786 Lublin had ninety Jewish tailors (against twelve Christian tailors), twenty-four furriers (six Christian), and thirty glaziers (one Christian). There were many Jewish goldsmiths and Jewish braziers.[9]

Eastern Poland

In general the pressure of the guilds on non-organized labor was less stringent in the towns of eastern Poland than in the western and central provinces, except in Vilna, however. There, too, the power of the guilds was broken in the course of the eighteenth century.

The Jewish artisan class in Minsk was relatively young, having originated in the second half of the seventeenth century. We find there saddlers, carvers and glaziers, furriers, lace makers and goldsmiths. The Jewish masters do not seem to have had any obligations, such as paying dues, toward the Christian guilds. The fact that they freely displayed brass plates and trade emblems in their workshops implies that the guilds were either too weak or did not feel endangered in their position. In Kovel, Volhynia, Jewish tailors and furriers were contributing to the maintenance of the guilds' churches (1618), according to some arrangements with the guilds. After 1650, there were Jewish artisans in the Christian guilds of Kovel.

A combined guild, referred to in a royal order of 1765, included Jewish tailors, furriers, weavers, lace and cap makers. The wardens were elected by Jewish and Gentile members.[10] In Vladimir-Volynsk all local craftsmen belonged to the guilds without distinction of creed and ethnic origin, the earliest reference to them dating from 1628.[11]

A rather unique arrangement is found in Pereyaslav, where a litigation between Jews and Ukrainians was settled in 1620 by mutual agreement according to which Jews were to enjoy the privileges of the Magdeburg Law and share all the burdens with the other inhabitants on an equal basis.[12] However, the Pereyaslav agreement was not more than a passing episode, chiefly because the history of the Jews in that city was of short duration. In 1648 they were murdered by the Cossacks of Bogdan Chmielnicky.

The Private Towns

As mentioned before, the position of the Jewish workingmen in the privately owned cities and villages was more favorable than in the royal cities. The guilds, as far as such existed in private towns, lacked the power to restrain the activities of non-members. The lord or his agent was anxious to see his people make a living and pay their taxes. The relationships between the Christian and Jewish groups, less affected by religious prejudice and economic competition, were conducted in a more amicable atmosphere. Conflicts were settled more effectively than in the king's lands.

A survey conducted in twenty-three towns and villages in Poland-Lithuania* gives the following picture: Jews, while having their own guilds, participated in the Christian guilds upon the order of the lord of the place. He took it upon himself to prompt the negotiations between the two parties. Jews were accorded masters' diplomas. They attended the guild assemblies and took part in the election of the wardens and other officers of the guild. In one town, Wengrow, the assembly was called for a weekday, out of consideration for the Jewish members who would not attend on the Sabbath. The Jews observed the guild rules concerning the production and sale of goods and the employment of journeymen; they assumed their part in defense duties. In some places they contributed to the quotas of wax for the churches along with the Christian members of the guild. Count Branicki, liberal owner of Bialystok, saw to it that the Jewish members of the local guilds were exempt from payments to the church.

Jewish members were not eligible for the post of guild warden. The same restriction applied to Protestant guild members. The formula of the oath concluding with the words: "So help me God and the Holy Trinity" (or "and all Saints"), which the elected

* These were: Berdichev; Bialystock; Brody; Chrzanow; Czortkow; Dubno; Keydany; Luboml; Nowy Sacz (Sonch); Opatow; Polonnoye; Rzeszow; Stanislawow; Tarnopol; Tykocin; Wengrow; Wieledniki; Zabludov; Zamosc; Zborow; Zloczow; Zolkiew.

warden had to pronounce, would have embarrassed a Jew. For similar reasons Jewish members were free from attending church affairs and funerals of Christian members of the guild. They made special payments to the guild in the same amount as did Christian members who had absented themselves from a church procession. We know of an instance of this sort in the city of Stanislawow.

It goes without saying that petty frictions between Jewish and Christian artisans could not be entirely avoided. There were the additional contributions to the guild which Jews resented. In the 1722 charter of the Jewish community of Czortkow, granted by the owner of the city, Count Stefan Potocki, it was stipulated that the tailors and furriers had to pay an entrance fee of six zloty, an annual fee of twenty-four groszy, and contribute a pound of wax to the church upon admission to the guild. Furthermore, the guild requested a bottle of brandy (*Schnaps*) of the best quality, and a cask of beer, or some other beverages. There was also the obnoxious rule requiring the applicant to stand bareheaded before the wardens at the registration. To a pious Jew, who was accustomed to cover his head out of reverence for his God, this was a highly repugnant practice. There were, in addition, the almost "traditional" harassments inherited from centuries of anti-Jewish feeling, such as when Gentile masters would intrude upon the premises of the Jewish workmen and damage their tools out of sheer malice.

As a result of these and similar grievances, the Jewish tailors and furriers of Czortkow resolved to set up a guild of their own. With the help of the elders of the Jewish community, they obtained a charter from the Austrian administration in 1781 (Czortkow had been incorporated into the Austrian monarchy in 1772) authorizing them to organize a guild.[13]

Mutual Concessions and No Solution

The Jewish fight for the right to work had lost much of its vehemence by 1795, the year of the final liquidation of the independent kingdom of Poland. A rather uncomfortable mode of co-existence had been secured in some places, with Jewish labor at least partially integrated into the fabric of the Christian guild. How little the acceptance and belonging to the guild really meant, may be inferred from the contemptuous terms "Lent fellows," or "quarterly fellows" *(suchedniarzy, kwartalnicy)*, used to designate the Jewish members of the guilds, owing to the fact that they made their payments to the guild either quarterly or during the period of Lent.

Some degree of real solidarity was probably achieved in situations of emergency, as when both Christian and Jewish members were fighting itinerant journeymen who undersold them and threatened their very existence.

Chapter XXIII

Relations Between Jewish Guilds and Jewish Community Councils in Poland-Lithuania: 1600-1800

Origins of the Jewish Guilds

Several factors combined to bring about the growth and development of the Jewish guilds in Poland and Lithuania. Jewish craftsmen living in the same place and plying the same trade tended to associate with each other. The purpose of such associations was to set up rules regulating working conditions and the relations with employers, fellow members, workmen outside the guilds, the Jewish community, and the governmental authorities. The guilds aimed at the protection of their members from competition both by outsiders and by the members themselves. They cared for the physical and spiritual welfare of the members and their families, encouraged the acquisition of technical skills, comforted and supported the sick, the widows, and the orphans, and concerned themselves with the religious needs of the group.

The government authorities were not opposed to the formation of Jewish guilds; rather they saw in them a means of strengthening the economic position of the Jewish workers and their ability to pay taxes. Frequently the authorities granted monopolistic rights to the Jewish guilds.

The establishment of the guilds was motivated to a large extent by the need for the Jewish working class to defend itself against the discriminatory policies of the Polish guilds which tended to deny Jewish craftsmen the right to work and to sell their goods to persons outside the Jewish fold. The Jewish workmen, not unlike those Christian workmen who were barred from the guilds, fought tenaciously, and by various means, for the right to work, until they came to realize that an effective self-defense could best be carried on by associations, or guilds, of their own.

In all probability the Jewish guilds originated toward the end of the sixteenth century—some two hundred years after the emergence of the Polish guilds—although documentary evidence does not go back further than the early seventeenth century. The guild statutes of the Jewish furriers (1613), and particularly those of the barbers of Cracow (1639), have been discussed in chapter XIX. We have records of a tailors' guild in Lwow, dated 1627, and of a tailors' guild in Vilna, which donated an iron portal to the Great Synagogue in 1640. The guild-book of the tailors in Przemysl refers to decisions adopted in the beginning of the seventeenth century.[1] It is reasonable to assume that more Jewish guilds were in existence in that period.

The rapid spread of handicrafts among Polish Jews at the close of the seventeenth century, and particularly during the eighteenth century, prompted the emergence of new guilds. Jewish craft guilds existed in most urban localities with a Jewish population, and in cities with a sizable Jewish community the number of guilds reached ten or more.[2]

Documentary evidence is available about Jewish guilds in more than fifty cities and towns. Nineteen guild statutes were preserved up to World War II.[3] This material, scanty as it is, offers an insight into structure, policies, and activities of the guilds.

The Guild and the Kahal

The guilds required approval by the government authorities in order to become institutions of public law. In the royal cities the Jews depended on the *voyevoda* (in Poland), or the *starosta* (in Lithuania), the king's representatives in matters of jurisdiction over the Jews and their self-government. In the private towns the Jews were ruled by the seigneurial lords and their administrators.

Before seeking recognition by the governing authorities, the

Jewish guilds had to obtain the approval of the local *Kahals,* the Jewish community councils.

The *Kahals,* on more than one occasion, had lent a hand to the artisans in their defense against the aggressive policies of the Christian guilds. Prior to any attempt on the part of the artisans to organize, the *Kahals* had frequently acted as spokesmen for the Jewish working people before the authorities. It is, therefore, not surprising that the Jewish guilds in Poland and in Lithuania, although in principle autonomous bodies, were tied in one way or another to the *Kahals* and became dependent upon them.

In this respect, the position of the Jewish guilds was different from that in Spain, where they enjoyed a high degree of autonomy in their relations to the community councils. We recall how the decisions of the guilds in Barcelona, supported by rabbinical authority, could not be invalidated by the community council.

In Poland a local *Kahal* could refuse to approve the statutes of a guild. In Cracow it withheld confirmation of the by-laws of a number of guilds for several years. It denied the butchers' guild the right to appoint its wardens (1595). On the other hand, the kerchief and ribbon makers' guild in Cracow (1683) enjoyed a broad autonomy and was in no way molested by the *Kahal.* In one point the *Kahal* was consistent. It forbade secessions from the guilds and warned the community elders "not to listen to him [the secessionist] even if he is prepared to pay a large sum of money."[4]

The interference of the *Kahal* was felt in many ways. In Przemysl the guild wardens were not to undertake any action and not to collect money for the guild's needs without the *Kahal's* knowledge.[5] In Poznan, the *Kahal* itself drafted the statute for the combined guild of several crafts (1737).[6] In the *Kahal's* justification, it may be said that it worked under high pressure. Its function, its only *raison d'être* in the eyes of the Polish government, depended on its ability to produce taxes. In 1646 the Poznan *Kahal* conceived the ingenious idea of setting up a tax on wearing apparel. The tailors were told to report to the *Kahal* the amount of the payment due to them from their patrons for every garment they were to deliver. Failure to do so might entail loss of the right to practice the trade, the tailors were forewarned. The warning was repeated in 1649.[7]

Cases of actual withdrawal of the right to work were by no means rare. The *Kahal* of Dubno forbade the baker, Seeb Wolf, a guild master, to work for an indefinite period (1765).[8]

Disputes within the guilds sometimes invited the intervention of the *Kahal.* This was the case in Zabludov (1752)[9] and in Dubno (1754)[10]. In Vlodava (1765), the *Kahal* brought about the reconciliation of the tailors, on the one hand, and the goldsmiths and furriers, on the other, keeping them together in the joint guild, but ruled that one of the wardens would henceforth be appointed by its authority.[11]

In Lithuania the guilds seemed to enjoy greater freedom. However, the *Vaad* of Lithuania resolved in 1670 that of the four wardens of a guild (*hevra*), two should be elected by the membership and two appointed by the local *Kahal.* This decision was amended in 1687. The two wardens from the *Kahal* were to be elected from the community at large.[12]

The Artisans' Position in the Community. Election Rights.

As has been mentioned, the *Kahals* were responsible for the collection of taxes to the government. In addition, they had to secure through taxes the upkeep of the communal institutions.

The election ordinances of the Jewish communities created barriers in the exercise of voting rights by the members of the community. The commanding posts in the communities were monopolized by men of substance, the large contributors who used their position in a ruthless way. Examples abound. In 1695 the Lithuanian *Vaad* instructed the electors that they must choose the community leaders from among those who had paid the tax in full.[13] This removed most of the artisans from positions of influence. The *Vaad* of 1761 also restricted the active election rights. In communities of more than three hundred families, artisans who had not participated in the elections before were not to be admitted to the electoral meetings which were to choose rabbis, cantors, ritual butchers, and communal officers[14]

The *Vaad* of White Russia ruled concerning the community of Petrovici that an artisan, to be eligible for a community post, had to be a high tax payer and house owner.[15] A man practicing one of the baser trades was not eligible, even if he paid over two per cent property taxes.[16] In the community of Ivenec, besides satisfying the property requirements, an artisan had to hold the honorific title of *morenu* (our teacher), in order to be considered for an elective community job.[17] An annual tax of 75 zloty qualified a man for the position of community elder, and a tax of 50 zloty for the position of a warden of the poorhouse in the community of Lwow. In Vilna, electors of the rabbi, cantor and sexton had to be holders of the titles of *morenu* and *haver* (companion). In several communities the number of persons having election rights was limited—in Poznan, to 21; in Dubno, to 55; in Leszno, to 71.[18]

The Kahal's Growing Interference with Guild Management

We have cited cases of guilds inviting the intervention of the *Kahal* to settle their conflicts. As a result, the *Kahal* strengthened its control over the guilds. In Kurnik, the guild had to submit its annual financial report to the *Kahal*. In the preamble to its by-laws the guild stated that the by-laws were adopted with the *Kahal's* approval (1754).[19] It submitted to the inevitable. In Vlodava, the *Kahal* threatened the guild in 1783 with excommunication.[20] In Dubno, the *Kahal* denounced the joint guild of weavers (probably tailors), butchers, and bakers to the Lord of the town, Count Jablonowski, and closed it down. There were a few exceptions, of course, as when the guild at Zabludov retained its prerogatives (1754).[21] However, in Minsk, where the guild disobeyed a verdict of the rabbinical court, the *Kahal* closed the artisans' synagogue.[22]

The Kahal's Privileged Artisans

The *Kahal,* not infrequently, circumvented the guilds in granting special favors to the more prosperous artisans who were in a position to pay for privileges.

A goldsmith in Cracow obtained the right to sell his own products and other wares in a store, while the guild—of which he was a member—usually denied this right. The goldsmiths were supposed to peddle in the streets.[23] A buttonhole maker, catering to an aristocratic clientele, was assured the right to retain the lucrative privilege for his children after his death.[24]

The social discrimination against the poorer artisans, and the *Kahal's* intrusion in the affairs of the guilds, did not fail to provoke profound bitterness which sporadically erupted into open defiance and rebellion.

Clashes between Kahals and Guilds

In 1777 a revolt broke out in the offices of the *Kahal* in Minsk. It was led by the artisans, who were joined by the impoverished elements in the community. The elders were physically attacked, the records were removed, and the insurgents proclaimed that they would henceforth take care of the affairs of the community. Subsequently both parties lodged complaints with the Polish court, and the outcome was that the *Kahal* returned to power.

However, this was not the end of the story. In 1782, the fight broke out again. The bone of contention was a *hazakah,* a privilege the guild had granted an artisan for a specified period and which was contested by the *Kahal.* The guild appealed to the government authorities. The *Kahal* resorted to a ruse. The leaders of the guild were invited to the synagogue to discuss the matter. When all were assembled, the doors of the synagogue were locked and one of the guild wardens was chained and flogged. The *Kahal* dismissed the other warden and seized the guild's files. The struggle of the Minsk artisans continued indecisively for a number of years.[25]

A similar outbreak occurred a year later in Vitebsk. The artisans complained to the city council, charging the *Kahal* with oppressive practices. The *Kahal* had some of the men flogged, and obtained a declaration from the artisans pledging "never again to revolt and disobey the *Kahal's* rules."[26]

The artisans' rebellion in Leszno in 1763 was provoked by excessively high taxes. The community was heavily indebted, and the *Kahal* had no other choice but to squeeze the taxes out of the people. The enraged masses dragged the community elders to the synagogue and made them swear that they would resign. However, the feudal lord of Leszno, Count Sulkowski, sided with the deposed heads of the community and had the leaders of the rebellion punished. Three of them were chained in the synagogue prison for three consecutive Sabbaths, and the fourth was sentenced to four weeks of hard labor.

In 1792, however, an ordinance issued by the *Kahal* of Leszno granted the artisans participation in community affairs. The ordinance provided that when matters of importance were to be decided, the elders were to summon to a meeting seven representatives of the vocational groups—the tailors, furriers, and goldsmiths. The artisans were to have seven votes and the community elders three. The assemblymen were to have the right to examine the community's finances, including the charity funds, every three months.[27] On the eve of the annexation by Prussia, the popular forces prevailed!

The artisans were successful in other cities of western Poland as well. In Inowroclaw (German: *Hohensalza;* Yiddish: *Leslau*), toward the end of the eighteenth century, a law was passed providing that the electors be chosen by the three classes: the wealthy, the middle class, and the artisans.[28] In Lublin the common people likewise obtained representation in the *Kahal*. In 1788 their delegates, called "people's counselors" (Polish: *radcy pospolstwa*), are known to have voiced opposition in a controversy within the *Kahal* concerning the lease of taxes in the Jewish community.[29]

These cases were an exception, however. The temporary victory of the artisans in Leszno, Inowroclaw, and Lublin finds its explanation in the fact that, according to the census of 1764-65, the artisans in these cities comprised about one-half of the registered Jewish families, namely, 50% in Lublin, 41% in Inowroclaw, and 40% in Leszno.[30] Accordingly, the *Kahal* was compelled to reckon with them. The situation was somewhat comparable in Vilna, the principal city of Lithuania, where the artisans obtained the right of participation in the affairs of the community during the bitter controversy between the elders and the rabbinate (1785-1790).[31]

In that period, various crafts—the tailors, furriers, passementerie workers, tinsmiths and others—were represented before the Jewish administrative and judicial authorities who dealt with the controversy. But in the vast, economically backward regions of Lithuania, White Russia, Volhynia, and other eastern provinces of Poland, where the percentage of artisans among the breadwinners in the Jewish community was considerably lower, they remained essentially without voice and representation.[32] Such was the case in Minsk, Vitebsk, Dubno, and Vlodava, among other places.

In private towns, where the will of the noble overlord was law, the situation depended on his relationship with the *Kahal*. The feudal owner looked with a jaundiced eye at the obligations of "his" Jews to pay taxes to the *Kahal*—which was likely to affect his income from his subjects! For instance, in 1732 the lord of Berdichev freed the Jewish tailors' guild from the supervision of the community, and warned the *Kahal* not to interfere in its affairs.[33] The lord of Veledniki, a town in the vicinity of Vilna, exempted the Jewish craftsmen's guild from the obligation of presenting the *Kahal* with holiday gifts.[34]

Relations between Jewish Artisans and Christian Guilds

A factor contributing to the lowering of the authority of the *Kahal* in the eyes of Jewish artisans is to be found in the relationship between the Jewish and the Christian guilds. Economically, the Jewish artisans were competitors of the Christian artisans, but once the Jewish artisan class was firmly established, the Christian craft guilds were interested in regularizing relations with them. This was particularly true in the seigneurial towns where the Christian guilds were weak and where the power of the *Kahal* was kept in bounds by the feudal lord. While Jewish merchants, the backbone of the *Kahal*, hardly ever belonged to Christian merchant associations and confraternities, Jewish artisans not infrequently were members of Christian craft guilds, with varying degrees of juridical allegiance and financial obligations.

In a great many instances, regular payments of dues to the Christian guilds were requested of the Jewish artisans. In return, the guilds granted them the right to ply their trades unmolested and the enjoyment of the guild's protection against unfair competition. In this way, the Jewish artisans became associated,—loosely, it is true—with the Christian guilds. But, in some instances, they even acquired membership, attended guild meetings, and voted in the election of guild elders. They never were elected as guild officers, however. Among the cities where Jews participated in the activities of Christian guilds, with more-or-less full membership rights, were the following: Keydany (1666), Kuty (1716), Czortkow (1722), Zloczow (1727), Zborow (1727), Novy Sacz (1742), Opatov (1769), Chrzanow (1781), and Rzeszow (date uncertain).[35]

Obviously, the contacts which were established between Jewish artisans' associations and the general guilds weakened the authority of the *Kahals*. Whereas, in the period of the bitter antagonism between Jewish and Christian guilds in the sixteenth and seventeenth centuries, the *Kahal* had played the role of mediator between the parties, and protector of the interests of the Jewish craftsmen, this role was reduced, and even reversed, during the eighteenth century, and toward the end of the century, it was definitely forfeited. The successive partitions of Poland undermined the institution of the *Kahal* as an organ of internal Jewish autonomy, along with other Polish institutions.

The unrelenting stubbornness with which the *Kahals* clung to their prerogatives hastened their end. On the other hand, the submission of Polish populations to Russian, Prussian, and Austrian administrations muted the rivalry between Christian and Jewish artisans and made them realize that a *modus vivendi* had become imperative. State legislation, opening the guilds to every qualified person, completed the process.

The status of the artisan in the Jewish community, as reflected in Jewish folklore, remained low. Only the profound socioeconomic transformation which set in toward the end of the nineteenth century, coupled with far-reaching ideological changes, altered the situation. In retrospect it is possible to recognize in the social unrest which gripped the Jewish laboring classes in the eighteenth century a harbinger of things to come.

Chapter XXIV

The Workshop Assistants: Apprentices and Journeymen

The System of Apprenticeship

The medieval guild system in western and central Europe had elaborate rules and provisions regarding apprenticeship, and these rules were taken over in large part by both the Christian and Jewish guilds in Poland and Lithuania. A family wanting to apprentice a boy to a master signed a written agreement with him, the so-called indenture. The master undertook to teach the boy the craft, feed and clothe him, watch over his health and morals, and punish him when he needed it. The boy became a member of the master's household and owed him loyal service and strict obedience. The term of apprenticeship in most European countries was two to seven years and at times more.

The problem of vocational training of youth was raised in a session of the Lithuanian *Vaad* in 1639. A number of orphaned and destitute children had drifted into Lithuania from other provinces in Poland, and the *Vaad* had to take care of them. It was resolved to distribute seventy-five boys among the communities, which would have to feed and clothe them and place them in schools; those unfit for scholarly studies would have to be apprenticed to artisans to be taught a trade. The need to take care of homeless children became particularly acute after the Chmielnicky pogroms of 1648 which devastated numerous Jewish communities in the Ukraine, Volhynia, Podolia, and Galicia. Nathan

Hanover, a native of Ostrog, Volhynia, mentions in his *Abyss of Despair* (*Yeven Metzulah,* Venice, 1653) that poor boys, chiefly vagrants, without family ties in the community, "were apprenticed to an artisan if they were willing to learn a craft."

Our information on the contents of artisan work contracts is derived chiefly from Jewish community records and guild minute books—original contracts having been lost. The guild by-laws also furnish some data on the working conditions of journeymen and apprentices. However, the guilds were mostly interested in ways and means of combatting competition between masters and securing cheap labor supply; their statutes, therefore, give an often one-sided picture of the position of the workshop assistants.

The earliest preserved materials on work contracts were found in the records of the Cracow community, which date from the period before 1650.

Conditions of Hiring

To obtain permission from the guild to engage a journeyman or an apprentice, the master had to satisfy certain conditions. Marriage was a prerequisite. Another was a certain duration of the master's membership. It varied in most statutes from one to three years. In Keydany, Lithuania, a ten years' membership was required.[1] Exceptions were made for sons and sons-in-law of guild members. There were cases when a guild, being in financial difficulties, would waive the restriction, for a contribution to the guild's chest.[2] In one case, in Kurnik, a tailors' guild prohibited the admission of apprentices for a period of six years while allowing the employment of guild members' children. This was clearly an attempt to convert the guild into a closed family corporation. Three years later, in 1776, the guild was compelled, upon the intervention of the *Kahal,* to revoke the regulation.[3]

The right to keep an apprentice or journeyman could be forfeited as punishment for disobeying a guild regulation, or because of insufficient qualification of the master.[4]

The number of journeymen and apprentices allowed to a master was fixed in the guild's by-laws. The tailors' guild in Plock (Plotzk) (1798), granted one apprentice to a master who had not yet completed a three years' membership, but no journeyman.[5] However, the arrangements varied. In 1722, the tailors' guild of Przemysl, liberalizing a regulation of 1704, allowed a master two journeymen and one apprentice, or vice versa. A master in a high tax bracket was permitted to hire three journeymen, and, in cases of emergency, as when a big order was given on short notice and had to be delivered before the holidays (Passover or Rosh Hashanah), permission was given to engage another master for day or piece work. This required the approval of the guild wardens and the guild's rabbi.[6]

The position of a master in the guild and in the community sometimes could be a determining factor. In Keydany a master, married eighteen years, a member for ten years, and a "lawmaker" (*i.e.* belonging to the guild hierarchy), was allowed two apprentices and one journeyman. Sons of masters were not restricted in the right to work for their fathers.[7] The guild in Lutzk apportioned workshop help in relation to the taxes paid by the master. An annual 150 zloty tax entitled a master to two journeymen and one apprentice. Those paying less got no help at all, and those paying twice that amount could hire as many as three journeymen, but only one apprentice. Then again, in Leszno, two apprentices were allowed.[8]

An agreement concluded in 1741 between the Christian and the Jewish cap makers in Vilna fixed the number of journeymen and apprentices to which a Jewish master was entitled.[9]

The tendency of the guild to limit the number of master assistants was based on the idea of securing a livelihood and equal opportunity for all. By the same token, the by-laws prohibited the hiring of additional journeymen for day or piece work, even for short terms.[10] As has been seen, the system was continually corroded from within and its intent frequently reversed. The more prosperous artisans and the guild officers were not held to the restrictions which were so rigidly imposed upon less affluent members. The former established themselves as a privileged group in violation of the very principles upon which the guilds were founded.

The labor contracts between masters and assistants had to be signed in the presence of the guild wardens and the guild rabbi, or before an appointed panel of seven to eight guild members.[11]

The apprentices were represented by their parents. The contracts were to be recorded in the guild books. Whether they always had to be recorded in the *Kahal* minute books is not certain. The Cracow community's minute books contain a number of contracts between masters and journeymen or apprentices.

Work Term, Remuneration, Promotion

The agreements usually indicate the terms of training (for apprentices) or employment (for journeymen). The minimal work term stipulated for a journeyman is one year.[12] The wages and other kinds of remuneration, such as food, shelter and clothing, are stated. In the case of an apprentice, pledges of parents to pay the master are recorded. The duties of journeymen and apprentices are delineated, sometimes with specification of the daily norm. There are provisions limiting the right of the master to use his workshop assistants for extraneous purposes. The agreements finally state the amount of dues to be paid by both parties to the guild, and the fines for breach of contract. In some statutes, provisions are made for a destitute master who is compelled to hire himself out as a journeyman, for a newlywed master, and for a journeyman who is getting married.[13]

The terms of training stipulated for an apprentice vary. The average duration is two years. In contracts recorded in the minute books (*pinkas*) of the tailors' guild of Kurnik, dating from the seventh decade of the eighteenth century, as many as six years appear to have been required for the proper training of an apprentice. The term was shorter for a boy trained by his father. After 1776, when many parents seemed to want their children to learn a trade but were discouraged by the long training, the term was generally reduced to three years, and the provisions for acceptance of applicants whose fathers were not guild members were liberalized.[14]

How long did a journeyman have to work to earn the title of master? Usually the contracts specify that journeymen had to hire themselves out for one to two years. Evidently, this was the required period for a journeyman to become a master. It is likely, however, that early marriage, then common among Polish Jews, shortened the term.

According to the statute of the tailors of Przemysl, a candidate for guild membership as a master had to prove that he had worked three years at his trade: two years as an apprentice and one year as a journeyman.[15] After satisfying certain conditions, such as being married and having paid a registration fee, he was to appear before the proper guild authorities to be admitted into the guild. The first three years he was considered a junior (*mlodszy*) and had limited rights. The tailors' guild in Plock, as already mentioned, allowed him an apprentice but no journeyman.[16] In Przemysl a junior tailor was forbidden to take his tape measure to the market with him as other tailors did. He had no election rights. Similar rules prevailed in Luboml.[17]

Mutual Obligations of Masters and Assistants

The contracts stipulate that the master should teach the apprentice all stages of the work without concealing any phase of it from him. Where the apprentice lived in the master's household, the boy's father paid for his room and board; where the boy went back at night to his family, a small remuneration might be stipulated. The obligations of the journeymen and apprentices included honesty, obedience, and working only for their masters. Almost all contracts and statutes forbade journeymen and apprentices to work for themselves.[18] This prohibition comprised all kinds of work, including assistance to the apprentice's own father. The Kurnik guild statute extended the restriction to outlying villages beyond the jurisdiction of the Kurnik community.[19]

However, the master could not dispose of his journeyman beyond certain limits. According to the by-laws of the tailors' guild in Luboml, a journeyman was to work only for the regular customers of his master. He was not to be compelled to do "Polish work," that is, occasional, extraneous work.[20]

A number of guilds forbade the masters to send their workshop assistants to the villages to get orders or to complete work there. The assistants were not allowed to appear at markets and annual fairs on their masters' behalf.[21]

These restrictions were meant not so much to prevent exploitation of the journeymen as to narrow the field of competition among the masters.

Working Hours

Neither the contracts nor the guild by-laws contain any provisions as to the length of the working day. The accepted practice was to work from sunrise to sundown in the summer, with additional evening hours in the winter. However, from Friday evening —the beginning of the Sabbath—until Sunday morning, the worker, apprentice or journeyman, was free. The same held true for the holidays. Only one case is known where an agreement was made between a master and an apprentice regarding the length of the working day.

In Cracow, in 1651, an apprentice pledged himself to work all day until five hours after sundown in the winter, and, in the summer, until such time when the inhabitants of Kazimierz (the Jewish quarter of Cracow) returned from the city, probably the time of the evening prayer (*Minha*). As a rule, the master could demand additional work but had to pay for overtime.[22]

Work Norm and Wages

(a) *Journeymen.*

The records are not specific with respect to the work norm for a journeyman. The only example at hand, the contract of a cap maker in Cracow and his journeyman (1723), stipulates somewhat vaguely that the journeyman should make three caps in a working day but may finish the job the following day, if not possible otherwise.[23]

Amounts of wages and conditions of paying were elastic. Payment, apparently depending on local and trade practices, was made weekly, quarterly, or semi-annually, except for piece work, where payment was on delivery.[24]

The amount of wages paid an advanced apprentice or journeyman varied in Cracow, from the middle of the seventeenth century to the beginning of the eighteenth century, between 15 and 48 zloty per year. The exceptionally high wage of 70 zloty stipulated in the above-mentioned agreement of 1723[25] reflects the devaluation of the Polish currency.[26]

The wages of the journeymen depended on the worker's efficiency and on local, as well as trade, conditions. In 1720 the maximum wage for a journeyman in the furrier and tailor trades in Lutzk was 40 zloty, with a heavy fine imposed on the master if he paid more.[27] In Kurnik, in the latter half of the eighteenth century, a tailor's journeyman received 20 to 30 zloty on the average. The minimum wage on record is 12 zloty; the maximum 54 zolty.[28]

In the same period, in Lublin, a journeyman in the goldsmith trade received 36 zloty annually. The statute of the furriers' guild in Leszno, approved in 1764, established a maximum journeyman's wage of 15 groszy per piece.[29] Generally, the wages of the journeymen were specified in the guild statutes, in order to prevent competition among the masters for the best workers, and disputes between masters and journeymen.[30]

The guilds seem not to have been opposed to the promotion of a journeyman to the status of a partner of his master. The 1640 statute of the barbers' guild in Cracow states that a master may hire an additional assistant with the approval of the majority of the guild, provided that he became a partner, sharing one-third of the master's profits.[31] Whether the status of a partner improved the journeyman's chances to become a master is not clear. At any rate, the journeyman was supposed to be treated with certain consideration. The food which he received in addition to his wages, was to be the same as that of the master and the master's family. His compensation included lodgings, clothes and laundering.[32]

(b) *Apprentices*

The contracts between the master and the apprentice, (actually the apprentice's father, mother or guardian) vary widely in terms and provisions. In some agreements the master pledges to provide food for the boy, in others the food allowance is shared by master and parents. The arrangements may be very specific, as when the father is to supply the food in the first half of the term, while the master takes care of it in the second half,[33] or when the father provides food and clothing during the first year of a five-year training period.[34] The apprentice's laundry, bed linen, and clothing are a matter of special arrangements between the master and the parents in the work contracts.[35] In several agreements we find a little touch which must have made the life of a young boy somewhat more pleasant: he was allowed to make himself a linen suit, apparently from the master's materials.[36]

Girl apprentices probably lived with their parents, but boys—particularly from out-of-town—frequently boarded in the master's house. One contract specifies that the boy has the right to go home after work.[37] Another contract stipulates that the master must not use the apprenticed boy to help with the housework.[38]

While working for food at first, the apprentice received a small wage after a while.[39] Some Cracow agreements provide for a wage of seven zloty semi-annually, payable every three months.[40] A Kurnik contract supplements the wages with thread, buttons, hooks, and other sewing accessories.[41] In one case, the father of a girl apprenticed to an embroiderer supplies the colored yarn needed for the first three months of her training by the master's wife.[42] In some contracts, the father pledges to pay for his son's training.[43] Quite interesting is the agreement of a youth from Florence, Italy, who undertakes to teach a Jewish man in Cracow the apothecary (alchemist) trade in a two-year term for a fixed remuneration.[44]

What was the procedure of promotion from apprentice to journeyman? Since nothing is known about tests, it must be assumed that an apprentice, after completing his training as fixed in the contract—and provided he was a good worker—would automatically become a journeyman. In Keydany he had to wait five years after termination of his apprenticeship. The Keydany guild had a clause according to which a contract with a journeyman could be revoked if a guild official raised objections on moral grounds involving the "honor of the guild."[45]

As a rule, a master could exercise the prerogative of hiring his former apprentice as a journeyman, in preference to other masters. In one case, a master claimed priority in hiring his former apprentice against a wage of as little as one half of the wage offered by other masters.[46]

Obligations of Masters and Assistants toward the Guild

Masters who employed workshop assistants had to pay special

dues to the guild chest. In the mixed guild of tailors and furriers at Kutno, a master paid four szelag (about four groszy) weekly for a journeyman, that is, double the amount paid by a master who worked alone.[47] The tailors' guild at Kurnik demanded five zloty from a master for an apprentice from out-of-town, and the tailors' guild at Przemysl as much as nine zloty for a three-year period.[48] These figures give us only an approximate idea of the amounts stipulated, because of the changing value of the zloty and its changing relationship to the grosz. On the average the zloty was the equivalent of thirty groszy.

The apprentices and journeymen contributed to the guild chest either a fixed amount, or a percentage of every zloty earned. Thus, in Leszno the journeyman's dues were one-half grosz a week; in Keydany, three groszy out of every zloty earned; in Czortkow, one grosz in 1721 and two in 1781 out of every zloty earned. In Kurnik, the journeyman paid one grosz out of every zloty and twenty-four groszy weekly when he worked for himself. In Miedzyrzecz, the annual dues was one zloty.[49]

Journeymen who entered a partnership with their masters—there were cases in Kurnik and Dubno (ca. 1750)—paid, in addition, community taxes like the masters (6%).[50]

Particularly vexing were the guild rules concerning out-of-town journeymen and apprentices. In Kurnik the entrance fee for a foreign apprentice was five times the amount paid by the son of a local guild member. An out-of-town journeyman had to pay, in addition to a fee to the guild treasury, a high community tax.[51] In Poznan, in 1723, a foreign journeyman could not be hired unless all the local journeymen were employed. His work permit was to expire after three years, regardless of the situation on the labor market.[52] The furriers' guild at Leszno provided in its by-laws, adopted in 1764, that both the foreign journeyman and the master who employed him were to pay ten zloty each to the guild for his right to work.[53]

Regulations Concerning Differences between Masters and Assistants

Guild statutes and labor contracts contain provisions for settling conflicts between the parties. Disputes were to be brought before the guild elders, or a rabbinical court, or a mixed tribunal of lay and rabbinical members. In Poznan the guild statute of 1723 stipulated that disputes among masters, journeymen and apprentices involving a sum no larger than ten zloty, belonged to the jurisdiction of the rabbi of the guild, who acted as judge, assisted by four guild wardens; when larger sums were involved, the parties could appeal to the *Kahal.*[54] In Kurnik, the guild statute of 1754 provided that differences between masters and journeymen regarding "tailors' business" were to be settled by the guild's elders, whereas disputes involving money were to be brought before a rabbinical court or the *Kahal.* While a verdict was pending, a journeyman was not to work for another master without the approval of the guild elders.[55]

A case where jurisdiction rested with the rabbinical court is reported from Lublin in the latter part of the eighteenth century. The circumstances are not known. The rabbinical court obtained the opinion of experts for determining the wage rate. The master, a goldsmith, was forewarned "not to beat the journeyman" and the latter, "to obey his master and not to cheat on the job." For offenses of this sort, he was threatened with excommunication.[56] The sources abound in complaints of masters about journeymen who had beaten them or beaten their wives and had committed thefts and other kinds of misdemeanors. In one case, the master appealed to the *voyevoda.* The journeyman was sentenced to pay a fine which was to be turned over to the *voyevoda's* court.[57]

The guild by-laws provided all sorts of fines for infraction of guild rules. The fines went to the guild or were divided between the guild and the *Kahal,* or else between the feudal lord and the injured party, or a combination of these. In the Cracow agreements fines were usually set aside for charitable purposes.

Rules Concerning Breach of Contract

The labor contract usually contained a clause on penalties for the breaking of the agreement. A workshop assistant, leaving his job in the middle of a work term, had to prove to the guild elders that the master was grossly negligent or unfair with regard to his obligations toward him.[58] If he was unable to substantiate his accusations, he had to return to his master; and since he was not allowed to accept work from other masters, the alternative was leaving the town.[59] The tailors' guild in Czortkow was less strict, and only temporarily suspended a recalcitrant journeyman.[60]

Some guilds fined a master for hiring a journeyman who had left his former master without legitimate reason. Others required the new master to obtain permission from the previous master before hiring the journeyman. If disputes were involved, the guild elders were to be asked to settle the matter.[61]

Walking out on the job was a serious problem reflecting the profound unrest among the workers. Some guilds tried in every possible way to compromise and avoid harsh measures. The guild in Plock ruled that a journeyman who had left his workshop in the middle of a season—not necessarily the middle of a work term—with a good reason, was to receive full wages for the time he put in during the summer months, two-thirds of his wages for work done during the winter months, and could hire out to another master.

If his former master had a legitimate complaint against him, the journeyman was still entitled to a compensation for work done. He was to receive one-third of his wages for the summer and one-half of his wages for the winter season. He was permitted to take on employment with another master but had to complete his work as stipulated in his contract with his old master.[62] On the whole, however, the guilds were inclined, as was the case in Kurnik, to fine the unruly journeyman, give him no payment whatsoever, and withdraw his right to work in the town.[63]

Social Status of Journeymen

In conclusion, one may say that the social status of the journeyman within the artisan group was low, and that it was still lower within the Jewish community as a whole.

Membership in the Jewish artisan guilds was predicated on high entrance fees and membership dues, and on considerations involving family status and morals. These conditions served the purpose of restricting the number of fully accredited masters. It must be assumed, therefore, that a substantial number of working artisans remained outside the guild organization. These outsiders (*partacze*), included the journeymen, along with a group of fly-by-night masters. Journeymen, generally, were denied membership in the guilds, yet were obliged to make certain payments to them. Apart from day-laborers, beggars, tramps, and other hand-to-mouth or charity cases, they were placed at the lowest rung of the social ladder in the Jewish group.

The heavy hand of the *Kahal,* hard-pressed by its fiscal obligations toward the authorities, was upon this under-privileged wage earner. The *Kahal* held down the wage rates (Cracow and Poznan, 1595 and 1621) and limited the chances of the journeyman to found a family. The *Kahal* of Poznan resolved in 1670 that only owners of a minimum of 400 zloty may obtain a marriage license without applying for the *Kahal's* permission.[64] Marriage, however, was a prerequisite for guild membership.

The story of Jewish artisanship in Poland was marked by a struggle on two fronts: a struggle against the Catholic guilds to obtain recognition of the right to work, and a fight within the Jewish community dominated by the more potent merchant element.

As time went by, the opposition of interests of the guild masters and their journeymen became manifest. The battle with the Christian guilds subsided in the late eighteenth century owing to the general decline of artisanship under the impact of the industrialization of production. But the inner struggle of the Jewish masters for a voice in the community management, and the Jewish journeymen's fight against both the guild leaders who restricted their promotion and the community leaders who would side with the masters continued unrelentingly.

The story of the Jewish guilds has its place in European guild history. Basically, the guild system was everywhere the same: in Florence, in Paris, in London, and in the Hansa cities—with its originally democratic ideals, its gradual yielding to favoritism, its oligarchic tendencies and attempts to make privileges hereditary, its restriction of promotions of journeymen, unjustified long duration of apprenticeship, inequality in social consideration of the "honorable" and the low trades.[65]

However, the Christian artisans usually had representation in the municipal councils and sometimes even dominated them. Whether high or low in the guild's ranks, a working man, a simple journeyman, had some voice in the guild assemblies. He had his social satisfactions too. He took pride in the guild hall of his city, decorated with the coats-of-arms of the crafts, the banners and the seals; he took pride in his church, built and run by the guilds. And he enjoyed the banquets, the impressive public ceremonies.

Even in Poland, where the guilds did not have the prestige they enjoyed in the west, they maintained a certain decorum and attached great value to display. An evidence is the *Codex Picturatus,* a collection of records of Cracow guild statutes compiled by the *cancellarius* of the city, Balthazar Behem, in 1505. The parchment manuscript is decorated with elaborate miniatures in the early Renaissance style, illustrating the activities of the various guilds. The text is in Latin interspersed with Polish and German terms.[66]

In Poland, too, the guild master, the *magister mechanicorum,* had an important role in the municipal councils.[67] It is true, there was discrimination against some Christian groups which were denied full guild membership. But the Jewish artisan, although not the only outsider, belonged to those tolerated the least.

Be it as it may, the Jewish craftsman had his satisfactions, too. His guild had a chamber in the synagogue for its own use.[68] It supported charitable work and made donations to the synagogue. In some places he was allowed to display his trade sign, and participated in official patriotic festivities carrying the badges, emblems, and banners of his guild.

The dissolution of the Polish state accelerated the downfall of the guilds. The differences between masters and journeymen in the Jewish guilds found their expression in the attempts of the journeymen to organize as a separate group. The earliest preserved document records the formation in 1832 of a tailor journeymen's association *(hevra)* in Jaroslaw, Galicia. The arrangement was made amicably. The *hevra* was set up with the blessings of the masters' guild and the approval of the rabbi. The founding act was recorded in the guild's minute book. According to the by-laws of the *hevra,* two of its officers were to be members of the guild. No resolution of the guild assembly was to be valid without their assent.[69]

There were similar attempts made by journeymen elsewhere. In Bialystok, journeymen of the tailors' guild set up an association, but dissolved it in 1850, under the masters' pressure, it would seem.[70] In Minsk, the *Kahal* stepped in to prevent the organization of the tailor journeymen (1841).[71]

It is interesting to note that the avowed aim of the journeymen in expressing their desire for an association was of a religious nature. They wished to set up their own *minyan* (quorum of no less than ten participants in a prayer meeting), actually their own religious service. They wished to engage their own *maggid* (preacher), and have their own place for study. It was understood that scholastic pursuits rather than secular studies were intended.

Economic incentives were, no doubt, a powerful factor in their aspirations. But the habit was strong to think of a professional gathering, of a craft's association, in terms of the traditional religious framework. These craftsmen wanted their own place in the Jewish house of worship not unlike those ancient Jewish craftsmen who had their special seats in the great synagogue at Alexandria.

It took another generation before a workers' movement took shape. Folkist-socialist and Marxist ideologies took hold of the working masses. From the 1870's onward, organized groups of Jewish workers appear in the northwestern provinces of Russia and in Congress Poland, in Warsaw, Bialystok, Vilna, and Minsk. They consisted chiefly of discontented journeymen. The first documented strike of Jewish workers occurred in a tobacco factory in Vilna in 1871. The first documented strike fund was set up by the hosiery workers in Vilna in 1882.[72] By that time, a large part of the Jewish artisan class, merges into the factory proletariat. Its history becomes indistinguishable from the history of the labor movement.

Appendices

APPENDIX I

Charter of the Jewish Shoemakers' Guild in Saragossa (1336) *

Let all men know by the present that to Us, Pedro, by the grace of God, King of Aragon, Valencia, Sardinia, and Corsica, and Count of Barcelona, there came [representatives] on behalf of certain Jews, members of the Brotherhood [guild] of the Benevolent Society of the Jewish shoemakers of the city of Saragossa, and there were granted to them certain by-laws for the advantage and improvement of the said Benevolent Society, as it is called, and these by-laws are as follows:

First, whenever any Jew of the Brotherhood shall make a wedding, and whoever fails to attend shall pay one *denarius* to the afore-said Benevolent Society. And if a son shall be born to him, [the members] shall be obliged to accompany [the father] to the ceremony of circumcision, and whoever fails to do so shall pay one *denarius* to the afore-said Society. Likewise if any of the afore-said brethren falls sick, the officers of the Benevolent Society shall visit him twice a week, on Mondays and Thursdays. And if [the ailing member] needs money or a loan requiring security, they may lend him up to five *solidi* from the treasury of the said Benevolent Society. And if it happens that the officers of the Society see indeed that he is in need, the said officers shall give him from the said treasury, as they may see fit, two *denarii* for each day [of his illness]. Also all the brethren shall be obliged to visit the said ill member every Saturday, and whoever fails to do so shall pay one *denarius* [for each missed visit] to the said Benevolent Society. Also, if one of the said Brotherhood [guild] should die, all the brethren shall be obliged to do him honor at the funeral, and whoever fails to do so shall pay two *denarii* to the said Benevolent Society. Also, if a member of the said Brotherhood dies and leaves something to the said Benevolent Society, it shall administer the trust honorably. Also, if the said brother should die by night, the said brethren shall lie down in the house of the deceased. Also, the brethren shall have these [articles] read twice a year so that everyone may know what is required of him. Also, any member of the brother-

* Translated from the Latin-Spanish original in the General Archives of the Kingdom of Aragon. Published by D. Manuel de Bofarull y de Sartorio in *Gremios i Cofradias de la antigua Corona de Aragon*. Barcelona, 1876, pp. 131-133.

hood who brings dishonor upon it or conceals [anything] from his brethren shall be suspended from the Brotherhood for one month, this in addition to any penalties exacted by justice and law for the said offense. Also, the said brethren shall be present in the house at the time that he departs his life. And the said brethren shall do this same thing for the closest relative of the deceased, say a prayer for the deceased in the synagogue on each of the eight days following his death, and whoever fails to do so shall pay one *denarius* to the said Society.

The afore-mentioned Jews, after the said by-laws had been granted them, humbly besought our royal favor to have these by-laws published and observed. Generously assenting to their plea, We have granted for Us and Ours in perpetuity, by the contents of this our present charter, with full knowledge, to the said Brotherhood and to those who are now its members or shall be in the future, the afore-mentioned by-laws and all things contained in them, and We publish, approve, ratify and confirm them, just as they are set forth above in better fashion and more fully. We order by the present document all Jews of the said Brotherhood, individually and collectively, both present and future, to uphold and preserve the said by-laws and the things expressed in them, and the penalties set forth in them shall be exacted from those breaking the provisions of the statutes, as often as they shall be broken; these [fines] shall be used for the benefit of the said Benevolent Society and shall not be evaded in any way. Moreover, we order the royal superintendent of Saragossa and our other officials or their lieutenants present and future firmly to adhere to our afore-mentioned grant; the by-laws inserted above and all the matters stated in them shall be kept by the said Jews and be observed inviolate and shall not be broken in any respect nor shall anyone be permitted to break them for any reason. In testimony of which we have ordered this our present charter to be drawn up and confirmed by our seal hereto appended.

Granted at Saragossa on this sixth day of the Ides of May, in the year of Our Lord MCCCXXX and six. G. de Villa, the mandate of the King having been made known by the vice-chancellor. Signed Pedro, King of Aragon, by the grace of God, etc. The witnesses are The Infante Jacobus Count Urgelli and Viscount Agerensis. His Reverence Peter Archbishop of Saragossa. Otho de Montecatheno. Lupus de Luna. Raymond Cornelius.

Written by Guillermus de Villa, the scribe of my Lord the King.

Appendix II

Apprenticeship Agreement concluded in Verdus, Aragon, in 1386*

July 6, 1386.

I, Izach [Isaac] Bonavia, son of Izach Bonavia, resident of San Martino [San Martino de Malda] do apprentice myself as tailor to you, Solomon Duyot de Serra, Jew of Verdus, from the date herein registered till the festival of the Birth of the Lord and from the said festival till the end of the year, and [I declare] that I will serve you well and faithfully and will not default; you, the said Solomon, shall faithfully provide me with food and drink, but the care of [my] shoes and stockings shall be my responsibility for the said period. And anything which depends on me I promise to attend to and to fulfill.

And I, the said Izach, twelve years old, renounce the benefit of minority and "restitution in pretextu"; and I swear on the Ten Commandments deposited in the hands of Bonuscujot Abenezech, Jew of San Martino, that I shall observe and fulfill all the afore-said [terms].

I, the said Solomon, for my part promise to teach you the said craft for the same period.

Witnesses: the venerable Père Guian, skilled in the law, and Vidal Channel, Jew of San Martino.

Appendix III

Apprenticeship Agreement Concluded in Rome in 1544**

We, the undersigned, witness that on this fifth day of the week

* Tr. from the Latin original published in *Boletin de la Real Academia de la Historia,* Madrid, 1914, vol. LXV, p. 250.

** Tr. from the Hebrew original published by A. Berliner, *Kobez al Yad,* IX (1893), 5.

which is the twenty-third day of Kislev 305 [1544] there appeared before us the bachelor [bahur] Samuel, son of the honorable Jacob and declared as follows: Be witness to the fact that I have made an agreement with the good woman Caracoso to have her son Michael stay with me for three years to learn the trade of tailoring. The said Samuel undertakes to defray the costs of food and drink; the mother agrees to provide the clothing. Moreover [it was agreed that the contract is valid] while Samuel stays in Rome. [But even] should he move from Rome, the boy is duty bound to follow him. And party failing to observe the agreement shall pay three scudi to the treasurer of the Vicario.

Witnessed by Siman Tov and Mordecai of Rosta.

Appendix IV

Privilege granted by the Grand Duke of Tuscany to operate workshops in Leghorn and Pisa, 1663.*

Ferdinand the Second by the grace of God, Grand Duke of Tuscany, etc.

Whereas for the public good we desire to accede graciously to the request of Efraim Cassuto, a resident of Florence, and of David Teglia, a resident of Livorno [Leghorn] both Jewish merchants, in which they set forth that they wished to be permitted to introduce into Our cities of Pisa and Livorno one or more contrivances for working diamonds and other stones (provided that they shall not be for inlaying), and accordingly were asking for the Privilege that none but they or their assigns should be permitted to make such kinds of contrivances in Our said cities, We, therefore, prompted by the public interest and Our customary benignity, do grant to the said Efraim Cassuto and David Teglia the Privilege and Favor that for the next ten years after today none but they or their assigns shall be permitted to keep or introduce contrivances for working diamonds or other stones (provided that they shall not be for inlaying) into Our said cities of Pisa and Livorno. We desire, however, that the aforesaid

* Tr. by Marco Treves, Florence, from the Italian original in the possession of Herman Davidowitz, New York.

men shall be required and obliged to hire qualified and skilled persons to exercise the said craft in the said cities within the time and term of one year, during which they must produce authentic justificatory certificates at the *Riformagioni* [a legislative drafting office] that they have begun to work or to make [their employees] work. In case of failure to do so and to continue to work and produce the abovementioned certificates from year to year, We intend that they shall be understood to have forfeited the present Privilege, it being left to Our discretion whether to grant it to others. We also intend that this Favor shall not take effect so long as it may have been granted by Us to others and still be in force, because We desire, as stated above, that none but the aforesaid men or their assigns shall be permitted to practice this kind of craft in the said places and [period of] time, under the penalty for any infringer (in addition to [other punishments at] our discretion) of the forfeiture of his contrivances and [a fine] of fifty scudi for each infringement, which shall go one quarter to the Exchequer and Great Ducal Treasury, one quarter to the men to whom this Privilege is granted, one quarter to the Accuser, whether secret or open, and the remaining quarter to the Magistrate who will convict and collect. We command, therefore, all the Magistrates, Mayors and Officers of Our States to observe and cause to be observed the present grant and Privilege inviolably, any law, statute, proclamation, or ordinance to the contrary notwithstanding, which of Our mere motion and certain knowledge and by Our ample and absolute powers We set aside completely and entirely as far as the aforesaid effects are concerned.

In witness whereof We have caused the present Privilege to be made, which shall be signed with Our hand, shall have Our customary leaden seal appended, and shall be subscribed by Our Counselor and Secretary whose name appears hereunder.

Given in Florence at Our Chief Palace on the seventeenth day of June in the year of the Salvation-bringing Incarnation of Our Lord Jesus Christ 1663, being the thirty-third year of Our reign as Grand Duke of Tuscany.

[The signature of the Secretary is illegible.]

Appendix V

Statutes of the Jewish Tailors' Guild of Prague, 1690*

1. No one shall seek permission to become a master, unless he has it in writing from the Jewish Elders of Prague that he is native of the place, and he shall previously furnish the Jewish Elders with a testimonial by guild Wardens to his [good] conduct.

2. After a [journeyman] has received permission in writing from four Wardens to become a master, he shall not take an apprentice for at least one year after his marriage, but shall employ one journeyman only. At the end of the year he may take one apprentice, but not more.

3. If a [journeyman] wishes to become a master, he must present himself at the Wardens' office and be inscribed in the guild book, which act shall be witnessed by the signatures of all the guild officers. Likewise, when an apprentice is admitted [to the guild] the several Wardens shall subscribe their signatures.

4. If a tailor is about to take the measure [of a patron], either in or outside the ghetto, and another tailor happens along, the latter shall immediately leave, but if he does not leave and tries to get the work for himself, he shall be liable to a fine of no less than two ducats, to be paid into the treasury of the Prague Jewish community.

5. The Warden of the month shall call a meeting of the Guild officers every Sunday on pain of incurring a fine of no less than 45 kreutzer, to be paid into the Guild treasury.

6. No one shall hold the office of Warden of the month longer than four weeks, on pain of paying a fine of one ducat into the treasury of the Prague Jewish community. If the Warden of the month has laid out money to defray certain expenses during his tenure of office, he shall not yield his office until his successor has reimbursed him for these payments.

7. When a Warden of the month relinquishes his office, the majority of the Wardens must witness this by their signatures, otherwise it is not valid.

* Tr. from the German original in the Prague Archives of the Ministry of Internal Affairs. Published by T. Jakobovits, in *JGGJCR*, VIII, 141-143.

8. If a tailor has a dispute with another tailor regardless of the matter [pertaining to the craft], they shall appear before the Wardens of the Guild to hear the verdict; but if one or the other refuses to abide by the verdict, he shall deposit a pledge of half a *schock* with the Warden of the month whereafter he shall have 24 hours to appeal to the *starsi* [superior wardens].

9. When a tailor hires a journeyman, he shall try him for a period no longer than three days on pain of paying a fine of two ducats into the treasury of the Jewish community, after which he shall have the journeyman registered in the Guild book, each party being required to pay a fee of 24½ kreutzer, or a total of 49 kreutzer.

Also, it is deemed right that all disputes concerning complaints of a Prague Jew [customer] of being overcharged by a tailor, or being asked to supply more [material] than is necessary, shall be settled by the Warden of the Guild sitting together with a representative of the Prague Jewish community appointed by the chief inspectors [of the Taendelmarkt]. In the event that the Prague Jew is not satisfied with the decision, regardless of whether he is justified or not, one or two Jewish judges shall be appointed to settle the dispute.

10. Every tailor who takes an apprentice to assist him, shall instruct him fairly in the craft as it is customarily practiced, so that the latter after his years of apprenticeship may become a journeyman.

11. Should it be found that an apprentice has not been taught the trade as it is customarily practiced, his master shall not only return the apprenticeship fee, but shall be forbidden to take another apprentice for a period of three years.

12. But, if a master has taught his apprentice the trade as it is customarily practiced, he shall be forbidden to take a new apprentice for a period of one year only [on pain of paying a fine of one ducat].

13. A master has the option of keeping a journeyman whom he has trained for three years; the latter, for his part, shall have the option [to leave] after one year, unless his master pays him as high a wage as he is offered by another master.

14. A journeyman shall work six years for a master before he is permitted to marry. By applying to the elders of the Prague Jewish community for permission to marry he shall produce a testimonial to his good conduct from the Wardens of the Guild.

15. A journeyman who is betrothed shall work for his master until his wedding day, even if he was working on his own wedding clothes.

16. Every journeyman is required to attend *shul* [synagogue] every day, especially on Mondays and Thursdays.

17. Also, ever journeyman and every apprentice shall have half an hour free to learn how to write.

18. Journeymen and apprentices shall work from 6 [AM] to 8[PM], as is the custom.

19. A journeyman when contracting to work for a master shall pledge to the Guild secretary his word that he will work faithfully and trustfully.

20. If a journeyman or an apprentice falls ill during his term of service, all the expenses involved shall be borne by his father.

21. If an apprentice dies, the partial payment which the master has already received shall be returned and the money still due him shall be foregone.

22. A foreign journeyman coming [to Prague] shall not go to work in a shop until he first reports to the Warden of the Guild. A master [hiring a foreign journeyman] shall also report.

23. No journeyman shall seize in pledge any of his master's property [for payment of his wages], but shall make a request in the regular way. Should he do it through ignorance, the pledge shall be deposited with the Warden of the month.

24. At the decision of the Wardens, no one shall be the secretary unless he has been married at least two years; no one shall be an elector who has not been a secretary, and no one shall be a Warden who has not been married at least ten years.

25. Newly elected Wardens are authorized with the concurrence of the Chief Inspectors to draw up a list of future expenditures.

It is deemed proper that all masters, journeymen, and apprentices should assemble every Sabbath to attend a lecture on Scriptures given by the Guild preacher. Each absence shall be penalized by a fine of half a liter of candles to be donated to the *shul*.

Lasser Bezallels — Beer Juda
Moyses Juda — Simone Ausch
Juda Loebl — Loebl Brandeis

Moyses Wehle, Guild Secretary

Appendix VI

Apprenticeship Agreement concluded in Cracow in 1650*

The honorable Judah Fikseles Katz articles his son Moses Eliah Fikseles Katz to the master tailor, the honorable Kopel Moses Keplish who undertakes to train [the youth] in sewing and cutting of every kind of garment. He shall not conceal anything from him, important or unimportant, and shall provide him board. The boy shall serve the full legal term of apprenticeship as it is established for all artisans in our community. When he shall have completed his term of apprenticeship he may take up mending and patching. The said Judah shall pay Kopel [the master] 10 Polish zloty as fee for his son before the 1st day of Kislev 411 [1650] and 10 zloty on the 1st day of Heshvan 412 [1651]. In the 4th year Kopel shall have the option for employing the youth at half the wages [offered him] by any [other] master tailor.

The transgressing party, God forbid, shall pay a fine of 10 taler to charity. The agreement is not subject to waiving nor is it to be considered an unreal promise. It was done according to the terms of a symbolic acquisition and drawn up on Tuesday which is the 1st day of Heshvan 411 [1650].

Moses Abraham Mattatiah Delakrut, Secretary of the Holy Community of Cracow.

The said Judah paid 10 zloty to Kopel. Attested by Mattatiah.

* Tr. from the Hebrew original published by F. H. Wettstein, "Kadmoniyot mi-Pinkassot Yeshanim," *Ozar ha-Sifrut*, ed. Graeber, Cracow, 1898, vol. IV, 623.

Notes

Notes to Chapter I

TRADES AND GUILDS IN ANCIENT ISRAEL

1. I. Mendelsohn, "Guilds in Babylonia and Assyria," *JAOS,* IX, (March 1940), 68-72.

2. Code of Hammurabi, §§ 188-189; Mendelsohn, "Free Artisans and Slaves in Mesopotamia," *BASOR,* 89 (February 1943), 26.

3. Mendelsohn, "Free Artisans and Slaves in Mesopotamia," *op. cit.,* p. 28.

4. A. Haldar, *Associations of Cult Prophets among the Ancient Semites,* Uppsala, 1945, pp. 38-89.

5. Mendelsohn, "Guilds in Babylonia and Assyria," *op. cit.,* p. 70.

6. *Idem,* "Guilds in Ancient Palestine," *BASOR,* 80 (December 1940), 17.

7. Albright, *The Archaeology of Palestine,* London, 1949, p. 127.

8. *Horesh* means wood, wooded height. See R. Grossman and M. H. Segal, *Compendious Hebrew-English Dictionary,* Tel-Aviv, 1938, p. 126.

9. G. E. Wright, "Iron in Israel," *BA,* I, 2 (May 1938), 5 ff.

10. W. F. Albright, *Archaeology and Religion of Israel,* Baltimore, 1942, p. 137.

11. N. Glueck, "The Excavations of Solomon's Seaport: Ezion-geber," *Annual Report of the Smithsonian Institution,* 1941; *idem, The Other Side of the Jordan,* New Haven, 1940, chs. III-IV; *idem,* "The Civilization of the Edomites," *BA,* X, 4 (December 1947), 77 ff.

12. *Idem,* "Explorations in Eastern Palestine," *AASOR,* XXV-XXVIII (1951), 231-232.

13. G. E. Wright, "Israelite Daily Life," *BA,* XVIII, 9 (September 1955), 57.

14. Albright, *The Archaeology of Palestine,* fig. 30.

15. *Ibid.,* p. 122.

16. Y. Yadin, "The Fourth Season ot Excavations at Hazor," *BA,* XXII, 1 (February 1959), fig. 11.

17. B. S. Isserlin, "Israelite Art during the period of the monarchy," *Jewish Art,* C. Roth, ed., Tel-Aviv, 1961, fig. 31. For version of this capital in lotus form from Ramat Rahel, see fig. 32. See also Y. Aharoni, "Excavations at Ramat-Rahel," *BA,* XXIV, 4 (December 1961), 98 ff.

18. K. M. Kenyon, *Archaeology in the Holy Land,* New York, 1960, p. 247.

19. E. Herzfeld, *Altpersische Inschriften,* Berlin, 1938, pp. 16-17; for Apollodorus of Damascus, see K. Woermann,

Geschichte der Kunst, Leipzig, 1915, vol. I, p. 478; for the architects of Hagia Sophia, *ibid.,* vol. III, p. 40.

20. Albright, *Archaeology and Religion of Israel,* pp. 130, 137 f.

21. C. C. McGown, "The Density of Population in Ancient Palestine," *JBL,* LXVI. 4 (December 1947), 434.

22. J. W. Crowfoot and Grace M. Crowfoot, *Early Ivories from Samaria,* with a note by E. L. Sukenik, London, 1938, p. 50 and *passim.* For the dating see also Albright, *The Archaeology of Palestine,* p. 129.

23. J. B. Pritchard, ed., *Ancient Near Eastern Texts relating to the Old Testament,* 2nd ed., Princeton, 1955, p. 279.

24. M. Hamilton Swindler, *Ancient Painting,* New Haven, 1929, fig. 206, center; Woermann, *op. cit.,* I, p. 225.

25. W. Stevenson Smith, *The Art and Architecture of Ancient Egypt,* Baltimore, 1958, pp. 129, 130, 131.

26. Sukenik, "Notes on Hebrew Letters on the Ivories," in Crowfoot, *op. cit.,* p. 7.

27. Crowfoot, *op. cit.,* p. 55.

28. Kenyon, *op. cit.,* p. 268.

29. J. L. Kelso and J. Palin Thorley, "Palestine Pottery in Bible Times, "*BA,* VIII, 4 (December 1945), 82-93.

30. Albright, *Archaeology of Palestine,* fig. 21.

31. *Ibid.,* fig. 22.

32. *Ibid.,* fig. 29.

33. Kelso, "The Ceramic Vocabulary of the Old Testament," *BASOR,* Supplementary Studies, nos. 5-6, New Haven, 1948, pp. 7, 9, and *passim.*

34. G. E. Wright, "Israelite Daily Life," *op. cit.,* p. 73.

35. *Ibid.,* pp. 71f.

36. *Ibid.,* pp. 65-68.

37. *Ibid.,* p. 68.

38. Albright, "The Excavation of Tell Beit Mirsim," *AASOR,* XVII (1938), 5.

39. J. L. Starkey, "Fourth Season's Work at Tell en-Duweir," *Palestine Exploration Fund Quarterly Statement,* LXVIII (October 1936), 188-189.

40. *Tell en-Nasbeh.* Excavated under the direction of the late W. F. Badè, I: "Archaeological and Historical Results," C. C. McCown ed., Berkeley and New Haven, 1947, p. 256, and plate 97.

41. A. Reifenberg, *Ancient Hebrew Arts,* New York, 1950, pp. 31-37, with illustrations.

42. Starkey, *loc. cit.*

43. Albright, "The Administrative Divisions of Israel and Judah," *JPOS,* V. 1 (1925), 50.

44. Mendelsohn, "Guilds in Ancient Palestine," *op. cit.,* pp. 17-21.

45. *Idem,* "Guilds in Babylonia and Assyria," *op. cit.,* pp. 68-69.

46. *Idem,* "Guilds in Ancient Palestine," *op. cit.,* p. 21.

47. Albright, "Tell Beit Mirsim," *AASOR,* XII (1930), no. 21.

Notes to Chapter II

CRAFTS AND GUILDS IN JUDEA DURING THE SECOND COMMONWEALTH (c. 538 B.C.E.-70 C.E.)

1. W. F. Albright, "A Brief History of Judah from the Days of Josiah to Alexander the Great," *BA,* IX, I (February, 1946), 8.

2. *Ibid.,* p. 13.

3. *Tell en-Nasbeh,* II, "The Pottery," by J. C. Wampler. Also G. E. Wright, "Tell en-Nasbeh," *BA,* X, 4 (December, 1947), 70.

4. *Aristeas to Philocrates,* Letter of Aristeas, ed. and tr. by Moses Hadas, New York, 1951, p. 147.

5. *The Apocrypha and Pseudepigrapha of the Old Testament in English,* ed. by R. H. Charles, I. *Apocrypha,* Oxford, 1913, pp. 452-454.

6. M. I. Rostovtzeff, "The Near East in the Hellenistic and Roman Times," *Dumbarton Oaks Inaugural Lectures,* Cambridge, (1941), ch. II, p. 35.

7. *Westminster Historical Atlas to the Bible,* ed. G. E. Wright, Philadelphia, 1956, Plates VIIA and XIIA.

8. For a description of the mausoleum see M. Cohen, "Jewish Art at the time of the Second Temple," *Jewish Art,* C. Roth, ed., p. 126.

9. C. C. McGown, "The Density of

Population in Ancient Israel," *op. cit.*, p. 425-426. See also J. Klausner, "How Many Jews Can Live in Palestine," *JSS*, XI (April, 1949), 127, where a figure of 3,000,000 is suggested; S. W. Baron, *A Social and Religious History of the Jews* (cited as Baron, *History*), 2nd ed., Philadelphia, 1952 I, 168, estimates that 2,500,000 people lived in Palestine before the destruction of the Second Temple, including about half a million Samaritans, Greeks, and Nabataeans.

10. L. Herzfeld, *Handelsgeschichte der Juden des Altertums*, Braunschweig, 1879, pp. 129-130.

11. *Ant.* XX, 9, 7; XX, 4, 3; J. Jeremias, *Jerusalem zur Zeit Jesu*, Leipzig, 1923, Part I, 9, 13; A. H. M. Jones, *The Herods of Judaea*, Oxford, 1938.

12. E. L. Sukenik, *Ancient Synagogues in Palestine and Greece*, London, 1934, pp. 69-70; S. Krauss, *Synagogale Altertuemer*, Berlin, 1922, pp. 200 ff.

13. P. Rieger, *Versuch einer Technologie and Terminologie der Handwerke in der Mischnah*, Berlin, 1894, part I; Krauss, *Talmudische Archaeologie*, (cited as Krauss, *Archaeologie*) 3 vols., Leipzig, 1910-12, *passim*.

14. H. L. Gordon, "The Basilica and the Stoa in Early Rabbinical Literature," *The Art Bulletin*, XIII, 3 (1931), 12f.

15. E. A. Urbach, "The Laws of Idolatry in the Light of Historical and Archaeological Facts in the Third Century," *Eretz-Israel*, V (1958), 189-205.

16. Jeremias, *op. cit.*, p. 6. See also Baron, *History*, I, 253.

17. L. Ginzberg, *Mekomah shel ha-Halakha be-Hokhmat Yisrael*, Jerusalem, 1931, p. 30.

18. F. M. Heichelheim, "Roman Syria," *An Economic Survey of Ancient Rome*, T. Frank, ed., (cited as Heichelheim, "Roman Syria"), Baltimore, 1938, IV, 197.

19. *Mishnah, Demai*, V, 3 and 4; cf. Herzfeld, *op. cit.*, p. 91; S. Louis, "Handicrafts and Artisans mentioned in Talmudical Literature," *Transactions of the Society of Biblical Archaeology*, VIII (1885), 404-405.

20. Krauss, *Archaeologie*, II, 256.

21. Quoted by Jeremias, *op. cit.*, p. 3; cf. also A. S. Herschberg, *Haye ha-Tarbut bi-Tekufat ha-Mishnah ve-ha-Talmud*, Warsaw, 1924, part I, Ha-Ereg ve-Taasiat ha-Ereg.

22. Jeremias, *op. cit.*, pp. 3 and 28.

23. *Ibid.*, pp. 3 and 4, cf. Krauss, *Archaeologie*, II, 258 and 625. According to Krauss, Tarsian garments were for the most part manufactured in Alexandria. See also A. S. Herschberg, *op. cit.*, p. 161. For the weavers' synagogue at Lydda, see Krauss, *Synagogale Altertuemer*, p. 209.

24. A. Rosenzweig, *Kleidung und Schmuck im biblischen und talmudischen Schrifttum*, Berlin, 1905, p. 48.

25. Herschberg, *op. cit.*, p. 313.

26. Jeremias, *op. cit.*, pp. 4 and 29; Krauss *Archaeologie*, I, 14.

27. S. Louis, "Handicrafts and Artisans mentioned in Talmuldical Literature," *op. cit.*, p. 399.

28. For the Tyche of Antioch see B. S. Myers, *Art and Civilization*, New York, 1957, fig. 110. See also Du Mesnil du Buisson, *Les Peintures de la Synagogue de Doura-Europos*, Rome, 1939, p. 119. For medieval representations, R. Wischnitzer-Bernstein, *Symbole und Gestalten der Juedischen Kunst*, Berlin, 1935, figs. 30 and 31.

29. G. M. A. Richter, *A Handbook of Greek Art*, New York, 2nd ed., 1960, p. 373; Heichelheim, "Roman Syria," p. 189.

30. Ginzberg, *op. cit.*, pp. 5-6.

31. Krauss, *Archaeologie*, II, 287.

32. Jeremias, *op. cit.*, pp. 27ff.

33. Heichelheim, "Roman Syria," pp. 197-198.

34. R. Dussaud, "Comptes d'ouvriers d'une entreprise funéraire juive," *Syria. Revue d'Art Oriental et d'Archéologie*, IV (1923), 241 ff; S. Klein, *Toledot ha-Yishuv ha-Yehudi be-Eretz Israel*, 1935, pp. 113-114; Sukenik, "The Cave of Bethphage and Its Inscriptions," *Tarbiz*, VII (1936), 102-109. Sukenik dismisses Klein's doubts as to the date of the inscriptions of the Bethphage ossuaries.

35. *Abbot de-Rabbi Nathan*, ed. S. Schechter, Vienna, 1887, p. 23a.

36. F. Delitzsch, *Jewish Artisan Life in the time of Jesus,* London, 1877, pp. 78-79; Krauss, *Archaeologie,* II, 254.

37. Baron, *History,* I, 256.

38. *Ibid.,* I, 276-277.

Notes to Chapter III

CRAFTS, GUILDS AND LABOR LEGISLATION IN PALESTINE (70-636)

1. A. Buechler, *The Economic Conditions of Judaea after the Destruction of the Second Temple* (cited as Buechler's *Economic Conditions),* London, 1912, p. 67.

2. S. Yeivin, *Milhemeth Bar Kokhba,* Jerusalem, 1952, 13-14; M. Avi-Yonah, *Bimei Roma u-Visantion,* Jerusalem, 1946, pp. 1-5; see also *Three Historical Memoranda, Submitted to the United Nations Special Committee on Palestine on Behalf of the General Council (Vaad Leumi) of the Jewish Community of Palestine,* Jerusalem, 1947, pp. 13-15.

3. The literature on weaving and its subsidiary trades is extensive. The following works have been used: Buechler, *Economic Conditions,* p. 50; E. Schuerer, *Geschichte des juedischen Volkes im Zeitalter Jesu Christi,* Leipzig, 1901, II, 77, n. 205; Krauss, *Archaeologie,* II and III; A. Rosenzweig, *op. cit., passim;* A. S. Herschberg, *op. cit., passim;* H. F. Lutz, *Textiles and Costumes Among the Peoples of the Ancient Near East,* Leipzig, 1923, p. 70; Heichelheim, "Roman Syria," *passim;* Mendelsohn, "Guilds in Ancient Palestine," p. 18; M. Avi-Yonah, "Ha-Mishar ve-ha-Taasiyah be-Eretz Yisrael be-Tekufah ha-Romaith ha-Bizantinith," *Sifriah le-Yediath Eretz Yisrael,* Jerusalem, 1937, pp. 96-98; *idem, Bimei Roma u-Visantion,* pp. 6-7.

4. J. Brand, "Pottery in Talmudic Literature," *Sinai,* X, 9-10 (June-July, 1946), 217-235; *ibid.,* X, 11-12 (Aug.-Sept., 1946), and passim (in Hebrew). Now in book form: *Klei ha-Heres be-Sifrat ha-Talmud,* Jerusalem, 1953; also Krauss, *Archaeologie,* II, 271. On Gerasa, Heichelheim, "Roman Syria," II, 208.

5. Avi-Yonah, *Bimei Roma u-Visantion,* p. 8.

6. Herzfeld, *op. cit.,* p. 96.

7. Avi-Yonah, *op. cit.,* p. 8; Baron, *History* II, 246.

8. Avi-Yonah, *ibid.,* pp. 8-9.

9. Krauss, *Archaeologie,* I, 13ff.

10. Sukenik, "History of Jewish Archaeology," *The Jewish People, Past and Present,* New York, 1946, I, 69; *Bulletin, Hebrew University Department of Archaeology* I-III (1949-1960).

11. Krauss, *Archaeologie,* II, 269ff.; Herschberg, *op. cit.,* p. 284 ff.

12. Sukenik, *op. cit.,* p. 77.

13. Krauss, *Archaeologie* II, 255; S. Kalischer, "Die Wertschaetzung der Arbeit in Bibel und Talmud," *Judaica. Hermann Cohen Festschrift,* Berlin, 1912, 579ff. H. Gollancz, "The Dignity of Labor as Taught in the Talmud," *The Imperial and Asiatic Quarterly Review,* N.S., II (July-October, 1891), 129-138; Buechler, *Der galilaeische Am-ha-Arez des zweiten Jahrhunderts,* Vienna, 1906, p. 237f.

14. Buechler, *The Political and Social Leaders of the Jewish Community of Sepphoris in the Second and Third Centuries,* Oxford, 1909, 72f.

15. Buechler, *The Economic Conditions,* p. 50, n.1.

16. *Berakhot* 35b.

17. Kalischer, *op. cit.,* p. 598.

18. *Massechtoth Kallah,* ed. by M. Higger, New York, 1936, p. 326.

19. Published by Tenuath Torah ve-Avodah, n.d.

20. A. S. Herschberg, *Pinkos Bialystok,* New York, 1950, II, 80 (Yiddish).

21. Quoted from Mendelsohn, "Guilds in Ancient Palestine," no. 80, p. 19.

22. Krauss, *Archaeologie,* II, 255-257 and 624.

23. *Ibid.,* p. 256.

24. This section is based mainly on I. Epstein, *Social Legislation in the Talmud,* London, 1943, See also S. Chononowicz, *Das Arbeiterrecht im Talmud.* Berlin, 1933, and surveys of labor legislation by M. Cohn, in *Encyclopaedia*

Judaica, III, *s.v.* Arbeiterrecht, and *Universal Jewish Encyclopedia*, VI, *s.v.* Labor.

25. Ginzberg, *op. cit.*, p. 25.

26. Baron, *History*, I, 265.

Notes to Chapter IV

JEWISH ARTISANS AND GUILDS IN THE DIASPORA (323 B.C.E.—640 C.E.)

1. S. Daiches, *The Jews in Babylonia in the Time of Ezra and Nehemiah. According to Babylonian Inscriptions*, London, 1910; A. Christensen, *L'Iran sous les Sassanides*, 2nd ed., Copenhagen, 1944; S. Funk, *Die Juden in Babylonien 200-500*, Berlin, 1902; J. Fuerst, *Kultur- und Literaturgeschichte der Juden in Asien*, Leipzig, 1849.

2. Pauly-Wissowa, *Realenzyklopaedie des Altertums*, s.v. "Babylonien."

3. Hiuen Tsiang, *Buddhist Records of the Western World*, tr. from the Chinese and ed. by S. Beal, London, 1884, II, 277.

4. Krauss, *Archaeologie, passim;* see also *Monumenta Judaica*, Monumenta Talmudica, ed. A. Wuensche, W. Neuman and M. Altschueler, 1st ser., no. 450 (Handwerke), 79-80; *Jewish Encyclopedia*, II, *s.v.*, "Artisans;" Heichelheim, "Roman Syria," pp. 189-198; *idem*, *Wirtschaftsgeschichte des Altertums vom Palaeolithikum bis zur Voelkerwanderung der Germanen, Slaven und Araber*, (cited as Heichelheim, *Wirtschaftgeschichte*), Leiden, 1938, *passim*.

5. R. Wischnitzer, *The Messianic Theme in the Paintings of the Dura Synagogue*, Chicago, 1948.

6. *The Itinerary of Benjamin of Tudela*, ed. by M. N. Adler, (cited as *Itinerary*), London, 1907, p. 57.

7. J. Obermeyer, *Die Landschaft Babylonien im Zeitalter des Talmuds und des Gaonats*, (cited as Obermeyer, *Landschaft Babylonien*), Frankfort-on-the-Main, 1929, pp. 194 f. and 334.

8. *Ibid.*, p. 195.

9. Quoted by Krauss, *Archaeologie*, I, 561.

10. Strabo, *Geography*, XVI, 2, §7.

11. Obermeyer, *Landschaft Babylonien*, p. 239.

12. *Ibid.*, p. 294 f.

13. A. Berliner, *Beitraege zur Geographie und Ethnographie Babyloniens in Talmud und Midrasch*, Berlin, 1884, p. 40 ff.

14. A. S. Herschberg, *op. cit.*, pp. 203-204.

15. *Ibid.*, p. 202 f.

16. H. Bluemner, *Die gewerbliche Taetigkeit der Voelker des klassischen Altertums*, Leipzig, 1869, p. 15, n. 5.

17. Pliny, *Nat. Hist.* VIII, 74, 196.

18. Rosenzweig, *op. cit.*, p. 45.

19. *Ibid.*, p. 57. For the Persian trousers of the Sassanian period see illustrations in F. Sarre and E. Herzfeld, *Iranische Felsreliefs*, Berlin, 1910. The trimmings on the trousers look like loops, but might be called fringes since they form loose edgings.

20. M. D. Judilowitz, *Haye ha-Yehudim bi-Seman ha-Talmud: Ir Pumbedita Bimei Ha-Amoraim* (cited as Judilowitz, *Pumbedita*), Tel Aviv, 1938, p. 11.

21. *Ibid.;* see also Herschberg, *op. cit.*, p. 313.

22. Judilowitz, *loc. cit.*

23. Obermeyer, *Landschaft Babylonien* p. 304; see also Krauss, *Archaeologie*, I, 142.

24. *Jewish Encyclopedia*, VII, s.v. "Leather."

25. Judilowitz, *Pumbedita*, p. 10; *idem*, "Ha-Ir Sura," (cited as Judilowitz, "Sura"), *Sinai*, I. 2 (1937), 172-173.

26. *Idem, Pumbedita*, p. 10.

27. J. Newman, *The Agricultural Life of the Jews in Babylonia between the Years 200 C.E. and 500 C.E.*, Oxford, 1932, *passim*.

28. Obermeyer, *Landschaft Babylonien*, p. 174; Christensen, *op. cit.*, p. 40.

29. N. S. Gezow, *Al Naharot Babel*, Warsaw, 1888, p. 58.

30. Judilowitz, "Sura," p. 174.

31. L. Rabinowitz, *The Herem Hayyishub*, London, 1945, pp. 27, 140-141; *idem*, "The Talmudic Basis of the Herem Hayyishub," *JQR*, N.S., XXVIII. 3 (Jan. 1938), 217-223; Heichelheim,

Wirtschaftsgeschichte, II, 1218-1219, dates the monopolistic tendencies of artisan groups in the Sassanian Empire from the early fifth century C.E., However, his argument is based solely on talmudic evidence compiled by Rabinowitz.

32. Krauss, *Archaeologie,* II, 255-256; Heichelheim, "Roman Syria," p. 198.

33. The Babylonian Talmud refers in this connection to physicians, midwives, perfumers, carpenters, fullers, and art metal workers. See Krauss, *Archaeologie,* II, 254.

34. Heichelheim, "Die auswaertige Bevoelkerung im Ptolemaeer Reich, *Klio,* Beiheft (cited as Heichelheim, *Klio*) XVIII, Neue Folge, V. (1925), 67f.

35. V. Tcherikover, *Hellenistic Civilization and the Jews,* Philadelphia, 1959, pp. 333ff.; L. Fuchs, *Die Juden Aegyptens in ptolemaeischer und roemischer Zeit,* Vienna, 1924, pp. 54-55.

36. J. Juster, *Les Juifs dans l'empire romain,* 1914, II, 306.

37. Bluemner, *op. cit.,* pp. 10, 15 n. 5; A. C. Johnson and L. C. West, "Byzantine Egypt; Economic Studies," (cited as Johnson and West, "Byzantine Egypt"), *Princeton University Studies in Papyrology,* no. 6 (1949), p. 119.

38. Fuchs, *op. cit.,* p. 55; Tcherikover, *op. cit.,* p. 519.

39. I owe this suggestion to the late Professor Chaim Tchernovitz.

40. Fuchs, *op. cit.,* p. 55. See also W. A. Thorpe's review of D. B. Harden's *Roman Glass from Karanis Found by the University of Michigan Archaeological Expedition in Egypt,* 1924-1929, in *Classical Review,* LI, 4 (Sept., 1937), 144-146.

41. Tcherikover, *op. cit.,* pp. 338, 520. See also Heichelheim, *Klio.*

42. Johnson and West, "Byzantine Egypt," p. 137.

43. Juster, *op. cit.,* II, 307.

44. *Ibid.,* I, 486.

45. *The Christian Topography of Cosmas Indicopleustes, an Egyptian Monk.* Tr. and ed. W. McCrindle, London, 1897, p. 122.

46. C. S. Hirschberg, *Israel be-Arav,* Tel-Aviv, 1946, pp. 183-184.

47. Juster, *op. cit.,* II, 306.

48. A. Kisa, *Das Glas im Altertum,* Leipzig, 1908, I, 99; M. L. Honey (Townbridge), *Philological Studies in Ancient Glass,* 1930, pp. 113, 117, 134.

49. C. Roth, *The History of the Jews in Italy* (cited as Roth, *Italy*), Philadelphia, 1946, pp. 23-24; see also Rosenzweig, *op. cit.,* p. 44; Baron, *History,* I, 194, and II, 261.

50. R. Wischnitzer-Bernstein, "Die Messianische Huette in der Juedischen Kunst," *MGWJ,* LXXX. 5 (September-October, 1936), 381 ff., and figs. 2, 4.

51. A. Reifenberg, *Ancient Hebrew Arts,* New York, 1950, pp. 153-154; E. R. Goodenough, *Jewish Symbols in the Greco-Roman Period,* New York, 1953, I, 168ff.

52. F. Neuburg, *Glass in Antiquity,* London, 1949, p. 49.

53. *Eraclius, Von den Farben und Kuensten der Roemer,* ed. A. Ilg, Vienna, 1873. Quellenschriften fuer Kunstgeschichte und Kunsttechnik des Mittelalters und der Renaissance, IV, part I, v; and part III, xlix.

Notes to Chapter V

JEWISH ARTS AND CRAFTS IN THE NEAR EAST (640-1500)

1. Gaon Sherira, *Iggeret,* ed. B. M. Lewin, Haifa, 1921; D. S. Sassoon, *A History of the Jews in Baghdad,* Letchworth, 1949, p. 7. Piruz Shabur on-the-Euphrates was founded or enlarged by Shabur II; today a village named Dimimima is probably all that remains of it. In the Babylonian Talmud it is called Be Shabur. Cf. Obermeyer, *Landschaft Babylonien,* pp. 57, 217.

2. J. Mann, "The Responsa of the Babylonian Geonim as a Source of Jewish History," *JQR,* N.S., X (1919-1920), 310f.

3. Sassoon, *op. cit.,* p. 50.

4. *Itinerary,* p. 39f.; Petachia of Ratisbon, *Sibub ha-Olam,* ed. by E. Gruenhut, Jerusalem, 1903, *passim;* G. Caro,

Sozial- und Wirtschaftsgeschichte der Juden im Mittelalter und der Neuzeit, Leipzig, 1908, I, 126, 272, 278; A. Strauss, *Toledot ha-Yehudim be-Mizraim ve-Syria Tachat Shilton ha-Mamelukim,* (cited as Strauss, *Toledot)* Jerusalem, 1944, I, 35.

5. D. W. Pearlman, Studies in the Economic Life of the Jews under the Caliphate of the Gaonic Age. A thesis submitted to the Jewish Institute of Religion, 1932, unpublished. Chapter III on crafts. Pearlman's main sources are the responsa of the geonim.

6. Pearlman, *op. cit.,* p. 55.

7. A. Harkavy, *Teshubot ha-Geonim,* Berlin, 1887, § 186, quoted from Pearlman, *op. cit.,* p. 69, 229, n. 29.

8. H. T. Bossert, *Geschichte des Kunstgewerbes aller Zeiten und Voelker,* Berlin, 1928-1935, IV, 361.

9. S. Assaf, *Teshubot ha-Geonim,* Jerusalem, 1942, p. 155.

10. Pearlman, *op. cit.,* p. 67.

11. *Itinerary,* pp. 41-42.

12. B. M. Lewin, *Ozar ha-Geonim,* Jerusalem, 1930, II, § 258, quoted from Pearlman, *op. cit.,* p. 66.

13. Pearlman, *op. cit.,* p. 69.

14. *Loc. cit.*

15. A. Neubauer, *Medieval Jewish Chronicles,* Oxford, 1887, I, 66.

16. *Ibid.,* II, 83.

17. R. Wischnitzer-Bernstein, *Encyclopaedia Judaica,* IV, *s.v.* Buchschmuck," also J. Leveen, *The Hebrew Bible in Art,* London, 1944, pp. 3-6.

18. J. Muller, *Halakhot Pesukot min ha-Geonim,* Cracow, 1893 pp. 14-15, cited from Pearlman, *op. cit.,* p. 60.

19. *Sefer Shaare Teshuba* (363 geonic responsa), Leipzig, 1858, § 215.

20. *Ibid.,* § 230; Lewin, *op. cit.,* II, 40, § 159; *Cf.* Pearlman, *op. cit.,* pp. 57-58.

21. Lewin, *op. cit.,* II, § 150; cf. Pearlman, *op. cit.,* p. 64, n. 60. The reference was corrected by the author.

22. D. Cassel, *Teshubot Geonim Kadmonim,* Berlin, 1848, p. 38 *recto.*

23. G. Le Strange, *Baghdad during the Abbasid Caliphate,* London, 1924, p. 156; Lewin, *op. cit.,* IV, 1-2, § 3; Assaf, *Teshubot ha-Geonim,* p. 93, § 179; cf. Pearlman, *op. cit.,* p. 71.

24. Harkavy, *op. cit.,* p. 86, § 190, cited from Pearlman, *op. cit.,* p. 71.

25. Pearlman, *op. cit.,* pp. 72, 238, n. 95.

26. A. Mez, *The Renaissance of Islam,* tr. S. K. Bukhsh and D. S. Margoliuth, London, 1937, p. 467; see also P. H. Hitti, *History of the Arabs,* London, 1949, pp. 414-415.

27. Harkavy, *op. cit.,* p. 28; Lewin, *op. cit.,* II, 78-79; Pearlman, *op. cit.,* p. 73.

28. Lewin, *op. cit.,* p. 64, § 207.

29. J. Finkel, "A Risala of Al-Jahiz," *JAOS,* XLVII, 4 (1927), 311-334. Finkel rightly emphasizes "that the occupations of the Jews were far from being limited to those mentioned by Jahiz". *Cf.* also Mez, *op. cit.,* pp. 27, 39.

30. *Description of Syria. Including Palestine,* by Mukaddasi, (circa 985 A.D.), tr. Guy Le Strange, London, 1886, p. 77.

31. *Itinerary,* p. 18.

32. His statement is quoted in Strauss, *Toledot,* I, 182; see also W. J. Fischel, *Jews in the Economic and Political Life of Mediaeval Islam,* London, 1937.

33. Strauss, *Toledot,* I, 34, 283; see also Hitti, *History of the Arabs,* p. 668.

34. Strauss, *Toledot,* II, 154; Hitti, *History of Syria,* London, 1951 p. 656.

35. J. Parkes, *A History of Palestine From 135 A.D. to Modern Times,* New York, 1949, p. 97.

36. *Itinerary,* p. 22; see also J. L. La Monte, *Feudal Monarchy in the Latin Kingdom of Jerusalem, 1100 to 1291,* Cambridge, 1932, p. 174.

37. E. Farchi, *Kaftor va-Ferach,* Venice, 1549; see S. Klein, *Encyclopaedia Judaica,* VI, *s.v.* "Farchi, Estori."

38. "The Roads from Jerusalem, by Isaac ben Joseph ibn Chelo (1334)," E. N. Adler, ed., *Jewish Travellers,* (cited as *Jewish Travelers*), London, 1930, pp. 130-150; Dillon, *Glass,* London, 1907, p. 148; Strauss, *Toledot,* I, 182.

39. Johnson and West, "Byzantine Egypt," pp. 263-264.

40. Strauss, *Toledot,* I, 234.

41. D. Neustadt, *Kavim le-Toledot ha-Kalkalah shel ha-Yehudim ve-Yeshuvom*

be-Mizraim bi-Yemei ha-Benaim, Zion, II, 3-4 (1937), 235; J. Mann, *The Jews in Egypt and in Palestine under the Fatimid Caliphs,* Oxford, 1922, II, 345; see also Strauss, *Toledot,* p. 184.

42. R. Gottheil, and W. H. Worrell, eds., *Fragments from the Cairo Genizah in the Freer Collection,* New York, 1927, p. 153.

43. S. A. Rosanes, *Dibre Yeme Yisrael be-Togarmah,* Jerusalem, 1931, II, 229; see also Neustadt, *op. cit.,* p. 55.

44. Strauss, *Toledot,* I, 179-180.

45. A. S. Tritton, *The Caliphs and Their Non-Muslim Subjects,* London, 1930, p. 92 f.

46. Mann, *op. cit.,* pp. 78-79.

47. Strauss, *Toledot,* I, 180.

48. R. Gottheil, "Tidbits from the Genizah," *Jewish Studies in Memory of Israel Abrahams,* Vienna, 1927, p. 164.

49. Gottheil and Worrell, eds., *op. cit.,* p. 161.

50. Strauss, *Toledot,* I, 183.

51. *Ibid.,* 185; see also Hitti, *History of the Arabs,* p. 696.

52. *Jewish Travellers,* pp. 171f; Strauss, *Toledot* II, 152.

53. Strauss, *Toledot,* pp. 243-245.

54. *Jewish Travellers,* p. 161 f.

55. V. Stassov and D Gunzburg, eds., *L'Ornement, Hébreu,* Berlin, 1905; R. Wischnitzer-Bernstein, *Encyclopaedia Judaica,* IV, *s.v.* "Buchschmuck." Among names mentioned in the colophons appear those of the calligraphers: Solomon Halevy Bar Buya, pupil of Sayyid bar-Fergai Balqouq and Samuel ben Jacob; see also F. Landsberger, "Illuminated Marriage Contracts," *HUCA,* XXVI (1955), 505, 508.

Notes to Chapter VI

JEWISH ARTS AND CRAFTS IN THE BYZANTINE EMPIRE

1. Southern Italy, Sicily, Crete, Corfu, Chios and Evvoia (Euboea) were lost to the Empire, at different periods, between the 9th and 14th centuries.

2. J. Starr, *The Jews in the Byzantine Empire, 641-1204, Texte und Forschungen zur Byzantinisch-Neugriechischen Philologie,* no. 30, (cited as Starr, *Byzantine Empire*), Athens, 1939, pp. 35, 36.

3. *Ibid.,* p. 28.

4. "Annales Cavenses," *Monumenta Germaniae Historica, Scriptores,* III, 192 (1839), 132. Quoted from Starr, *op. cit.,* p. 223.

5. Starr, *loc. cit.*

6. J. W. Thompson, *Economic and Social History of the Middle Ages, 300-1300,* (cited as Thompson, *Middle Ages*), New York,, 1959, I, 453.

7. R. S. Lopez, "Silk Industry in the Byzantine Empire," *Speculum,* XX. 1 (1945), 23.

8. *Itinerary,* p. 10.

9. Starr, *Byzantine Empire,* p. 29.

10. W. Miller, *The Latins in the Levant. A History of Frankish Greece, 1204-1566,* London, 1908, p. 93.

11. Thompson, *Economic and Social History of Europe in the Later Middle Ages, 1300-1530,* (cited as Thompson, *Later Middle Ages*), New York, 1931, p. 365; Miller, *op. cit.,* p. 495.

12. *The Pilgrimage of Arnold von Harff, Knight from Cologne, through Italy, Syria, Egypt, Arabia, Ethiopia, Nubia, Palestine, Turkey, France and Spain, which he accomplished in the years 1496-1499.* Tr. and ed. Malcolm Letts, London, 1946, p. 81.

13. Thompson, *Later Middle Ages,* p. 365.

14. Starr, *Romania: The Jewries of the Levant after the Fourth Crusade,* Paris, 1949, pp. 82-83.

15. Starr, *Byzantine Empire,* p. 198.

16. U. Cassuto, *Encyclopedia Judaica,* X, *s.v.* "Kreta;" Starr, "Jewish Life in Crete under the Rule of Venice," *Proceedings of the American Academy for Jewish Research,* XII (1942), 90 and 60, n. 5. For Meshullam's report, *Jewish Travellers,* pp. 202-203.

17. Starr, *Romania,* p. 86.

18. *Jewish Travellers,* p. 217.

19. Starr, *Romania,* pp. 28-29.

20. *Ibid.,* p. 67.

21. Starr, *Byzantine Empire,* p. 28.

Notes to Chapter VII

JEWISH TRADES IN SOUTHERN ITALY IN THE MIDDLE AGES (500-1500)

1. In 1931 the figure for southern Italy was 1,034 Jews and for Sicily and Sardinia 230. See F. Zander, *Die Verbreitung der Juden in der Welt,* Berlin, 1937, pp. 104, 106.
2. C. Roth, *Italy,* pp. 229, 276.
3. Thompson, *Middle Ages,* pp. 406, 453.
4. *Allgemeine Enzyklopaedie der Wissenschaften und Kuenste,* ed. by J. S. Ersch and J. G. Gruber., XXVII, 142.
5. *Ibid.,* 143; see also W. Cohn, *Das Zeitalter der Hohenstaufen in Sizilien,* Breslau, 1925, p. 81.
6. M. Camera, *Memorie Storico-Diplomatiche del' Antica Citta e Ducato di Amalfi,* Salerno, 1876, I, 347; R. Straus, *Die Juden im Koenigreich Sizilien unter den* Normannen und Staufen (cited as Straus, *Sizilien*), *Heidelberg,* 1910, p. 66.
7. Aquinas, *Selected Political Writings,* ed. d' Entrèves, Oxford, 1948 p. 87.
8. *The Chronicle of Ahimaaz,* ed. M. Salzman, New York, 1924, p. 44.
9. *Encyclopedia Britannica,* XX, *s.v.* "Silk and Sericulture;" A. J. Doren, *Italienische Wirtschaftsgeschichte,* Jena, 1934, I, 494; Hitti, *History of the Arabs,* p. 607; Thompson, *Later Middle Ages,* p. 251.
10. A. Schaube, *Handelsgeschichte der romanischen Voelker,* Munich, 1906, p. 473.
11. M. Guedemann, *Geschichte des Erziehungswesens und der Cultur der abendlaendischen Juden waehrend des Mittelalters und der Neueren Zeit,* Vienna, 1880-1888, II 68, n. IV. On Amalfi see n. 6 (above).
12. Straus, *Sizilien,* p. 71.
13. F. Edler de Rovere, "Lucchese Silks," *Ciba Review,* 80 (June 1950), 2902, 2907.
14. Straus, *Sizilien,* p. 67; Schaube, *op. cit.,* p. 302; Caro, *op. cit.,* p. 490.
15. Schaube, *op. cit.,* p. 585.
16. *Ibid.,* p. 477.
17. Guedemann, *op. cit.,* II, 312-313, n. v; Straus, *Sizilien,* pp. 68-69; Roth, *Italy,* pp. 87-88.
18. Doren, *op. cit.,* p. 447; W. Cohn, *op. cit.,* pp. 111, 138; Roth, *Italy,* 87-88.
19. Roth, *Italy,* p. 234.
20. *Ibid.,* p. 229.
21. J. van Wyck Osborne, *The Greatest Norman Conquest,* New York, 1937, p. 191; Roth, *Italy,* p. 86.
22. Thompson, *Middle Ages,* p. 451.
23. A. Freimann, "Jewish Scribes in Medieval Italy," *Alexander Marx Jubilee Volume,* New York, 1950, Engl. Section, pp. 231-342; C. Bernheimer, *Paleografia Ebraica,* Florence, 1924; E. Munkacsi, *Miniature Painting in Italian Libraries. Hebrew Codices* (in Hungarian), Budapest, 1937; *idem,* "The Canon of Avicenna with Miniatures," *Mult es Jovo* (Jan. 1935), 1 ff.; see also F. Landsberger, "Jewish Artists before the Period of Emancipation," *HUCA,* XVI, 1941; *idem,* "New Studies in Early Jewish Artists," *HUCA,* XVIII, 1944.
24. J. Starr, "The Mass Conversion of Jews in Southern Italy," *Speculum,* XXI (Jan. 1946), 203-211.
25. N. Ferorelli, *Gli Ebrei nell' Italia Meridionale dall'eta romana al secolo XVIII,* Turin, 1915, pp. 125-128; G. Guerrieri, *Gli Ebrei a Brindisi ed a Lecce, 1409-1497,* Turin, 1900, p. 8.
26. Roth, *Italy,* p. 229.
27. *Jewish Travellers,* pp. 210-214.
28. *Codice Diplomatico dei Giudei di Sicilia,* eds., B. and G. Lagumina, Palermo, 1884, I, 505.
29. Roth, *Italy,* pp. 256-259; A. Milano, "The Number of Jews in Italy," *JSS,* XV, 1 (January, 1953), 31-32.
30. La Lumia, "Gli Ebrei Siciliani 1492," *Studi di Storia Siciliana,* Palermo, 1870, II. Cf. also Guedemann, *op. cit.,* II, 288; Roth, *Italy,* p. 229.
31. G. Spano, "Gli Ebrei in Sardegna." *Vessillo Israelitico,* XXVII (1879), pp. 115 ff.; Roth, *Italy,* pp. 262-268 (no references given).

Notes to Chapter VIII

JEWISH TRADES IN SOUTHERN FRANCE IN THE MIDDLE AGES

1. G. B. Depping, *Les Juifs dans le moyen-age. Essai historique sur leur état civil, commercial et littéraire,* Brussels, 1844, p. 315.
2. *REJ,* XXII (1891), 272 f; XXIII (1891), 265 ff.
3. L. Bardinet, "Les Juifs du Comtat Venaissin au moyen age," *Revue Historique,* V, Tome XIV (Sept.-Dec., 1880), 39-40; see also *REJ,* XLVII (1903), 72 (for Marseilles).
4. Perpignan came under the rule of Aragon in the early thirteenth century.
5. L. Bardinet, *op. cit.,* p. 40, n. 5.
6. *REJ,* XX (1891), 266.
7. *Ibid.,* XLVI (1903), 45. *Lapis*—may mean a building stone, a tombstone, a pumice stone, or a precious stone.
8. *Ibid.,* XLVII (1903), 222.
9. *Ibid.,* XLVI (1903), 46.
10. *Loc. cit.,* Caro, *op. cit.,* I, 243.
11. Bardinet, *op. cit., passim.*

Notes to Chapter IX

JEWISH CRAFTS IN GERMANY, NORTHERN FRANCE AND ENGLAND IN THE MIDDLE AGES

1. *Germania Judaica,* I, part 2, XXXII; Caro, *op. cit.,* pp. 71, 75.
2. See, for instance, the privilege granted to the Jews of Speyer by Bishop Ruediger in 1084 and confirmed by emperor Henry IV in 1090 (*Germania Judaica,* I, part 2, pp. 329 and 349).
3. O. Stobbe, *Die Juden in Deutschland waehrend des Mittelalters,* Braunschweig, 1866, p. 105.
4. H. J. Zimmels, *Beitraege zur Geschichte der Juden in Deutschland im 13. Jahrhundert,* Vienna, 1926, p. 48; see also *Germania Judaica,* I, 2, XXXII.
5. A. Berliner, *Aus dem Leben der deutschen Juden im Mittelalter,* Berlin, 1900; A. Riemer, *Die Juden in niedersaechsischen Staedten des Mittelalters,* Goettingen, 1907, p. 41; *Germania Judaica, loc. cit.,* and p. 319, where reference is made to salt-making by Jews in the tenth century on the Saale, a tributary of the Elbe river.
6. *Sefer Hasidim,* ed. J. Freimann (Hebrew), Frankfurt a.M., 1924, p. 179, §§ 680, 681, 682.
7. M. J. Husung, "Ueber den sogenannten juedischen Lederschnitt," *Soncino Blaetter,* I (1925), 29ff.; B. Italiener, "Isak b. Secharia, ein juedischer Lederschnittkuenstler des 15. Jahrhunderts," *Festschrift fuer Aron Freimann,* Berlin, 1935, p. 159 f.; for bibliography, Landsberger, "The Cincinnati Haggadah and Its Decorator," *HUCA,* XV (1940), 543 ff.
8. E. Moses, "Juedische Kult-und Kunstdenkmaeler in den Rheinlanden," *Rheinischer Verein fuer Denkmalpflege,* I (1931), 193 f.; B. Italiener, ed., *Die Darmstaedter Pessach-Haggadah,* Leipzig, 1927; R. Wischnitzer-Bernstein, *Universal Jewish Encyclopedia,* V, *s.v.* "Illumination of Manuscripts," (for bibliography); Landsberger, articles in *HUCA* for 1941, 1944, 1948 and 1950/1.
9. *Zeitschrift fuer die Geschichte des Oberrheins,* ed. Mone, XVII (1865), 245-255.
10. *Germania Judaica,* I, 2. XXXII, 397, 482; S. Dubnow, *History of the Jews in Russia and Poland,* Philadelphia, 1946, I, 42.
11. J. M. Rigg, ed., *Select Pleas, Starrs, and other Records from the Roll of the Exchequer of the Jews, 1220-1284,* London, 1902, p. XI.
12. *Evreiskaya Entsiklopedia,* II, *s.v.* "Anglia;" see also Roth, "The Jews in the Middle Ages," *Cambridge Medieval History,* VII, 655.

Notes to Chapter X

JEWISH ARTS AND CRAFTS IN THE IBERIAN PENINSULA UNTIL 1931: SPAIN, NAVARRE, PORTUGAL

1. C. E. Chapman, *A History of Spain,* New York, 1931, p. 36.
2. S. Katz, *The Jews in the Visigothic and Frankish Kingdoms of Spain and*

Gaul, Cambridge, 1937, *passim;* Y. F. Baer, *Toledot ha-Yehudim bi Sfarad ha-Nozrit* (cited as Baer, *Toledot*), Tel Aviv, 1944/45, vol. I, 15-20.

3. Baer, *Toledot,* p. 20

4. E. Lévi-Provençal, *L'Espagne Musulmane au X-ième siècle,* Paris, 1932, pp. 183-185; see also Hitti, *History of the Arabs,* 59f.

5. Jose Amador de los Rios, *Historia social, politica y religiosa de los judios de España y Portugal* (cited as Amador, *Historia*), Buenos Aires, 1943, vol. I, 154.

6. A. Neuman, *The Jews in Spain. Their Social, Political and Cultural Life during the Middle Ages* (cited as Neuman, *Spain*), Philadelphia, 1944, pp. XXV and XXX.

7. "Sefer ha-Kabbalah," A. Neubauer, ed., *Medieval Jewish Chronicles,* Oxford, 1887, I, p. 69.

8. R. Dozy, *Histoire des Musulmans d'Espagne,* Leiden, 1932, Tome II, book 2, p. 174; Lévi-Provençal, *op. cit.,* p. 233.

9. Edrisi [M. Idrisi], *Description de l'Afrique et de l'Espagne,* tr. R. Dozy and M. J. de Goeje, Leiden, 1886, pp. 252-253.

10. Baer, *Toledot,* I, p. 20.

11. Hitti, *op. cit.,* pp. 542-543.

12. Thompson, *Later Middle Ages,* p. 347.

13. Y. F. Baer, *Die Juden im Christlichen Spanien,* part II: *Kastilien,* (cited as Baer, *Kastilien*), Berlin, 1929-1936, pp. 2, 41, 55, and 56.

14. Baer, *Toledot,* I, p. 129 f.

15. *Ibid.,* p. 137.

16. *Ibid.,* p. 336.

17. Asher ben Yehiel migrated to Castile after his flight from Germany in 1303, and became rabbi in Toledo in 1305.

18. Asher ben Yehiel, *Responsa,* Venice, 1607-8, XVIII, 14; LXXXIX, 12, and CIV, 2, and 3; Baer, *Toledot,* p. 336; C. W. Reines, "Labor in Rabbinical Responsa," *Israel of Tomorrow,* L. Jung, ed., New York, 2nd ed., 1949, pp. 143-145.

19. Baer, *Toledot,* I, pp. 140-141. See also F. Bofarull Y Sans, *Los Judios en el territorio de Barcelona (siglos X al XIII) Reinado de Jaime I 1213-1276, Barcelona,* 1910, p. 4 f.

20. *Amador, Historia,* III, 71.

21. Baer, *Die Juden im Christlichen Spanien,* Part I: *Aragonien und Navarra,* (cited as Baer, *Aragonien*), Berlin, 1929, p. 318.

22. *Ibid., passim.*

23. *Ibid.,* pp. 411-415; see also M. Serrano y Sanz, "Notas acerca de los judios aragonenses en los siglos XIV y XV," *Revista de Archivos, Bibliotecas y Museos,* (cited as Serrano, "Notas"), Año XXI, Tomo XXXVII (1918), 327.

24. I. Epstein, *The "Responsa" of Rabbi Solomon ben Adreth of Barcelona (1235-1310) as a Source of the History of Spain,* London, 1925, pp. 39, 108.

25. Baer, *Toledot,* I, pp. 275, 289 and 298

26. Baer, *Aragonien,* pp. 625.

27. Quoted by C. R. Markham, *Story of Majorca and Minorca,* London, 1908, p. 9.

28. M. Wischnitzer, *Die Juden in der Welt,* Berlin, 1935, p. 92.

29. Baer, *Toledot,* I, p. 133.

30. A. Morel-Fatio, "Notes et documents sur les juifs des Baléares," *REJ,* IV (1882) 43; Baer, *Studien zur Geschichte der Juden im Koenigreich Aragonien waehrend des 13. und 14. Jahrhunderts,* (cited as Baer, *Studien*), Berlin, 1913. p. 167.

31. Baer, *Aragonien,* p. 495.

32. F. L. May, *Hispanic Lace and Lace Making,* New York, 1939, p. 292; see also Landsberger, "Jewish Artists before the Period of Emancipation," *op. cit.,* p. 342.

33. A. L. Isaacs, *The Jews of Majorca,* London, 1936, p. 268.

34. *Ibid.,* p. 108.

35. B. Braunstein, *The Chuetas of Majorca,* Scottdale, 1936, p. 129; See also Wischnitzer, *Juden in der Welt,* p. 93.

36. Baer, *Toledot,* I, pp. 283, 359; *idem, Encyclopaedia Judaica,* V, *s.v.* "Cresques, Abram;" Isaacs, *op. cit.,* pp. 89, 96, 222; A. Libman Lebeson, "Jewish Cartographers," *Historia Judaica,* X. 2 (October, 1948), 155-157.

37. M. Kayserling, *Die Juden in Navarra, den Baskenlaendern und auf den Ba-*

learen, Berlin, 1861, pp. 59, 73; Baer, *Aragonien,* pp. 927, 942, 946-948, 975-976, 982, 999.

38. E. J. Hamilton, *Money, Prices and Wages in Valencia, Aragon and Navarre, 1351-1500,* Cambridge, 1936, pp. 178-179.

39. M. Kayserling, *Geschichte der Juden in Portugal,* Leipzig, 1867, p. 59. See also H. V. Livermore, *History of Portugal,* Cambridge, 1947, pp. 215-217.

40. E. H. Lindo, *The History of the Jews of Spain and Portugal* (cited as Lindo, *History*), London, 1848, p. 318.

41. M. L. Margolis and A. Marx, *A History of the Jewish People,* Philadelphia, 1941, pp. 474-75.

Notes to CHAPTER XI
JEWISH CRAFT GUILDS IN SPAIN IN SPAIN

1. J. Klein, "Medieval Spanish Guilds," *Facts and Factors in Economic History* (in honor of E. F. Gay), Cambridge, 1932, pp. 173-174; R. Leonhard, "Ueber Handwerkergilden und Verbruederungen in Spanien," *Jahrbuecher fuer Nationaloekonomie und Statistik,* III. Folge, XXXVII (1909), 742.

2. Klein, *op. cit.,* p. 178; see also J. Uña y Sarthou, *Las Asociaciones obreras en España,* Madrid, 1900, p. 143 f.

3. Klein, *op. cit.,* p. 19.

4. Chapman, *op. cit.,* p. 105.

5. Klein, *op. cit.,* p. 19.

6. Baer, *Aragonien,* pp. 647 and 877.

7. *Idem. Kastilien,* p. 382.

8. Neuman, *Spain,* I, 182.

9. M. Serrano y Sanz, *Origenes de la dominacion española en América* (cited as Serrano, *Origenes*), Madrid, 1918, XVI-XVII; see also Uña y Sarthou, *op. cit.,* p. 144.

10. The statutes of the Jewish shoemakers of Saragossa, preserved in the general archives of the kingdom of Aragon, were published by M. de Bofarull y de Sartorio, *Gremios y cofradías de la antigua Corona de Aragón,* Barcelona, 1876, vol. I, pp. 131-133. Collección de decumentos inéditos del archive de la Corona de Aragón, vol. XL. M. Kayserling published an abridged German translation, "Ein Verein der juedischen Schuhmacher in Saragossa," *Allgemeine Zeitung des Judentums,* LVI (1892), 438.

11. There are a number of statutes of Jewish guilds from Czechoslovakia, Poland and Lithuania dating from the early modern period.

12. For the Saragossa guild statutes see Appendix I.

13. Serrano, *Origenes,* XLIV. *Hasguafim* is a distortion of *Ashkafim* (shoemakers, in Hebrew). Acach is Isaac. Gallur was a common family name.

14. Serrano, *op. cit.,* XLII.

15. G. Bergman, *Ha-tzedakah be-Yisrael Toldoteha U-mosdoteha,* Jerusalem, 1944, p. 73; Baer, *Toledot,* I, p. 286; F. Cantera Burgos, *Sinagogas Españolas,* Madrid, 1955, pp. 353 ff.

16. Thompson, *Later Middle Ages,* p. 360.

17. Bergman, *op. cit.,* pp. 73, 154.

18. Adret, *Teshubot ha-Rashba ha-meyuhasot le-ha-Ramban,* Warsaw, 1883, no. 105. See also Reines, "Labor in Rabbinical Responsa," *op. cit.,* p. 144.

19. Baer, *Toledot,* I, p. 337.

20. J. Segura, "Costumes de Catalonia," *Jochs Florals de Barcelona,* 1885, p. 148.

21. Klein, *op. cit.,* p. 184.

22. Solomon ben Abraham ibn Adret, *She'elot u-teshubot,* Vilna, 1881, vol. IV, § 185. For an English translation of Ibn Adret's decision see also Neuman, *Spain,* I, p. 183.

23. H. Heaton, *Economic History of Europe,* New York, 1948, p. 210 f. The role of the guilds in the city management may be derived from the fact that in Barcelona, in 1445, representatives of twenty-five guilds sat in the Great City Council. See A. Ebert, *Quellenforschungen aus der Geschichte Spaniens,* Kassel, 1849, p. 28 f.

Notes to CHAPTER XII

DECLINE AND EXPULSION OF THE JEWS OF SPAIN AND PORTUGAL

1. Baer, *Aragon,* pp. 162, 409, 495 and *passim.* For *Pictor pannorum lane,* see p. 411.

2. A. Castro, *The Structure of Spanish History*, tr. E. King, Princeton, 1954, p. 514.

3. E. P. Cheyney, *The Dawn of a New Era*, New York, 1936, p. 75.

4. Baer, *Kastilien*, pp. 210 f., 231 f., 244 f.

5. M. Mendez Bejarano, *Histoire de la Juiverie de Séville*, Madrid, 1922, pp. 116-120; see also M. Wischnitzer, *Evreiskaia Entsiklopedia*, VIII, *s. v. Ispania.*

6. Amador, *Historia*, III, 306; Lindo, *History* p. 196; Baer, *Kastilien*, p. 263 f.; *idem, Toledot*, II, 448, 569.

7. Baer, *Toledot*, II, 408; *idem, Kastilien*, p. 270.

8. *Idem, Toledot*, II, 451.

9. Lindo, *History*, p. 221.

10. For the ordinance in English translation see Lindo, *History*, pp. 221-226; Neuman, *Spain*, I, 185-190; Baer, *Kastilien*, p. 312.

11. Baer, *Kastilien, passim.*

12. Heaton, *op. cit.*, pp. 264-265.

13. Baer, *Aragonien*, pp. 617-624. King Martin confirmed these municipal regulations in 1409 upon the request of representatives of the *aljama.*

14. Serrano, *"Notas," passim.*

15. Baer, *Toledot*, II, 387.

16. Thompson, *Later Middle Ages*, p. 360.

17. Baer, *Aragonien*, p. 847.

18. W. H. McCarthy, "An Outline of the History of Bookbinding," *A History of the Printed Book*, ed. L. C. Wroth, New York, 1938, p. 454.

19. Baer, *Studien*, p. 168; *idem, Aragonien*, p. 415.

20. *Idem, Aragonien*, p. 321.

21. R. Wischnitzer-Bernstein, "Ein juedischer Buchmaler des 15. Jahrhunderts," *Jahrbuch fuer juedische Geschichte* und *Literatur*, XXX (1937), 84-94,

22. Baer, *Aragonien*, p. 839, 842, also 797.

23. Serrano, *Origenes*, I, Appendices, CCCLXII; Ebert, *op. cit.*, p. 28 f.

24. Baer, *Toledot*, II, 485-486, 573 and n. 42.

25. *Ibid.*, I, 136, 178.

26. *Ibid.*, II, 582.

27. A. Marx, "The Expulsion of the Jews from Spain. Two New Accounts," *JQR*, XX (Jan., 1908), 240 f.

28. Baer, *Kastilien*, pp. 477-545; *idem, Toledot*, II, 516-519.

29. Klein, *op. cit.*, p. 186.

30. Lindo, *History*, p. 285.

31. I. de Asso, *Historia de la Economia Politica de Aragón*, Saragossa, 1798, pp. 210, 214, 256, 282, 284; see also Amador, *Historia*, III, 310.

32. Lindo, *History*, p. 321.

33. *Ibid.*, p. 295.

34. Klein, *op. cit.*, p. 186, n. 1.

35. J. Hammer-Purgstall, *Geschichte des Osmanischen Reiches*, Pest, 1846, II, 14.

36. F. Beaujour, *Tableau du commerce de la Grèce*, Paris, 1880, I, 150.

37. Quoted in Lindo, *History*, p. 300. Mojeron's work was not accessible to the author.

38. Thompson, *Later Middle Ages*, p. 347; also J. L. Barcelo, *Historia Económica de España*, Madrid, 1952, p. 174; J. Contreras y Lopez de Ayala Lozoya, *Los gremios españoles*, Madrid, 1944.

CHAPTER XIII

JEWISH CRAFTS IN THE OTTOMAN EMPIRE (1500-1800)

1. Baer, *Toledot*, II, 556; Marx, *op. cit.*, 252.

2. *De vita et scriptis Eliae Kapsali.* Likutim shonim me-sefer debe Eliahu, ed. M. Lattes, Padua, 1869, p. 7; Wischnitzer, *Die Juden in der Welt*, pp. 104-106.

3. I. M. Molko, "Kehilat Saloniki bedorot ha-rishonim," *Sinai* XIV, 7/8 (1944), passim.

4. I. S. Emmanuel, *Histoire des Israélites de Salonique* (cited as Emmanuel, *Israélites*), Salonica, 1936, I, 111.

5. *Idem, Histoire de l'Industrie des Tissus des Israélites de Salonique* (cited as Emmanuel, *Industrie*), Paris, 1935, p. 14.

6. S. di Medina, *Responsa*, Salonica, 1797-98, IV, nos. 45, 130, 139; H. Shabetai, *Torat Hayyim*, Salonica, 1713, I,

no. 63; S. A. Rosanes, *Dibre Yeme Yisrael be-Togarmah,* III, 384-396; Emmanuel, *Industrie,* pp. 16-17. For dye ingredients, see already Pliny, *Nat. Hist.* IX, 64, 138.

7. Heaton, *op. cit.,* p. 308.

8. Emmanuel, *Industrie,* p. 18; Rosanes, (*op. cit.,* III, 392) gives a description of the different cloth produced in Salonica.

9. H. Dernschwam's *Tagebuch einer Reise nach Konstantinopel und Kleinasien 1553-1555,* ed. F. Babinger, Munich, 1923, p. 107.

10. Evliya, *Narrative of Travels in Europe, Asia and Africa in the XVIIth Century,* tr. by Joseph von Hammer (cited as Evliya, *Travels*) , London, 1834, 1846. 2 parts; part ii, 166; for second passage. see part i, 124.

11. Emmanuel, *Industrie,* pp. 41-42; *idem, Israélites,* p. 122.

12. Heaton, *op. cit.,* pp. 169-170.

13. Emmanuel, *Industrie,* pp. 19-20.

14. *Ibid..* p. 20.

15. *Ibid.,* p 27.

16. *Ibid.,* p. 45.

17. J. Nehama, *Histoire des Israélites de Salonique. Salonica,* 1936, vol. IV, p. 53.

18. Emmanuel, *Industrie,* pp. 20-21; Mustafa ben Abdalla Hadshi Halfa, *Rumeli und Bosna geographisch beschrieben.* tr. by J. Hammer, Vienna, 1812. Not seen by the author.

19. Emmanuel. *Industrie,* pp. 55-56.

20. N. Iorga, *Geschichte des Osmanischen Reiches,* Gotha, 1908-1913, vol. IV, 365.

21. M. V. Coronelli, *A Historical and Geographical Account of the Morea, Negropont, and the Maritime Places as far as Thessalonica.* tr. R. W. Gent, London, 1687, pp. 223-224.

22. Rosanes, *op. cit.,* III, 39.

23. E. M. Cousinéry, *Voyage dans la Macédoine,* Paris, 1831, vol. I, 49.

24. Emmanuel, *Industrie,* p. 111; Nehama, *op. cit,* vol. IV, 55.

25. A. H. Lybyer, *The Government of the Ottoman Empire in the Time of Suleiman the Magnificent,* Appendix I: The Second Book on the Affairs of the Turks, by Ramberti, Venice, 1543, pp. 131-146. (The appendix is a translation of Ramberti's *Libre Tre della Cosi di Turchi,* 1534).

26. N. de Nicolay. *Les Navigations, pérégrinations et voyages faits en Turquie,* Antwerp, 1577, p. 245.

27. Nehama, *op. cit.,* IV, 54, n. 30.

28. *Ibid.,* pp. 54-55.

29. P. Belon du Mans, *Les Observations de plusieurs singularitéz et choses mémorables, trouvées en Grèce, Asie, Judée, Egypte et autres pays estranges,* rédigées en trois liures, Paris, 1553, pp. 45 f.; see also Ami Boué, *La Turquie d'Europe,* Paris, 1840, vol. IV, 377; D. Urquhart, *Turkey and Its Resources,* London, 1833, p. 178; Emmanuel, *Israélites,* p. 111; Nehama, *op. cit.,* IV, 56-58.

30. Nehama, *op. cit.,* p. 54.

31. Emmanuel, *Israélites,* pp. 57-58, 113; Nehama, *op. cit.,* pp. 52-55.

32. Emmanuel, *Israélites,* p. 112.

33. Rosanes, *op. cit.,* II, 41; Emmanuel, *Industrie,* pp. 23, 45, 57.

34. Lybyer, *op. cit.,* pp. 131-146.

35. Dernschwam's *Tagebuch* (see n. 9) . Quoted here from the English translation in *The Jew in the Medieval World, A Source Book, 315-1791,* by J. R. Marcus, Cincinnati, 1938, p. 412.

36. Hammer-Purgstall, *op. cit.,* III, 213.

37. Evlyia, *Travels,* part ii, pp. 165, 191, 207, 181, and 240 f.

38. G. Vajda, "Les Corps de métiers en Turquie d'après deux publications de V. Gordlevskij," *Revue des Études Islamiques,* I (1934) , 79 f.

39. E. Biliotti and Abbé Cotret, *Histoire de l'Ile de Rhodes,* Paris, 1881, p. 563. See also A. Galanté, *Histoire des Juifs de Rhodes, Chio, Cos. etc.,* (cited as Galanté, *Rhodes*) , Istanbul, 1935, p. 55.

40. J. Starr, *Romania,* p. 89.

41. A. Harkavy, "Neuaufgefundene Hebraeische Bibelhandschriften," *Mémoires de l'Académie Impériale de St. Pétersbourg,* viie série, XXXII, 8 (1884), 27; see also Starr, *op. cit.,* p. 90; Marx, *op. cit.,* p. 264.

42. Carlier de Pinon, "Rélation du

voyage en Orient," *Revue de l'Orient Latin,* XII (1910-11), 370.

43. Galanté, *Rhodes,* pp. 57-58; Rosanes, *op. cit.,* II, 4, 136-137; III, 216.

44. S. di Medina, *op. cit.,* IV, no. 249; Rosanes, *op. cit.,* II, 121.

45 Galanté, *Rhodes,* p. 57.

46. *Ibid.,* Galanté does not indicate the source. *Oka* is a Turkish weight, ca. 2¾ lbs.

47. Emmanuel, *Israélites,* p. 236; Nehama, *op. cit.,* pp. 200-201; Galanté, *Histoire des Juifs d'Istanbul depuis la prise de cette ville en 1453 par Fatib Mehmed II, jusqu' à nos jours,* Istanbul, 1941-42, *passim;* S. Schechter, *Studies in Judaism,* second series, Philadelphia, 1945, p. 231; Rosanes, *op. cit.,* vols. II and III, *passim.*

48. E. Schwarzfeld, "The Jews of Rumania from the Earliest Times to the Present Day," *The American Jewish Yearbook* (1901-1902), pp. 45-47; I. N. Angelescu, *Histoire Économique des Roumains,* Geneva, 1919, pp. 250-252; N. Ghiulea, *Les Corporations de Métiers en Roumanie,* pp. 9, 17.

49. Rosanes, *op. cit.,* II, 131; L. A. Frankl, *Nach Jerusalem,* Leipzig, 1858, I, 24.

50. S. Assaf, *Mekorot le-toledot ha-hinnuk be-Yisrael,* Tel Aviv, 1936, III, 82, 84.

51. *The Six Travels of John Baptiste Tavernier, Baron of Aubonne, through Turkey and Persia to the Indies during the space of forty years.* Tr. by J. P., London, 1684, ch. xxii, p. 253. The French ed.: *Les Six Voyages de J.-B. Tavernier, Ecuyer, Baron d'Aubonne, en Turquie, en Perse et aux Indes,* Paris, 1679, book v, p. 749, was used (R. W.).

52. Carleton S. Coon. *Measuring Ethiopia and Flight into Arabia,* Boston, 1935, p. 235.

53. H. A. R. Gibb and H. Bowen, *Islamic Society and the West,* London, 1950, part I, pp. 294, 296, 297, n. 299; B. Lewis, "The Islamic Guilds," *Economic History Review,* XVIII. 1 (November 1937), 20-37; M. Clerget, *Le Caire,* Cairo, 1934, II, 278; Rosanes (*op. cit.,* II, 229) refers to Radbaz' responsum.

54. *Iggrot Eretz Yisrael,* ed. A. Yaari, Jerusalem, 1943, p. 157.

55. *Shibhe Yerushelaim,* ed. Jacob ben Mose Hayyim Baruch, Leghorn, 1784, p. 16.

56. Schechter, *op. cit.,* second series, p. 230; J. Knaani, "Ha-Haim ha-Kalkaliim bi-Zefat Uvesvivoteha" (Economic Conditions in Safed), (cited as Knaani "Zefat"), *Zion,* old series, VI (1934), 172-217.

57. "A Letter by Moses di Rossi from Palestine, dated 1535," ed. D. Kaufmann, *JQR,* old series, IX (1897), 491-499; cf. also Knaani, "Zefat," pp. 195, 197.

58. Knaani, "Hapoalim ve-ha-Pekidim bi-Zefat Uvesvivoteha," *Sinai* XII (1943), 94-100; *idem,* "Zefat," p. 195.

Notes to CHAPTER XIV
JEWISH TRADES IN ITALY IN THE EARLY MODERN PERIOD

1. The first Italian ghetto was established in Venice in 1516. Ghettos were instituted in the Papal States in 1555.

2. C. Roth, *Italy, passim. A.* Berliner, *Die Geschichte der Juden in Rom,* (cited as Berliner, *Rom*), Frankfurt, 1893; H. Vogelstein and P. Rieger, *Geschichte der Juden in Rom* (cited as Rieger, *Rom*), Berlin, 1895-96, II; M. A. Shulvass, "The Jewish Population in Renaissance Italy," *JSS.* XIII, 1 (January, 1951), 3-24.

3. M. Stern, *Urkundliche Beitraege ueber die Stellung der Paepste zu den Juden,* Kiel, 1893, pp. 48-50, no. 44.

4. U. Cassuto, *Gli Ebrei a Firenze nell'eta del Rinascimento,* Florence, 1918, p. 194.

5. Rieger, *Rom.* II, 25.

6. Roth, *Italy,* p. 188.

7. *Ibid.,* pp. 199-200.

8. M. Steinschneider, "Juedische Typographie und Juedischer Buchhandel," Ersch-Gruber, *Allegemeine Enzylopaedie der Wissenschaften und Kuenste,* Vol. XXVIII.

9. Rieger, *Rom,* II, 436-438.

10. A. Berliner, "Aus schweren Zeiten," *Jubelschrift zum siebzigsten Geburtstag des Dr. Israel Hildesheimer,* Berlin, 1890,

p. 160; see also Rieger, *Rom,* II, 118.

11. G. Vasari, *Lives of the most eminent Painters, Sculptors, and Architects,* tr. by A. B. Hinds, London, 1927, IV, 121; see also R. Wischnitzer, "Passover Art and the Italian Renaissance," *The Reconstructionist,* XXIV. 4 (April 4, 1958), 7.

12. Published by A. Berliner in the Hebrew original in *Kobez al Yad,* IX (1893), 5.

13. Rieger, *Rom,* II, 118-119.

14. A. Wolf, "Etwas ueber juedische Kunst und aeltere juedische Kuenstler," *MJV,* IX (1902), 17; F. Landsberger, "Jewish Artists before the Period of Emancipation," *HUCA,* XVI, 371; see Thieme-Becker, *Lexikon der Bildenden Kuenstler,* XI, *s. v.* "Fideli, Ercole de'."

15. Roth, *Italy,* p. 376; M. Lattès, "Documents et notices sur l'histoire politique et littéraire des Juifs en Italie," *REJ,* V (1882), 219-237.

16. Wolf, *MJV,* IX, 17.

17. Landsberger, *op. cit.,* p. 374; Wolf, *MJV,* XXIV (1907), 108.

18. Landsberger, *op. cit.,* p. 373; Wischnitzer-Bernstein, "Studies in Jewish Art," *JQR, new series,* XXXVI, 1 (1945), 59; *idem,* "Passover Art and the Italian Renaissance," *op. cit.,* p. 10.

19. D. Kaufmann, "Le peintre vénitien Mose dal Castellazo," *REJ,* XXII (1891), 290-293; I. Sonne, "Nouveaux éclaircissemens sur la personnalité de Moïse dal Castellazzo," *REJ,* XCIV, 187 (Jan.—March, 1933), 196 ff.; Landsberger, *op. cit.,* p. 372.

20. Rieger, *Rom,* II, 119-120, 181; Roth, *Italy,* pp. 193-201, 375; J. R. Marcus, *The Jew in the Medieval World,* pp. 399-400, 478.

21. Berliner, *Rom,* II, 2, 23; Rieger, *Rom,* II, pp. 180, 181.

22. Roth, *Italy,* pp. 371-372, 374; *idem, Venice,* Philadelphia, 1930, p. 282.

23. Quoted from *De morbis artificum Bernardini Ramazzini Diatriba. Diseases of Workers, The latin text of 1713.* Revised with English translation and notes by W. C. Wright, Chicago, 1940; Roth (*Italy,* pp. 374-375) quotes from the Italian edition.

24. Rieger, *Rom,* II, 231; see however, E. Rodocanachi, *Le Saint-Siège et les Juifs. Le Ghetto à Rome,* Paris, 1891, p. 70.

25. Levi's account was published in *Israelietische Letterbode,* X and XI. Also Berliner, *Rom,* II, 86.

26. Rieger, *Rom,* II, 321, n. 2.

27. *Ibid.,* 322.

28. A. Berliner, *Aus den letzten Tagen des roemischen Ghetto.* Berlin, 1886, pp. 21-22.

29. Rieger, *Rom,* II, 322, n. 2.

30. Berliner, *Rom,* II, 99-102.

31. Roth, *Italy,* pp. 345-346; U. Cassuto, *Encyclopaedia Judaica,* X, *s.v.* "Livorno."

32. Thanks are due to Mr. Herman Davidowitz, New York, for putting the privilege of 1663 in his possession at my disposal.

33. Roth, *Italy,* pp. 223-227; D. W. Amram, *The Makers of Hebrew Books in Italy,* Philadelphia, 1909, pp. 53-54.

34. S. Assaf, *Mekorot le-toledot ha-hinnuk be-Yisrael,* II, 208.

Notes to CHAPTER XV

JEWISH ARTISANS IN BOHEMIA AND MORAVIA FROM THE MIDDLE AGES TO THE END OF THE THIRTY YEARS' WAR

1. "On the Early Slavs. The Narrative of Ibrahim ibn Yakub," tr. S. Rapoport, *Slavonic and East European Review* (cited as "Ibrahim ibn Yakub"), VIII, 23 (December 1929), 331-341. Cf. G. Vernadsky, *Kievan Russia,* New Haven, 1948. pp. 329, 338.

2. K. Krofta, *A Short History of Czechoslovakia,* New York, 1934, *passim;* A. F. Pribram, "Das boehmische Commerzcollegium und seine Taetigkeit. Ein Beitrag zur Geschichte des boehmischen Handels und der boehmischen Industrie im Jahrhunderte nach dem Westfaelischen Frieden," *Beitraege zur Geschichte der Deutschen Industrie in Boehmen,* Prague, 1898.

3. J. Aronius, *Regesten zur Geschichte der Juden in Deutschland,* Berlin, 1893, no. 130; G. von Below, "Zur Raffelstetter

Zollordnung," *Vierteljahrschrift fuer Sozial- und Wirtschaftsgeschichte,* XVII (1924), 349; S. Steinherz, "Die Einwanderung der Juden in Boehmen," *Die Juden in Prag,* ed. S. Steinherz, Prague, 1927, pp. 7-58; J. Brutzkus, "Der Handel westeuropaeischer Juden mit dem alten Kiev," *Zeitschrift fuer die Geschichte der Juden in Deutschland,* III, 2/3 (1931), 97 ff.

4. "Ibrahim ibn Yakub," p. 335.

5. Steinherz, *op. cit., passim;* H. Tykocinski, *Germania Judaica,* I, part 2, pp. 269-281, *s. v.* "Prag."

6. The charter was published by J. Celakovsky in *Codex juris municipalis* regni Bohemiae, I, 5 f., reprinted in G. Bondy and F. Dworsky, eds., *Zur Geschichte der Juden in Boehmen, Maehren und Schlesien von 960 bis 1620,* Prague, 1906, I. 17-22.

7. R. Kestenberg, "Hussitentum und Judentum," *JGGJCR,* VIII, 11-25.

8. H. Flesch, "Urkundliches ueber juedische Handwerker in Maehren," (cited as Flesch, "Maehren"), *MGWJ,* N. S., XXXVIII. 5/6 (May-June 1930), 197 f.

9. Bondy and Dworsky, eds., *op. cit.,* I, no. 363.

10. F. Kamenicek, *Zemske Snemy a Sjezdy Moravske,* Brno, 1905, III, 230; A. Engel, "Die Ausweisung der Juden aus den koeniglichen Staedten Maehrens und ihre Folgen," *JGGJCR,* II, 50-96; B. Heilig, "Ziele und Wege einer Wirtschaftsgeschichte der Juden in der Tschechoslovakischen Republik," *JGGJCR,* IV, 25 f.

11. Bondy and Dworsky, eds., *op. cit.,* I, no. 347; II, no. 1060; see also R. Wenisch and E. Krakauer, "Geschichte der Juden in Komotau," *Die Juden und die Judengemeinden Boehmens,* ed. H. Gold, Bruenn, 1934, I, 299-304; Z. Winter, *Dejiny remesel a obchodu v Cechach* v XIV a v XV stoleti (cited as Winter, *Dejiny*), Prague, 1906, p. 410.

12. Winter, *Remeslnictvo a zivnosti XVI veku v Cechach, 1526-1620* (cited as Winter, *Remeslnictvo*), Prague, 1909, p. 13.

13. *Idem, Dejiny,* p. 410. Prague had three districts: the "Old City," the "New City," and "Klein Seite;" the ghetto was located in the "Old City."

14. Bondy and Dworsky, eds., *op. cit.,* I, no. 348.

15. *Ibid.,* I, nos. 356 and 404; T. Jakobovits, "Die juedischen Zuenfte in Prag," (cited as Jacobovits, "Zuenfte"), *JGGJCR,* VIII, p. 72 and *passim.*

16. Bondy and Dworsky, eds., *op. cit.,* II, no. 1267.

17. *Ibid.,* I, no 526; see also *Zeitschrift fuer die Geschichte der Juden in Deutschland,* I (1886), 178 f.

18. Winter, *Cesky prumysl a obchod v XVI veku* (cited as Winter, *Cesky prumysl*), Prague, 1913, pp. 58 and 158.

19. Bondy and Dworsky, eds., *op. cit.,* I, nos. 698, 708, 711, 729; Jakobovits, "Zuenfte," pp. 63-64.

20. Winter, *Remeslnictvo, p.* 525; M. Rachmuth, "Die Juden in Neuhaus," *JGGJCR,* III, 188.

21. Winter, *op. cit.,* 525; *idem, Dejiny,* p. 500.

22. Winter, *Remeslnictvo,* 525.

23. K. Koepl, "Urkunden, Akten und Regesten aus dem k. k. Statthalterei-Archiv in Prag," *Jahrbuch der Kunsthistorischen Sammlungen des Allerhoechsten Kaiserhauses,* XII (1891), nos. 8175, 8236; Bondy and Dworsky, ed., *op. cit.,* II, nos. 767, 837; Winter, *Dejiny,* pp. 414-415.

24. *The Jewish Museum of Prague.* A Guide, by H. Volavkova, Prague, 1948, p. 32, no. 31.

25. For Prague, see Winter, *Dejiny,* p. 410; for Chomutov, articles by Louny and Nachod in *Die Juden und die Judengemeinden Boehmens;* for Nikolsburg, Maehrisch-Budwitz and Maehrisch-Schoenberg, *Die Juden und Judengemeinden Maehrens in Vergangenheit und Gegenwart,* ed. H. Gold, Bruenn, 1929.

26. Winter, *Remeslnictvo,* p. 423.

27. L. M. Popper, *Die Inschriften des Alten Prager Judenfriedhofes,* ed. M. Popper, Prague, 1893, p. 23; D. Gans, *Tzemah David,* Prague, 1592, Part I, p. 46; R. Krautheimer, *Mittelalterliche Synagogen,* Berlin, 1927, pp. 234 ff.; F. Landsberger, "Jewish Artists before the Period of Emancipation," *HUCA,* XVI

(1941), 390; H. Volavkova, *The Pinkas Synagogue,* Prague, 1955.

28. Volavkova, *The Synagogue Treasures of Bohemia and Moravia,* Prague, 1949, pp. xi, 6; Jakobovits, "Zuenfte," pp. 57, 119.

29. Winter, *Remeslnictvo,* p. 624; *idem, Cesky prumysl,* p. 184; *idem,* "Kulturhistorischer Teil," in I. Herrmann et al., eds. *Prager Ghetto,* Prague, 1903, pp. 72-73; Jakobovits, "Zuenfte," pp. 67-68.

30. Winter, "Kulturhistorischer Teil," *op. cit.,* p. 41.

31. Jacobovits, "Zuenfte," pp. 62-67; Winter, *Cesky prumysl,* p. 61.

32. J. Prokes, "Der Antisemitismus der Behoerden und das Prager Ghetto in Nachweissenbergischer Zeit," (cited as Prokes, "Antisemitismus") *JGGJCR,* I (1929), 63-64.

33. K. Spiegel, "Die Prager Juden zur Zeit des Dreissigjaehrigen Krieges," *Die Juden in Prag,* pp. 130, 180.

34. S. H. Lieben, "Der Hebraeische Buchdruck in Prag im 16. Jahrhundert," *Die Juden in Prag,* pp. 88-106; Winter, *Remeslnictvo,* p. 310; For Jung Bunzlau, see *Juden und Judengemeinden Boehmens,* p. 210; Bondy and Dworsky, eds., *op. cit.,* I, 522 and II, nos. 875, 1208, 1209; H. Flesch, "Aus Juedischen Handschriften in Maehren," *JGGJCR,* II, 292; Winter, *Remeslnictvo,* p. 329.

35. Heilig, *op. cit.,* p. 25; Flesch, "Maehren," p. 197 f. For data on crafts plied by Jews in Moravian cities, see articles in *Juden und Judengemeinden Maehrens.*

36. Spiegel, *op. cit.,* pp. 107-187.

37. Jakobovits, "Zuenfte," pp. 68-70.

38. *Ibid.,* pp. 70-72.

39. For the German text of the charter of 1648 see J. Wertheimer, *Die Juden in Oesterreich. Vom Standpunkte der Geschichte, des Rechts und des Staatsvorteils,* Leipzig, 1842, Part I, pp. 200-211; see also Jakobovits, "Zuenfte," pp. 73, 139.

40. Winter, *Cesky prumysl,* p. 434.

Notes to CHAPTER XVI

EXPANSION OF JEWISH ARTISANSHIP IN BOHEMIA AND MORAVIA (1650-1780)

1. M. Wischnitzer, *Yevreyskaya Entsiklopedia,* IV, *s. v.* "Bogemia."

2. Prokes, "Antisemitismus," I, 41-62.

3. *Ibid.,* pp. 72-73, 97 f.

4. Pribram, *op. cit., passim;* Prokes, "Antisemitismus," I, 199.

5. Prokes, "Antisemitismus," p. 226.

6. *Ibid.,* pp. 236 f., 261; see also *Juden und Judengemeinden Maehrens,* p. 593.

7. J. Bergl, "Das Exil der Prager Judenschaft von 1745 bis 1748," *JGGJCR,* I, 263-331.

8. Jakobovits, "Zuenfte," pp. 90-98.

9. *Ibid.,* pp. 110, 141.

10. Prokes, "Die Prager Judenkonskription vom Jahre 1729," *JGGJCR,* IV, 297-332.

11. Schudt, *Juedische Merckwuerdigkeiten,* 1717, part IV, iii Continuation, pp. 151, 156.

12. Prokes, *op. cit.,* p. 326; see also Jakobovits, "Zuenfte," p. 128.

13. Winter, *Remeslnictvo,* p. 6.

14. Prokes, "Antisemitismus," pp. 327-328.

15. Jakobovits, "Zuenfte," pp. 129-131.

16. Popper, *op. cit., passim.*

17. R. Kestenberg, "Mifkad yehudei behm shemehutz li-Prag bishnat 1724," (cited as "Mifkad 1724"), *Zion,* IX (1944), pp. 15-20, 22, 23; K. Krenek, "Dejiny zidu v Libovicich," *Juden und Judengemeinden Boehmens,* p. 374.

18. Krenek, *op. cit.,* pp. 374-375.

19. Estimates based on data given in *Juden und Judengemeinden Maehrens,* 303.

20. Heilig, "Die Vorlaeufer der maehrischen Konfektionsindustrie in ihrem Kampf mit den Zuenften," *JGGCR,* III, 388.

21. L. Moses, "Nikolsburger Studien," *Zeitschrift fuer die Geschichte der Juden in der Tschechoslovakei,* V. 2. (1938), 85-108.

22. V. Zacek, "Die Juedischen Ger-

bereien in Maehren zu Beginn des achtzehnten Jahrhunderts," *JGGJCR*, V, 175-197.

23. Flesch, "Maehren," p. 216.

24. J. Bronner, "Die Maehrischen Juden im Goldschmiedehandwerk," *Zeitschrift fuer die Geschichte der Juden in der Tschechoslovakei*, I. 4 (1931), 243-247.

25. Landsberger, Huca, XVI, p. 365 f.

26. G. Wolf, *Die Alten Statuten der Juedischen Gemeinden in Maehren samt den nachfolgenden Synodalbeschluessen*, Vienna, 1880.

27. Kestenberg, "Mifkad 1724," *Zion*, IX (1944), 23; *idem*, "Toledot ha-kalkalah shel Yehudei Behm shemehutz li-Prag bamea ha-17 weha-18," *Zion*, XII (1947), 64.

28. F. Hillel, *Die Rabbiner und die verdienstvollen Familien der Leipniker Gemeinde im 17., 18. und 19. Jahrhundert*, Maehrisch-Ostrau, 1929, pp. 107-111.

29. Kestenberg, "Mifkad 1724," *Zion*, XII (1947), 62.

30. Heaton, *Economic History of Europe*, pp. 140, 346.

Notes to CHAPTER XVII

SURVEY OF JEWISH CRAFT GUILDS IN BOHEMIA AND MORAVIA (1600-1780)

1. Winter, *Remeslnictvo*, p. 725.

2. A. Gindely, "Das Zunftwesen in Boehmen vom 16. bis ins 18. Jahrhundert," *Sitzungsberichte der k. boehmischen Gesellschaft in Prag*, Prague, 1884, pp. 55-83.

3. Jakobovits, "Zuenfte," pp. 119, 141-143.

4. Popper, *op. cit.*, pp. 6-7.

5. The Statutes are published by G. Kisch, *Die Prager Universitaet und die Juden, 1348-1848, Maehrisch-Ostrau*, 1935, pp. 152-153.

6. Jakobovits, "Zuenfte," p. 119; Volavkova, *The Synagogue Treasures of Bohemia and Moravia;* Spiegel, *op. cit.*, p. 132.

7. Schudt, *op. cit.*, p. 153.

8. Kisch, *op. cit.*, pp. 82-83 see illustrations of the pageants of 1716 and 1741, following p. 16). For illustrations of the trades emblems see *Universal Jewish Encyclopedia*, I, *s. v.*. "Artisans."

9. *The Old Jewish Cemetery of Prague.* A Guide through the Cemetery, Prague, 1947, p. 9; Popper, *op. cit., passim.* The burial brotherhood (*hevra kadisha*) in Prague—not a guild—may be mentioned here. At its fraternal meals it used wine beakers in enameled glass decorated with scenes illustrating the services of the brotherhood, such as carrying the bier, etc. Specimens of seventeenth and eighteenth century beakers are preserved in the New York Jewish Museum and in other collections.

10. Kisch, *op. cit.*, pp. 152-153; Jakobovits, "Zuenfte," pp. 141-145; see also the statutes of the shoemakers' guild published by S. Adler in *Selbstwehr*, no. 20 (1932).

11. Jakobovits, "Zuenfte," p. 130.

12. Winter, *Cesky prumysl*, p. 127.

13. Jakobovits, "Zuenfte," p. 124.

14. Kisch, *op. cit.*, p. 103.

15. *Ibid.*, pp. 47, 160-165.

16. *Casopism Musea Kralovstvi Ceskeho*, LXVIII (1894), 220; Bondy and Dworsky, eds., *op. cit.*, II, no. 1331, p. 1042; Winter, *Remeslnictvo*, p. 714; Spiegel, *op. cit.*, p. 133.

17. Jakobovits, "Zuenfte," p. 86; Winter, *Dejiny*, p. 86.

18. B. Bretholz, "Die Judengemeinde von Ungarisch-Brod und ihr Streit mit dem Grundherrn Grafen Leo Wilhelm von Kaunitz, gest. 1655," *JGGJCR*, IV, 107-181; the statutes of the Jewish tailors' guild on pp. 161-162.

19. Heilig, *op. cit.*, pp. 350 ff.; Flesch, "Maehren," p. 205-209.

20. Flesch, *op. cit.*, p. 207; Heilig, *op. cit.*, p. 351.

21. *Juden und Judengemeinden Maehrens* (Nikolsburg), p. 425.

22. Flesch, *op. cit.*, p. 205.

23. Heilig, *op. cit.*, p. 338 f.

24. *Ibid.*, p. 353 f.; Hillel, *op. cit.*, pp. 53-54.

25 Heilig, *op. cit.*, pp. 373-374.

Notes to CHAPTER XVIII

JEWISH TRADES IN WESTERN EUROPE IN THE EARLY MODERN PERIOD

1. W. Sombart, *The Jews and Modern Capitalism,* Glencoe, 1951, tr. M. Epstein, p. 181.

2. H. J. Koenen, *Geschiendenis der Joden in Nederland,* Utrecht, 1843, pp. 234-235; H. Bloom, *The Economic activities of the Jews in Amsterdam in the seventeenth and eighteenth centuries,* Williamsport, Pa., 1937, passim; *Geschiedenis der Joden in Nederland,* ed. H. Brugmans and A. Frank, Amsterdam, 1940, pp. 568, 571-576, 594, 598-660; N. W. Goldstein, "Die Juden in der Amsterdamer Diamanten-Industrie," *Zeitschrift fuer Demographie und Statistik der Juden,* III. 12 (December, 1907), 178-184; J. S. da Silva Rosa, *Geschiedenis der Portugeesche Joden te Amsterdam,* Amsterdam, 1925, *passim;* H. Poppers, *De Joden in Overijsel,* Utrecht, 1926, pp. 63-68; E. Voet, Jr., *Haarlemsche goud-en zilversmeden en hunne merken,* Haarlem, 1928; S. Seeligmann, "De Gilden en de Joden," *De Vrijdagavond,* V (June 1, 1928), 135 f.; C. Roth, *A Life of Menasseh ben Israel,* Philadelphia, 1945, p. 73 f.; R. Wischnitzer, "Jewish Art," in *Jewish People, Past and Present,* III, 283.

3. C. Roth, *The Great Synagogue, London 1690-1940,* London, 1950, pp. 66, 70-71, 121; *Treasures of a London Temple,* compiled by A. G. Grimwade et al., London, 1951, pp. 17, 53-54.

4. E. Schnurmann, *La Population Juive en Alsace,* Paris, 1936, p. 7; S. Posener, *Encyclopaedia Judaica,* IV, *s. v.,* "Bordeaux;" S. Kahn, "Les Juifs de Nîmes au XVIIe et au XVIIIe siècles," *REJ,* LXVIII (1914), 235.

5. I Freund, *Die Emanzipation der Juden in Preussen,* Berlin, 1912, II, no. 4, pp. 22-60; English translation of the passage in J. R. Marcus, *The Jew in the Medieval World,* p. 89; H. Jolowicz, *Geschichte der Juden in Koenigsberg in Preussen,* Posen, 1867, p. 49; S. Stern, *Der Preussische Staat und die Juden,* Berlin, 1925, I, part i, pp. 131, 143-144, see also new ed., Tuebingen, 1962; Baer, *Das Protokollbuch der Landjudenschaft des Herzogtums Cleve,* Berlin, 1922, I, 65, 77; M. Koehler, *Beitraege zur neueren juedischen Wirtschaftsgeschichte. Die Juden in Halberstadt und Umgebung bis zur Emanzipation,* Berlin, 1927, pp. 25-28; A. Wolf, "Die Gutachten des Senats der Universitaet Jena," *MGWJ,* N. S. VI (1898), 473 f.; A. Human, *Geschichte der Juden in Sachsen-Meiningen-Hildburghausen,* Weimar, 1939, 2nd ed., p. 69; M. Brann, *Geschichte der Juden in Schlesien,* Breslau, 1896, pp. 1-40.

6. S. Haenle, *Geschichte der Juden im ehemaligen Fuerstenthum Ansbach,* Ansbach, 1867, p. 173; A. Wuerfel, *Historische Nachricht von der Judengemeinde im Hofmarkt Fuerth,* Frankfurt a. M., 1754, pp. 26-27.

7. Landsberger, "Old-Time Torah Curtains," *HUCA,* XIX (1946), 371-387.

8. Schudt, *op. cit.,* p. 252.

9. E. Toeplitz, "Die Malerei in den Synagogen," *Beitraege zur juedischen Kulturgeschichte,* Heft III, Frankfurt a. M., 1929.

10. A. Jaraczewsky, *Die Geschichte der Juden in Erfurt,* Erfurt, 1868, p. 61.

11. A. Wolf, *Jewish Encyclopedia,* V, *s. v.* "Engraving"; Landsberger, "Jewish Artists before the period of Emancipation," *op. cit.,* p. 400; R. Wischnitzer, "Jewish Art," *op. cit.,* p. 290; S. Kirschstein, *Juedische Graphiker,* Berlin, 1918, p. 15; S. Stern, *The Court Jew,* Philadelphia, 1950, *passim.*

12. A. Pribram, *Urkunden und Akten zur Geschichte der Juden in Wien,* Vienna, 1918, I, 494 f., for the English translation of this reference see R. Mahler, *Jewish Emancipation. A Selection of Documents,* New York, 1941, p. 19.

Notes

Notes to CHAPTER XIX

JEWISH ARTISANS IN POLAND AND LITHUANIA (1350-1648)

1. S. Dubnow, *History of the Jews in Russia and Poland,* Philadelphia, 1946, I, ch. 2; M. Wischnitzer, "Survey of the Political and Social History of the Jews in Poland and Lithuania," in *History of the Jews in Russia,* (cited as Wischnitzer, "Survey,"), Moscow, 1914, p. 23 f. (in Russian).

2. J. Lelewel, *Guillebert de Lannoy et ses Voyages en 1313, 1414 et 1421,* Brussels, Poznan, 1844, p. 42; Dubnow, *op. cit.,* I, 58 f.; M. Wischnitzer, "Di Geshikhte fun Yidn in Lite fun Mitlalter bis ershte Weltmilkhome," *Lite,* M. Sudarsky and U. Katzenelenbogen, eds., New York, 1951, I, col. 43-57.

3. L. Charewiczowa, Ograniczenia gospodarcze nacyj schizmatyckich i zydow we Lwowie XV i XVIw.," *Kwartalnik Historyczny* (1925), 216; I. Schipper, *Studja nad stosunkami gospodarczymi zydow w Polsce podczas sredniowiecza,* Lwow, 1911, pp. 252-255; J. Shatzky, *Geshikhte fun Yiden in Varshe,* New York, 1947-53, I, 37; Wischnizer, "Jewish Artisans and their Guild Organization," in *History of the Jews in Russia,* (cited as Wischnitzer, "Artisans,"), 287-288 (in Russian); R. Mahler, "Di Yidn in Amolikn Poyln," in *Di Yidn in Poyln,* (cited as Mahler, "Yidn in Poyln"), New York, 1943, col. 78.

4. Schipper, "Distribution of the Jewish Population in Poland and Lithuania," in *History of the Jews in Russia,* pp. 112-114 (in Russian); Mahler, "Yidn in Poyln," col. 46.

5. Wischnitzer, "Survey," p. 35; *idem,* "Artisans," p. 292; Mahler, "Yidn in Poyln" cols. 80-83; for shoemakers, see the Christian shoemakers' in Lwow complaint of 1599 that the Jewish shoemakers damage their guild. The shoemaker craft was not popular among Jews, however. P. Kramerowna, "Zydowskie cechy rzemeslnicze w dawnej Polsce," *Miesiecznik Zydowski,* II, 7-12 (July-December, 1932), 296; for bookbinders see record in files of the Grodno municipal court of 1578-79, published in Bershadski, *Litovskiye Yevrei,* St. Petersburg, 1883, pp. 409-410: "Owing to an error of the Jew bookbinder, this section is set here while it actually belongs farther down under the head of the Three Kings."

6. Russko-Yevreiski Archiv, I, no. 179; *Regesty i Nadpisi,* Svod materialov dlia istorii yevreyev v Rossii, St. Petersburg, Publication of the Jewish Historic-Ethnographic Society, 1910, vol. II, 137-139, no. 1385.

7. Wischnitzer, "Artisans," pp. 289-290; Dubnow, *op. cit.,* pp. 74-78.

8. M. Balaban, *Zydzi lwowscy na przelomie XVI i XVII wieku,* Lwow, 1905. p. 482; *idem, Historia Zydow w Krakowie i na Kazimierzu,* Cracow, 1928, I, 298 f.; W. Lozinski, *Patrycyat i mieszczanstwo lwowskie w XVI i XVII wieku,* Lwow, 1892, pp. 193-194; M. Schorr, *Zydzi w Przemyslu do konca XVIII wieku,* Lwow, 1903, p. 62.

9. Wischnitzer, "Artisans," pp. 292-293; *idem,* "Die Juedische Zunftverfassung in Polen und Litauen im 17. und 18. Jahrhundert," *Vierteljahrschrift fuer Sozial- und Wirtschaftsgeschichte,* XX. 3 and 4 (1928), 433 ff. For barbers' guild statute see F. H. Wettstein, *Kadmoniyot mi-Pinkassot yeshanim: takanot ha-Balbirer* (cited as Wettstein, *Kadmoniyot*), Cracow, 1892, IV, 604-605; tr. J. R. Marcus, *The Jew in the Medieval World,* pp. 446-449; apprenticeship contracts were published by Wettstein, *op. cit.,* and in his "Debarim Atikim," *Eschkol,* II (1899), 172.

10. Marcus, *op. cit.,* p. 449.

Notes to CHAPTER XX

THE SPREAD OF JEWISH HANDICRAFTS IN POLAND-LITHUANIA AFTER 1648

1. The Jews of Lithuania had their

own Council (Vaad) ; however, in matters of common interest requiring intercession with the Crown and the Diet, the "Council of the Four Lands" acted alone.

2. S. Luzzatto, *Discorso circa il stato degl' hebrei, et in particolar dimoranti nell' inclita citta di Venetia,* Venice, 1638, p. 90 Hebrew edition: *Maamar al Yehudei Venezia,* Jerusalem, 1951; M. Isserles, *Responsa,* no. 95.

3. Wischnitzer, "Survey," pp. 67-81; also Dubnow, *op. cit.,* I, 144 ff.; Mahler, "Yidn in Poyln," col. 161 ff.; I. Halpern, *Pinkas Vaad Arba Aratzot,* Jerusalem, 1945, p. 88, n. 1.

4. In addition to sources in Wischnitzer's "Survey," cf. *Menasseh ben Israel's Mission to Oliver Cromwell,* ed. L. Wolf, London, 1901, p. 87; Schipper, "Distribution of the Jewish Population in Poland and Lithuania," *op. cit.,* 113-114. M. F. Vladimirski-Budanov, "Peredvizhenye yuzhno-russkago naseleniya v epokhu Bogdana Khmielnitskago," *Kievskaya Starina, VII* (1888).

5. Halpern, *op. cit.,* Appendix, pp. XVIII-XIX, no. 17; *idem,* "Al Sakanat Gerush li-Klal Yisrael be-Poyln ve-Lita be-mahatsit ha-sheniyah shel ha-meah ha-shva-esre," *Zion,* XVII (1952) , 65.

6. Balaban, *Die Judenstadt von Lublin,* Berlin, 1919, pp. 50 and 106.

7. A. Szelagowski, "Rozwoj ekonomiczny i spoleczny w Polsce do roku 1795," *Polska, Obrazy i Opisy,* Lwow, 1909, vol. II, 672 J. Rutkowski, *Historia Gospodarcza Polski* [up to the partitions], 3rd ed., Poznan, 1947, p. 91; French ed.: *Histoire économique de la Pologne avant les partages,* Paris, 1927.

8. W. Surowiecki, *O Upadku przemyslu i miast w Polsce,* Warsaw, 1811, p. 221; T. Korzon, *Wewnetrzne dzieje Polski za Stanislawa Augusta,* Cracow, 1897-98, II, 10; J. Kolaczkowski, *Wiadomosci o fabrykach i rekodzielach w dawnej Polsce,* Cracow, 1881, p. 7.

9. M. Bersohn, *Dyplomatarjusz dotyczacy zydow w dawnej Polsce na zrodlach archivalnych osnuty, 1388-1782,* Warsaw, 1910, nos. 179 and 281.

10. Halpern, *Pinkas Vaad Arba Aratzot,* pp. 148 ff., § 352.

11. *The Memoirs of Ber of Bolechow (1723-1805)* , ed. M. Vishnitzer, Oxford, 1922. See Introduction and pp. 18 ff., 36, 142 ff., on the disintegration of the Polish state in the eighteenth century.

12. Mahler, *Yidn in Amolikn Poyln in Likht fun Tsifern,* Warsaw, 1958, pp. 30-37.

13. T. Czacki, *Rosprawa o zydach i karaitach,* Cracow, 1860, p. 117. The first edition appeared in 1807.

14. Mahler, *op. cit.,* 193.

15. *Ibid.,* 123-134.

16. *Pinkas ha-Mdinah o Pinkas Vaad ha-Kehilot ha-Rashiyot bi-Mdinat Lita* (cited as *Pinkas ha-Mdinah*) , Berlin, 1925, § 728 and § 360.

17. Mahler, *op. cit.,* col. 118.

18. *Pinkas ha-Mdinah,* § 322 (1637) .

CHAPTER XXI

JEWISH ART-CRAFTS PARTICULARLY IN POLAND AND LITHUANIA

1. W. R. Zaloziecky, *Gotische und barocke Holzkirchen in den Karpathenlaendern,* Vienna, 1926, p. 9 ff.

2. M. and K. Piechotka, *Wooden Synagogues,* Warsaw, 1959; R. Wischnitzer, *The Architecture of the European Synagogue,* Philadelphia, 1964.

3. The inscription was first published in *History of the Jews in Russia* (see ch. XIX, n. 1.) , pl. facing p. 392.

4. El L. [Lissitzky], "The Synagogue of Mogilev," *Rimon,* no. 3. (1923), 9 ff. (in Hebrew) ; *Milgroim,* no. 3 (1923) , 9 ff. (in Yiddish) .

5. A. Breier, M. Eisler and M. Grunwald, *Holzsynagogen in Polen,* Baden-Vienna, 1934, p. 13.

6. S. Zajczyk, "Architektura barokowych boznic murowanych w Polsce, "*Biuletyn Naukowy,* I, 4 (June, 1933) , 195.

7. M. Bersohn, "Einiges ueber die alten Holzsynagogen in Polen," *MJV,* XIV, 2 (1904) , 19.

8. M. Diamant, *Juedische Volkskunst,* Vienna, 1937, p. 22.

9. *Encyclopaedia Judaica,* VII, *s. v.* "Grab," cols. 631 ff., plates, cols. 614-618.

10. Bersohn, *op. cit.*, VIII, 2 (1901), 182.

11. Zajczyk, *op. cit.*, p. 192.

12. *Idem*, "Boznica w Kepnie," *Biuletyn Zydowskiego Instytutu Historycznego*, no. 43-44 (July-December, 1962), 63-83, notes 19 and 23. For illustrations see A. Grotte, "Deutsche, boehmische und polnische Synagogentypen," *Mitteilungen der Gesellschaft zur Erforschung juedischer Kunstdenkmaeler*, VII-VIII (1915), figs. on p. vii and nos. 20 and 20a. Grotte's remarks on p. 46 ff. are superseded by Zajczyk's findings.

13. E. Toeplitz, "Die Malerei in den Synagogen," *Beitraege zur juedischen Kulturgeschichte*, III (1929).

14. Landsberger, "Old Hanukkah Lamps," *HUCA*, XXV, 366.

15. Balaban, *Zabytki historyczne zydow w Polsce*, Warsaw, 1929, p. 15.

16. Bersohn, *op. cit.*, VIII. 2, 170; *ibid.*, XIV. 2, 10.

17. R. Wischnitzer, "Der Siddur der Altstaedtischen Synagoge in Rzeszow," *Festschrift fuer Aron Freimann zum 60. Geburtstage*, ed. A. Marx and H. Meyer, Berlin, 1935, pp. 77-80.

18. Balaban, *op. cit.*, p. 82.

19. F. Siarczynski, *Obraz wieku panowania Zygmunta III*, Posen, 1858, II, 121.

20. F. Piekosinski, ed., *Prawa, przywileje i statuta miasta Krakowa*, Cracow, 1892, ii, part 2 (year 1610).

21. T. Mankowski, "Mecenat Jana III w Zolkwi," *Prace Komisji Historii Sztuki*, IX (1948), 127-152, particularly 130, 131, 148.

22. The most recent publication on the engraver Herszko Lejbowicz is T. Dobrowolski, *Polskie Malarstwo Portretowe*, Cracow, 1948, p. 69.

23. Quoted from an unpublished biographical note on Dornhelm by W. Lozinski of 1911 by M. Goldstein and K. Dresdner, *Kultura i Sztuka ludu zydowskiego na ziemiach Polskich*, Lwow, 1935, p. 118 ff. See also pp. 116 ff.

24. *Encyclopaedia Judaica*, II, *s. v.* "Antokolski, Mark."

25. Schudt, *op. cit.*, I, 14, 218; also VI, 34, 284.

26. Balaban, *Zydzi lwowscy na przelomie XVIgo i XVIIgo wieku*, pp. 533-534.

27. According to a decree of King Stefan Batory of 1582, cited in J. Stutschewsky, *Klezmorim*, Jerusalem, 1959, p. 66 (in Hebrew).

28. Lewin, *Geschichte der Juden in Lissa*, Pinne, 1904, pp. 16, 23, and 24.

29. A. Z. Idelsohn, *Jewish Music*, New York, 1929, p. 215.

30. J. Stutschewsky, *op. cit.*, p. 60.

31. Illustrated in G. Liebe, *Das Judentum in der deutschen Vergangenheit*, Leipzig, 1903, facing p. 8.

32. P. Nettl, *Alte juedische Spielleute und Musiker*, Prague, 1923, p. 41.

33. Cod. Hebr. 1333, Bibliothèque Nationale, Paris, fol. 38, illustrated in D. H. von Mueller and J. von Schlosser, *Die Haggadah von Sarajewo*, Vienna, 1898, fig. 5.

34. S. Tomkowicz, *History of Music in Cracow*, 1907, cited by Stutschewsky, *op. cit.*, n. 109, without the original title and without page number. Tomkowicz' book was not available to the author.

35. Nettl, *op. cit.*, p. 4.

36. *Ibid.*, p. 6; A M. Rothmueller, *The Music of the Jews*, tr. H. C. Stevens, London, 1953, pp. 93, 98.

37. Nettl, *op. cit.*, p. 39; the engravings are reproduced in G. Kisch, *Die Prager Universitaet und die Juden*, following p. 16.

38. For the guild statutes see, Nettl, *Beitraege zur boehmischen und maehrischen Musikgeschichte*, Brunn, 1927, pp. 80 ff.

39. *Ibid.*, p. 71.

40. *Ibid.*, p 78. The expression used is: "unsere erlehrnte (sic) Nahrung" (our livelihood earned by skilled work).

41. C. Sachs, *Our Mutual Heritage*, New York, 1955, p. 273.

42. *Ibid.*, p. 304.

43. I. Rabinovitch, *Of Jewish Music, Ancient and Modern*, tr. from the Yiddish, Montreal, 1952, chapters XVIII-XXI.

44. M. Beregovski, *Yiddishe Instrumentale Folksmusik*, Kiev, 1937, p. 4. (In Yiddish).

Notes to CHAPTER XXII

THE STRUGGLE FOR THE RIGHT TO WORK

1. S. Kutrzeba, *Historia ustroju Polski w zarysie,* 2nd ed., Lwow, 1908, I, 96), refers to royal regulations of 1423 and 1438 which were intended to abolish the guilds because they were regarded as a factor in the rise of prices. He adds, however, that these regulations were never carried out in practice.

2. Surowiecki, *op. cit., p.* 175.

3. *Ibid.,* 189.

4. M. N. Gelber, "Toledot Yehudey Brody," *Arym ve-Imahot be-Yisrael,* Jerusalem, 1955, VI, 31-32.

5. K. Chodynicki, " O Stosunkach wyznaniowych w cechach wilenskich od XVI do XVIII wieku," *Ksiega Pamiatkowa ku czci Oswalda Balzera,* Lwow, 1925, I; J. Jablonowski, *Zrodla Dziejowe,* V, 41; L. Charewiczowa, *Lwowskie Organizacje zawodowe za czasow Polski Przedrozbierowej,* 1929, p. 88; S. Herbst, *Torunskie cechy rzemieslnicze,* Torun, 1933, pp. 14, 63, 68 ff.

6. Rutkowski, *op. cit.,* 141-142.

7. H. Wolczacka, "Rzemioslo szklarskie w Wilnie do konca XVIII wieku," *Alma Mater Vilnensis. Biblioteka,* III (1933), 52-68, particularly pp. 55 f., 61, 65, 67.

8. *Regesty i Nadpisi,* 1913, III, no. 2234; I. Klausner, *Toledot ha-Kehila ha-Ivrit be-Vilna,* Vilna, 1938, I, 14-21, 34, 35, 38 and 39.

9. Balaban, *Die Judenstadt von Lublin,* pp. 40-41, 65; I. Trunk, "Bletlekh fun der fergangenhayt," *Dos Bukh fun Lublin,* Paris, 1952, pp. 25, 37-43.

10. M. Kremer, "Der Ontayl fun Yidishe Baaley-Melokhes in di kristlekhe tsekhn in amolikn Poyln," *Bleter far Geshikhte,* II (1938), 13-14.

11. Jablonowski, *op. cit.,* pp. 145-146.

12. *Ibid.,* 216-217.

13. "A Historisher dokument," *Yubileum-Bukh fun der 40-yoriker egzystents funem Chortkover Shpiro-Ferayn,* New York, 1932, pp. 37-39, also pp. 64-65.

Notes to CHAPTER XXIII

RELATIONS BETWEEN JEWISH GUILDS AND JEWISH COMMUNITY COUNCILS IN POLAND-LITHUANIA (1600-1800)

1. Balaban, *Zydzi lwowscy na przelomie XVI i XVII wieku,* see Appendix: Materialy, no. 75; Klausner, *op. cit.,* 123; Schorr, *op. cit.,* 63; P. Kon, "Yidishe tsekhn in Vilne onhoub 19. Yorhundert," *Shriftn far Ekonomik un Statistik,* I (1928), 89-90.

2. Balaban, *op. cit.,* 469-488.

3. Up to World War 11, guild bylaws were preserved of the following cities: Bilgoraj, Drohobycz, Czortkow, Gniezno, Jaroslaw, Luboml, Kejdany, Kobylin, Kurnik, Kutno, Luck [Lutzk], Minsk, Mikolajew, Mogilev, Malin, Plock [Plotzk], Pavoloch, Sokolow, Sedlikow [Sedlishche?].

4. Wettstein, *Kadmonyot,* p. 15; *idem,* "Divrey Hefets," *Measef,* I (1902), no. 27.

5. Schorr, *op cit.,* pp. 64.

6. W. Feilchenfeld, "Eine Innungsordnung fuer die juedischen Handwerker zu Posen von dem Gemeindevorstande im Jahre 1737 erlassen," *Zeitschrift der Historischen Gesellschaft fuer die Provinz Posen,* X (1895). 310 ff.

7. B. Weinryb, *Teudot le-Toledot ha-Kehilot ha-Yehudiyot be-Poyln,* New York, 1950/51, p. 162. The tax ranged from 2 zloty to 7.5 groszy.

8. C. Z. Margoliot, *Dubno Rabosi* Warsaw, 1910, p. 90.

9. Halpern, "Hevroth Baaley-Melokhot Yehudim be-Poyln ve-Lita," (cited as Halpern, "Lita,"), *Zion,* I (1937), 88; *Historishe Shriftn,* II (1937), 580-586.

10. I. Levitats, "Der Pinkas fun Dubner Kohel," *Historishe Shriftn,* II, 102.

11. Weinryb, *op. cit.,* pp. 227.

12. *Pinkas ha-Mdinah,* § 681 (for 1670), § 817 (for 1687). An exception was made only for the Burial Brotherhood which enjoyed autonomy in the community.

13. *Pinkas ha-Mdinah,* § 899 (for 1695).

14. *Pinkas ha-Mdinah,* § 983 (for 1761).
15. Trunk, "Geshikhte fun Yidn in Vitebsk," *Vitebsk Amol,* New York, 1956, pp. 15. 16.
16. *Idem,* "Vaad Medinat Russia (Raysn)," *YIVO-Bleter,* XL (1956), 80.
17. I. Sosis, "Yidishe Baalmelokhes un zeyere Arbeter in Lite, Vaisrusland un Ukraine," *Tsaitshrift,* IV (1930), 21.
18. Mahler, "Yidn in Poyln," col. 303; Pinkas of the Poznan community, p. 21, cited from E. Kupfer, "Di Batsiyung fun Kohel tsum Baalmelokhe un Uremshaft," *Bleter far Geshikhte,* II, 1-4 (1949), 209; Levitats, *op. cit.,* p. 86; Lewin, *op. cit.,* p. 85.
19. Pinkas of Kurnik. Hevra Baaley-Melokhot, manuscript at the Jewish Theological Seminary, Accession no. 63964, pp. 13 and 63.
20. Weinryb, *op. cit.,* pp. 222, 227.
21. Halpern, "Lita," *loc. cit.;* Margoliot, *loc. cit.*
22. Sosis, *op. cit.,* pp. 20-21.
23. Wettstein, *Kadmonyot,* no. 33.
24. *Idem,* "Divrey Hefets," *Measef,* XXXIX (1902), 32, 33, and 44.
25. Bershadski, *op. cit.,* pp. 46-48; Kon, "Der Bunt fun Minsker Amkhu kegn Kohel, 1777," *Historishe Shriftn,* II, 608-614.
26. *Yevreiskaya Starina,* XII (1928), 88.
27. Mahler, "Yidn in Poyln," cols. 340-342; Lewin, *op. cit.,* pp. 92-93.
28. A. Hepner and I. Herzberg, *Aus Vergangenheit der Juden und der Juedischen Gemeinden in den Posener Landen,* Bromberg, no. 11 (1906), 432-433.
29. Trunk, "Toledot Yehudei Lublin," *Entsiklopedia shel Galuyot. Lublin,* V (1957), 67.
30. Mahler, *Tabeln-Bailage tsum Bukh Yidn in Amolikn Poyln in Likht fun Tsifern,* Tables VI and VI A.
31. *Akty izdavayemye vilenskoyu komissiyeyu dla razbora drevnikh aktov,* Vilna, 1902, XXIX, 473; Mahler, "Yidn in Poyln," cols. 340-341.
32. Mahler, "Yidn in Poyln," cols. 94-96.
33. *Regesty i Nadpisi,* II, no. 1742.
34. Cited from Shatzky, "A Geshikhte fun der Kehile," *YIVO Bleter,* XXIII (1944), 283.
35. Kremer, *op. cit.,* pp. 13-27.

Notes to CHAPTER XXIV

THE WORKSHOP ASSISTANTS: APPRENTICES AND JOURNEYMEN

1. The by-laws of the tailors' guild in Kurnik (1754) required one year membership; those of the furriers' guild in Lissa (1764) two years after marriage; Luboml, Plock and Przemysl three years. Cf. Pinkas of Kurnik (see ch. XXIII, n. 19); Lewin, *op. cit.,* § 5, p. 354; Halpern, "Pinkas ha-Hevra shel Baaley-Melokho be-Lubomla" (cited as Halpern, "Lubomla"), *Yediyot Arkheon ve-Museon shel Tnuat Avoda,* II (1935), 11; E. Ringelblum, "Pinkas fun der Hevra Hayotim," *Economishe Shriftn,* II (1930), 6; Schorr, *op. cit.,* p. 266; a rule of the guild in Przemysl of 1722 allows the wardens to make an exception for younger members, see Schorr, *ibid.,* Appendix: Materialy, no. XIII.
2. Kremer, "Yidishe Baley-Melokhes un Tsekhn in Amolikn Poyln," *YIVO Bleter,* XL (1956), 92.
3. Pinkas of Kurnik, fol. 20a and 20b.
4. Statut polaczonego cechu zydowskiego, Kutno (tailors' and furriers' guild), Manuscript at the Warsaw Archiwum Glowne Akt Dawnych, part 91, book 26/36, 1783, § 14.
5. Ringelblum, *loc. cit.*
6. Schorr, *op. cit.,* Materialy, no. XIII.
7. M. Wischnitzer, "Der Pinkas fun Keydaner Bal-Melokho Tsekh," *Bleter far Yidishe Demografie, Statistik un Ekonomik,* V (1925), 75-77 § § 19, 45, 47.
8. Y. Krashinsky, "Me-Pinkasei Lutsko," *Measef,* I (1902), p. 289 § 21; Lewin, *op. cit.,* 355, § 16.
9. Klausner. *op. cit.,* p. 35.
10. Krashinsky, *loc. cit.;* for Czortkow (1721) see *Yubileum Bukh fun 40-yoriker egzystents funem Czortkover Shpiro Ferayn;* also our ch XXII, n. 13. for

Przemysl, Schorr, *op. cit.*, Materialy, no. XVIII ff.

11. Wischnitzer, *op. cit.*, § 23; Krashinsky, *op. cit.*, § 5; Lewin, op. cit., p. 20.

12. The work term agreed upon in Cracow was one year (Wettstein, *Kadmonyot*, p. 52), in Plock (Ringelblum, *op. cit.*, § 27) and in Lissa (Lewin, *op. cit.*, § 6) only six months. In Przemysl (Schorr, *op. cit.*, Materialy, no. XVIII), and Luck (Krashinsky, *op. cit.*, § 22) three-month arrangements are to be found.

13. Schorr, *op. cit.*, pp. 65, 66 and Materialy, no. X (1704), no. XIII (1722), and no. XVIII (1743); also Statut . . . Kutno, *op. cit.*, § 18; Feilchenfeld, *op. cit.*, § 8.

14. Pinkas of Kurnik, see our n. 1.

15. Schorr, *op. cit.*, Materialy, no. X.

16. Ringelblum, *op. cit.*, § 6.

17. Schorr, *op. cit.*, Materialy, no. XV (1729); Halpern, "Lubomla," p. 11.

18. Krashinsky, *op. cit.*, § 5; Schorr, *op. cit.*, Materialy, no. X, p. 268; Feilchenfeld, *op. cit.*, § 7.

19. An exception was made for a journeyman or apprentice for a period of four weeks before his marriage (Pinkas of Kurnik, fol. 46a).

20. Halpern, "Lubomla," p. 12.

21. Statut . . . Kutno, *op. cit.*, § 20; Wettstein, *Kadmonyot*, no. 21 (1650); Ringelblum, *op. cit.*, § 20; In Przemysl the journeyman was forbidden to sell clothes made in his master's shop in the streets and markets (Schorr, *op. cit.*, Materialy, no. VI (1690).

22. Wettstein, *Kadmonyot*, no. 24.

23. *Ibid.*, no. 31.

24. In Kurnik the journeymen were paid annually; in Cracow semi-annually (Wettstein, *Kadmonyot*, nos. 10 and 35), annually, (*ibid.*, no. 25), trimonthly (*ibid.*, no. 24) and weekly (*ibid.*, 31); also per piece work (*ibid.*, no. 21); In Lutzk, trimonthly (Krashinsky, *op. cit.*, § 27) and in Lissa, per piece work (Lewin, *op. cit.*, §17).

25. Wettstein, Kadmonyot, nos. 10, 25, 31, 35.

26. Korzon, *op. cit.*, II, *passim.*

27. Krashinsky, *op. cit.*, § 28.

28. Kremer, "Yidishe Baley-Melokhes un Tsekhn in Amolikn Poyln," *op cit.*, p. 101; Pinkas of Kurnik fols. 30a, 30b.

29. Trunk, "Toledot Yehudey Lublin," *op. cit.*, p. 68; Lewin, *op. cit.*, p. 355,

30. Krashinsky, *op. cit*, § 27; Statut . . . Kutno, *op. cit.*, § 22; Feilchenfeld, *op. cit.*, § 9.

31. Wettstein, *Kadmonyot*, no. 9 (1640).

32. *Ibid.*, nos. 25, 31, 35 (1650).

33. *Ibid.*, nos. 23, 24, 29.

34. Wischnitzer, *op. cit.*, contract of 1815.

35. Pinkas of Kurnik, fols. 26, 30b, 33b, 35a.

36. *Ibid.*, fols. 30a, 33b, 34a.

37. Wettstein, *Kadmonyot*, § 24; according to a provision in the Pinkas of Kurnik (fol. 25a), the apprentice was allowed to go to his teacher for an hour daily for religious study.

38. Pinkas of Kurnik, fol. 33b.

39. Wettstein, *Kadmonyot*, no. 29; Pinkas of Kurnik, fol. 37a; for the latter half of the year the apprentice received wages (7.5 zloty).

40. Wettstein, *Kadmonyot*, no. 10, 24.

41. Pinkas of Kurnik, fols. 30a, 37a, 37b, and *passim.*

42. Wettstein *Dbarim Atikim*, Cracow, 1901, no. 33.

43. *Idem*, *Kadmonyot*, no. 23.

44. *Ibid.*, no. 25 (1650).

45. Wischnitzer, *op. cit.*, § § 45, 61.

46. Lewin, *op. cit.*, § 15, p. 355; Wettstein, *Kadmonyot*, no. 23.

47. Statut . . . Kutno, *op. cit.*, § 30.

48. Pinkas of Kurnik, by-laws for 1754, § 4; Schorr, *op. cit.*, Materialy, no. XIX (1744).

49. Lewin, *op. cit.*, § 9, p. 354; Wischnitzer, *op. cit.*, § 23; Czortkow Pinkas (1721), § 8 and (1781), § 19 (see our n. 10); Pinkas of Kurnik, § 6, fol. 46a; M. Hendel, "Mezritcher Pinkasim," *YIVO Bleter*, VIII (1935), 64; Kremer, "Yidishe Baley-Melokhes un Tsekhn in Amolikn Poyln," *op. cit.*, p. 98.

50. Levitats, *op. cit.*, § § 8 and 9 (for 1750). Wages up to 20 zloty were tax free; in the taxation rules for 1717, journeymen were not even mentioned

(*ibid.*, p. 97).

51. Pinkas of Kurnik, fol. 58b.

52. Feilchenfeld, *op. cit.*, § § 10 and 11.

53. Lewin, *op. cit.*, § 19, p. 355.

54. Feilchenfeld, *op. cit.*, § 3.

55. Pinkas of Kurnik, § 6.

56. Trunk, "Toledot Yehudey Lublin," *op. cit.*, p. 68.

57. Z. Pazdro, *Organizacja i praktyka sadow podwojewodzinskich,* Lwow, 1903, pp. 66, 121.

58. Wettstein, *Kadmonyot,* no. 31.

59. Pinkas of Kurnik, § 6.

60. Czortkow Pinkas, § 21 (1781).

61. Statut . . . Kutno, *op. cit.*, § 23; Pinkas of Kurnik, fol. 38a (1778); Halpern, "Lubomla," p.13.

62. Ringelblum, *op. cit.*, § 36.

63. Pinkas of Kurnik, § 6, fols. 30a, 38a, 59a.

64. Wettstein, *Kadmonyot,* pp. 15-16; Weinryb, "Al Yakhson shel ha-Kehilot be-Poyln," *Yediyot Arkheon ve-Museon* shel *Tnuat Avoda,* II (1935), 18.

65. G. Renard, *Guilds in the Middle Ages,* tr. D. Terry, ed. with introduction by G. D. H. Cole, London, 1919, *passim.*

66. B. Bucher, ed., *Die Alten Zunft- und Verkehrsordnungen. Nach Balthazar Behems Codex Picturatus in der k. k. Jagellonischen Bibliothek,* Vienna, 1889. The only reference to Jews in the Codex is a prohibition of the furriers' guild to give out to or take from Jews furs for sale. The penalty was three marks and loss of the goods. For Polish trades emblems, see A. Chmiel, *Godla Rzemieslnicze i Przemyslowe Krakowskie od polowy XIV w., az do XX w.,* Cracow, 1922.

67. J. Mazurkiewicz, *Poczatki Ustroju Cechowego w Lublinie,* Lublin, 1948, pp. 11, 12, 16.

68. The "Vorstadt" synagogue of Lwow, built in 1632 was sometime later remodeled to make room for several guild chambers. See A. Grotte, *Deutsche, Boehmische und Polnische Synagogentypen vom XI. bis Anfang des XIX. Jahrhunderts,* Frankfurt a.M., 1915, plate 5.

69. Kremer, "Yidishe Baley-Melokhes un Tsekhn in Amolikn Poyln," *op. cit.*, pp. 118-119.

70. Halpern. "Lita," I, 84.

71. J. Brafmann, *Das Buch vom Kahal,* Leipzig, 1928, II: Das Buch von der Verwaltung der Juedischen Gemeinde, pp. 254-255, no. 1046.

72. A. Menes, "Di Yidishe Arbeter-Bevegung in Rusland," *Historishe Shriftn,* III 1939), 10-11; A Kirznis, *Sotsialistishe Literatur af Yidish 1875-1897,* Minsk, 1935, pp. 37-38.

Publications of Dr. Mark Wischnitzer on Jewish Crafts and Craft Guilds

1 "Remeslenniki" (Artisans), *Yevreyskaia Entsiklopedia,* XII (1911/12), 430-437.

2 "Yevrei-remeslenniki i tsekhovaia organizacia ikh," (Jewish artisans and their guild organization), *Istoria Yevreev v Rossii* (History of the Jews in Russia), Moscow, 1914, pp. 286-29.

3 *Yidishe balmelokhe tsekhen in Polen un in Lite* (Jewish craft guilds in Poland and Lithuania), Berlin, 1922.

4 "Der Pinkas fun Keydaner bal-melokho tsekh," (The Minute book of the Keydany craft guild, *Bleter for Yidisher Demografie, Statistik un Economic,* 5 (1925), 72-77.

5 "Die Juedische Zunftverfassung in Polen und Litauen im 17. und 18. Jahrhundert," *Vierteljahrschrift fuer Sozial-und Wirtschaftsgeschichte,* XX.3-4 (1928), 433-451.

6 "Di Struktur fun Yidishe tsekhen in Poland, Lite un Weissrussland inem 17.un 18.Jahrhundert," (The Structure of the Jewish Guilds in Poland, Lithuania and White Russia in the 17th and the 18th centuries), *Zeitshrift,* II-III (1928), 73-88.

7 "Handwerk. Vom Ausgang des Altertums bis zur Mitte des 19. Jahrhunderts," *Encyclopaedia Judaica,* VIII (1931), cols. 951-970.

8 "Handicrafts," *Universal Jewish Encyclopedia,* V (1941) cols. 201-204.

9 "Traditional Judaism and Manual Labor," *ORT Economic Review,* II. 4-5 (July-Oct. 1941),12-15.

10 "The Spread of Arts and Crafts among Jews," *ORT Economic Review,* III. 1 (January-February 1942), 14-20.

11 "Notes to a History of the Jewish Guilds," *HUCA,* XXIII. 2 (1950-1951), 245-263.

12 "Origins of the Jewish Artisan Class in Bohemia and Moravia 1500-1648," *Jewish Social Studies,* XVI. 4 (1954), 335-350.

13 Reviews of books on Jewish economic history published in *Yevreyskaia Starina* (Jewish Antiquities). For a list of these articles see A. G. Duker, "'Yevreiskaia Starina,' a Bibliography of the Russian-Jewish Historical Periodical," *HUCA,* VIII-IX (1931-32), *passim.* To the items signed with the full name are to be added those signed with the initials M. V., which are also by Mark Wischnitzer.

Index

Index

Index

Index

www.ingramcontent.com/pod-product-compliance
Ingram Content Group UK Ltd.
Pitfield, Milton Keynes, MK11 3LW, UK
UKHW041131071026
15587UKWH00009B/416

9 780824 604745